EMANCIPATION OF DALITS AND FREEDOM STRUGGLE

EMANCIPATION OF DALITS AND FREEDOM STRUGGLE

Editor
H.C. Sadangi

ISHA
Isha Books
DELHI-110009

Emancipation of Dalits and Freedom Struggle

Rs. 850

ISBN: 81-8205-481-8

Published in 2008 in India by
Isha Books
B-63, Ist Floor,
New Gupta Colony, Near
DDA Market,
Delhi-110009
E-mail: kalpaz@hotmail.com
Phone : 9212729499

Lasser Type Setting by : Quick Media, Delhi
Printed at : Vishal Kaushik Printers, Delhi

CONTENTS

Preface

The book—*Dalit Identity Struggle*—analyses the transition period of India, in both political and social terms. The mentioned transition covers the efforts of Indian nation to overthrow the British rule for establishing an independent India and also the transition efforts of low castes on behalf of elevating their social position until they are equalized with any other Indian citizen.

Being one of the oldest civilisations of the earth, Indian civilizations emergence can be traced back least 5,000 years. Initially Aryan tribes invaded lands of Dravidians around 1.500 BC and cultures of these two foreign civilisations merged. These lands of attraction received many other incursions as well. Aryan invasion was followed by the assaults of Arabian, Turkish and European ones. Those diverse cultures melted in the pot of Indian lands and formed the present day Indian culture.

One of the most distinctive characters of the Indian culture is the *varna* or the caste order. This order categorizes Indian people into five groups. The first four groups are almost sharing intrinsic qualities. They are from top to bottom *Brahman, Kshatriya, Vaishya and Shudra*. Roughly the first group, *Brahmans* are the priests for spiritual guidance and intellectual nourishment of Indian society. *Kshatriyas* are the warriors to secure and govern India. *Vaishyas* are traders and deal with agricultural and commercial undertakings. *Shudras* are the labour class. Besides those mentioned four castes, there is one other group who are considered as outcastes. They are the Untouchables. The Untouchables are deprived of several basic human rights. They are considered to be impure to touch, to live together, to use public possessions or even to pray together.

Naturally, the Untouchables suffered the most by this social order. Even though there had been several attempts to conclude this implementation, they were unsuccessful weak attempts.

The new consciousness of the Untouchables were inspired by Mahatma Phule and initiated *de facto* by Babasaheb Ambedkar. Those were the times of British India. India was governed and economically exploited by the British powers. India, under the leadership of Mahatma Gandhi, was carrying a resistance against the British influence. Nevertheless, there was a group of Indians, who benefited the existence of the British. They were the Untouchables, because the British bestowed them several facilities, from education to career. Now it was the right time for Untouchables to achieve their own liberty. It was the right time for the reason that upper caste Indians were fighting for own freedom and to establish a new India. Before a new India was formed, the Untouchables had to move quickly and prevent founding of the old social order once again. They were willing to finish the degrading *varna* order and become ordinary, equal citizens. Initially all downtrodden people of India unified, including the Untouchables, and became the Dalits, as far as it indicated their political awareness and then they maintained constitutional safeguards for themselves. Under the light of the legal arrangements, the Dalits converted from Hinduism to Buddhism to cease their social integration successfully.

The book explains this process of Indian freedom movement and the Dalit Movement that paved the way to the emergence of modern India. Both movements were against exploitation at all levels; on the other hand while one was realized on behalf of India's revival in all means, the other one was an anti-systemic one. Upper castes Indians were contesting the British exploitation and manipulation in India. They were trying to consolidate their sovereignty by expelling the British. Simultaneously, the Untouchables were historically downtrodden by the upper castes and now they wanted to destroy this order for reaching their own freedom. They were seeking their self-determination in regard to political participation, economic strategy, social and religious freedom.

The book is arranged in sixteen chapters. *The first chapter* provides a brief political history of India beginning by the colonization period to the end of independence movement.

In *The second chapter,* deals with two bhakti modes for legitimacy for modern change. In the third chapter, an attempt has been made to highlight the 19th century background of the Mahar movement. The fourth chapter throws light on untouchability, scheduled castes and nation building. In the fifth chapter, the Dalit Movement has been highlighted with its prominent leader. The sixth chapter highlights the leadership of B.R. Ambedkar, the architect of Indian Constitution. In the seventh and eighth chapters, an attempt has been made to throw light on the Mahars of Maharashtra, and Buddhism and Politics in Maharashtra respectively.

The ninth chapter is about the attitude of Gandhi and the Congress on the subject of Dalit Movement. In the tenth chapter, conversion movements along with 22 vows of B.R. Ambedkar have been covered. The eleventh and twelfth chapters cover the revival of Buddhism in India and religion and legitimization in the Mahar Movement respectively. The thirteenth chapter highlights the role of Ambedkar in innovation in contemporary Indian Buddhism. The fourteenth chapter covers Buddhist sects in contemporary India.

The fifteenth and last chapter of the book analyses the Buddhist literature of modern Maharashtra.

1

India on the Eve of Independence

Caste

The tremendous geographical diversities of India, from snowy mountains in the north to tropical rain forests in the south, from arid desert in the west to alluvial flood plain in the east, correspond with the diversity of human cultures. These cultures exhibit diverse social modes.[1] Stratification of Indian culture is diversified as other Asiatic communities; yet, India's social formation is perceived to be the most developed form of the caste system.[2] Occupation, functions and skin colour are imperative role-players, in addition to class, caste, tribe, kinship relations, socioeconomic conditions and heredity, of this hierarchical formation.

The word caste has its origins in Portuguese as *casta*, which means specie, race or tribe. However, this term does not actually cover the meaning that the Sanskrit word *varna* provides, because, *varna* is the symbiote of Hinduism, and has a religious stratification of the Indian society. It implies the four main and social classes in addition to two outsider groups and all those classes have numerous sub-classes called *jat* or *jati*. *Jati* means birth.[3] The word caste is far from illustrating the caste distinctions, *varna ashramas* in Sanskrit, but just collect all of them under one label.[4] *Jatis* are kinship groups and the members of each, perform very similar occupations. As local *jatis* denote, occupational identity, common customs, taboos and traditions, some sociologists argue *jatis* to be more meaningful unity than *varnas*.[5]

Varnas

This system is the most deep-rooted organization of Indian society, that is why even though the system is the order of discrimination, such enlightened[6] social reformers as Mahatma Gandhi never dared to attack it, because his faith taught him that *varnas* cannot undergo changes, their number and what they were to be were unalterably set in *Vedic* days and described in the sacred books.[7] Albeit *varna* has its origins in Hinduism, the Hindu caste system has become a part of Indian social life including other religious and ethnic groups as Muslims, Christians, Jews, Mongoloids, Dravidians etc., as well. It is because, several different ethnic and religious groups live together in India and each is as much an Indian as a Hindu. Whether Muslim, Hindu, Christian, Jain or Parsi, the cult of solidarity and tolerance is cultivated there to its utmost.[8]

The *varna* structure is explained by the *Purusha Sukta* myth.[9] Among Hindus it is believed that, *varnas* are separate body parts of the creator Brahma and this sacrificial myth of creation takes place in Rig Veda[10], which is one of the four main holy *Vedas*[11] of Hinduism.[12]

> When the gods spread the sacrifice with the Man as the offering, spring was the clarified butter, summer the fuel, autumn the oblation.
>
> They anointed the Man, the sacrifice born at the beginning, upon the sacred grass.
>
> When they divided the Man (Purusha)...His mouth became the Brahmin; his arms were made into the Warrior, his thighs the People, and from his feet the Servants were born.[13]

The ancient code of India, the *Laws of Manu*, sets the rights and duties of Hindu society. This sacred Hindu book of law was written in circa 400BC. Laws of Manu give the details of religious obligations, basic rituals, ceremonies as birth, death, marriage, dietary, etc. This code prescribes the traditional caste system, as well. One of the leading political figures of India, Dr. Babasaheb Ambedkar utter in a speech that Manu had proclaimed the gospel, which Nietzche sought to preach, long before Nietzche was born. This is a religion, which is not intended to establish liberty, equality and fraternity. It rather proclaims the worship of the superman, who is the Brahmin, by the rest of the Hindu society. It propounds that the class of the Brahmin are born to live and to rule. The rest of the society are born just to serve them.This gospel proposes that they have no night of their own life, and no right to develop their own personality.[14]

Carla Power labels the caste system as a religiously sanctioned form of segregation.[15] Analysing this verse, three deductions are made. First is, because *varna-vyavastha* is mentioned in the book, *varnas* are least five thousand years old. Secondly, this system is divine, because Rig Veda utters that; sections of Hindu society are body parts of the God. Lastly, for the reason that each *varna* is a different piece of *Virat Purush*, then those *varnas* also have a hierarchy within themselves.[16]

Meaning of Varna: The definite meaning of the word *varna* is colour. It is maintained in plentiful sources that, distinctions were made to distinguish Aryan invaders from non-Aryans, where Aryans were fair but the indigenous populace were brunette. There are stories about *varnas* being composed in accordance with skin colours. Mahabharata Brigu classifies four *varnas* respectively as fair, reddish, pale and black. Still this proposal is not applicable; it is impossible to match *varnas* with specific ethnic groups since fair-skinned people, Australians, Mongoloids and blacks are basic elements of India's ethnic *mixtum compositum*; and all are assorted with each other. The early inhabitants of Indian sub-continent are thought to be Negritos, and others as Proto- Austroloids like Australian aborigines. As for the recent ages, the dominant ethnic breeds are of Aryan origins, which make Indians to resemble Europeans than Chinese and other Asians. The Mongoloid type people can be detected only in the line bordering China. Still, invasions that India pulled all through the history, brought diverse people to India besides the mentioned types. Even supposing marriage restrictions prevented those types to be blended, yet some marriages occurred, producing a hybrid strain.[17] This is why the Untouchables believed that the only way to destroy casteism is to make marriage within one's caste unlawful.[18] The correlation between language and ethnic roots is rough. In the northern parts of India, Indo-Aryan and in southern parts Dravidian is spread; the Himalayan tribes speak mainly Tibeto-Burman languages. All those languages have local splinter languages and dialects. Except linguistically homogeneous areas, which are small peasantry places, bi-lingualism or tri-lingualism is common.[19]

Varnas and Jatis: Within each of the *varnas* and *jatis*, members possess different rights, liberties and different practices of daily life and religious obligations. Some enjoy many privileges, whereas others are limited by a number of restrictions. Thus, the system is much abused.[20] For instance the *Shatapatha Brahman* lays down different sizes of the funeral mound for the four classes.[21] The caste distinctions, *varna ashramas*[22] are determined by purity and high exclusivism. Higher castes are lofty, because of their purity, whereas the lowers are there due to their impurity. This cleanliness is used both for physical and spiritual connotations. Therefore the inter-caste or inter-*jati* relations are also regulated, according to status of each. In order to prevent *jatis* merging, endogamy is enforced. If this rule was broken, then those people became outcaste. Caste of a newborn is predetermined, because caste is hereditary. Moreover, it is impossible and intolerable to change the caste one belongs to, thus each individual lingers within that caste until death.[23] In theory, the position of individuals and the ascriptive groups to which they belonged were fixed, though in practice, each caste developed myths, which made exceptions for itself, and some quite successfully altered their relative status.[24] Due to the rigidity of this caste system, the social relations between castes are weak and limited. Superior classes even do not eat with inferior standings. If the rule restricting the marriage among different *jatis* is broken, then the society prohibits this family, they are excluded and sinful. The Hindu caste system is thus the most strict one among other correspondents.

For the reason that each *varna* and *jati* has a certain profession, there is a direct correlation between the economic status and social strata. The traditional caste system, while in many ways unique in its cultural features, was nevertheless very clearly a 'pre-modern' system. It was correlated with an economic and political structure that is aptly characterized as a 'feudal' one. The strictly designed economic relations constituted challenge towards modernisation. Caste economy was based on village economy. That made modernisation difficult. Because the penetration degree was limited.[25] Higher groups enjoy spiritual, administrative and such major jobs, where lower *varnas* and *jatis* are mostly craftsman. The jobs that higher caste member do is non-polluting for the lower groups. For some scholars, caste was useful for formation of the Indian society, but as the time passed by, bonds among layers changed, they tightened and the relations became so much limited as upper classes wanted to set power relations with lower classes, so defined limits for the inferior classes as well as themselves. Caste, according to Kasambi, originally had a positive function which enabled Indian society to be formed out of many diverse and even discordant elements, with the minimum use of violence.[26]

The four castes are Brahman, Kshatria, Vaishya and Shudra, hierarchically. Roughly they are priests; rulers, aristocrats and warriors; landlords and businessmen; and peasants. Duties of the priests, who are namely the Brahmins are to preserve and protect the eternal laws of the Dharma, which is the universe. Dharma is also the destiny and it is the task of each person to follow own Dharma. If the person manages to be a good one, then after death her/his Dharma may reborn as an upper caste member. The class of rulers and warriors namely the Kshatriyas are the defenders and the guarantors of the safety and security of the community. As for the business people *Vaisyas*, they are the conservers and distributors of wealth. And the fourth *varna* is the division for labourers, they are *Shudras* and they are the working majority involved in the production of essential commodities. Actually, even though there is a clear partition between the twice-born groups as the first three *Varnas*; the Brahman, Kshatria and Vaishya; the last caste is referred as once born since they are considered to be so dirty to born again and in most districts of India, they are almost equal with the Untouchables, and the distinction among them is not precise.[27]

In the hierarchy, the ruling class has a lower status than the religious people. The sacred and political functions were separated well and clearly, where importance of political was second degree due to well distinction between royalty and priestly-hood.[28] Even though there was a dichotomy between ruling and religious classes, sometimes the ruler asked for more sacred position. So he caused conflict with Brahmanical order. For instance the founder of Jainism was the ruling prince Mahavir, who asked for more sanctified claims and set off a conflict with Brahmans.[29]

Outcastes: Still there are two other groups, who are not worthy to fall within the caste system so they are outcastes: Panchamas (fifths) - who were later known as the Untouchables - and foreigners. *Malecha* tag is used for the foreigners or invaders. The Untouchables are the polluting populace, thus they are entitled with polluting services as dishwashing, grave digging, body washing, cremating, cleaning, etc. Foreigners are recognized same as the Untouchables in some places; in diverse parts of India they are treated differently. In his article Clarke maintains that; when the Indian society is investigated through the lens of caste, then two distinct and distinguishable components of society comes out.[30] One is the Untouchables and the other is *varna* members.These two components exist within their own geographical, cultural, social, political and economic worlds, and their interaction is proscribed by centuries of religio-social constraints and constrictions.[31]

Colonization

Asia continent, with all its abundant products, wide spread trade, well established culture and traditions, was the most precious centre of the world. The mist of its religions and culture, the exoticy of its languages, the wealth and progressiveness of Asia drew Europeans to itself. In the middle of the seventeenth century, Asia still had a far more important place in the world than Europe.[32] The special conditions of Europe, particularly in England and France, pushed them in a nation state building process. As a result of this process, industrial developments and capitalism emerged. It was possible for those states to obtain cheap and copious raw material from the lands of Asia in addition to cheap labour. India offered more of these boons for United Kingdom. This is why; the British named India 'Jewel in the Crown'. India remained under the British rule from 1858 until 1947.

> The riches of Asia were incomparably greater than those of the European States. Her industrial techniques showed a tradition that the European handicrafts did not possess. And there was nothing in the more modern methods used by the traders of the West countries that Asian trade had to envy. In matters of credit, transfer of funds, insurance and cartels, neither India nor Persia nor China had anything to learn from Europe.[33]

All through its history, India experienced several conquests from all geographical directions, owing to its richness. Besides the material wealth, India was prosperous with literature, architecture and arts. The early Indian civilization, beginning in the Indus Valley and almost newly unearthed cities of Harappa and Mohenjodaro, which are the lands that we now recognize as Pakistan, can be compared to Sumerian, Mesopotamian or Egyptian civilizations, because it was developed as much as them. Such a high-culture was an ocean wherein what is hidden is not known to anybody,[34] this attracted attentions of various civilisations, and was invaded for several times. In early times of history, North of India was invaded by Central Asian tribes. Huns were the next invaders of India and they defeated the Gupta Empire by coming together with other Central Asian tribes. And then, Muslim conquests began. Especially Persian occupations left an everlasting mark in India. As for the 15th century, following the Muslim take over, Portuguese traders started entering into India. For the Portuguese, the experience of passing through the lands, where herbs were born,[35] was extremely important. While the Portugal state was funding navigations to explore economical routes in the direction of India, publishers within the Portugal were occupied in publishing booklets[36] about this country and geographical findings for those willing to cruise towards India. By mid 16th century a new empire was rising in territories of India, the Mughal Empire. European traders, the British,

French and Dutch were coming to India in early 17th century. Among the European powers, the British managed to consolidate their own rule in India and initiated a new era, whose impact is still visible in the contemporary India. The British achieved to settle their own political rule and introduced Western culture, life style and technology there. So, India met numerous conquests among its aged history, and the colonial trend beginning with the 15th century, which left a different mark on present-day India.

The verb 'to colonize' does not mean 'to exploit' but means 'to make your home somewhere' and implies conveying Christianity and 'civilization'. However, this was not the case.

> A 'colonizing activity', we have called it, but we must add that the word 'colonizing' is not meant in the popular sense; or perhaps we should say that, on the contrary, it was true colonization. Is not peaceful penetration, both economic and cultural, and occurring with the full consent of those colonized, for whom it proves beneficial and lasting in its effects, is not this, in fact, real colonization?[37]

By the 15th century, European states began conquering and settling in diverse areas of the world, particularly in Africa, Asia and Latin America. This trend has political, economic and social aspects. Especially, after the European states managed to form modern nation states and this nation state formation process ended up with capitalism and the colonizing process emerged due to raw material necessity. The colonizers not only spoiled the natural sources, but also the cultural, historical remains, belief systems and social organization styles.

After the first travel of Columbus, who is considered to be the one who broadened the borders of the world,[38] Kings of Spain and Portugal shared the world. They had drawn an imaginary line on world map with Tordesillas Agreement signed in 1494. Consequently, Portuguese became the possessors of the lands beyond Eastern border of Spain and Spanish became the possessors of the lands beyond Western border of Spain. The Portuguese immediately launched geographical discoveries. They promoted their existence in India and arrived in Indian

Ocean by the year 1498 by using the most lucrative route passing through the East and South Africa and the Persian Gulf. Without encountering other European powers, the Portuguese enjoyed power in India for about a hundred years and made huge profits of the spice trade from Asia to Europe. Afterwards, traders of other European countries' arrived in India. Following the Dutch, Danish, English and French appeared in India. Among those the British and the French became significant and as a result of the rivalry between these two states, the British became the winner of India. As the Munghal Empire began to collapse, the British Company, the East India Company, was the forerunner of European companies to rush in and to settle factories in diverse parts of India. The British achieved this via offering some profits for the local merchants. Moreover, the British appeared so insistent about obtaining trade concessions by the Indian government. Actually, the British existence in India began via the East India Company.

Dr. Ambedkar, who is the chief architect of Indian Constitution and the leader of the Dalit movement, in his writing entitled 'India on the Eve of the Crown Government' lays the justification of the British imperialism.

> Unlike the Greeks who did not have even a word for imperialism, the Romans were the world's first and greatest imperial people and they coined a justification for imperialism that became the heritage of their successor. They proclaimed that they were a people of superior race with a culture too high to be compared with any other, that they had better system of administration, that they were versed in the arts of life. They also proclaimed that the rest were people of inferior race with a very low culture and were absolutely devoid of the arts of life, and that their administration was very despotic. As a logical consequence of this the Romans argued that it was their divine mission to civilise their low lying brethren, nay to conquer them and superimpose their culture in the name of humanity. The British have justified their imperial policy in India by similar argumentation.[39]

Even though the aim of the British was to make profit of their rule in India, since they began dominating Indian trade and politics, via using the raw material cultivated on Indian lands in manufacturing done in British lands and then by exporting the manufactured goods back to India, on the other side they contributed to the modern development of Sub-Continent. The European rulers of India brought advanced systems of postage, printing, transport. The mentioned developments brought the country together, facilitated the political organization of castes in terms of exchange of views, to inform affiliates of the developments, to coordinate and realize meetings, to record and archive political achievements to transmit the forthcoming generations. The language that British introduced in India served as the link language among different districts. The British also familiarize the Indians with the civil and penal codes. This endorsement brought new principles, be it justice, freedom and equality. Many castes have their constitutions printed by taking the new values in to account. It can be even said that the British existence in India paved the way to a modern social system, by softening the strict caste interactions.[40]

Nationalism in India

When nationalism in India is mentioned, the first name appearing is Raja Ram Mohan Roy, who is recognized as the 'father of Indian nationalism'. All through his life, he worked to melt Indian traditions and Western values in the same pot.

The nationalism was interpreted mainly in two ways in the Indian National Congress and represented by Moderates and Extremists. According to moderates, who dominated Congress for long years, India had to be much more westernized via adopting European style institutions, be it the field of health, justice or education. They wanted to establish local legislative foundations to lift self-government appreciation. As for the Extremist wing of the Congress, they were hesitant in adopting western values, since they were afraid of damaging the Hindu traditions. They were also after modernisation; however they were willing to preserve the Hindu beliefs and customs while modernizing. They were impatient with the small steps that moderates were taking as local legislatures, but they sought full independence; they pronounced their intention to use force if needed to achieve independence. Moreover, Lord Curzon's partition of Bengal in 1905 strengthened the nationalism ideas as all-encompassing Indian nationalism delivered by Gandhi's support in Khilafat movement.

Mohandas Karamchand Gandhi

History of Mohandas Karamchand Gandhi is always considered to be the history of India. He is the father of the Indian nation and the hero of Indian nationalism. He is the one who dared to wage an independence war against the continuous British imperialism and to free India from its dominion. He marked his era with an exceptional style of non-violence.

> Mohan Das Karam Chand Gandhi gained first-hand experiences in the continents-Europe, Africa and Asia. He was well-versed in the traditions and teachings of the major religions of the world. No wonder, he developed into an enigma. He was a peculiar mixture, of the oriental and the occidental, of the ancient and the modern.[41]

Gandhi is the Indian leader, who led the independence movement of India from the British colonial rule. He is best known for his philosophy of non-violence called Satyagraha. Satyagraha means the true path. According to his presupposition, there is no difference between religious and realistic doings. They are combined with the non-violence principle. He imbibed his philosophy into his political vision, as well.

It is known that this thought of him is inspired by diverse faith systems, be it Christianity, Buddhism or Hindu in addition to a novel of Russian author Leo Tolstoy, The Kingdom Of God Is Within You, 1894.[42] For Tolstoy, 'a Christian enters into no dispute with his neighbour; he neither attacks nor uses violence; on the contrary, he suffers himself, without resistance, and by his very attitude towards evil not only sets himself free, but helps to free the world at large from all outward authority'. This idea might have inspired the Great Soul Gandhi and might have echoed his own thoughts.[43] Sinha's explanation clarifies this idea and method. He thinks all living things have the will to live, so the non-violence notion is the logical outcome of this will. The spirit feels its own unbreakable autonomy and understands the others autonomy feelings. She/he wants to survive, and understands the others wish of living. So no one wants to be hurt or killed or to suffer at the hands of others.[44]

Gandhi was born in Porbandar city of Gujarat district. He belonged to the *Bania* division of *Vaishya* caste. The Vaishya caste is the third caste among four castes, so Mohandas Karamchand Gandi was not a member of a high caste. The caste that Gandhi belonged is known to be dealing commerce and especially they are grocers and the name Gandhi indicates this occupation. Gandhi was son of the Chief Minister of Porbandar. Within his childhood memoirs, Gandhi sorrowfully mentions his child-marriage experience.[45] At the age of fourteen he was married to a thirteen age-old young girl Kasturba and this marriage was a piece of their customs.[46]

Mohandas Karamchand Gandhi left India, to study law in London. After experiencing a number of unsuccessful job attempts, he attended in an Indian firm for a post in South Africa, where he faced discrimination several times, because he was an Indian. Regardless of caste or education level, Indians were badly disgraced by the British in South Africa, which was also the territory of the British Empire. As he came across with apartheid there, he initiated his first resistance in South Africa in order to improve the conditions of Indians resident there. This is how his political views began to be formed.

Satyagraha

His silent and calm confrontation was corresponding to his Satyagraha attitude. It was a passive, non-violent resistance. Gandhian non-violent satyagraha was a method of direct action, which allowed for non-cooperation against the government for a temporary period without resort to violence.[47] Those people performing this practice resistance are called satyagrahis. The method they used was rejecting and opposing to the unfair situation silently, by breaking the rule and suffering for the outcome of protesting it. It is also called as the soul force. Gandhi's policy was to avoid humiliating the enemy at all costs.[48]

At the end of this silence struggle, they managed to persuade those in South Africa to negotiate about the status of Indians. Afterwards he returned to India in 1915 and supported the British army during the war. However, when he was fed up with the British intimidating attitude towards Indians and passing the Rowlatt Act, he stopped supporting them. The Rowlatt Act let the government to arrest Indians without trial. Immediately he initiated his passive resistance once again, nonetheless he could not prevent the violence. On April 13, 1919, the innocent and naturally unarmed three hundred *satyagrahis* were killed and thousands of them were wounded by the fire of the British. The order of fire was given by General Reginald Dyer, whose explanation of this horrible massacre was; he planned punishing the *satyagrahis* and he wanted to make a wide impact on them.[49] Actually this struggle ended with the Amritsar Massacre of 1919. Albeit the Amritsar Massacre was something that Gandhi never wished happened and accused himself of having made a mistake, this event paved the way for the defiance of British rule in India.

Khilafat Movement

In the same year, 1919, Gandhi provided support for the Khilafat Movement of Muslims. Ottoman Sultan Abdülhamit II pioneered the Khilafat Movement. The Ottoman Sultan was the caliph of entire Ottoman Muslims. Anyhow, Abdülhamit II affirmed the Ottoman caliph to be the universal caliph, embracing entire Muslims in the world. He had several aims in doing this. His paramount endeavour was preventing the disintegration process of Ottoman Empire via pan-Islamism idea. The second aim was to impede the occupation and colonization activities towards Muslim countries. Many Muslim groups all around the world, including India, easily accepted this *ummah* solidarity. Since it was at the same time a campaign against colonization, Gandhi did not hesitate to support the Indian lap of the Khilafat Movement. This led Hindus and Muslims forming an alliance versus the British rule in India. Already, Khilafat leaders were eager for Hindu-Muslim unity, without which any non-cooperation movement involving boycott of services was evidently impossible.[50] It is also underlined by Minault that the Khilafat was the symbol indicating different things to different people, but the anti-British spirit of the movement provided the same consistency for all its components.[51] Gandhi set his non-cooperation and non-violence resistance in this movement and put it like that:

> I know that withdrawal of cooperation is a grave thing. It requires ability to suffer. I know that it is the right of the citizen to withdraw his cooperation from the state when that cooperation means his degradation. It is a tangible form of showing one's displeasure at the acts of one's government.[52]

By the year 1920, Gandhi concretely commenced his non-cooperation or in other words the non-alignment movement against the British. The aim was to challenge British via pullout of Indian espousal. The initial step of this movement was to set up a total consciousness against the British colonialism in India and to topple it. He called for a nationwide strike, *hartal.* During the movement, Indians boycotted the imported clothing besides the institutions, be it schools or courts, taxes established or introduced by the British. The non-violence movement became very popular within India. Gandhi asserted that the movement he initiated was their constitutional right and in the letter he gave to the Viceroy on June 22, 1920 he reminded the Viceroy of subjects right to refuse the assisting a ruler who is believed to misrule the country. As a result of this non-violence movement, Gandhi became the hero of Indian nationalism and independence deed. The civil disobedience of Gandhi made a substantial impact on the British government in India. It endangered governmental administrations in a number of Provinces and in that sense it embarrassed the government, which was hesitant to come down heavily upon non-violent resistance.[53]

On the other hand, this movement caused him being sentenced to his longest detainment course. It is known that, Gandhi had the best times, to develop his ideas, in prison. During his detainment, he read the book Civil Disobedience (1849) by Henry David Thoreau and decided to try this method, but he did not get constructive and affirmative results.[54] Gandhi was at the age of forty-four, and he was carrying out painstaking struggles since over twenty years. He was experienced enough to initiate a real battle now.[55]

Indians burned their clothes and any other pieces of import. Now they were spinning their own cotton fibres via the customary *charkha,* the wooden spin machine, which became a symbol of Indian nation and is present in the Indian flag. From educated urban people to rural backward folks the *charkha* program was taken as the path towards *swadeshi* –self reliance- and also it constructed somehow solidarity between masses and elite,[56] that's why this movement was the all-India movement. The texture spun short, the *khadi,* became the brand of Gandhi. Besides, Gandhi fasted, for the well being, peace and independence of the Indian nation.

The next target of Gandhi was to topple the colonial rule and liberate India. In his great effort he was allied with two other prominent names of the Indian liberation struggle, who were Gopal Krisha Gokhale, whom Gandhi was to regard as his *guru*[57] and Hindu Bal Gangadhar Tilak besides Rabindranath Tagore, who is considered to be the one that called Gandhi as Mahatma. Mahatma has a religious, spiritual connotation and it means the 'Great Soul'.

> Mahatma Gandhi was not only a political saint, as he is often projected in some writings, but he was more than that a cool and calculating strategist and shrewd realist. His phenomenal success can be gauged from the fact that he was able to communicate his conviction of the superiority of moral and spiritual power over physical force to all.[58]

Gandhi initiated the liberation struggle by taking up concrete measures like protests. He and his supporters rallied for rights of various groups; be it women, indigo growers or textile workers. Fasting was the best way to achieve their political, social and economic demands.

It was 1925, when he was elected the president of the Indian National Congress, which became a great social occasion as well as a political assembly.[59] By his presidency, he fasted for the good of the Indian public, organized meetings concerning British rule and related issues besides protesting some Hindu traditions like child marriage. He was also deeply apprehensive with the new language spreading among people, English. He made efforts to promote usage of their national language, Hindi. By 1928, he aroused his rallies especially as a result of the latest Indian constitution imposed by British, without consulting even one Indian. The young politicians were not believers on Gandhi's non-violence policy. Mahatma Gandhi was then called *Bapu* Gandhi, which means 'Grandfather Gandhi', by the young and modern Indian politicians, who were ready to replace the Great Soul Gandhi. They were impatient with British undertakings and initiated violent upcomings. Unavoidable, those upheavals were silenced by the British forces severely. Mahatma persuaded the Congress about accepting the British Raj until the last day of 1929. At the same time he appealed the British government to give India dominion[60] status by the end of the announced period. Otherwise he declared to initiate new non-cooperation campaigns. He planned to use this interim period to travel around India, explaining people the way to independence, to stop child marriages, to prevent consumption of alcohol, the price of British rule, how to resist and how implement non-violence.

Dandi March

Since British persisted on their exploits of India, Gandhi initiated his famed Dandi March in 1930. This Satyagraha was a protest of the British salt taxes. Followed by numerous Indians, the Great Soul Gandhi walked from Ahmedabad to Dandi, which counts almost four hundred kilometres, to produce own salt and to protest paying salt taxes. The foreseen production of salt was illegal, however object of the march was to annihilate the law preventing Indians producing own salt. Even though this demonstration was also of non-violence school, aggressive incidents happened that effected son of Mahatma Gandhi, as well. Gandhi, by this protest rally, managed to convince the British government in negotiating as a result a series of conferences were arranged. In the first round table meeting, Indians were represented by Mohammad Ali Jinnah. However, this situation was harshly criticized by the Congress as far as Jinnah was the leader of Muslims in addition to his position against the policies of Gandhi. Because this situation attracted the disapprovals of Hindus, Gandhi was present to represent the Congress. As a result of the negotiations, the Delhi Pact, in other words Gandhi-Irwin Pact was signed between Mohandas Karamchand Gandhi and Lord Irwin,[61] in March 1931. By the pact, the British Government consented to free the prisoners detained after the salt demonstrations. Besides, salt production was legalized by means of this agreement. Lastly, another conference was approved. However, the conference, which was held in London, was satisfactory neither for Gandhi nor for other Indian independence seekers. The agenda of the conference did not include any title on power transfer, but rather other topics. It dealt with minorities that caused a catastrophic outcome that each group; Hindus, Muslims, Christians, Sikhs, Parsees all asked for separate electorate. He was again imprisoned when he was back to home and the latest viceroy, Lord Freeman Willingdon refused to debate with Gandhi. In jail he heard that Dalits and various religious groups granted separate elections by the new constitution and Gandhi warned the government about annihilating it or he would fast to death. Dr. Ambedkar consented to argue with Gandhi on this case and Gandhi managed to convince Dr. Ambedkar. This did not prevent the progress in the status of Dalits. Dalits were now allowed to enter the Hindu temples and as the pollution understanding was partly changed, the upper caste people started accepting food from those traditionally Untouchables. He was still in prison in the year 1933 and that year he founded and edited a newspaper namely *Harijan*. He did not support the orthodox Hindus, who sought prevention of Dalits entering the temples. After his release, he began pursuing policies about reforming India. Gandhi resigned his seat in Congress and he totally stopped his engagement with politics whilst World War II was beginning.

World War II and Quit India Movement

Very close to the invasion of Poland in 1939 by Nazi's, The Second World War exploded. Mahatma Gandhi was advising his own method, non-violence and noncooperation, to the wounded sufferers of the war and especially to the victims of fascism. His famous saying advises world people non-violence: An eye for an eye just leaves world blind. His hatred towards Hitler and Mussolini, who was called 'the man with cat eyes' by Gandhi, is well known.

Gandhi did not avoid making deals with Britain by asking them proving their real goal was democracy in that war, as they declared. He meant leaving India totally free. Certainly the British authorities did not accept his proposal. Thus, Gandhi denied being a plaintiff in the war. He began pushing for independence more firmly then. These demands paved the way to the Quit India Movement.

Quit India Movement, *bharat chhodo*, began completely in year 1942, when the Congress passed an enactment seeking complete freedom by confiscating the British reign in India.

Winston Churchill sent Sir Richard Stafford Cripps to India in order to ensure British possessing India and to undermine the insufferable half-naked fakir.[62] The thought of Churchill about India is best described by Catherine Clement, who said "When he wanted to justify the Raj, Winston Churchill would say calmly, 'India is an abstraction'." And how could independence be granted to an abstraction?[63] British wanted to keep India, especially against Japan during the war. However, demands for independence aroused within India at the same time. Sir Cripps promised India independence, if India accepts the British dominion till the end of the World War. On the other side Japan was threatening India by invading. Because India was not strong enough to resist both pushes, it had to make a choice out of two bad things, and India picked the British option.

Such a dilemmatic situation irritated Gandhi a lot. His goal was clear: to free India. He just decided to make moves towards this ambition, the coined the famed slogan 'Quit India'. The followers of Gandhi were making rallies all around India for aspiring their liberation expressing their impatience with jingles of 'freedom has to come not tomorrow but today'. Gandhi encouraged all citizens of India to join the civil disobedience movement and certainly advised to keep in the frames of nonviolence principles. This time he wanted to make their wish more visible, thus he called everybody to open rebellion. Because the British did not want to encounter another rebellion in war time, Gandhi was imprisoned again, this time Kasturba too. Moreover, the rebellions were suppressed via brutal bloody ways that Gandhi would never wish.

As a result, the Quit India Movement was a tremendous defeat for Gandhi and Indians, who aimed to obtain their freedom. This was a huge disillusement for the Indians in search of self-determination. Britain took this opportunity to blame Gandhi of the violence. Gandhi fasted to deny this claim. His adopted son –at the same time his first secretary- died of acute bronchitis and his death was followed by Kasturba's. Gandhi was about to die, too. Churchill decided to release him of the prison. However, Gandhi did not die, but healed.

The Partition of India

The new Prime Minister of Britain was Clement Attlee after the end of World War II, in 1945. He was planning to free India; however his concern was to divide India into two regions; one for Muslims and one for the others. Mohammad Ali Jinnah was one of the greatest supporters of this idea, as the leader of Indian Muslims. Jinnah was willing to establish a separate state of Muslims; 'the country of pure: Pakistan'.[64]

The Shimla Conference was held to make negotiations about the partition of India. In June 1945 at Shimla, the Viceroy held separate interviews with Jinnah and Nehru. Gandhi was not a delegate in this conference, and Nehru represented the Hindu segment and still Gandhi was present in Shimla. Especially the Muslim party was so much striving in this conference and the viceroy rejected the requests of the Muslim side. Besides, the Pakistan foreseen in the conference was found ungovernable, because Pakistan itself would be divided into two segments separated by more than a thousand kilometres.[65] The Shimla Conference ultimately failed in its objective. It showed that neither the Viceroy Wavell nor the Congress were ready to answer the demands of Muslims, like separate electorate in the coming elections. This Conference adjusted the attitude of Congress towards the British friendly.[66]

The new leader of India was Nehru, who was charged by the Viceroy Wavell. Nehru proposed a ministry for Mohammad Jinnah, but it was refused by him. Moreover, Jinnah decided to take some more severe measures to make people understand how Muslims are decisive on having a separate state. This was ended by bloody, brutal and extremely violent acts. In his book, Clement narrates that Muslims forced many Hindus to convert and massacred them.[67] Even though Gandhi was no more an actor of politics; he fasted to put an end to this bloodshed and cruelty.

As for the Dalits, their most prominent leader, Dr. Ambedkar favoured this partition as far as he believed that the population density was not corresponding to the city and state boundaries of India. Ambedkar regarded Muslims as a distinct nation, but they were a minority within Indian borders. This partition would result in altering the boundaries of places where Muslims and Hindus lived, and free the minority group from the domination of Hindus. Gandhi and his deputy, Jawaharlal Nehru denied existence of a religious communal problem. Actually, Dr. Ambedkar was neither supportive of Muslims nor their opponent. For him, India had a problem of minorities. He felt that the minorities could be left at the mercy of aggressive majority. Like the Muslim case, a similar communal problem was present among downtrodden classes and upper castes of India.

The Freedom Movement

India's way to freedom was long and slow. Under the guidance of Gandhi, India exhausted a lengthy and controversial process. Three key episodes during this process are the milestones recognized within this gradual course. Those are the times, when the British Government enacted new laws regarding India in the years 1909, 1919 and 1935.[68]

The 1909 *Morley-Minto Reforms* of Lord Morley led to the establishment of provincial legislative councils, where the members were elected. Those were not legislative councils but only advisory bodies. The legislative power was held by the Viceroy. Morley underlined that he did not realize those reforms to pave the way towards a parliamentary democracy.[69] Already some MPs were challenging the establishment of a parliamentary democracy in India, because they were not clear about giving India a kind of self-rule since they could not estimate where would it end and they were afraid of the British Empire's disintegration.

> If it could be said that this chapter of reforms led directly or necessarily to the establishment of parliamentary system in India, I for one would have nothing at all to do with it.[70]
>
> *Lord Morley*

The next Viceroy of India, Samuel Montagu planned and announced to establish new bodies in order to penetrate self-governing, responsible institutions working in coordination with the British authorities. Thus, he run *Montagu-Chelmsford Reforms* and released the India Act of 1919. As a result there was a diarchy system. This meant that in provincial level legislative bodies were founded, where the native Indians carried the legislation function. Those provincial were given the right to enact laws in particular fields. Still, this given right to legislation does not mean that British gave up dominating the Indian politics. In the newly found provincial legislative bodies, the MPs could enact laws concerning education, agriculture, health, etc. Nonetheless they were not allowed to enact laws pertaining to monetary or fiscal policies like taxes. Those mentioned financial policies were made by the British. Moreover, the British government, represented by the Viceroy, held the right to veto any law enacted by the provincial legislatures.[71]

The third important move is the *India Act of 1935,* which put an end to the diarchy giving the provincial legislative bodies the right to enact laws in any subject. Now the provincial councils were responsible for the Central Government and the Viceroy only dealt with foreign affairs and defence matters. This was the utmost progress en route for self-determination.[72]

On one hand, there was the Congress Party, and on the other the Muslim league, where respectively one was led by Mohammad Ali Jinnah and Pandit Motilal Nehru, who can be recognized as the father of Jawaharlal Nehru — the most important fellow freedom-fighter of Gandhi's struggle for India's independence.[73] The two groups were acting together since especially the Mutiny of 1857. The two parties met in December 1916 and declared their unity with the Congress – Muslim League Pact or the Lucknow Pact. The aim was to establish a united achievement in the national emancipation. This move was not found anxious by the British, and even a declaration was made saying that the unity among Indian citizens pleasures Crown as far as India is an integral part of the United Kingdom. Certainly British did not responded rigorously, because they were making preparations for the largest concessions to be taken via the Act of 1919.

By the Morley-Minto Reforms; in other words, by the Government of India Act of 1919, new and Western political notions were brought in India. The reforms provided partial roles to the Indians within legislative councils of India's provinces. The members of the legislative councils were elected, while the members of the central council were appointed. Besides, the governor general was not responsible to the legislative councils. On the other side, Britain provided herself the largest allowances by making the viceroy in India only responsible to the Crown and the government in London but not the legislative and judicial bodies of India. The Indians, who bodied the opposition by getting conscious about the developments, were silenced by the British. Sometimes the British took severe measures towards the opposition, and the events resulted with the massacre in Amritsar. Unavoidably, they earned the annoyance of Indians, among those who were protesting this event, Jawaharlal Nehru and Mohandas Karamchand Gandhi. The Muslim league protesters were excited and their nationalist ideas aroused when caliphate resident in Ottoman Empire was abolished. As they became more enthusiastic for independence and self-rule, they began mobilizing the masses for this purpose. The Muslim movement did not become a distinctive process but they joined in the lines of freedom struggle on entire India basis. The Muslims participated in the movement of Gandhi and in return Gandhi backed the Muslim demand for the caliph. Turkey rejected the Muslim dream of caliphate, since she became a secular republic. The unrest within India continued until the World War II and then the way towards the independence got clearer. Those were the times, when dispute amongst Hindus and Muslims was taking place after the failure of Simla Conference and Gandhi disappeared from active politics. He was now the *Bapu* Gandhi, walking with his stick and travelling from one village to another, talking, staying with all Indians, be it a Hindu or a Muslim and advising them solidarity and freedom, rather than British dominion and partition. In his speeches, he made citations also from Koran and Bible. Those were the days that people were talking about the Muslim partition, thus Gandhi's reciting of Koran was criticized by some Hindus and they called him 'Mohammad Gandhi'.

> On 15th August 1947, the Indian flag was raised in place of the Union Jack. The colours of Congress –orange, white and green- bore Emperor Ashoka's wheel in place of Gandhi's spinning wheel. Speeches all through the night paid homage to 'the Father of Nation' and crowds, drunk on freedom, shouted: 'Victory to Mahatma Gandhi!' The Mahatma himself called the day a 'spiritual tragedy' and spent it fasting.[74]

References

1. Ramachandra Guha and Madhav Gadgil, *State Forestry and Social Conflict in British India,* Past and Present no. 123 (May 1989) p. 123.

2. Raja Jayaraman, *Caste and Class Dynamics of Inequality in Indian Society* (Delhi: Hindustan Cooperation, 1981) p. 9.

3. Stanley Wolpert, *India* (Berkeley: University of California Press, 1991) p. 118.
4. Vedantam Vatsala, *Still Untouchable,* Christian Century, 6/19/2002.
5. Sumit Sarkar, *Modern India: 1885-1947* (London: Macmillan, 1992), p. 54.
6. Wolpert, *op. cit.,* p. 118.
7. S.V. Desika Char, *Caste, Religion and Country: A View of Ancient and Medieval India* (New Delhi: Sangam Books, 1993) p. 47.
8. Catherine Clement, *India: Of Crowds and Democracy in* ed. Geeti Sen (New Delhi: Sage Publications, 1993), p. 53.
9. Vena Das, *Structure and Cognition: Aspects of Hindu Caste and Ritual* (Delhi: Oxford University Press, 1990) p. 10.
10. Shanti Swarup Gupta, Varna, *Castes and Scheduled Castes: A Documentation in Historical Perspective,* (New Delhi: Concept Publishing Company, 1991) p. 13.
11. Rig Veda, Sama Veda, Yajur Veda and Atharva Veda. Still some other books are mentioned to be holy books, for instance Ramayana and Mahabharta are widespread.
12. Beatrice Lamb, *India: A World in Transition* (New York: Frederick A. Praeger Inc. Publishers, 1964).
13. Wolpert, *op. cit.,* p. 117.
14. B.R. Ambedkar, Ranade, Gandhi and Jinnah: Address delivered on the 101st Birthday Celebration of Mahadev Govind Ranade Held on the 18th January 1943. In the Gokhale Memorial Hall, Poona, (Bombay: Thacker and Co., Ltd., 1943) Chapter V.
15. Carla Power, *Caste Away,* Mother Jones, 03628841, (Jul/Aug 2001).
16. Gupta, Varna, *Castes and Scheduled Castes: A Documentation in Historical Perspective,* pp. 13-4.
17. Lamb, *op. cit.,* pp. 14-6.
18. Sophie Baker, *Caste: At Home in Hindu India* (London: Jonathan Cape, 1990) p. 139.
19. O.H.K. Spate, *India and Pakistan: A General and Regional Geography* (London: Methuen and Co. Ltd., 1954) pp. 124-25.

20. Vedantam Vatsala, *Still Untouchable,* Christian Century, 16/19/2002.
21. Govind Sadashiv Ghurye, *Caste and Race in India,* (Bombay: Popular Prakashan, 1969).
22. Vatsala, *op. cit.*
23. Barbara R. Joshi, *Ex-Untouchable: Problems, Progress and Policies in Indian Social Change,* Pacific Affairs, Vol. 53, No. 2, (Summer, 1980) p. 195.
24. Gail Omvedt, *Cultural Revolt in a Colonial Society: The Non-Brahman Movement in Western Indian 1873 to 1930,* (Bombay: Scientific Socialist Education Trust, 1976) p. 66.
25. *Ibid.,* p. 41.
26. *Ibid.,* p. 40.
27. Sathianathan Clarke, *Dalits Overcoming Violation and Violence,* Ecumenical Review, 00130796, (July 2002, Vol. 54, Issue 3).
28. Omvedt, *op. cit.,* p. 41.
29. *Ibid.,* p. 59.
30. Clarke, *op. cit.*
31. *Ibid.*
32. Auguste Toussaint, *The History of the Indian Ocean* (London: The University of Chicago Press, 1066) p. 88.
33. *Ibid.,* p. 131.
34. An ocean in which what is hidden is not known by anyone.
35. Pasar a donde nascen las especerias (Port.): To pass through the lands, where herbs are born.
36. Portolano (It.): A booklet analysing a coasts climate, sea, etc. features.
37. Toussaint, *op. cit.,* p. 61.
38. Amplificator mundi (Lat.): The one who broadens the borders of the world.
39. http://www/ambedkar.org, *India on the Eve of The Crown Government.*
40. M.H. Srinivas, *Caste in Modern India,* (The Journal of Asian Studies, Vol. 16, No. 4 Aug., 1957) pp. 530-31.

41. R.K. Sinha, *Gandhian Non-Violence and the Indian National Struggle,* (Delhi: H.K. Publications, 1992) p. 5.
42. Mohandas K. Gandhi *autobiography: The Story of My Experiments with Truth,* (New York: Dover Publications Inc, 1948), p. 77.
43. 1992: 48.
44. Sinha, *op. cit.,* pp. 11-2.
45. Gandhi, *op. cit.,* pp. 1-11.
46. Clement, *op. cit.,* p. 30.
47. V.T. Patil, *Mahatma Gandhi and the Civil Disobedience Movement: A Study in the Dynamics of the Mass Movement* (Delhi: Renaissance Publishing House, 1988) p. 115.
48. Clement, *op. cit.,* p. 48.
49. *Ibid.,* pp. 61-2.
50. Sarkar, *op. cit.,* p. 196.
51. Gail Minault, *The Khilafat Movement: Religious Symbolism and Political Mobilization in India* (New York: Columbia University Press, 1982) p. 67.
52. Clement, *op. cit.,* p. 62.
53. Patil, *op. cit.,* p. 115.
54. Clement, *op. cit.,* pp. 46, 65.
55. *Ibid.,* p. 49.
56. Sarkar, *op. cit.,* p. 204.
57. Lamb, *op. cit.,* p. 76.
58. Gisela Bonn, *Ways of Perception: Between Effusiveness and Rejection Perceiving India* edited, Geeti Sen (New Delhi: Sage Publications, 1993) p. 26.
59. Sarkar, *op. cit.,* p. 89.
60. As the colonies of British Empire accomplished constitutional progress, then the British Empire allowed self-governance; be it a real or a virtual one.
61. Edward Frederick Lindley Wood, the Viceroy of India from 1926 to 1931.
62. Clement, *op. cit.,* p. 96.

63. Geeti Sen (ed.), *Perceiving India: Insight and Inquiry* (New Delhi: Sage Publications, 1993) p. 54.
64. Clement, *op. cit.,* p. 100.
65. *Ibid.,* p. 100.
66. Syed Shameem Hussain Kadri, *Creation of Pakistan* (Lahore: Wajidalis, 1982) pp. 303-16.
69. *Ibid.,* p. 74.
70. *Ibid.*
71. *Ibid.*
72. *Ibid.*
73. Bonn, *op. cit.,* p. 27.
74. Clement, *op. cit.,* p. 105.

2

Chokhamela and Eknath's Protests on Untouchability

Chokhamela, a thirteenth-fourteenth century Maharashtrian *sant*[1] in the Bhakti tradition, and Eknath, a sixteenth century *sant*, are both revered figures in the *warkari sampradaya,*[2] the tradition of pilgrimage to Pandharpur which marks the important Bhakti movement in the Marathi-speaking area. The lives of both are known by legend; their songs are sung by devotees on the pilgrimage and in *bhajan* sessions. Chokhamela was a Mahar, the only important Bhakti figure in Maharashtra from an Untouchable caste. Eknath was a Brahman from the holy city of Paithan who wrote about Chokhamela, ate with Mahars, allowed Untouchables into his *bhajan* sessions, and wrote poems in the persona of a Mahar who was wiser in spiritual matters than the Brahmans.

Both, then, offer models for contemporary change in regard to untouchability: even though an Untouchable, Chokhamela, achieved sanctity and a place among the Bhakti pantheon of *sants;* Eknath, even though a Brahman from a distinguished, scholarly family, showed by his actions that there was equality among the true Bhaktas. This study as explores the thought and the actions of both the Bhakti figures in an attempt to determine their basic social and religious ideas, and then note the contemporary attempts to legitimize change through reference to these earlier religious figures.

Chokhamela

Chokhamela was born in the second half of the thirteenth century, probably about the time that Dnyaneshwar, who is considered the founder of the Bhakti sect in Maharashtra, was born. He died in 1338 in Mangalvedhe, a town in Sholapur district, not far from Pandharpur. Chokhamela and his family seem to have followed the traditional village duties of a Mahar. The legend of his birth involves his parents' carrying mangoes to Pandharpur on the orders of the village headman, a duty expected of the Mahar village servant who was at the beck and call of the *patil*. On their journey, God Vitthal (or Vithoba), worshipped as the central divinity by the *warkari sampradaya,* disguised as a Brahman, begged for a fruit from the woman. He tasted it, found it sour and returned it to her. She tucked it into the folds of her sari and delivered the other mangoes to the priests at Pandharpur. When the fruit was counted and one was found missing, she pulled the half-bitten mango from her sari only to find that it had become a lovely child—Chokhamela.[3]

The legend of Chokhamela's death also involves traditional Mahar work and God's grace. He and other Mahars were called to repair the wall at Mangalvedhe—another traditional Mahar duty. As they worked on it, it collapsed, burying them. Namdev, a Bhakti *sant* from the *shimpi,* or tailor community who was Chokhamela's most devoted friend, went to the village to claim Chokhamela's body. He found the bones that murmured "Vitthal, Vitthal" and took them to Pandharpur, where they were buried near the steps of the temple.[4]

The legends, of course, can do no more than suggest that Chokhamela and his family were thoroughly and uncomplainingly involved in the traditional work of the Mahar caste, with divine intervention only to allow that work to proceed more smoothly. In even the lowliest of duties, that of dragging dead cattle out of the village, God Vitthal appeared to help Chokhamela.[5] There is no evidence to suggest that Chokhamela ever protested the traditional limits of Mahar village work.

The internal evidence of Chokhamela's *abhangas* (Bhakti songs) suggests some protest, however, about the concept of untouchability, even though the greater number reveal only the traditional devotion and piety of the *bhakta*. The printed collection of Chokhamela's *abhangas* contains 211 songs,[6] some of them obviously spurious since the names of later *sants* appear in them. The collection was prepared for popular use, and no substantive scholarly work has been done on the manuscripts [allegedly] held at Pandharpur. It seems, however, that an authentic voice does come through these songs, however corrupt the text may be.

All but thirty-two of Chokhamela's over two hundred songs could have been written by any of the *sants*. They are simple, direct, without reference to his caste, such as this one :

Why do you need a mirror
    to see the bangles on your wrist?
Have faith in the Name of Vitthal.
You don't need to think about ritual;
Chant the Name of Vitthal.
The path of the Yogi is not filled with clutter;
    the chant is free;
    do it first.

Chokha says: there is bliss in the company
    of the saints;
chant the Name every night, every day. *Abhanga 4*

The *abhangas* which do refer to untouchability, however, reveal that Chokhamela was probably profoundly troubled by his despised place in society. At times he was accepting, at times rebellious.[7]

If You had to give me this birth,
    why give me birth at all?
You cast me away to be born; you were cruel.
Where were You at the time of my birth?
Who did You help then?
Chokha says: O Lord, O Keshava, don't let me go.

Abhanga 6

O God, my caste is low; how can I serve You?
Everyone tells me to go away; how can I see you?
When I touch anyone, they take offense.
Chokhamela wants Your mercy.

Abhanga 76

The only impurity is in the five elements.
There is only one substance in the world.
Then who is pure and who is impure?
The cause of pollution is the creation of the body.
In the beginning, at the end, there is nothing but pollution.
No one knows anyone who was born pure.
Chokha says, in wonder, who is pure?

Abhanga 11

One abhanga seems to relate to one of the legends about Chokhamela, a legend of rejection in the temple and acceptance by God which is also commonly told about other Untouchable Bhakti *sants* in other traditions. In the Marathi version, Chokhamela sits on the banks of the Bhima river behind the temple after having been driven away by the temple priests, the Badve. Vitthal himself comes to comfort him, and Chokhamela offers him curd. A priest following Chokhamela overhears him address his companion as "Vithoba", an affectionate name for God Vitthal, and slaps his face. When he returns to the temple, the priest finds the image of Vitthal with a swollen cheek and curd spilt on his garment.[8] The *abhaga* which follows leaves out the miraculous, but indicates the Badve's interference with Chokhamela's attempts to worship Vithoba.

Run, run, Vithu, don't come slowly.
I am beaten by the Badve for some transgression:
They ask: "How can you wear the garland of Vithoba?"
They abuse me and curse me: "Why have you polluted God?"

I, Chokha, hands clasped, beg You, O God,
Don't be angry with my importuning.

Abhanga 5

However, Chokhamela more often than importuning God simply uses the symbols of his Maharness to reinforce the idea of his devotion to Vitthal as well as to weave his own tradition, his own work, into the life of the devotee. In the following *abhanga,* the word *call* in the last line is a translation of *daundi,* which means the proclamation the village Mahar servant makes in the centre of the village to call people together for an announcement:

Clap hands, raise flags.
take the road to Pandhari.[9]
The marketplace of Pandhari, the marketplace of joy!
There pilgrims meet in ecstasy,
So many flags they cannot be counted!
The banks of the Bhima resound with joyous shouts.
Let unbelievers come;
    let them go back pure.
Chokhamela gives this *call* from his heart.

Abhanga 54

Chokhamela even uses the customary right of the Mahar to receive any discarded food as a way to worship Vitthal. In this *abhanga,* he also uses the customary address of a Mahar to a superior *Johar,* as a salutation to Vitthal, here addressed as *May-Bap* (Mother and Father).

Johar, May-Bap, Johar.
I am the Mahar of Your Mahars.
I am so hungry I have come for Your leavings.
I am full of hopes; I am the slave of Your slaves.
Chokha says: I have brought a bowl for Your
    left-over food.

Abhanga 71

In contrast to his *abhanga* on impurity, Chokhamela in another *abhanga* accepts his low status as his *karma,* the result of bad action in a previous life. [The reference to Nila in the following *abhanga* is probably to King Nila who fought against the Pandavas in the Mahabharata war, but there are many puranic and epic figures named Nila. At any rate, the meaning is clear.]

Pure Chokhamela, always chanting the name.
I am a Mahar without a caste, Nila in a previous birth.
He showed disrespect to Krishna; so my birth as a Mahar.
Chokha says: this impurity is the fruit of our past.

Abhanga 4

The ultimate reconciliation Chokhamela seems to have made was to consider himself fully an Untouchable in the eyes of men, without hope of acceptance as anything but impure, but just as fully a beloved of God. The most popular of all his *abhangas* raises his own defect of body (or caste) into a universalized concept: even the ugly, the deformed, the outwardly unacceptable, can be holy. Iravati Karve, in her narration of a pilgrimage to Pandharpur,[10] tells that the Brahman group in which she was travelling sang this song by the Untouchable Bhakta Chokhamela :

> Cane is crooked, but its juice isn't crooked,
> Why be fooled by outward appearance?
>
> The bow is crooked, but the arrow isn't crooked,
> Why be fooled by outward appearance?
>
> The river is twisting, but its water isn't crooked,
> Why be fooled by outward appearance?
>
> Chokha is ugly, but his feelings aren't ugly,
> Why be fooled by outward appearance?
>
> *Abhanga 52*

Protest and question though he did, it would seem that Chokhamela lived in his traditional role as a Mahar and with its traditional limitations. The spirit of most of the *abhangas* is delight in the Lord, delivery from life's suffering through devotion. Even though agony is there, the central message is that Chokha, even though a Mahar, could experience the grace of God.

The Role of Bhakti Movement

With the growth of nationlism and the awakening of interest in Maharashtra's past, the Bhakti movement, still very much alive, came to serve a new purpose. Mahadeo Govind Ranade, a Brahman, a judge and a member of the reformist religious group, the Prarthana Samaj, as well as a leading nationalist, wrote in 1900 of the historic importance of the Bhakti movement:

> . . . like the Protestant Reformation in Europe in the sixteenth century, there was a Religious, Social and Literary Revival and Reformation in India, but notably in the Deccan in fifteenth and sixteenth centuries. This Religious Revival was not Brahmanical in its orthodoxy; it was heterodox in

> its spirit of protest against forms and ceremonies and class distinctions based on birth, and ethical in its preference of a pure heart, and of the law of love, to all other acquired merits and good works. This Religious Revival was the work also of the people, of the masses, and not of the classes. At its head were Saints and Prophets, Poets and Philosophers, who sprang chiefly from the lower orders of society—tailors, carpenters, potters, gardeners, shop-keepers, barbers, and even *mahars*—more often than Brahmans.[11]

Ranade's interpretation of the Bhakti movement served as legitimization for modern ideas of social justice, but his interpretation has been disputed. One reprint of Ranade's *Rise of the Maratha Power* includes a disclaimer in the introduction by R.V. Oturkar:

> It must further be emphasized, as Professor G.B. Sardar has done, that while the saints in Maharashtra released the people from the thralldom of rituals they did not raise a revolt against Chaturvarna [the four Classes] and the Caste system. Their revolt was more or less of a conceptual character, severely confined to the field of religious thinking...[12]

The supposed equality of the Bhakti movement continues to be a much used concept, however, chiefly by those not directly involved in the political or religious aspects of the contemporary attempt of ex-Untouchables to gain equality. W.B. Patwardhan, as quoted by R.D. Ranade in *Pathways to God in Marathi Literature,* stated what still is probably the general popular impression:

> The gates of the Bhakti school were ever open. Whoever entered was hailed as a brother—nay more—was honored as a saint.... All separatism tendencies vanished ... all were equal.... For five successive centuries, Maharashtra was the abode of that noblest and truest of all Democracies, the Democracy of the Bhakti school.[13]

This conception was echoed as recently as 1964 by the then Supreme Court Justice, P.B. Gajendragadkar, as he inaugurated the canopy he had presented for the main temple at

Pandharpur. He called for a spirit of equality and brotherhood in Maharashtra today of the same sort that the *warkari* tradition had taught. And he claimed that he called for equality and brotherhood with the same intensity that Chokhamela had cried out his grievances at the feet of Vithoba.[14]

In the 1930s, when the Mahar movement for religious rights was at its height, the message of Pandharpur was invoked to call for a lessening of the practice of untouchability by C.B. Agarwal:

> One of the greatest reformers in Maharashtra was Dnyaneshwar. According to the Shastras, the Harijans were debarred from hearing or reading the sacred Vedas.... Dnyaneshwar opened the gates of Vedic spiritualism to the Hindu masses including the Harijans .. . We have only to read the writing of Chokhamela, the untouchable Saint and follower of Dnyaneshwar, to get an idea of the tremendous joy he felt....Certainly those persons who Dnyaneshwar thought good enough to share our spiritual heritage cannot be unworthy of our touch.[15]

In the first third of the twentieth century, Mahars themselves seem not to have called for social justice in the name of the Bhakti saints as did the higher caste reformers, but to invoke the name of Chokhamela as their claim to a place in past religious life and past greatness. Apart from Chokhamela[16] and some legends of a hero in the days of the Muslims Sultanates,[17] there was little in the Mahar past that could serve the necessary purpose of legitimizing their worth. And so many new efforts to improve their position in society carried the name of Chokhamela. A night school run by Mahars in Poona intermittently from about 1912 to 1933 was called the Chokhamela Vidhyawardah Mandal. A hostel started in 1914 in Nagpur by an educated Mahar, G.A. Gawai, was called the Chokhamela Hostel, and the Government Hostel now in Nagpur continues with that name. There was a Chokhamela Reform Society in Vidarbha in the early 1920s which asked for a new temple which would be open to all. According to a ballad written about the Mahar-led *satyagraha* in Poona in 1929, Untouchables attempted to climb the holy hill to the Parvati temple singing the names of Lord Shankar, Shivaji Maharaj (the seventeenth century Maratha king), Dr. Ambedkar (by that time the most important leader of the Mahar movement) and Chokhamela.

The best known early leader of the Mahars in the Vidarbha area was Kisan Fagu Bansode, whose work in the 1920s and early 1930s stressed attempts to claim religious rights. Even though the Bhakti movement did not have a strong history in the area, Bansode made pilgrimages to Pandharpur, collected Chokhamela's *abhangas,* wrote a play on Chokhamela's life, and created at least one poem invoking the image of Chokhamela to encourage, bravery:

> Why do you endure curses?
> Chokha went into the temple resolutely,
> Why do you, ashamed, stay far off?
> You are the descendants of Chokha.
> Why do you fear to enter the temple?
> Brace yourself like a wrestler, come,
> Together let us conquer pollution.[18]

Rise of Ambedkar as Mahar Leader

With the rise of Dr. Ambedkar as the leader of the Mahars, however, the use of Chokhamela's name dwindled in importance. Being Western educated, Dr. Ambedkar was, from the beginning, more confident of political means to raise status and effect improvements than of religiously oriented methods. His first newspaper, *Muknayak* (the voice of the dumb), begun in 1920, carried under its title an *abhanga* by Tukaram in which the poet reminded men that the shy, the dumb, the bashful, were never noticed. While Ambedkar occasionally quoted Tukaram or Dnyaneshwar, he did not speak of the piety of Chokhamela as an example to Mahars, even in the days when he encouraged Untouchables to enter temples, put on the sacred thread, hold Vedic ritual weddings, and join in the public Ganapati festival.

In 1929, Ambedkar presided over a meeting at Trymbak, a pilgrim centre at the source of the Godavari river, which discussed the building of a temple there in the name of

Chokhamela. The meeting decided, after discussion, that a "real memorial consisted in devoting themselves with unflagging energy to the removal of the blot of untouchability".[19] In 1932, Ambedkar elaborated on the ineffectiveness of religious piety:

> The appearance of Tulsi leaves around your neck will not relieve you from the clutches of the moneylenders. Because you sing songs of Rama, you will not get a concession in rent from the landlords. You will not get salaries at the end of the month because you make pilgrimages every year to Pandharpur.[20]

Ambedkar's family were followers of the Kabir and Ramananda Bhakti sects, but his wife's family led her to a devotion to Pandharpur. She wanted to make a pilgrimage there, but Ambedkar would not allow her to go because she would have been allowed no farther into the temple than the *samadhi* of Chokhamela at the foot of the temple steps. Ambedkar's biographer reports that he consoled his wife with these words:

> What of that Pandharpur which prevents its devotees from seeing the image of God? By our own virtuous life, selfless service and spotless sacrifice in the cause of downtrodden humanity we would create another Pandharpur.[21]

In the 1936 speech to the Mahar Conference that called for Untouchables to leave Hinduism and convert to another religion, Ambedkar told his audience:

> If someone asks you what your caste is, you say that you are a *Chokhamela* or *Harijan;* but you do not say you are a *Mahar.* Nobody changes his name unless there is need for it. But there is no meaning in adopting a name like *Chokhamela* or *Harijan.* The stench of the old name will stick to the new and you will be forced to change your name continually. Then why not change it permanently?[22]

Conversion to Buddhism

The permanent change was not to come until 1956, when Ambedkar converted to Buddhism, followed in the next months by over three million people, most of them former Untouchables. The reasons for a group as united, as educationally eager, and as politicized as the Mahars to opt for

Buddhism instead of Chokhamela and the Bhakti *panth* are clear. The Bhakti movement in the twentieth century was without any social protest or social reform content, with a few exceptions such as saint Gadge Maharaj.[23] Even more to the point, Chokhamela had accepted his place in the village hierarchy, while the twentieth century Mahars saw no option but to leave what they then saw as servility, a part and parcel of untouchability. Chokhamela had accepted the concept of sins in past lives resulting in low birth, but most twentieth century ex-Untouchables reject this rationale.[24] Chokhamela had found joy in equality with other *bhaktas* and in God's eyes; the new generation wanted equality in social and political matters.

Buddhism offered scriptural justification for worth achieved by mind and action, not by birth. And since Ambedkar's interpretation of the history of the, Untouchables was one in which they had been Buddhists, who were isolated and denigrated once Hinduism regained its authority, there was now a glorious past of great accomplishments to reinforce current ideas of their potential as a worthy and creative people.

The change seemed swift, but the ground had been well prepared. In 1955, Dr. Ambedkar had been invited to come to Dehu Road, a small town near Pune, where some Untouchables who had made some money through their employment at a local ammunition depot wanted him to dedicate a temple to Chokhamela. Ambedkar agreed to come only if he could dedicate the temple to Buddha, and since Ambedkar's ideology, not Chokhamela's, had become important, his suggestion was accepted. On Christmas Day, 1955, he arrived with a Buddha image and a Buddhist monk to make the Dehu Road temple the first Buddhist structure of the coming conversion movement. Less than a year later, when crowds gathered in Nagpur for the actual conversion day, local newspapers reported that the scene seemed like "another Pandharpur".

Although there is still pride in Chokhamela, interest in the Bhakti sect among educated Buddhists is primarily academic: efforts to find Chokhamela's authentic *abhangas* and to trace the influence of Buddhism on the development of the Bhakti ideology. In contrast, the Chambhars of Maharashtra, a smaller ex-Untouchable caste which works with leather, did not join Ambedkar's movement en masse and continue to celebrate the Chamar *sant* of the Hindi-belt, Rai-das or Ravidas [or Rohidas], as their patron saint. The doors of the temple at Pandharpur are now open to all, forced open after Independence by a Brahman socialist, Sane Guruji, who sat fasting in the temple doorway. A silver head of Chokhamela marks his burial place at the foot of the temple stairs. The Mahars who traditionally tend it have not converted to Buddhism, and there are still a few Mahar *warkaris* who find great meaning in their Bhakti faith. But for the caste as a whole, Chokhamela's life and message cannot serve as a model for the kind of change they have come to feel is theirs by right.

Eknath

The background of Shri Eknath Maharaj (c.1533-1599) was completely different from that of Chokhamela. He belonged to a Brahman family of considerable fame, living in the "Benares" of the Marathi-speaking area, Paithan. His great grandfather, Bhanudas, was a Bhakta and a poet, credited with bringing back the image of Vitthal from the state of Vijayanagar, after it had been taken there to reinforce the Vijayanagara King's piety—or dominance. The scholarly learning which surrounded Eknath by virtue of his family and his birthplace was reinforced by worldly knowledge. Paithan had been an ancient capital and in the sixteenth century, was a trading centre of great importance, producing exquisite silk saris known as Paithani.

The political world around Eknath was also dissimilar to the fourteenth century world in which Chokhamela lived. Chokhamela was probably a very young man when Alla-ud-din Khilji stormed Devagiri (modern Daulatabad) in 1296, bringing the creative energy of the Yadava period to an end. His time period also witnessed the raids of Muhammad Tughlaq, who shifted his capital to Daulatabad in 1327, but Chokhamela died before the stable Bahmani kingdom was created in 1347. One senses little of the political life around Chokhamela from either his *abhangas* or the legends about him. Mangalvedhe seems to have been a backwater, unaffected by the to-ing and fro-ing of armies.

Eknath lived at the time of the Ahmadnagar Sultanate. Its influence can be seen in the number of Persian words which Eknath used in his writings, in the Muslim terms for administration which he wove into the poetry which used obligations to government as an analogy for debts to God. He was in contact with many Muslims, a fact verified by his use of Muslim holy men as figures in his dramatic poems and by his inclusion of Hindustani in those poems. An even more telling fact is that Eknath's own guru, Janardan Swami, was both an acknowledged holy man and the keeper of the Daulatabad fort! At one time, according to legend, Eknath even took Janardan's place at the head of the Muslim ruler's army when the fort was attacked and Janardan was deep in meditation.

Eknath's Works

Eknath's massive volume of work shows all these influences: his Brahmanical training, his interest in scholarship, his tradition of devotion to the Pandharpur Bhakti sect, his knowledge of a very heterogeneous world in a religious centre and market city crossed by several trade routes. He was in the unusual position of living in a highly orthodox and closed Brahmanical world and yet being in contact with the foreign, the non-Sanskritic, indeed all manner of men. His devotion to the lowly, his insistence on using Marathi instead of Sanskrit, his unorthodox behavior in performing charitable acts for all men, meant that he was often ostracized and lived under the threat of excommunication. But in part because of the grace of the God of Pandharpur, in part because he never challenged the right of Brahman privileges for other Brahmans, he lived his life fairly peacefully in Paithan and took samadhi there; his home is now a temple which serves as a pilgrimage centre even today.

Eknath's scholarly work does not concern us here, except for its primary purpose of bringing the highest of philosophical thought and moral teaching to the people of his area through the common language, Marathi. One of the basic texts of the Bhakti devotees is the "Eknathi Bhagavata", a translation of the eleventh book of the *Bhagavata Purana* from Sanskrit to

Marathi.[25] Unlike those parts of the *Bhagavata Purana* which tell of the love between Krishna and the Gopis and are popular in the Northern Bhakti tradition, this expresses a stern morality. Eknath also began a Marathi version of the *Ramayana,* commented on the Vedantic philosophy of the ninth chapter of the second book of the *Bhagavata Purana,* corrected the 250 year old text of the *Dnyaneshwari* (the foundation stone of the Bhakti movement), and produced a number of philosophical works. He is also credited with some four thousand *abhangas,* but these never achieved the poetic intensity of the more popular *abhangas* of Tukaram.

Eknath's Bharuds (Drama Poems)

But Eknath is not only the most scholarly and prolific of all the *sants* in the Marathi Bhakti tradition, he is also the most conscious of the presence of Untouchables in society and of their spiritual capabilities. His most unusual contribution to the "performance genre"[26] of Bhakti literature are some three hundred *bharuds,* drama poems meant to be acted out, and of these almost fifty are written as if an Untouchable were the author. Forty-seven *bharuds* seem to come from the mouths of Mahar men or women; one is written in the name of a Mang, one of the three important Maharashtrian Untouchable castes.

The *bharud* form has been used by a number of poets, both in Karnataka and Maharashtra. It requires a symbol or a metaphor to carry the message of the poem; this can be not only a particular caste, but a dog, a Muslim fakir, a wandering acrobat, an unhappy wife, a demi-god, a prostitute, a game, a bird, a notification of debt collection, a symbol drawn from almost any aspect of ordinary life. Eknath's *bharuds* contain references to Vedantic philosophy and stories from the Epics and the Puranas, but their importance here is as a reflection of Eknath's omniscient eye and his all-encompassing compassion. No orthodox Brahman, no peasant appears in his *bharuds;* instead they reflect the non-Sanskritic street life he must have seen in the busy town of Paithan.

The poems in which the Mahar is the speaker are Johar poems, beginning with the greeting used by Mahars to their superiors. Most are very different from the poems of

Chokhamela; in Eknath's *bharuds,* the Mahar not only preaches to others about morality, the necessity for a guru and the company of the *sants,* but also of the calamity of rebirth that is inevitable for those who do not take the Bhakti path, and of the false lives of the pseudo-pious.

There are many ways to interpret these Johar poems. Eknath can be seen as the Mahar of the Lord, one who does His work faithfully and with devotion. Some poems suggest that the life of the Mahar is so difficult it stands for the hardship of constant rebirth. The fact that the Johar poems are often harsh and vulgar indicates that Eknath may have taken on this voice in order to preach a fundamentalist kind of Bhakti—the certainty of rebirth for non-devotees being a sort of hell-fire and damnation threat. What is clear, however, is that Eknath has closely observed the work of the Mahar, and seems to try to put himself into the Mahar's skin. These poems also indicate a deep belief that the faith of the true Bhakta is true wisdom, and that the devout Mahar can speak with clarity and truth about the evils of the world and its people.

The following *bharud* shows the Mahar in his typical role: doing anything that is necessary, begging for food, sweeping, announcing officials—the official in this case is the God Rama:

> Johar, May-Bap, Johar.
> My Johar to all the Saints.
> I am the Mahar of Ayodhya City,
> Of Ramji Baba's court, ki ji May-Bap.
>
> Ramji Baba's work is the
> rule of Ayodhya city;
> There this lowly servant's work
> is to do all the good, all the bad.
>
> I wake early in the morning
> and ask Sita for food.
> I sweep the court and
> throw the dirt outside.

When Ramji Baba comes to Council
I go ahead to announce him.
In truth, Eka Janardan
Offers Johar, ki ji May-Bap.[27] *Bharud* 3864

The Mahar in the next *bharud* also belongs to Rama, but his name is *Atmanak (atma,* meaning soul, and *nak,* the suffix to their names used by Mahars until the beginning of this century).[28] The poem is addressed to the *patil,* the headman of a village which is used as a metaphor for the human body. Each being must live through eighty-four hundred thousand lives, each time dying painfully and being beaten by the Lord of Death before being born again. Only the true Bhakta is not reborn. The "ki ji May-Bap" at the end of each stanza is literally,' "O mother and father", "O master", but has been retained in its Marathi rhythmic form.

Johar, May-Bap, Johar.
I am sun-born Rama's Mahar.
My name-Atmanak Mahar.
I do all the work of the Lord, ki ji May-Bap.

What will remain in the broken hut ?
Your feel will fall into the trap of bones.
If you hide your face, you'll lose your honor.
Then what's the use of living ? ki ji May-Bap.

Ruin is drawing near?
Eighty-four hundred thousand creditors—
watchmen of the Lord of Death [are coming]—
and they will beat you and beat you, ki ji May-Bap.

Johar, Honorable Patil.
Are you pleased with the Darbar?
Today they have come to tell you
The balance of your debt is due, ki ji May-Bap.

The due date comes near.
A warning must be given.
So many have been beaten and taken away.
I am speaking the truth, am I not? ki ji May-Bap.

Leave your body-village ?
Shave your head, change your name ?
Leave the house and stay in the temple ?
Better keep your staff in your hand! ki ji May-Bap.

Eka-Janardan Mahar [says]
Johar to the Company of Saints.
They have felt the endless treadmill
of Births and Deaths, ki ji May-Bap[29]

Bharud 3877

In the following *abhanga,* which is full of puns and of the typical shouts or calls of certain religious performances, which the audience undoubtedly shouted in unison, Eknath's Mahar criticizes all religious fakery. The exclamations have been left in Marathi, since, like "Bravo" or "Whoo-pee", they carry a tenor and a sense of occasion which cannot be translated.

Johar, May-Bap, Johar.
Good guru Janardan's Mahar says
Listen attentively to a thought
about the Age of Kali, ki ji May-Bap.

Among the four chief Ages
the Age of Kali is the best
Good deeds should be done, praise to God sung,
the Name should be remembered.[30]

Perform the nine kinds of Bhakti;
Then you will miss the cycle of 84 hundred thousand lives.
Believe in what I say
or you will be trapped!

There should be an altar of basil by the door.
You should worship the uninvited guest.
Take shelter with the saints.
This is the sign of Bhakti.

Wear the tulsi beads around your neck,
put the mark of sandal on your forehead.
Chanting the Names should be the
garland of the mouth.

Observe the fast of the eleventh day,
keep vigil all night.
On the twelfth day eat sweets,
drink milk with respect and love.

These are the signs of Vaishnava Bhakti.
I have told you all the marks.
He who does not know the secret
follows the non-religious way.

There are eighteen kinds of castes.[31]
I will tell you what they think.
Listen carefully, without doubt;
don't be angry.

We are Brahmans, they say,
But they don't bathe, pray to the sun, read the Vedas,
They perform impure deeds by chanting
to kill and bind, fascinate and hold.

They say, in this world we have attained the end,
but they are far from even the means.
They are involved with other women,
kulululu, ki ji May-Bap.

I have become a Sannyasi, they say,
but the six enemies are in their hearts.[32]
Their minds, night and day, are on
Other people's money, other people's food....

He became a Fakir for the sake of his stomach.
His life was spent saying Allah, Allah.
He wore "faultlessness" like a garment,
calling *haydosh haydosh...* [33]

They say, "We have become Lingayats".
Yet they do not worship Shiva.
They beg for the sake of their stomachs.
They blow the conch: *bham, bham, bham....*

They say, "we have become saints"
They put on garlands, sandal paste.
Taking a lamp in their hands,
They cry *udo udo...* .[34]

They do kirtan for the sake of their stomachs.[35]
They teach the "meaning of all" to the people.
They cheat their ignorant devotees.
They do not know the secret of kirtan....

Do the one kind of Bhakti.
Don't wait for anything else.
Good and bad come in their own way.
They are the proof of past deeds.

As in the mind of a faithful wife,
The final measure is the husband's,
So to understand the causes and the remedies,
Take the Lord as Measure...[36]

Bharud 3891

Many of the Johar *bharuds* are repetitious; many concern themselves with officials and different aspects of life in the village; many use the complex numerology of the initiate: the five elements, the six great enemies, the nine doors to the body, etc. Throughout, however, the Mahar preaches, and Eknath deliberately uses him as both metaphor and actual Untouchable, indicating several times that the Mahar as Mahar should be listened to:

A Mahar speaks—so you turn away in arrogance.
But you should do what is good for you!
O you men! Don't close your eyes!

Bharud 3880

One of the most popular *bharuds* is a conversation between a Mahar and a Brahman, in which the Mahar teaches the arrogant Brahman about the formless God and the grace of the Saints.[37] This might seem to be bolder than it actually is, since another amusing dialogue takes place between a Brahman and a dog, with the same sort of authority given the dog. It is clear that Eknath's basic message is that even dog, or a Mahar, can share God's grace. Or is it? The very daring of this sort of dialogue must have fascinated Eknath's audiences, and the device is still striking today, when the *bhajan* members, sometimes in costume, act out the *bharud*.

Brahman	:	Come here, doggie, come here.
		Don't pollute me—
		Just take your food.
Dog	:	Give it to me, give it.
		The pollution is in you—
		pull your robe back.
Brahman	:	Now this dog has gotten arrogant! .. .[38]
		Look, I'll let you die without food.
Dog	:	So what! Everything is nectar!
Brahman	:	You have only one home—
		What will you eat in the morning!
Dog	:	Where will you yourself be tomorrow?
Brahman	:	Where did you get this wisdom?
Dog	:	It is the great gift of my guru.
Brahman	:	What! You have a guru?
Dog	:	He is in everybody.
Brahman	:	But we call you a dog!
Dog	:	You're fooled by ignorance.
Brahman	:	Call a Brahman ignorant?
Dog	:	If you are so great, why do you die?
		The devotees of God are immortal!
Brahman	:	How do you know that?
		I would like to become immortal!
Dog	:	Then why don't you?
		Don't even look at caste or lineage.
Brahman	:	How did you come by this knowledge?
Eka Janardan	:	I learned it by the grace of the guru.

Bharud 3792

The whole Maharashtrian Bhakti tradition, and probably the Bhakti tradition everywhere, makes it clear that there is no caste distinction in the sight of God. Dnyaneshwar, the founder of the Bhakti sect in the Marathi speaking area, put this very plainly in his commentary on the *Bhagavad Gita,* the *Dnyaneshwari:*

> There is a distinction between the Khaira and the Chandana trees only so long as they are not put into fire; but as soon as they are put inside it, they become one with it, and the distinction between them vanishes. Similarly, the Kshatriya, the Vaisyas, the Sudras and Women are so called only as long as they have not reached Me. But having reached Me, they cease to be distinguished; as salt becomes one with the ocean, even so they become one with Me.[39]

Eknath put it in simple, colorful terms, using the names of Non-Brahman *sants* from both Maharashtra and Northern India:

> God baked pots with Gora,
> drove cattle with Chokha,
> cut grass with Savata Mali,
> wove garments with Kabir,
> colored hide with Ravidas,
> sold meat with butcher Sajana,
> melted gold with Narahari,
> carried cow-dung with Janabai
> and even became the Mahar messenger of Damaji.[40]

The concept of living according to caste in non-religious aspects, however, was not challenged. Each caste was expected to do its duty; even the corrupted Brahman, according to Eknath, was to be shown respect. Birth in a low caste was in accord with past deeds, and the only way out was a life of devotion and duty which would obviate the necessity of rebirth. Eknath's message was by no means one of social protest: his basic views on caste and the position of Brahmans were quite orthodox. But his vision of God's presence in all humanity and his compassion lifted his orthodoxy into the kind of creative approach shown in the above *bharuds* and from time to time, according to legend, into most unorthodox action.

Eknath's Compassion

Mahipati, the eighteenth century biographer of all the *sants,* tells many legends of Eknath's compassion, the following being one of them. On the day of the worship of ancestors, Eknath invited Brahmans to his house for the feast. An Untouchable sweeper and his wife working in the alley smelled the food, but told each other they could never have such a splendid feast, and on this holy occasion even the food left on the plates would be buried, not given to them. Eknath overheard them and went out to invite all the Untouchables in the town to the feast, serving them himself. The Paithan Brahmans were furious and excommunicated Eknath. But Lord Krishna, who was working in Eknath's house as a menial Brahman, known as Shri Khandya, said, "Serve a feast to the ancestors anyway". And so the ancestors came, and the local Brahmans saw the splendid heavenly Brahmans eating the feast at Eknath's house. Added to this, Eknath cured a leper even as he was performing the penance imposed on him for this deed by the Brahmans, and so they said to him, "You are indeed the avatar of Vishnu."[41]

A long story in Mahipati's *Bhaktalilamrta* tells of Eknath dining with a pious Bhakta, Ranya Mahar, and his wife. Ranya had been a worshipper of Vishnu, but through some fault was reborn as a Mahar. He sat outside Eknath' s *kirtans,* swept a path to his bath, etc. Ranya Mahar's pious wife wanted Eknath to come to their house to eat, and Eknath accepted, quoting this verse from the *Bhagavata Parana* (VII:9:10):

> A dog-eating outcaste, who has made an offering to God of his mind, his words, his actions, his property and his very life, is to be considered far superior to a Brahman, who, although gifted with the twelve characteristics of a Brahman, has turned away from the feet of God. The former purifies his whole family, not so the latter puffed up with pride.

Hearing the Sanskrit verse, the Paithan Brahmans were enraged. "Why do you repeat a sloka to this unmentionable?" Eknath replied, "I am convinced that he has the right to philosophic knowledge. By his reverent devotion he has made the Supreme Brahma, existing in the form of Shri Hari, subject to him." Eknath submitted himself to the penance imposed by the Brahmans, but even as he stood penitentially in the river, he again accepted Ranya Mahar's invitation to dine at his home. He went to the Mahar quarters for dinner, but as the Brahmans went to check on him, they also saw him eating at his own home. God Vitthal had taken Eknath's form and eaten at the house of Ranya Mahar.[42]

Eknath and his wife also took in a starving Mahar thief after he was let out of the jail, and kept him in their house for many days, converting him from a life of crime to that of piety by their kindness.[43]

A legend that still has power because it involves the all-important matter of touch concerns Eknath's pity for a small boy, left crying on the hot sands on the banks of Godavari river during the summer heat. He picked him up and carried him to the hovel the child pointed out to him, realizing only when he saw the child's mother that he held a Mahar boy. He put the boy down at his home, returned to the river and bathed with all his clothes on. None of the Brahmans saw him, but the deed became known, according to God's plan. A learned Brahman with leprosy was told by God that Eknath had performed an act of special goodness. If Eknath would give that good deed to the Brahman, he would become whole. Hearing this, Eknath smiled, put a little water in the leper's hand, and the leper's body became beautiful.[44]

It is Eknath's generosity, his liberality of spirit, his imagination, his kindness that is moving, not his piety. It is these qualities that make him an important figure in contemporary times, and it is the actions stemming from his all-encompassing compassion that offer a model for modern day elite reformers.

Eknath's compassion does not have much appeal to the ex-Untouchables themselves. A couplet reading "I am the bastard Mahar, son of the Lord",[45] may be moving to a Brahman, but not to a Mahar. I have found no reference to Eknath in any of the writings of the early Mahar movement, and none during the period since the Buddhist conversion, nor is there much interest in Eknath's vision of humanity. That vision seems to bear some similarity to that of Mahatma Gandhi, whose views on caste were only somewhat less orthodox and whose humanitarianism was closely linked with charity. Gandhi's vision and methods have been rejected by most of those drawn into the more radical Ambedkar movement.

Indeed, some Dalit[46] poets reject the Bhakti idea as totally useless. In a very avant-garde poem, Namdeo Dhasel speaks of "Crumpled-paper Pandurang-dindi goes on singing, winding, the sweet notes flute", and in the next line speaks of prostitutes on Juhu beach. The image of procession to Pandharpur is mocked as unreal, while the life of the city poor is a reality the Pandharpur pilgrims do not see.[47] Daya Pawar also picked up this theme of neglect of humans in pursuit of the divine [or the pious care of animals] in a poem called "Pay" (legs or feet), in which the theme is that those born from the feet of the primordial being, the Shudras, are at the bottom of a crushing pyramid of castes. The poem ends with the pyramid being sanctified, but the sanctifying water is given to a thirsty donkey: "The pitchers of Ganges water come and are poured into the mouth of a donkey".[48] The original legend of the Ganges water given to a thirsty donkey is the one told of Eknath.

But for the elite reformer, the wise and scholarly Brahman whose compassion allows him to rise above caste distinctions is a powerful image. One of the most interesting and effective ways in which the figure of Eknath was used in a modern context was in the film on his life produced by the Prabhat Film Company in Poona. Using traditional Maharashtrian themes as the basis for very popular movies, this young, highly intellectual and socially committed group of the film makers produced a number of excellent films during a "Golden Age" of Marathi films in the late 1930s and early 1940s. The film on Eknath was called *Dharmatma* (the soul of righteousness). In it, the miraculous events of Eknath's legendary life were downplayed to allow a more realistic picture of a good and pious householder who loved and cared for everyone. Some of Eknath's *abhangas* and *bharuds* were sung in the film in the context of anyone at all being able to give the message of Bhakti. And one of the most dramatic high points of the movie was the scene in which Eknath goes to the Maharwada and eats in the house of Ranya Mahar!

A recent pamphlet for children, *Don mahan sant* (Two Great Saints) by Datta J. Kulkarni (Pune: Aragade Kulkarni Prakashan, 1968), illustrates another possible use of Eknath as a model for social consciousness. The two saints are Gadge Maharaj, the twentieth century wandering holy man whose social teachings on the evils of drinking, practicing untouchability, and putting ritual above social good were extremely strong and effective, and the sixteenth century *sant,* Eknath. The washerman Gadge Maharaj, rough, unlearned, homeless and completely unorthodox, and the pious Brahman Eknath are unlikely companions. Linking them is an effective device for legitimizing modern reformist social attitudes.

Of all the *sants,* only Eknath could have served as legitimacy for protesting orthodoxy in the incident of the 1977 Marathi Literary Conference in Pune. The Marathi Sahitya Sammelan is not only the literary event of the year, but one of the most prestigious gatherings in all Maharashtra. To be elected President is a recognition not only of literary worth but of real presence on the Maharashtrian scene. When a man known for his conservative views and his religious orthodoxy, P.B. Bahave, was elected President over liberal candidates, there was a charge that the election committee was fixed, and the radical student groups of Pune disrupted the last day of the Conference with a demonstration. The shout of the procession which prevented the Conference President from speaking was: "Eknath carried a Mahar child on his shoulder, but all you Brahmans want is power".[49]

The popular Sunday edition of the Pune newspaper, *Sakal,* picked up this theme in its edition of 25 March 1979, with an article entitled "On the banks of the Godavari Eknath showed the light of equality", illustrated by a picture of the *sant* in full Brahman regalia with a dark child in his arms. [A number of recent popular pamphlets picture Eknath in this pose].

Pandharpur Pilgrimage

It should be emphasized that the living Bhakti sect in Maharashtra today is not a force for change. The *warkaris* themselves, those who actually wear the tulsi beads, go on pilgrimage to Pandharpur, eschew liquor and meat in order to live pious lives, have not initiated any sort of social reform campaign. They continue to make the distinctions between equality in the sight of God and equality in daily life that the *sants* made through the centuries. In her essay on the Pandharpur pilgrimage, Iravati Karve wonders that the songs sung so vigorously preach equality of all the Bhaktas, and the pilgrims preserve caste groups in the procession as they are singing them.[50]

However, it is equally clear that the Bhakti Movement and its literature is still a reservoir of living ideas.[51] The lives of the poets of Pandharpur are known to everyone, even the children, and there is material in this common pool of regional ethos which can serve many purposes.

There is a possibility that Chokhamela will be revived, not as a "sanskritizing process" in the usual Srinivasian sense of upward mobility within the caste system,[52] but as "sanskritization" in the broader sense of participation in the recognized higher intellectual culture. The current interest in Chokhamela, his wife and son, may be academic, but the result may be new editions of his *abhangas* and those of his family, perhaps some theater, perhaps some use of the legends about him in poetry. After all, Chokhamela represents a clear and important participation of Untouchables in the past culture of the area, and although he no longer serves a model for emulation, he may well become once again a theme of inspiration as a creative figure from the past.

The figure of Eknath also has a real but limited appeal. What was unusual about him was his observant eye, his enormous ability to see things as they were and to act according to human need. The idea that one so scholarly and so wise could be so quick to understand the life around him and so human is a forceful idea. The message, however, seems limited to those who are "scholarly and wise"-to the intellectuals and the elite. But interpreted with imagination and skill, the figure of Eknath can become an enabling force; his synthesis of the worldly and the spiritual has the capacity to be understood today. The future importance of Eknath as a social force depends largely on the ability of the educated elite who emulate him to affect the social tenor of life today.

References

1. *Sant* can easily by translated "saint". I have kept the Marathi word, however, because it is used only for the saints in the Bhakti tradition, not for all holy men.
2. *Warkari sampradaya* "Tradition of the pilgrims". The finest study in English of this tradition as a whole is G.A. Deleury's *The Cult of Vithoba* (Poona: Deccan College Postgraduate and Research Institute, 1961). I have tended to use the term "Bhakti Movement" in this paper rather than the usual Marathi designation or Deleury's term in order to stress the continuity of the line of *sants,* who wrote their poetry over a five hundred-year period, and in order to link the movement with Bhakti traditions in other language areas.
3. *Chokhamela abhang gatha.* (Collection of Chokhamela's Abhangas.) (Bombay: Balkrishna Lakshman Pathak, 1950), pp.1-2.
4. See R.D. Ranade, *Pathway to God in Marathi Literature* (Bombay: Bharatiya Vidya Bhavan, 1961; originally published in 1933) for a slightly different version of this legend.
5. Nicol Macnicol, *Psalms of the Maratha Saints* (Calcutta: Association Press and Oxford University Press, 1919). p. 23.
6. The references to Chokhamela's abhangas in this paper are from *Chokhamela abhang gatha* (Bombay: Balkrishna Lakshman Pathak, 1950). A newer collection, *Shrisant Chokhamela Maharaj yanche charitra va abhang gatha,* edited by S.B. Kadam (Bombay: Mandakini S.Kadam, 1969) contains 349 *abhangas.*
7. A.K. Ramanujan has informed me that *Abhangas 6* and 11 need not refer to untouchability since similar songs appear

in the work of caste Hindu *sants* in the South. However, since some of Chokhamela's songs do refer to untouchability, a phenomenon which seems not to appear in the words of other Untouchability *sants*. I think *Abhang* 6 can be interpreted as protesting his low birth and *Abhang* 11 as protesting the concept of untouchability.

8. See Justin E. Abbott and Narhar R. Godbole's translation of Mahipati's *Bhaktavijaya* (Ch. XXIII, pp. 6-60) in *Stories of Indian Saints* (Poona: Office of the Poet Saints of Maharashtra 1933) for a slightly different version of this legend.
9. Pandhari - Pandharpur.
10. Iravati Karve, "On the Road", *Journal of Asian Studies*, XXII: 1 (1962), pp. 13-29. The translation of *Abhang* 52 is by Maxine Bemtsen. R.D. Ranade translates the "ugly" of the last line as "untouchable". (See Ranade *op. cit.*, p. 161), [The usual translation of "feelings" in the last line is "devotion" *(bhav).*]
11. M.G. Ranade, *Rise of the Marathi Power and Other Essays* (Bombay: University of Bombay, 1961, first published in 1900), p. 5.
12. R.V. Oturkar, Introduction to M.G. Ranade, *op. cit.*, pp. VI-VII. The work of G.B. Sarkar to which Oturkar refers has been translated by Kumud Mehta as *The Saint-Poets of Maharashtra (Their Impact on Society)* (New Delhi: Orient Longmans, 1969).
13. R.D.Ranade, *op. cit., p.* 165.
14. *Kesari* (Pune), 27 December, 1964.
15. C.B. Agarwal, *The Harijans in Rebellion* (Bombay: Chhotelal Bhagwandas, 1934), p. 64. "Harijan", i.e., people of God, is Mahatma Gandhi's term.
16. Chokhamela's wife, Soyrabai, his sons, Karmamela and Banka, and his daughter, Nirmala, are all considered saints and poets. Their *abhangas* have been collected by S.B. Kadam, *op. cit.*
17. For the legend of the hero Amrutnak, see my article "The Leadership of Babasaheb Ambedkar", in this volume and in B.N. Pandey ed., *Leadership in South Asia (New* Delhi: Vikas, 1977), which analyzes the cultural images of the Mahar past.

18. Kisan Fagu Bansode, *Pradip* (Nagpur: Jagruli Prakashan, no date), p. 48.

19. Dhananjay Keer. Dr. *Ambedkar, Life and Mission* (2nd ed. Bombay: Popular Prakashan, 1962), p. 126.

20. *Ibid.,* p. 218.

21. *Ibid.,* p. 247.

22. *The Depressed Classes A Chronological Documentation* (Kuseong: St. Mary's College, 1930), p. 103.

23. The life of this contemporary *sant* should be studied, since he seems to be the only figure who revived both the idea of castelessness among the Bhakti devotees and the radical actions of the earlier saint-poets. There are a number of popular pamphlets in Marathi on his life, including *Gadge Maharaj* by Amrendra (Bombay: Vora, 1959). See also a book—length study, *Shri Gadge Maharaj,* by Gopal Nilkanth Dandekar (Bombay: Majestic Book Stall, 1976 and 1982). *A Kirtan* of the radical saint has been ranslated by Maxine Bernsten for Eleanor Zelliot and Maxine Berntsen eds., *The Experience of Hinduism* (Albany: State University of New York Press, 1988).]

24. For non-acceptance of re-birth as an explanation for untouchability, see Bernard S. Cohn,' 'Changing Traditions of a Low Caste", in Milton Singer ed., *Traditional India: Structure and Change* (Philadelphia: The American Folklore Society, 1959); and Pauline Mahar Kolenda, "Religious Anxiety and Hindu Fate". *Journal of Asian Studies,* XXXIII (1964), pp. 71-81.

25. The 23rd chapter of the *"Eknath Bhagavata"* has been translated by Justin E. Abbott as *Bhikshugita: The Mendicant's Song* (Poet-Saints of Maharashtra series No. 3, Poona, 1928). [Hugh van Skyhawk submitted a Ph.D. thesis on Eknath's Rhagavata in 1988 to the University of Heidelberg.]

26. The phrase is from Kunta Narayan Jagdale, "The Use of Symbols in Bharud Literature" *(Journal of the Shrimati Nathibai Damodar Thackersey Women's University,* V, 1975. It is useful in distinguishing Bhakti literature meant to be sung or acted out in a group, such as *abhangas* and *bharuds,* from literature intended to be recited or read.

27. There is no critical edition of Eknath's *bharuds*. The edition I have used is *Shri Eknath Maharaj Yanoya Abhangachi Gatha,* collected and edited by Brahmibhut Shrinanamaharaj Sakhre (Poona: Indira Prakahan, 1952).

28. In other *bharuds* the term 'Vithnak' is used as the name of the Mahar, a combination of the name of God Vithal and the traditional Mahar ending of a name.

29. All Eknath's *bharuds* are signed with a shortened version of his name combined with that of his guru, Janardan. In the Johar *bharuds,* he makes it clear that Eka-Janardan speaks as a Mahar.

30. The *Kaliyug* or Age of Kali is traditionally the worst of the four yugas. Here, Eknath calls it the best because it is the age in which Bhakti can lead men to salvation from rebirth. The phrase *karve haribhajan,* literally *"the bhajan to Hari* should be done", is translated "praise to God sung". The *bhajan* is a sort of musical prayer meeting; Hari is a name for Vishnu.

31. There are traditionally eighteen castes in Maharashtra, Eknath uses the words *varna-yati* here, but delineates types of religious figures, not castes, in the stanzas following.

32. The six enemies are hypocrisy, passion, anger, greed, pride and envy. Eknath makes frequent use of this concept in the *bharuds,* either by name or number.

33. "Haydosh" (O friend) is an exclamation used in the processions of the Shiite observance of Mohurram. *Dosh* in Marathi means "fault", and Eknath has combined it with a variant pronunciation of the Persian *dost* here to make a pun.

34. *Udo, Udo,* meaning "awake" or "arise" is exclamation used by the worshipper of the Goddess.

35. *Kirtan,* like *bhajan,* is a group gathering in which *abhangas* are sung, but there is also usually a leader who recites from scripture or gives a sermon. Eknath's *kirtans* in Paithan were famous far and wide.

36. A number of stanzas have been omitted from this translation. Other religious figures whose hypocrisy is criticized in the *bharud* are Jogis, members of the Mahanubhav sect, Dev Rishis who heal by magic, followers of Khandoba, worshippers of the demi-gods Vetal and Mahishasur and even imperfect Bhaktas.

37. [For a translation of this *bharud,* see Eleanor Zelliot, "Eknath is Bharude: the *Sant* as a link between Cultures", in *The Sants: Studies in a Devotional Tradition of India,* edited by Karine Schemer and W.H. McLeod. Berkeley: Religious Studies Scries; Delhi: Motilal Banarsidass, 1987.]

38. The three lines following "Now this dog has gotten arrogant!" are not clear and have been omitted.

39. Quoted in R.D. Ranade, *op.cit.,* p. 88. For a full translation of Dnyaneshwar's classic, see the *Jnaneshvari (Bhavarthadipika),* translated by V.G. Pradhan and edited by H.M. Lambert, in two volumes (London: George Alien and Unwin, 1967 and 1969). [This translation has been recently reprinted by State University of New York Press, which has also published a translation by Swami Kripananda. Dnyaneshwar's name is often spelled Jnaneshwar.]

40. Adapted from the translation in R.D. Ranade, *op. cit.,* p. 177.' A similar *abhang* is credited to"the great seventeenth century *sant,* Tukaram. The story of Damaji concerns a Bhakta who was a revenue official for the Muslim Sultan of Bedar. He gave away all the storehouses of grain in Mangalvedhe during a great famine, and was arrested by the Sultan for looting his property. God Vitthal, disguised as a Mahar whose traditional duty is to carry taxes to the capital, brought gold to pay for the grain. See *Stories of Indian Saints,* Vol. II, translated by Justin E. Abbott and Narhar R. Godbole from Mahipati's *Bhaktavijaya* (Poona: Office of the Poet Saints of Maharashtra, 1934); Chapter XL, pp. 85-99.

41. See Mahipati's *Bhaktavijaya.* Chapter XLVI, pp. 45-128; English translation as in footnote 40, pp. 176-81.

42. Mahipati's *Bhaktalilamrita,* Chapter XLVI, pp. 138-240; see Justin E. Abbott's translation in *Eknath* (Poet-Saints of Maharashtra No. 2, Poona, 1927), pp. 139-49. '

43. *Ibid.,* Chapter XX, pp. 168-203; pp. 166-69 in Abbott's translation.

44. *Ibid.,* Chapter XXII, pp. 124-49; pp. 201 -04 in Abbott's translation.

45. *Abhang* 3867:1.

46. *Dalit* means "ground down, broken, depressed". It is the term by which many ex-Untouchables, chiefly those converted to Buddhism, refer to themselves.

47. "Darulate glasat ambar" in *Golpitha by* Namdeo Dhasal. (Poona: Nilkant Prakashan, 2nd edition, 1975). [A translation of this poem, entitled "Amber/Sky Alcohols in the Glass", appears in the *Journal of South Asian Literature* XVII: 1 (Winter, Spring 1982), pp. 97-8.]

48. "Pay" in *Kondwada,* by Daya Pawar. Poona: Magowa Prakashan, 1974.

49. Communication from Gail Omvedt-Patankar.

50. Iravati Karve, *op. cit.*

51. For a comprehensive review of Bhakti literature in the context of all pre-modern Marathi literature, see Shankar Gopal Tulpule, *Classical Marathi Literature* (Vol. IX, Fasc. 4, in the History of Indian Literature series; Wiesbaden: Otto Harrassowitz, 1979).

52. M.N. Srinivas's basic concept of "Sanskritization" is presented in a chapter with that title in *Social Change in Modern India* (Berkeley: University of California Press, 1966).

3
The Mahar and Non-Brahman Movements in Maharashtra

Two large and effective protest movements flowered in Maharashtra in the twentieth century. The Non-Brahman movement which grew chiefly among the dominant agricultural castes of the Marathas resulted in a quiet and almost total takeover of the Congress Party in the mid-century decades. The Mahar movement brought that much smaller [and Untouchable] caste into a degree of awareness and unity that enabled them to create a political party; a system of hostels, schools and colleges; and an effective Buddhist conversion movement before the death of its leader, Dr. B.R. Ambedkar, in 1956. The organizational triumphs of these movements were dependent on the democratizing processes of the period of political reforms, 1921-1939, but both had roots reaching back to an apolitical period in the last half of the nineteenth century. This study is a speculative one, attempting not so much to find why these movements began but what qualities of the Maharashtrian soil allowed both to come to fruition.

Non-Brahman movements and attempts of Untouchable castes to organize for social and political purposes have occurred in other parts of India. The Non-Brahman movement of Madras actually has a more coherent history and an earlier period of successful political activity than that of Maharashtra.[1] There was also a movement, or a group of movements, among the Untouchables of Madras, although neither this movement nor others among the Ilavas of the Malabar coast, the Chamars of Chhattisgarh area, the Depressed Classes of the Punjab or the Namashudras of Bengal, were as sustained and all-encompassing as that among the Mahars of Maharashtra.[2] The juxtaposition of movements among both Non-Brahmans and Untouchables in Maharashtra suggests an assortment of factors conducive to social change.

The Mahar Movement: Factors Inducing

What role these factors played in the rise of the Mahar movement in the nineteenth century, and the extension of this thesis to the early Non-Brahman movement, is the subject of this study. The term "nineteenth century" has been stretched to cover the early period of movement, ending when Dr. Ambedkar's effective and dominant leadership began in 1920.

The essential factors in the processes by which the Mahar movement grew were :

1. A leadership released from traditional service [and followers with some economic freedom].
2. Grievances understood and felt by both the "elite" members of the caste and the masses.
3. Some form of legitimization of the new non-traditional Mahar ambition both within the caste and among members of the elite in the larger society.
4. A group of "brokers" — men who could serve as links between the caste and the institutions of power in society, or who knew how to use modern channels of change.
5. Channels for communication, both within the group and from the group to the public.
6. Some form of protection for protesters when the overstepping of traditional boundaries brought retaliation.

Without any one of these factors, the Mahar movement would have taken a different path, or would have narrowed its aims, or would have remained a minor protest. The first four of these factors will be considered at length, the last two briefly noted. Similar conditions affecting the Non-Brahman movement will be briefly discussed.[3]

Leadership Released from Traditional Service

The traditional role of the Mahar was, in British official parlance, that of "inferior village servant". Every village in the Marathi-speaking area had its *Maharwada,* Mahar quarters somewhat removed from the village proper. Mahars had no special skill or craft, but performed necessary duties for the village as watchmen, wall-menders, messengers, removers of cattle carcasses, servants of any passing government official, aides to the *patil* (headman) in boundary disputes, tax or police matters. The Mahar service was hereditary, with those families which inherited the position filling it in turn. It carried with it a small amount of *watan* land as a badge of public office, and this watan land bound the Mahar to his village still more firmly.

Whenever excessive numbers of Mahars or the implementation of a cash economy threw this village role out of balance, Mahars entered other occupations. The coming of British administration also reduced the importance of the Mahar village role as many village functions were removed from local control; however, at the same time, it also opened new fields of occupation. The new freedom from the traditional village service almost invariably brought some social changes. The Khandesh Gazetteer for 1880 defines the traditional Mahar as a "lazy", "unthrifty" but "intelligent" village servant, and notes that other Mahars "make excellent railway gang labourers and have gained almost a monopoly of the unskilled railway labour market...." The implications of the occupational change are also noted :

> Of late between landholders and village Mahars complaints and feuds have grown very common...the railway has done much for the Mahars.... Some of them, gathering capital as petty contractors and moneylenders, show much independence, and manage their business without the help of any high caste clerks. Of late too, they have begun to send their boys to school.[4]

The upward thrust of the Mahars was especially noticeable in the nineteenth century in Vidarbha, the eastern part of the

Marathi-speaking region. Here the percentage of Mahars approached nearly twenty per cent of the population, in contrast to three or four per cent along the coast and an average of nine per cent over the entire area. This larger percentage could not be absorbed as village servants and in these eastern parts Mahars were also weavers, petty traders, carpenters and cultivators. A report on the Land Revenue Settlement effected during 1890-1895 in the Nagpur area commented prophetically on the Mahar venture into new fields :

> They turn their hands to anything and everything....The rise of the Mahar will probably be one of the features of social change in this district during the next fifty or a hundred years. He at present lacks education and a sense of self-respect, but these will come and the day may not be far distant when a Mahar will be found among the ranks of the native magistrates.[5]

New occupations and the concomitant upward thrust created a new sort of Mahar and the pioneering leadership for the larger movement came from a group which lacked neither education nor a sense of self-respect. With one exception, this early leadership came from those Mahars who had entered the British army. From sometime in the late eighteenth century until the last decade of the nineteenth, thousands of Mahars particularly from the Ratnagiri area, the coastal strip south of Bombay, entered the army, and some advanced to high non-commissioned ranks.

Gopal Baba Walangkar, a pensioned soldier from Ratnagiri, began the first Mahar newspaper, attempted to send a petition to the British protesting against the closure of army service to Untouchables, and addressed a plea for better treatment publicly to Hindu leaders. Subhedar (captain) Bahadur Gangaram Krishnajee of Pune was the President of the earliest conference of Mahars, which met in 1903. Subhedar Savadkar, an ex-soldier, was instrumental in securing the cooperation of village Mahars for the historic 1927 Mahar conference, a meeting planned by Dr. Ambedkar and his associates but dependent on Savadkar's work for its local support. Ambedkar himself came from a Ratnagiri family whose men had served in the army for several generations, and he gave credit for the Mahar thrust toward new rights to the education received by army men and their children. While ex-army men formed the new "aristocracy" of the western Mahars, one other new English related occupation produced a major leader. Shivram Janba Kamble, organizer of most of the petitions, conferences, night schools, temple and hotel entry movements in the Pune area from 1903 to 1930, was a butler in the Masonic Hall in the Pune Cantonment.

Later Mahar elite came from a new breed of primary school teachers, arising sometime after 1920, and from traditional Watandar families who made good use of their land or extended their traditional role into governmental supply and contracting work. The early movement was dependent upon those who had freed themselves from economic or psychological subservience to the existing village structure.

Just as Mahar leadership did not come from those still bound in the village system, so the early Non-Brahman leadership did not come from traditional Maratha headmen *(patils)*. The Maratha was a farmer, and although the administration of the British in the nineteenth century affected the political structure of his village, it is not clear how much his indebtedness, loss of land or economic situation was affected. It is clear that the *patils* lost much in power and status, and although this created a grievance among Marathas which was widely shared, it did not seem to produce a new movement towards regaining power.

Two events of the same period, the 1870s, illustrate the point of the necessity for non-traditional leadership. The Deccan Riots, the stirring of the peasant masses in the areas around Pune and Ahmadnagar in 1875, were led by traditional village leaders. They were directed, however, at the foreign element in the village, the Gujarati or Marwari merchants and moneylenders, not toward the British or the Brahmans, nor were they a precursor of a plea for a change of system.

Non-Brahman Movement: Leaders: The first Non-Brahman organization, the Satya Shodak Samaj (Truth-seeking Society), was founded in Pune in 1873, just before the Deccan Riots. It is this organization which is seen as the earliest sign of the modern Non-Brahman movement. The group gathered around Jotirao Phule, the founder of the Satya Shodak Samaj, is striking in that it consisted chiefly of non-Marathas and of those urban and not village based. Phule himself was a Mali, a member of a gardening caste whose farming practices adapted well to the new irrigation systems introduced by the British. He was first a school teacher in a Christian school, then ran an agency for monlds for types, and finally supported himself well through contracting work for British public enterprises. In later years he returned to the Mali role at a high level by purchasing a 200 acre irrigated farm near Pune.[6]

Phule's associates include other Malis, Krishnarao Pandurang Bhalekar and N.M. Lokhande; two Telugu-speaking Malis, Ramayya Vyankayya Aiyyavaru and P. Rajanna Lingu; V.R. Gholay, a Gawli (cowherd), Eliaya Soloman, probably from the Bene Israeli group of Jews which fit the Teli (oil-presser) caste category; Dhondiram Namdeo Kumbhar (a potter), and Tukkaram Tatya Padval, a Bhandari (toddy-tapper).

Biographical information on later Non-Brahman leaders indicates that many were not directly associated with the village. Shahu Maharaj of Kolhapur, who kept the movement alive from the turn of the century until his death in 1923, was obviously above any traditional village ties; Bhaurao Patil, the Jain educator of Satara and the southern districts, was a tutor and a salesman for Kirloskar Brothers industries, although his name indicates a village headman background; Bhaskarrao (B.V.) Jadhav, the first Maratha minister in Bombay under the Montagu-Chelmsford reforms, had been in the administration of Kolhapur State. The early Non-Brahman leadership did not come from those directly affected by the decline of Maratha power. Those who first protested the loss of Maratha status and the omnipresent power of the Brahmans were not from the old Maratha leadership (with the obvious exception of the Maharaja of Kolhapur), but from a new middle class, urban-based and with some perception of Western organizations.

Grievances Understood by both Elite and Mass

In both Non-Brahman and Mahar movements, there seems to be a double set of grievances, one a longing look back at past glory, the other a protest at current treatment in the light of current standards and opportunities. In the early Mahar movement there was little sense of past glory, just an occasional reference to pre-Aryan "Lords of the Land", and no sense of pride at all in their current village status, even though early British commentators held their role to be important.

Although Mahar history is not well documented until the modern period, a few indications of protest against the untouchable status are in evidence. The fourteenth century Mahar poet-saint Chokhamela speaks generally of devotion to God, but occasionally a note of anguish enters his poetry. He laments his being turned away from the temple in one poem; he cries out, "O God, who is pure?" in another.[7] Legal evidence indicates later protest of a more practical sort. Mahars in Junnar in the seventeenth century appealed for the privilege of having Brahman priests officiating at their weddings, an appeal which was refused by Aurangzeb on the basis of the preservation of custom. This decision was quoted by the Peshwa's government in the late eighteenth century in support of that government's refusal to allow Mahars in the Konkan a similar request.[8]

In the mid-nineteenth century, a Mahar boy from Dharwar applied for admission to a government school. Upon being refused, he appealed to the Education Department of Bombay Province, and in 1857 to the Government of India at Calcutta, but his petition was not granted on the grounds that opposition from higher castes was too strong.[9]

The grievances: It is difficult to extrapolate any widespread sense of grievance or ambition from such evidence. In 1890, however, Gopal Baba Walangkar, the retired army leader from Ratnagiri, petitioned "the Shankaracharya and other Hindu leaders" for redress of grievances, and from this point on such grievances are noted often enough that a common sense of deprivation among these Mahars can be surmised. In language "vigorous ... though not always correct", Walangkar listed the disadvantages of the Untouchable: difficulty in getting education, exclusion from *dharmshalas* (pilgrims' and travelers' guest houses), discrimination while traveling, ban on participation in trade, social stigma even when army service pay might allow the Untouchables to better their conditions, revulsion towards the Untouchables because of their handling of dead cattle.[10] Most of these disadvantages were experienced by the non-traditional Mahar. The last not on "revulsion", however, applies both to the Mahar in the new occupation and the village Mahar. Moving out of the traditional Mahar work did not affect the Mahar's ritual status, and resentment of treatment received both in village and town seems to have tied both those who stayed in it together. A word used frequently in the movement in the twentieth century indicates this tie: *manuski* (of man, i.e., self respect, humane attitudes) figures so often in Mahar speech-making that it seems to stand for a widely understood emotional grievance.

Among the Marathas, so recently a people of power and prestige, a loss of glory or, in more down-to-earth terms, of authority in the village was combined with resentment of the dominance of the Brahmans. Maureen Patterson reports that documentation for Brahman-Non-Brahman conflict is in evidence from the thirteenth century onward." The movement emerging in an organized form in the nineteenth century built upon this age-old conflict, but was expressed in terms that dealt with the modern world and with the village situation as it existed in the last half of that century.

The early Satya Shodak Samaj movement stressed two things: education for the masses and the reduction of Brahman ritual power. Phule himself was a creative pioneer in education, and he and other Samaj members not only worked in actual educational enterprises but used every channel available to them to urge the Government to take more responsibility for mass education. The most amusing example of this occurred when the Prince of Wales was greeted on his visit to Pune in 1889 with a sign hung from the Din Bandhu Sarvajanik Sabha free school for boys :

Tell Grandma we are a happy nation.
But 19 crores are without education.[12]

The jingle picks up a stress on masses, on the majority, which was common in the Non-Brahman movement. *Bahujan*

Samaj, the majority society, was often used as a synonym for Non-Brahman. And education was seen as the way by which members of that majority could enter the elite.

The pledge of the Shodak Samaj reflects its anti-Brahman bias only in its denial of the need for a priest in the relationship of a human being to God :

> All human beings are the children of one God. They are my brothers, and I shall always try to act upon this principle. I shall not entertain the services of any intermediary at the time of adoring, worshipping and meditating upon God and at the time of performing a religious ceremony, and I shall always try to induce others to follow the same practice. I shall always be loyal to the British Government. I shall not neglect to educate my boys and girls...[13]

The effort to do away with reliance on Brahman priests was part of a larger emphasis on reducing the combined ritual-administrative power of the nineteenth century Brahman. It was the power of the Brahman in both the secular and ritual worlds that elicited the attack on Non-Brahmans. The Maharashtra Brahmans' extraordinary ability to take advantage of the opportunity offered by the British administration and the westernizing process of the nineteenth century Maharashtra brought them into a position of dominance beyond that of the Peshwa times.

Usurption of Patil's Power by Kulkarni: The link between resentment of Brahmanical power on the part of the urbanized middle castes and the peasants of the village seems to be the figure of the *kulkarni,* the village accountant. As the *patil* was traditionally a Maratha, the village *kulkarni* was traditionally a Brahman. British methods of administration and revenue collection reduced the power of the *patil.* An official description of the *patils* in mid-century :

> They may be considered as the relics of a brighter era of a national prosperity; and they have in most instances profited by the mutability and continual changes of succeeding governments ...but the present change of system has effected a corresponding change in the circumstance of

> the Patel: each individual ryot being alone responsible for the assessment on his holding, the principal onus is removed from the Patel, and he is deprived of uncontrolled action, and shorn of a portion of his dignity.[14]

Resentment was turned not so much against the new system as against the village figure who seemed to profit by the recent change, the Brahman *kulkarni.* Phule's words on the usurption of the *patil's* power by the *kulkarni* indicate this treatment :

> The Patil of a village, the real head, is in fact a non-entity. The Kulkarni, the hereditary Brahmin village accountant... moulds the Patil according to his wishes. He is the temporal and spiritual advisor of the ryots, sawkar (money-lender) in his necessities and the general referee in all matters.[15]

Anti-kulkarni protest can be found at all levels: in the non-Brahman newspapers of the nineteenth century, in petitions to British administrators against the power of Brahman clerks, in poems and polemics. It seems to have served as a symbol for a deep-seated sense of lessened stature and frustration over an inability to deal as well with the new regime as did the Brahmans. It reached it apogee not in the nineteenth century or even in the early days of the political reforms when the Legislative Assembly became the platform for protest against Brahman dominance. In 1948, when a Maharashtrian Brahman assassinated Mahatma Gandhi, almost every village in the *desh* (plains) area of Maharashtra erupted in violence against the Brahmans of that place.

Legitimization

The eventual legitimization for the Mahar movement was the acceptance of a Western (or modern) view of democracy and the equality of man. Before the establishment of this credo with Ambedkar's rise to power, several other forms of justification for the Mahar's protest and claims to rights were put forward. The writing of the earliest modern leader, Gopal Baba Walangkar, reflects two things: the claim of *kshatriyahood* (which was abandoned early, probably because the Marathas pre-empted the field), and the contradictory but more popular claim of dominant status in the area before the advent of the

Aryans. This sort of prestige became basic to the movement of Untouchables in South India, where the term Adi-Dravida (original Dravidians) was sought and gained as Census nomenclature. In Maharashtra, however, the concept seems to have been discarded as early as 1910, when Shivram Janba Kamble based his petition to the British on a simple human rights issue.[16] Later, Ambedkar refused to use the pre-Aryan "Lords of the Land" claim, which he felt might result in permanent separation of the Untouchable and the caste Hindu. As political action became the most successful channel to social change, the legitimization of the movement in terms of "liberty, equality and fraternity" sufficed.

Legitimization of the movement in the eyes of the elite took the forms of sympathy, denial of inherent inferiority in the Untouchable, claims that through the Bhakti movement and the saint Chokhamela the Mahar had already proved his worth, and adherence to a belief in equality that had a western base. Maharashtra was especially rich in justification of social change, and the very Brahmans castigated by both Mahar and Maratha provided the public encouragement for their movement upward. A few examples show the range of the nineteenth century and early twentieth century attitudes. They reflect an openness and a radicality which was not widespread, but which was found among very influential men. A poem from the nineteenth century by Krishnaji Keshav Damle (Keshavsut), a Brahman revered as the first modern Marathi poet, illustrates this unusual quality of empathy :

The First Question of the Untouchable Boy

The children of untouchables,
poor, gay, playing on the roadside -
A Brahmin came from far
to the simple kids what should he say:
'O you brats of *Mahars,* move away,
be gone! What are you playing at, you louts?
Run and give way to the Brahmin!'
The boys fled — who would dare stay!

One amongst them did;
the wicked Brahmin brandished his club and shouted,
'Ass! thy shadow must not fall on me,
get thee gone, or else this "Sweet present"!'
The kid too slunk homewards,
musing—
'What if my shadow fell on him,
what's so wrong about it?'
At home he asked the question of his mother.
The poor mother said:
"We are low and they are high,
when you see them, you had 'better step aside'.
She said so - simply.
How should she know
that highness in this world is built
on sin and glory
on the degradation of others![17]

Another quotation indicates a view far ahead of its time. Dr. R.G. Bhandarkar, the eminent Sanskritist, told the Indian Social Conference in 1895 about a Mahar *haridasa* who had performed a *kirtan* [combined sermon and music] at his house, ending the story thus: "... and I believe from the opportunities I have had of observation, that the despised Mahar possesses a good deal of natural intelligence and is capable of being highly educated. So that to continue to keep him in ignorance is to deprive the country of an appreciable amount of intellectual resources."[18] Quotations which offered support to the Mahar movement can be found in the work of Mahadev Govind Ranade, Gopal Ganesh Agarkar, the novelist Hari Narayan Apte and other eminent figures of the nineteenth and early twentieth centuries. They offered an intellectual climate for change which was not often expressed in action but which encouraged among the Mahars an expectation that their own efforts for a better place in society would have elite support.

In the long run, the same idea of participatory democracy that justified the Mahar movement came to dominate the Non-

Brahman movement. However, it took sixty years between the founding of the Satya Shodak Samaj and the realization that democracy could mean majority control. In the intervening period, those in the Non-Brahman movement were, in general, loyal to the British and often battled against increased extensions of the democratic process, such as the granting of the vote to women, on the grounds that such innovations would only increase Brahman power.[19] The concept of *bahujan samaj* — the majority, however, was present in the movement from the first.

The traditional legitimization for many castes' claim to better status was the attempt to secure Kshatriya status. The Marathas as warriors considered themselves to be Kshatriya and it had taken some effort for the king of the seventeenth century Maratha empire to have himself crowned Chhatrapati Shivaji by a Brahman in true Kshatriya style. But while a number of sacred thread ceremonies are recorded there seems to have been no major attempt to secure a Census listing of the Maratha caste as Kshatriya. In a sense the Marathas needed no such legal bolstering of their claim to power and worth; the memory of Shivaji's empire was not dead. The first Non-Brahman glorification of Shivaji in the modern period seems to have been Mahatma Phule's Shivaji ballads of 1888.[20] The extent of pride in Shivaji in rural areas in the late nineteenth century is not known, but the current knowledge of Shivaji and his accomplishments is so widespread that one must presume either a constant folk memory or a thorough resurrection which met a ready response. One anthropologist's findings indicate that a greater percentage of village residents could correctly identify Shivaji rather than Nehru in the 1950s.[21]

Shivaji was also essential to the nationalists' image of India. The writings of Mahadev Govind Ranade and Bal Gangadhar Tilak, both Brahmans, reactivated pride in the Maratha past and also offered reinforcement for the Non-Brahman's claim to a greater share of contemporary power. The writing of the elite on the Maharashtrian Bhakti (devotional religion) movement centred on Pandharpur also added legitimacy to the Non-Brahman's concept of his proven worth. While saints from all castes entered into the movement in its period of creativity from the thirteenth through the seventeenth century, the most popular by far was the Shudra Tukaram, a poet-saint of Shivaji's period and, according to some, the spiritual source of his greatness.[22]

The reform associations of the Brahmans contributed to the intellectual justification of the Non-Brahman movement. Western India's religious reform movement, the Prarthana Samaj, allowed its ceremonies to be conducted by Marathas. The Poona Sarvajanik Sabha, a social and political organization which was the most important predecessor of the Indian National Congress in the Maharashtra area, attempted for a time to use Marathas from the landed aristocracy as its figureheads and also took on the presentation of peasant grievances to the Government. Jotirao Phule was extremely critical of both Prarthana Samaj and Sarvajanik Sabha, considering them both to be too much under Brahmanical control to be of any service to Non-Brahmans. Nevertheless, these elite attitudes could be used to justify Non-Brahman aims.

Brokers

While leadership within caste ranks and tacit intellectual approval on the part of the elite was necessary for the development of the Mahar movement, a group of "brokers"—men who formed links with power sources or who could perform the duties members of the caste were not yet able to undertake — seems to have been essential. This is especially clear in the early period of Ambedkar's leadership, from 1925 to 1935, when members of the Chandraseniya Kayastha Prabhu (C.K.P.) caste were of great importance in the development of his institutions. The presence of this group, highly educated and yet considered Shudras by the Brahmans, working both from a reformist commitment and in their own self-interest in the twentieth century, has caused a search for similar "brokers" in the nineteenth. An easily defined group cannot be isolated, but it is clear that a number of individuals participated meaningfully in the earliest stages of movement.

Jotiba Phule himself served as a link between Mahars and the larger society. His schools for Untouchable children in Poona in the 1850s were among the earliest non-missionary efforts on behalf of the Depressed Classes. Vithal Ramji Shinde, himself a Maratha reformer who devoted much of his life to the education of the Depressed Classes, reported that Jotiba Phule, Baba Padmaji and others helped and guided Walangkar in his early effort to petition the British for redress of the ban on Untouchables' recruitment in the army.[23] Shivram Janba Kamble is said to have received help from the Gaikwad of Baroda in his various efforts at securing rights for the Untouchables. Just before Ambedkar came on the scene to represent Untouchables directly, two Mahars were brought before the Secretary of State for India, Edwin Montagu, on his 1917-1918 tour of India. Montagu reports :

> Then we had Rai Bahadur Dougre on behalf of the depressed classes. He was a very nice fellow, taking a great interest in the depressed classes. He is a caste Hindu, and he brought along with him two Untouchables, who struck me, although one did not speak English, by their extraordinary intelligence. He thinks that communal representation for them is necessary....[24]

The incident is an illustration of the necessary form of brokerage. Dougre was a Non-Brahman, anxious to serve that cause while aiding the Depressed Classes. While there was much paternalism extended to lower castes and Untouchables in many parts of India, and many instances of this in Bombay province, there was also a form of aid more conducive to the growth of a movement in the depressed group itself. That category of help which has been catalogued as "brokeage" was responsive to the initiative of the depressed group itself, allowed leadership when possible to direct the action taken, and contained a healthy clement of self-interest.

In the Non-Brahman movement, reformist Brahmans generally served this role as friends, aids and associates of Mahatma Phule. There is also some indication that at the village level members of the C.K.P. caste quite early took on some responsibility in the Non-Brahman movement. The necessity of "brokers" is clearer in the history of the Mahar movement than in the Non-Brahman. Both movements, however, needed men more literate, more sophisticated, better able to approach the thrones of authority than the men actually of those movements in the nineteenth century. And in Maharashtra at every turn such men quietly performed that service.

Communication and Protection

These two necessities are obvious, and although communication was an all important and interesting development in both movements, perhaps it is sufficient to say here that in Maharashtra the newspaper was the *sine qua non* of any movement. Even before Ambedkar's sophisticated leadership began in 1920, at least four newspapers had emerged from the Mahar movement. And the Non-Brahman movement produced *Din Bandhu* (Brother of the Poor), a Marathi weekly, within four years of the establishment of the Satya Shodak Samaj in 1877.

References

1. See Eugene F. Irschick, *Politics and Social Conflict in South India: The Non-Brahman Movement and Tamil Separatism, 1916-29* (Berkeley: University of California Press, 1969) [See Addendum].
2. Although there is much material in censuses and in anthropological studies, there was no historical monograph on an Untouchable caste movement when this essay was written except my Ph.D. thesis, 'Dr. Ambedkar and the Mahar Movement" (University of Pennsylvania, 1969). Owen Lynch's study of the Jatavas in Agra, *The Politics of Untouchability* (New York: Columbia Univers ity Press, 1969) does cover the history of that segment of the Chamar caste which became related to the Mahar movement in 1940s through Dr. Ambedkar's leadership. [There is now a study of Ad-Dharm in the Punjab in Mak Juergensmeyer's *Religion as Social Vision: The Movement against Untouchability in 20th Century Punjab* (Berkeley: University of California, 1982). The Ilava

movement of Narayana Guru has now been covered in at least a dozen recent books.]

3. The chief sources in English for Non-Brahman history when this essay was written were Dhananjay Keer, *Mahatma Jotirao Phooley* (Bombay: Popular Prakashan, 1964); A.B. Latthe, *Memoirs of His Highness Shri Shahu Chhatrapati Maharaja of Kolhapur, 2* Vols. (Bombay: The Times Press, 1924); Anjilvel V. Mathew, *Bhaurao Patil* (Sztara: Rayat Shikshan Sansta, 1957); and Maureen L.P. Patterson's unpublished M.A. thesis, "A Preliminary Study of the Brahmin versus Non-Brahmin Conflict in Maharashtra" (University of Pennsylvania, 1952). See the Addendum for the flood of recent material.
4. *Gazetteer of the Bombay Presidency.* Vol XII: Khandesh. Compiled by James M. Campbell, William Ramsay and James Pollen (Bombay: Government Press, 1880), pp. 116, 119.
5. *Report of the Land Revenue Settlement of the Nagpur District in the Central Provinces.* Compiled by R.H. Craddock (Nagpur: Government Press, 1899), p. 28.
6. Biographical information on Jotirao Phule has been drawn from Dhananjay Keer's biography, *Mahatma Jotirao Phooley* [For more recent studies, see the *Addendum* to this essay.]
7. *Cokhamela abhang gatha* (Bombay: Balkrishna Lakshaman Pathak, 1950). See *Abhangas* 5 and 11 and the essay on "Chokhamela and Eknath" in this volume.
8. See Hiroshi Fukazawa, "State and Caste System (Jati) in the Eighteenth Century Maratha Kingdom", *Hitotsubashi Journal of Economics,* IX: 1 (June 1968), p. 43.
9. See Syed Nurullah and J.P. Naik, *History of Education in India* (Bombay: Macmillan, 1951), pp. 421-22.
10. *Indu Prakash* (Bombay, 5 May 1890), p. 4. j
11. Maureen L.P. Patterson, *op. cit.*, p. 1. [More recent scholarship suggests that Brahman-Maratha cooperation was more common than competition, but a change in areas of power and dominance would throw caste interdependence into competition.]

12. Dhananjay Keer, *op. cit.*, p. 240. According to Census figures, there were 580 literate males per 1000 among Brahmans, 43 in 1000 among Marathas, and 7 in 1000 among Mahar males in 1901. No significant change in these proportions appeared until the 1931 Census when literate males per 1000 were: Brahman, 788; Maratha, 223; Mahar, 63.
13. *Indian Statutory Commission*. VII. Memorandum submitted by the Government of Bombay (London: H.M.S.O., 1930), pp. 227-28.
14. R.N. Gooddine, *Report on the Village Communities of the Deccan* (Selections from the Records of the Bombay Government, No. IV) (Bombay: Government of Bombay, 1852), p. 15.
15. Quoted in Ravinder Kumar, *Western India in the Nineteenth Century* (London: Routledge & Kegan Paul, 1968), p. 307 from Jotirao Phule's *Gulamgiri* (slavery).
16. The petition is reproduced in H.N. Navalkar, *The Life of Shivram Janba Kamble* (Poona: S.J. Kamble, 1930.)
17. Translated by Prabhakar Machwe in his short biography, *Keshavsut* (New Delhi: Sahitya Akademi, 1966), pp. 45-6.
18. R.G. Bhandarkar, *Collected Works*, Vol. II, edited by Narayan Bapuji Utgikar (Poona: Bhandarkar Oriental Institute, 1928), p. 491.
19. *Bombay Legislative Council Debates*, Vol. I (1921), pp. 358-61.
20. Dhananjay Keer, *op. cit.*, pp. 100-01.
21. William A. Morrison, "Knowledge of Political Personages held by the Male Villagers of Badlapur", *Sociological Bulletin*, X: 2, pp. 1-26 and XII: 2. pp. 1-17.
22. The popular view of Tukaram as saint in Shivaji's time is vividly shown in the Marathi film, *Sant Tukaram*, produced by Prabhat Film Company Poona in 1936. [Tukaram's problems with orthodox Brahmans and his eventually winning their approval and Shivaji's devotion are the high point of the film.]
23. Karamvir Vithal Ramji Shinde, *Majhya athavani va anubhav* (My memories and experiences) (Poona: R.B. Andre, 1958), p. 214.
24. Edwin S. Montagu, *An Indian Diary*. Edited by Venetia Montagu (London: William Heinemann, 1930), p. 306.

4
Untouchability Then and Now

Society in India is based on a unique form of social order known as the 'caste system.' Indian society is divided horizontally and vertically into thousands of castes. The castes are further divided into sub-castes or sub-sub-castes. Each caste is an endogamous unit. At the lowest rung of the ladder sit the people who are called and treated as 'Untouchables', and in some parts as unapproachable and unseeable. They are considered to be outside the pale of Hinduism. Unfortunately, even the 'Untouchables' are divided into hundreds of castes and sub-castes and they are mutually 'Untouchable.' This has made their unity difficult and exploitation and oppression by others easy. Instead of rebelling against the system and against the religion which degrade them and deny them the hope and the opportunities for elevating their social status, and improving their economic conditions, they have been, for centuries, endeavouring to carve a niche in the dilapidated mansion of Hinduism, and strengthening the chains of slavery around them by imitating the customs, rituals and ceremonies of the upper caste Hindus.

Hindus consider not only the so-called lower castes people engaged in occupations like scavenging, sweeping, tanning, shoe-making, midwifery, butchery, pig and poultry keeping, basket making, etc., as 'Untouchables.' For them, Moslems, Jews and Christians are also 'Untouchables.' In Hindu homes separate utensils are usually kept for the members of these religious communities. Orthodox Hindus do not touch the utensils used by the guests or the visitors from these communities. After a visit by Louis Mountbatten, the last Viceroy and Governor General of India, a temple in South India was washed, cleaned and was purified for seven days with *Punch Gavya* (a concoction made of cow's urine, dung, milk, curd and butter), because a Christian white man had polluted the temple.

The practice of untouchability has also political implications. Untouchability was one of the reasons which led to the creation of Pakistan and the partitioning of India. It may lead to another partitioning of India if Hindus do not change their attitude towards the 'Untouchables' and other minorities. The 'Untouchable' groups all over India have become more aware of their rights and dignity as human beings, and are getting organised everywhere to defend their rights. The Hindus can ill-afford to ignore this emerging phenomenon.

Nobody knows about the origin of untouchability or of the caste system itself. Some historians try to trace the origin of the caste system to the Vedas, the ancient religious books of the Hindus. The Purusha Sukta in the Rig Veda mentions about the creation of four varnas, namely the Brahmin, the Kshatriya, the Vaishya and the Shudra. Outside the varna system were the indigenous people who continued to fight against the invading Aryans. They were exterminated or subjugated and made serfs and slaves when the Aryan invaders established themselves in this land. In order to preserve the purity of blood, social intercourse was prohibited with the members of the vanquished group. Those who did not follow this rule as well as those who opposed or violated it were outcasted and forced to live away from the dominating group. According to one explanation, those who were forced to live outside the villages became outcastes and later 'Untouchables.'

Gradually, the Hindu varna system became more rigid and upward mobility became difficult, if not impossible. Strict religious, social and economic measures were introduced by the priestly caste and enforced through the warrior castes to perpetuate the system. Inter-marriage and inter-dining were strictly prohibited. Society was divided into small endogamous units which were further divided into water-tight compartments, giving fewer opportunities to meet and discuss common problems. Those who violated the law of endogamy and restrictions on dining, were awarded deterrent punishment and were excommunicated. The outcastes had no alternative but to accept lowly jobs like dragging the dead animals, removing excreta, sweeping the streets and drains, flaying the animals, and guarding the cremation grounds. Wars, famines, epidemics and natural calamities like flood and earthquakes made more people homeless. This forced many to join the ranks of the outcastes.

The outcastes were known as *'antyaja,' 'antvasin,' 'chandala,'* and *'asprshya.'* The Brahmin law makers and the Kshatriya rulers condemned them to live outside the villages and towns, in ignorance, poverty and destitution. The law makers were not content with banning social intercourse with these people but also prescribed that their touch, their breath, their sight, even their shadow, polluted the upper caste Hindus. They were not allowed to enter cities or have contact with the nobility. Fahien, the famous Chinese traveller, who visited India during the sixth century and spent many years as a guest of the kings and Boudh *Viharas* wrote: 'The *chandalas* are named "evil men" and dwell apart from others; if they enter a town or market, they sound a piece of wood in order to separate themselves; then men, knowing who they are, avoid coming in contact with them.'

Even in Buddha's times *chandalas* were treated as 'Untouchables.' However, from the Theri Gatha and Thera Gatha and other books of Tripatika, it appears Buddha admitted *chandalas* and other lower caste people in his *Sangha.* It seems that some *chandalas* also joined the Jain Sangh of Mahavir. Harikesh Bal, son of a *chandala* rose to be a famous and learned Jain Bhikkhu. There was no discrimination against the *Chandalas* or *Antyajas* in the Bhikkhu Sangh of the Buddha.

In the later Puranik period, when Hinduism once again became powerful, Bouddh Bhikkhus were ridiculed and treated as 'Untouchables.' According to an incident mentioned in Vishnupurana, a Raja had to take birth as a crow, a dog, a donkey and a pig because of the sin of talking to a Bouddh Bhikkhu on his way back from a river. His wife, of course, dutifully avoided looking at the Bhikkhu and ultimately rescued her husband from further degradation.

Untouchables during the Islamic and the British Period

Ibn Batuta, the Moslem scholar who accompanied Mahmud Ghaznavi, mentions about the stratification of Hindu society and the untouchability practised by them. Moslem invaders, according to him, at first treated all Indians alike but later took advantage of the cleavages existing in Indian society. It was the Moslem invaders who opened the gates of their cities to the 'Untouchables' living outside the cities. Many of the 'Untouchables' and low caste people embraced Islam and joined the invaders, partly to avoid persecution and partly in search of better status and fortunes. Those who embraced Islam and joined the armies of Moslem invaders imitated the customs and manners of their new masters. They gradually became merged and integrated into Moslem society. Besides those who formally embraced Islam, whether voluntarily or under compulsion, there were millions of those who belonged to the artisan castes like weavers, mason, carpenters, blacksmiths, shoe-makers, basket makers, potters, dyers etc., who came in contact with the Moslems. For a long time they remained nominal converts to Islam. Until the beginning of the 19th century their religious status remained ambiguous. Compulsions of twentieth century politics led them to declare themselves Moslems or Hindus according to the pressures from these two religious groups.

The British, who came as traders, recruited some 'Untouchables' as watchmen in factories. Later on, they raised a trained army from among them. They recruited anybody who volunteered himself for service as a soldier under the East India Company and appeared to be strong enough to handle arms. After the battle of Plassey, many soldiers belonging to the Brahmin, Rajput and other upper castes from the neighbouring provinces of Oudh, Bihar and Central India, began to join the Bengal Army of the East India Company. Their main attractions were better wages, security of service, attractive uniform and pensionary benefits. As the number of upper caste Hindus in Bengal Army increased, the soldiers belonging to the

'Untouchable' castes and other lower castes were gradually eased out of service. The military policy of the British underwent several changes according to political needs and expendiency. Armies manned by the 'Untouchables' were ultimately disbanded by the end of the nineteenth century. The doors of employment in the army were finally closed on them excepting the lowly ranks of sweepers, washermen, domestic servants, butlers, bearers and cooks.

For a long time education was the monopoly of the Brahmins. Buddhist Bhikkhus were perhaps the first to open the doors of education for all, irrespective of caste or race. Buddhist Viharas and monasteries became great centres of learning where people from different parts of India and the neighbouring countries came to study. Moslems during their rule, did not introduce any system of public education, nor did the ordinary people feel any necessity of education save for reading the Koran which was written in Arabic. Only men belonging to the upper classes studied Persian and Arabic.

It was the Christian missionaries who liberated education. The missionaries admitted in their schools boys and girls belonging to all classes including the 'Untouchables.' Many 'Untouchables' embraced Christianity and many more who got education in the missionary schools became aware of their miserable condition. The demobilised soldiers and the young men who got the benefit of education in Christian institutions furnished the early leadership among the 'Untouchables.'

The British, with a view of strengthening their administration, began collecting information about the social system, religious customs, rituals, traditions and superstitious beliefs of their subjects. Census Reports, Gazetteers and Settlement Reports furnished valuable information in this regard. Educated classes in India also became aware of the plight of their countrymen. Hindus, for the first time, became aware that their population was constantly decreasing and that of the Moslems, Sikhs and Christians, was rapidly increasing. This was mainly due to a large number of 'low-caste' people embracing Christianity, Islam and Sikkhism. The lower castes of Hindus learnt that a handful of Brahmins, barely three per cent of the total population, held more than eighty per cent of the government jobs and wielded enormous power. The Moslems learnt that even though they ruled over the country until the end of the nineteenth century, owing to their backwardness in education, they had become backward in all respects. They had very little share in the administration. The upper classes among them, organised themselves and demanded a share in the administration in proportion to their population. They also demanded exclusion of 'Untouchables' from the category of Hindus. As a result of demands made by the Moslems and also by the leaders of the 'Untouchables,' these groups were enumerated in the Census as 'menial and vagrant castes,' 'exterior castes' and later as 'Depressed Classes.' When numbers became politically important, each religious group began to look for converts. It was only from among the 'Untouchables' and other low castes that converts could be found and all religious groups tried to woo the 'Untouchables' to their respective religions.

The Arya Samaj, a reform movement founded in the middle of the nineteenth century, started the Shuddhi movement to check the egress of 'Untouchables' and to reconvert those who had embraced Sikhism, Christianity and Islam. It could not reconvert many Moslems or Christians or even Sikhs during the early years of its struggle, but it succeeded in checking the migration of 'Untouchables' to other religions especially to Christianity in Northern India. The orthodox Hindus, who were more concerned with their religious status and ritual purity, tried to consolidate their position by insisting on the separation between 'touchable' and 'untouchable.'

The Arya Samajists, on the other hand, encouraged the 'Untouchables' to return to their fold. In their zeal to increase their strength, the Arya Samajists converted a large number of 'Untouchables'—Meghs, Chamars, Rahatias, and Julahas (weavers)—and bestowed on them the right to wear tuft *(choti),* sacred thread *(Janyoo)* and to enter the Arya Samaj temples. However, they soon realised that it was easy to give the new converts Vedic names like 'Ved Prakash,' and 'Om Prakash' and the right to wear sacred thread, but difficult to give them equal status in Hindu society. An Arya Chamar (leather worker) remained a Chamar and a Arya Bhangi remained a Bhangi (scavenger). In order to wriggle out of this difficult situation, they declared that there was no question of Shuddhi for Chamars etc., since they were already Hindus for all purposes. Shuddhi, they explained, was necessary only for conversion of people from other religions like Islam and Christianity. Instead of converting the 'Untouchables' through 'Shuddhi' they encouraged Hinduisation of the 'Untouchables.' The 'Untouchables' were asked to give up beef eating, to cremate their dead instead of burying them, and to perform their religious ceremonies according to Brahminic rites.

Sweepers were embracing Christianity *en masse* in Punjab. It was necessary to check these mass conversions if the sweeper class was to be preserved. The sweepers followed a religion which was very much independent. Lal Beg was their patron saint. They called him Bala Shah and sometimes identified him with Balmiki, the legendary composer of the *Ramayana*. They introduced the names of the prophets of the Old Testament, and Hindu and Moslem dieties in their prayers, which were known as 'Kursinamas.' Brahmin leaders of Arya Samaj, instead of converting the sweepers, converted their patron saint and gave him the name 'Balmiki,' the author of the Ramayana. Pandit Amin Chand, a Brahmin preacher, wrote a small book entitled *Valmiki Prakash* to further strengthen the belief in their minds that Lal Beg was actually the corrupted name of Balmiki. They, however, took care to stress the point that they were the followers, not descendants of Maharshi Valmiki. Lal Beg was gradually forgotten and all sweepers became Hinduised. Mass conversions were checked and the spirit of rebellion among the Sweepers of Punjab was weakened. From Punjab, the movement and the new name 'Balmiki' spread to other parts of north India. The sweepers employed in the army played a significant role in this.

Non-Arya Samajist social reformers also exhorted the 'Untouchables' to give up beef eating and burial of the dead and encouraged cremation of their dead in separate crematoria. Some of the affluent Hindus even helped the 'Untouchables' to meet the expenses of cremation and for building separate temples and shrines for them. As a result, some of the lower castes, especially in north India, sent representations to the government against their names being included in the list of the Depressed Classes. They claimed to be Kshatriyas and Brahmins. Jatavs in western Uttar Pradesh asserted that they were Kshatriyas, progeny of Krishna, and some began to affix the word Yadava to their names.

The Search for a New Name

The term 'Depressed Classes' was not acceptable to many organisations and leaders among the 'Untouchables' themselves. At the Round Table Conference held in London, 1930-32, Dr. B.R. Ambedkar, who represented the 'Untouchables,' demanded the removal of this nomenclature.

Gandhiji used a new word, 'Harijan.' Actually he did not coin the word. One Narsi Mehta, a Vaishnava Saint, in one of the poems, had used the word 'Harijan' to refer to the 'Untouchables'. One of the correspondents of Gandhiji suggested to him the adoption of this name. The name appealed to Gandhiji and he readily adopted it and popularised it. Not many among the 'Untouchable' leaders and organisers favoured the word 'Harijan,' however. Dr. Ambedkar vehemently opposed it. Yet, Gandhiji and his followers continued to use it. It was not officially adopted by the makers of the Constitution.

The British Government was, at this time, preparing a list of the socially, educationally and economically backward castes, who were to be given special assistance. Those castes, who suffered from disabilities arising from untouchability and had no objection to their names being included in the list of 'Untouchables' were listed separately. This list was appended as a schedule to the Government of India Act, 1935. Because of the inclusion of these castes in the schedule, they were called the 'Scheduled Castes.' At the time of drafting the Constitution, the name 'Scheduled Castes' was adopted and incorporated in the Constitution.

The right to include or exclude any caste in the list of the Scheduled Castes was given to the President of India. According to the list of the Scheduled Castes released by the President in 1950, only those who professed Hinduism were considered to be Scheduled Castes. Converts to other religions were excluded. However, under pressure from the Sikh leaders, 'Untouchables' who were converted to Sikhism were included in the list of 'Scheduled Castes' and all concessions reserved for the Scheduled Castes were extended to them. The British had recognised the 'Untouchables' as a separate entity. The 'Untouchables' were also becoming increasingly conscious of their condition. They knew who was responsible for their degradation and exploitation and who was opposing them, and why. They knew who was their friend and who their enemy. They had a charismatic leader in Dr. B.R. Ambedkar, who was the most highly educated leader born among them. There was nobody to match him even among the Hindus.

Hindu leaders were also beginning to realise that it was no longer possible for them to deny the 'Untouchables' their human, civic and political rights even though many Hindus were not prepared to treat them as human beings. Untouchability and caste system had religious sanction behind them. Hindu leaders did not want to lose them to Christians and Moslems but they could not stem the rebellion fast growing in the minds of 'Untouchables,' which manifested itself in the form of confrontation and as conversion to other religions. At the same time the Hindu intelligentia did not want the 'Untouchables' to become independent, get united and organised under the banner of Dr. Ambedkar. Prosperity and affluence of upper caste Hindus depended on the ignorance, poverty, disunity and general backwardness of the 'Untouchables' who provided them with cheap labour and performed all unpleasant duties. Awakening of the 'Untouchables' was fatal to the Hindu interests.

Hindu Leaders Strategy Towards Untouchables

Hindus were aware of the weaknesses of the 'Untouchables' which they exploited to their best advantage. They developed a strategy strictly according to the injunctions of the Shastras. It included: (1) weaning away the 'Untouchables' from the leadership of Dr. Ambedkar and creating misunderstanding and distrust between the leader and his followers; (2) creating disunity among the 'Untouchables' by pitting one caste against the other (Chamars were pitted against the Mahars in Maharashtra and Bhangis were pitted against the Chamars in north India); (3) Encouraging Hinduisation of the 'Untouchables' and keeping the Moslems away from them; (4) adopting illiterate leaders with little knowledge or understanding of politics from among them as party candidates for legislatures; (5) admitting young untouchables in colleges and schools run by Hindu organisations like Arya Samaj, Hindu Mahasabha etc., in order to train them in the Hindu way; (6) encouraging the worship of patron saints, gods and goddesses etc., so as to combat Christian missionary work among them.

It is easy to find traitors in backward communities and nations. Congress and other Hindu organisations found them in abundance among the 'Untouchables.' The strategy of the Hindus bore fruit and they succeeded in keeping the Scheduled Castes backward and disunited and also proved to the world at large, on the basis of the election results, that majority of the Scheduled Castes were with Gandhiji and with the Congress.

According to the latest Census Report, Scheduled Castes in India account for about 100 million. They are divided into about 1000 castes. Each caste is an endogamous unit. It is an artificially created minority which can be easily scrapped with a stroke of pen by deleting the word 'Scheduled.' There is nothing to bind them excepting the Schedule appended to the Constitution. Even in times of adversity, they do not unite.

The Scheduled Castes occupy 78 out of the 542 seats in the Lok Sabha. These seats are reserved for them. There is no reservation in the Rajya Sabha but some persons are nominated or indirectly elected to represent the Scheduled Castes. Out of the 3997 seats in the State Assemblies, 540 are reserved for the Scheduled Castes. Besides the Legislature, 15 per cent of the seats in all categories, are reserved for them in the Administration. Even in posts filled by promotion, 15 per cent of the seats are reserved for them in almost all categories, barring the highest posts. Seats are also reserved in Corporations, autonomous bodies and public undertakings as well as aided institutions. Because of the resistance from the upper castes, these provisions made under the Constitution have not been implemented. In the rural areas, where more than 80 per cent of the population live, they work as landless labourers, artisans, menial servants etc. In spite of the ceiling laws, land has not been allotted to them. If allotted, it is very difficult to make vacant land available to the allottees. Many murders and atrocities are committed on the 'Untouchables' owing to the allotment of land or for their demand for better wages or for refusing to do 'begar' (work without wages).

Dr. Ambedkar and a New Vision

The main theme of the Hindu leaders including Gandhiji was to protect and strengthen Hinduism. They wanted to keep 'Untouchables' within the Hindu fold. Owing to their numbers, 'Untouchables' who were disowned both by the Hindus and the Moslems, until the 18th century, had become politically important. Hindus were not serious about their upliftment. They were only interested in keeping them within the Hindu fold for economic and political reasons and with that object in view, they allowed some concessions. They, of course took care, and devoted more time and money for publicity here and abroad, to show to the world that they had removed the curse of untouchability. Gandhiji was given credit for this great 'achievement.'

Dr. B.R. Ambedkar, on the other hand, wanted to emancipate the 'Untouchables' and liberate them from the slavery of Hinduism. He wanted to achieve equal rights—human, civic and political—for the 'Untouchables.' He wanted them to grow into a third force beside the Hindus and Moslems in free India and share power with them. It was only then, he believed, that they would be able to fight against the wrongs done to them by an unjust society.

Dr. Ambedkar came on the scene in 1927 and led a mass movement of 'Untouchables' to take water from a public tank at Mahad. It was for the first time in the history of India that the 'Untouchables' under their own leader launched a struggle for their rights. He was preceded by Rao Bahadur M.C. Rajah in the Presidency of Madras. Rao Bahadur Rajah and

Dr. Ambedkar both came from families who had served in the British Army. Dr. Ambedkar started his public life in Maharashtra but his participation in the Round Table Conference held in London, where he championed the cause of the 'Untouchables' of the whole of India, made him the acknowledged leader of the 'Untouchables.' Rao Bahadur Rajah lacked the knowledge and perspective and a broader vision. Out of jealousy, he joined the Congress camp and continued to oppose Dr. Ambedkar until 1943, when he was disillusioned with the Hindu leaders and once again came closer to Dr. Ambedkar. Dr. Ambedkar did not want to depend on the charity of Hindus. As a student of history, he knew that the oppressed people had to struggle and pay the price for freedom. For some time he tried to work for amelioration of the condition of the 'Untouchables' within the Hindu fold. But he soon realised that the Hindus were not prepared to change their attitude or behaviour towards the 'Untouchables.'

Dr. Ambedkar tried to unite the 'Untouchables' under one banner in order to fight for justice and equality. 'Their wrongs could be righted,' he told them, 'only when they got a share in the political power and in the administration of the country.' He realised that for achieving both these ends, education was most crucial. So, from 1932 onwards, he devoted considerable time and energy in promoting education for the 'Untouchables' by setting up educational institutions and, getting sufficient financial aid for them, from the government.

The method and strategy adopted by Dr. Ambedkar and his followers were not liked by many Hindus. The separate electorate granted to the 'Untouchables' by the British Government through what is known as the 'Communal Award' was vehemently opposed by the Hindu leaders while it was accepted for the Muslims and other minorities. On the issue of separate electorate for the 'Untouchables,' Gandhiji, as a true Hindu leader, undertook a 'fast unto death.' It was not so much to help the 'Untouchables' as to save Hinduism and Hindu society. Owing to the pressure from the Hindu leaders and in order to save Gandhiji's life, an agreement was signed between the Hindu leaders and Dr. Ambedkar. This agreement is known as the Poona Pact.

According to the Poona Pact, the 'Untouchables' lost their right for separate electorate to choose their own political representatives. Instead, they were given a larger number of seats to be filled by joint electorates. Since there was no constituency in which the 'Untouchables' were in majority, this meant that only those 'Untouchable' leaders who were acceptable to the Hindu majority and who were sponsored by political parties controlled by the Hindu leaders would be elected. Dr. Ambedkar realised this and later remarked, that it would have been better for the 'Untouchables' if they had fewer seats reserved for them, to which they could send their own representatives. Under the Poona Pact, the Hindus secured the right to choose the representatives of the 'Untouchables.' The same arrangement continues to be followed under the Constitution adopted in 1949. Dr. Ambedkar did try to make a change in this but the Scheduled Caste members of the Constituent Assembly refused to support him for fear of offending their party bosses. Today most of the 'Untouchable' politicians join the parties which readily adopt them and finance their elections. They seldom join Communist organisations because Communist parties are cadre-based parties and demand active participation in their activities. Scheduled Caste men and women having political ambitions, usually join Capitalist supported Hindu organisations like the Congress, or the Jan Sangh. These Hindu dominated organisations have enormous resources at their disposal. The Republican Party of India (RPI) having its base among the Scheduled Castes succeeded in returning about eight men to the Parliament in 1957 when they entered into alliance with Samyukta Maharashtra Dal comprising Communists, Socialists etc. Owning to the lack of funds and poor organisation, it has not been able to make an impact, yet it has many sympathisers among the Scheduled Castes and Backward Classes throughout India. Dr. Ambedkar believed that, in order to have power, 'Untouchables' and minorities must have a party of their own. But his successors could not make it a strong party. One by one the leaders deserted it. Very few non-Scheduled Castes,

Christians, Mohammedans or Backward Classes joined the RPI.

Abolition of Untouchability

Untouchability was abolished by the Constitution. On the 27th November 1947, a provision abolishing untouchability was passed and Article 17 was incorporated in the Constitution.

Nobody had any clear idea as to what was being abolished. For reasons better understood by the students of sociology, the political leaders, especially the Hindus, felt shy of defining untouchability. Untoucbability is not a mere touch-me-not-ism. It is a prejudice sanctioned by Hindu religion which manifests itself in the form of discriminatory treatment against a large number of people, who are believed to have been born among certain castes, as punishment for the sins committed against Brahmins and their religion in their past births. Hindus practise untouchability against Christians and Mohammedans also, but, this does not fall within the orbit of law framed under Article 17 of the Constitution.

However, untouchability was abolished and its practice was made an offence under the law. The law, however, was passed some seven years after the incorporation of the Article in the Constitution. When the law was ultimately passed in 1955 under the title of 'Untouchability (Offences) Act, 1955,' it suffered from many defects. It was a very mild Act because the Gandhian legislators did not want to make it a harsh one. As a result of these deficiencies, majority of the cases were ignored by the authorities or ended in compromises under pressure. Very often the Police did not Register the cases under the Act. The judiciary, dominated by upper caste Hindus tended to treat cases of untouchability very lightly, and awarded minor punishment. If untouchability is practised against a person belonging to Scheduled Castes who has embraced Christianity or Buddhism, the offence is not punishable under this law.

Untouchability is still being practised throughout India. In states like Uttar Pradesh, Bihar and Madhya Pradesh, it is practised in the worst form. In these states cases of offences are often not even registered by the police. In an interview, published in the Harijan Sewak Sangh, Delhi, a police officer from Tamil Nadu stated that if proper action was taken under the Untouchability (Offences) Act, half of the people in Tamil Nadu would be in jail.

Owing to the multiplication of incidents of atrocities, a commission was appointed under the chairmanship of Elayaperumal to study the problem. On the basis of the recommendations this Commission submitted in 1969, representations made by Scheduled Caste organisations and suggestions from the Commissioner for the Scheduled Castes and Scheduled Tribes, the original law was amended in 1976. The new Act is known as the 'Protection of Civil Rights Act 1955.' 'More teeth were added to the law' but again the government did very little to implement the law or even to give it wide publicity. Lamenting the inaction on the part of the Government and the ineffectiveness of the law, Justice Krishna lyer remarked: 'What was abolished was the name not the practice, for Untouchability still thrives and is widely practised.'

Like the laws forbidding child marriage and dowry, the law forbidding the practise of Untouchability too is not respected by the people at large. Deep rooted traditions cannot be easily replaced by secular laws. Courts have also been very slow in meting out punishment to the offenders. Due to the cumbersome court procedures, and expenses and time involved, the victims often do not report the cases, or if they do, they find it difficult to pursue them. Law alone cannot bring about social reform. It must be properly and earnestly implemented. But those who are expected to implement the law, namely the police and the judiciary, are often controlled by the dominant upper castes or political interest groups, who are prejudiced against the Scheduled Castes.

In a past case in Gujarat, the lower court imposed a ridiculous fine of Rs. 2 on an offender under the Untouchability Offences Act 1955. The complainant went in appeal before the High Court and the Gujarat High Court finally enhanced the fine to Rs. 50. The Elayaperumal Commission Report also confirmed that in many places the police did not possess a copy of the Untouchability (Offences) Act. Many of them had not even heard of this law. Much can be achieved if this law could be included in the course for police officers and its importance impressed upon them. In the same way, the textbooks used in schools and colleges could be used to expose social evils such as the practice of Untouchability.

The Ministry of Information and Broadcasting can also do much in the matter of social education. Unfortunately, one gets the impression that much of what is being done in this area is done with the object of defending and strengthening Hinduism rather than for the abolition of Untouchability or the caste system. The Caste system is an essential aspect of Hinduism. It is the caste system which has kept Hinduism alive. If caste goes, Hinduism cannot survive. No class or group is bad enough to cut its own throat. The average Hindu does not find anything wrong with the custom of Untouchability. Purity, for a Hindu, is more important than cleanliness. Ascribed status of an individual on the basis of caste is more important than his merit, virtues or acquisitions. Social status is determined on the basis of birth. In India, even today, a Brahmin rickshaw puller or dish-washer or a cook is addressed as Punditji (learned one), but a learned member of sweeper (Bhangi) or leather worker caste (Chamar), even if he is holding a high office, is contemtuously referred to as 'Chamar' or 'Bhangi.'

Legislation can, undoubtedly, be of help but in a country like India where laws are not respected, and where even an ordinary case takes years in the police station and law court to decide, it is not likely to be of much help to remove this curse. Untouchability is sanctioned by religion, yet nothing has been done to educate people against it. Gandhiji was the only leader of stature who kept reminding the Hindus to change their attitude towards the 'Untouchables' even though he was careful not to offend the sensitivities of his Hindu followers or to weaken Hinduism in any manner. He believed that there was nothing wrong with Hindu religion or the caste system. Untouchability, according to him, was an excrescence on Hindu society which should be removed. Much more could have been achieved, had the government used education as a weapon to annihilate the demon of untouchability, and concentrated on the education of children. A whole generation of people which rose after independence would have been educated against this abominable practice which is against the security and progress of the country. The UNESCO in one of its pamphlets on Prejudice, has made the following recommendation :

> A tradition on which prejudice is based can be maintained only by being transmitted to children. If the transmission of prejudice through the home and play group can be counteracted by the school and Church while the child's mind is still flexible, prejudice cannot survive long. Also, if the public can be led to consider that the manifestations of prejudice are shameful, many parents will refrain from displaying their prejudice in front of their children.

Unfortunately, our government is more concerned with protection and promotion of Hinduism, Sanskrit, Hindi and Brahminic culture rather than with taking effective measures to remove prejudice, superstition, caste system, untouchability or communalism from public life. What is required is to change the mind of the prejudiced and also to strengthen the will and capacity on the part of the victim to resist and to assert his rights. Government has been concentrating on economic uplift of a small section of 'Untouchables' and has ignored the main object. Perhaps their object is different.

Reservation in Services

In India common people's language was never the language of the state. In ancient times, Sanskrit was the language of the political and religious aristocracy. During the Turkish and the Moghul regime, it was Persian. The British introduced English in 1835-37. Upper caste Hindus, Brahmins in Madras and Bombay Presidencies and the Brahmin, Baidya and Kayastha castes in Bengal, who had literary traditions, immediately started learning English as they had learnt Persian during the Moghul regime because it was necessary to enter the administration. During the early decades of the British rule, the Moslems treated English as the language of the infidels and refused to learn it. After some time, they realised that they were excluded from the administration and had become backward. All important positions in the administration had by that time been monopolised by upper caste Hindus. The 'Untouchables,' of course, never had any share in the administration. It was only through English education imparted by the Christian missionaries in their schools that some of them could acquire sufficient knowledge to enter the government service.

The Moslems, Christians and other minorities also began to demand a share in the administration. The British rulers, keeping in view their political interests and administrative efficiency, introduced a quota system. All minorities, religious groups, and identifiable social groups were granted a share proportionate to their population. The 'Untouchables' were ignored on the plea that educated people were not available among them. Some 'Untouchable' organisations like the Depressed Classes Association and the Depressed Classes Federation, Caste organisations like Somavanshi, Mahar Association and Adi-Dravida Sabha, in different provinces began to demand reservation in services and other facilities. Dr. Baba Saheb Ambedkar put his demands in more concrete form in the public meetings, conferences, in the legislative assembly and finally before the Round Table Conference at London. This was also one of the demands which the Hindu leaders agreed to in the Poona Pact, although it was never honoured by the dominant Hindu group.

The All India Scheduled Castes Federation was founded in 1942 by Dr. Ambedkar in order to struggle for the political rights of the Scheduled Castes. At the annual conference of the Federation, held in September 1943, besides other things, Dr. Ambedkar stressed the need for having a share in the administration because, without having their own men in services, the policies and programmes meant for their amelioration could not be implemented. Advising his people he said: 'You should demand that a number of posts in the public services shall be reserved for the Scheduled Castes, subject of course to the rule of minimum qualification.'

As a member of the Viceroy's Executive Council, Dr. Ambedkar submitted a Memorandum demanding reservation for the Scheduled Castes in services, and scholarships and financial aid for the promotion of their education. Lord Linlithgow, Viceroy and Governor General, made favourable recommendations and referred the Memorandum to the Secretary of State in London. The Government accepted the recommendations, and in 1943 reservation in services in favour of the Scheduled Castes became effective.

After independence, Dr. Ambedkar was made the Law Minister and Chairman of the Drafting Committee to draft the Constitution. His presence in the Constituent Assembly greatly facilitated making suitable provisions in the Constitution in favour of the Scheduled Castes and aboriginal people of India. While reservation in the legislature and in services for other religious minorities was abolished, reservation in favour of Scheduled Castes and Tribes was allowed to continue for indefinite period in services and for a period of ten years in legislature in the first instance. Reservation in the legislature has since been extended upto 1990. Fifteen per cent of the posts in all categories of services are also reserved for the Scheduled Castes. In some states the percentage is higher and in some it is lower, depending on the population of the Scheduled Castes. The Central Government, State Governments, Corporations and public-aided institutions and undertakings also have to reserve quotas for the Scheduled Castes. But so strong is the prejudice and the opposition within the services that even after sixty five years, the full quota has not been filled. In the early years following Independence, the plea was that 'suitable candidates are not available.'

Later on, when large number of educated Scheduled Castes candidates came forward to claim these posts, the caste Hindu heads of the departments gave other reasons for rejection, such as 'available but not found suitable.' Posts were dereserved and filled up by appointing candidates belonging to the upper castes of Hindus and Sikhs. In some states 'reservation' has been challenged in law courts on the plea that it violates the principle of equality enshrined in Article 14 and Article 16 of the

Constitution. There is no law to punish those who refuse to implement the government orders in regard to the reservation. Several ministries and departments blatantly flout the orders and instructions of the Government and even refuse to give replies to letters issued by the Commissioner for Scheduled Castes and Tribes, an officer appointed under the Constitution to supervise the implementation of the provisions of the Constitution and orders of Government. Private sector does not accept the members of the Scheduled Castes except in low paid jobs.

The Government is the only agency which systematically employs the Scheduled Caste people. As a result of continuous struggle of the people and their organisations and the will of the people to assert their rights coupled with the liberal provisions made in the Constitution, a considerable number of people belonging to the Scheduled Castes have entered government services and are participating in the nation building activities. Reservation has not been earnestly implemented, as is evident from the following table, taken from the Scheduled Castes Commissioner's Report.

Percentage of reserved jobs held by the Scheduled Castes in Central Government as on 1.1.79

Category of Class	*Percentage of jobs held by the Scheduled Castes*
Class I	4.75
Class II	7.37
Class III	12.55
Class IV	19.32

In terms of numbers, out of a total of 3,092,551 employees under the Central Government, 467,712 belonged to the Scheduled Castes. The lowest number was employed in Class I, only 4.75 per cent. (The percentages for other classes were: Class II: 7.37; Class III: 12.55; and Class IV: 19.32). The worst offenders were the Lok Sabha and Rajya Sabha Secretariats. Hitherto, members of the upper castes, who had been enjoying the monopoly of government services for centuries, opposed the entry of Scheduled Caste men and women. Since organised resistance has been started, some political parties who have their base among the middle classes of Hindu society, have been supporting them. The press has not been very objective in its approach, for fear of losing clientele among the upper castes. Riots have also been engineered to pressurise the government to abolish reservation. At the same time, a large number of caste Hindus enter government services and colleges, using fake Scheduled Caste certificates. Very few are caught. When caught, the culprits are treated kindly and let off with a warning.

Armed Forces

Prior to the Mutiny of 1857, which, some historians now prefer to call the 'War of Independence,' the 'Untouchables' accounted for a large percentage in the British Army. The army in Bombay and Madras freely recruited 'Untouchables' such as Pariahs, Malas, Madigas, Mahars, Mangs, Mehtars, Dosadhs, Dhusias, Dhanuks, and Bhils. In the beginning, the Bengal Army was also not fastidious about caste. Those who fought under Clive in the Plassey battle, belonged to the 'Untouchable' castes of Bihar, Oudh and neighbouring states.

This situation did not last very long. Better wages, attractive uniform, pensionary benefits and better service conditions attracted a large number of soldiers from the neighbouring states who belonged to the upper castes like Brahmins, Rajputs and Pathans. As the number of upper castes in the army increased, the life of 'Untouchable' soldiers was made miserable. They were often humiliated and harrassed by the Brahmin and Rajput soldiers who looked down upon their 'Untouchable' colleagues. They were gradually assigned inferior jobs of batsman, cooks and bearers, barbers, stretcher bearers, messengers, band players, porters, sweepers and dishwashers.

Most of the mutinies were initiated and led by the Brahmin soldiers. Yet, the British preferred to have tall, well built upper caste men in the Bengal Army. After the mutiny they changed their recruitment policy. At first they were reluctant to admit Sikhs, but when the recruitment areas fell under the control of mutineers, the British had to recruit soldiers from other states like Punjab. Soon, the British changed their recruitment policy again. A false and pernicious theory of 'martial' and 'non-martial' races was propounded and many castes and classes of Indian people were excluded from military service.

The worst affected were the 'Untouchables.' The British began to recruit Sikhs, Muslims, Jats, etc., from educationally and economically backward regions, while Mahars, Mangs, Chamars, Mehtars, Kolis, Dosadhs, etc., were demobilised and their regiments disbanded. In Northern India only the Mazhbi Sikhs (converts from sweepers) and Ramdassi Sikhs (converts from Chamar-leather workers) were considered martial and recruited in the Army. In times of adversity, the British declared the 'Untouchables' 'martial' but as soon as the emergency was over, they were once again relegated to the category of 'non-martial.'

During World War I, when there was shortage of able bodied men for recruitment as soldiers, a Mahar Regiment was raised but was disbanded after the hostilities were over. During World War II, again a Mahar Regiment was raised partly out of necessity and partly due to the pressure from the Mahars led by Dr. Ambedkar, who was the member in-charge of the Labour Department in the Viceroy's Executive Council. This was not disbanded and it continues to play a very important role even today, although now it is not, like many other class regiments, manned exclusively by Mahars and Mangs. A Chamar regiment was also raised during World War II but was disbanded after the War.

The present policy of the government is not to have caste regiments. Theoretically, any able bodied man can be recruited as a soldier, sailor or airman, but, in practice, the young men from the lower castes are rejected either by the recruiting officers or by the medical officers on some flimsy grounds. There have been instances of people who are rejected, when they tell the truth in respect of their castes, but are found fit and recruited when they state that they are Christians, Moslems or Buddhists. Most of the recruiting officers usually belong to castes like Rajput, Maratha, Ahir and Jat, and are highly prejudiced against the Scheduled Castes. The dominating group in the Defence Ministry is not in favour of having Scheduled Caste men in the Army, especially in the infantry, in spite of the fact that the Scheduled Caste people have proved that they do not lack in physical strength, intelligence, courage and valour. Even sweepers in different wars, in spite of being non-combatants, have valiantly fought side by side with other soldiers and won recognition and awards for gallantry.

Performance of Legislators

The Scheduled Castes, as stated earlier, have 78 members in Parliament (House of the People) and 540 members in various State Assemblies. Unfortunately, the performance of these members has not been satisfactory. The vast majority of them belong to different political parties, especially to the ruling party and are dependent on them for their political existence.

Another reason for their poor performance is the method of election in reserved seats. Very few Scheduled Caste candidates get elected against general seats. Since the non-Scheduled Caste people constitute the majority in every constituency, they have the power to decide. Moreover, owing to general poverty and lack of resources, Scheduled Castes have not been able to build up a strong political party. Most of the men and women join political parties or the problems of the Scheduled Castes. They prefer to remain silent most of the time for fear of offending the party bosses. Scheduled Caste masses generally feel that, had there been separate electorates system, they could have returned better people to the legislatures. Scheduled Caste legislators' performance on the floor of the house is usually not satisfactory, but in the committees some of the better educated ones play an important role. The government departments do not attach any importance even to the letters sent by the Scheduled Caste legislators.

Atrocities and Harassment

Atrocities are committed on the 'Untouchables' in the villages and small towns and the incidents of such cases are showing an upward trend. Atrocities are committed by the members of land holding castes, like Vellalas and Thewars in

Tamil Nadu; by Kappus, Reddies and Kammas in Andhra; by Marathas and Kunbis in Maharashtra; by Bhumihars and Thakurs in Bihar; by Jats, Gujars, Ahir and Rajputs in Uttar Pradesh, Rajasthan and Madhya Pradesh; by Jats and Rajputs in Haryana and Punjab. Most of the policemen in these states are recruited from the peasant castes and the police have also joined hands with the upper caste men in committing atrocities on the 'Untouchables' in the villages as well as in the police stations. They have abused their power and knowledge of law to terrorise and oppress the 'Untouchables.'

The Scheduled Castes in India are estimated to be about 100 million. About 80 per cent of them live in the villages and the vast majority of them are illiterate. Nearly 80 per cent of them live below the poverty line. They depend for work and food on the upper caste people who own land and employ Scheduled Castes as labourers on wages determined by the landlords. Many of these labourers have been reduced to the status of bonded labourers redeeming their paltry debts taken for performing religious or social ceremonies like marriages, or feasts after the death of some older member of the family. Each state has a dominating caste of Hindus and each state has also numerous castes of 'Untouchables.' The numerical strength can often be an asset but can also provoke jealousy from the upper castes.

Atrocities on Scheduled Castes

During the recent years, atrocities on the Scheduled Castes have increased. Often these atrocities are committed for flimsy reasons. A young man belonging to Balmiki caste was murdered because he affixed the word 'Chauhan' to his name. 'Chauhan' is the name of a Rajput tribe but 'Chauhan' and 'Patar Chauhan' are also two of the 1370 gods of sweepers in north India. Two 'Untouchable' women were crushed under boots because they wore rings *(bichhwas)* on their toes. Some men in Rajasthan were murdered because they brought water from the Ganga and offered it to the deity in a Hindu temple. The devotees belonged to the Chamar caste. In Tamil Nadu near Tirunelveli atrocities were committed because the 'Untouchable' women put on sandals and walked through the Hindu street.

In Marathawada, in 1969, houses of the Mahar and Buddhist followers of Dr. Ambedkar were burnt down and many people killed or beaten by the caste Hindus, following the decision of the government to change the name of Marathawada University to Ambedkar University. According to the figures given by the Commissioner for Scheduled Castes and Tribes (Report 1977-78), 777 cases of atrocities were reported. This included 22 murders, 13 rapes, 40 burnings, 651 serious cases of beatings and 51 cases of untouchability. This, however, represents only the tip of the ice-berg. Incidents of mass murders were reported in Deoli, Sadhupur, Mainpuri and Kanpur involving many people belonging to the Chamar and Pariah castes, who were murdered by caste Hindus. Not even old women and infants were spared.

Often one caste is singled out for victimisation. The 'Untouchables,' who are divided into numerous castes and sub-castes, are seldom capable of taking a united action against the assailants. Atrocities are often committed with the connivance of the non-Scheduled Castes of the village who provide the raiders with food and shelter. After the incident, the villagers even provide money and protection to the murderers. When the police arrive, they usually stay as guests in the upper caste homes far away from the place of the incident. It is very seldom that the assailants are punished. Owing to the lack of evidence, many go free, or are acquitted by the high courts for want of evidence.

Protection of Civil Rights and Self Defence

The government has set up special cells to protect the rights of the Scheduled Castes and Tribes. The Protection of Civil Rights Act 1955 has also prescribed stringent punishment to those who violate the law. But these measures have so far brought about little change in the behaviour of upper caste men, as is evident from the recent events following mass conversion of 'Untouchables' in Tamil Nadu and brutal mass murders in Uttar Pradesh. There are few organisations to defuse the issue or to settle the dispute in a peaceful manner getting justice to the wronged. Age old prejudices against the 'Untouchables,' religious approval for discriminations against them enshrined in the Hindu scriptures like the *Ramayana*, the *Mahabharata*, the Dharma Shastras etc., easy availability of arms, domination by the police and the judiciary, lack of respect for law, poverty and disunity among different castes of 'Untouchables' themselves, absence of political support to the oppressed: these are some of the factors which give encouragement to the oppressors. The 'Untouchable' groups are gradually learning to organise themselves for self-defence. They are also joining political parties with revolutionary programmes. But the smaller number in the villages and lack of leadership among them is impeding the progress in this direction.

Dr. Ambedkar was the only leader who seriously thought of finding a long term solution. He suggested migration of the 'Untouchables' to urban areas, setting up separate villages for the 'Untouchables,' and reorganisation of villages. He believed these measures would go a long way to help to solve their problem. He also suggested nationalisation of the land and allotment of land on cooperative or collective basis instead of creating small holdings and peasant proprietors.

The government however, choose to create small land holdings resulting in fragmentation of land and multiplication of land disputes and court cases. Whatever can create unity among the Scheduled Castes does not seem to find favour with the government in power. Whenever an incident of mass murder or atrocities is reported in the papers, the Central government issues a circular to the state governments. Law and order is a State subject under the Constitution. There is little that the Centre can do except showing sympathy and holding out promises of better protection in future. Unless the Scheduled Castes, Scheduled Tribes and the other backward classes join together in united action to defend themselves in the villages, they cannot put an end to the atrocities and brutalities being committed by the upper caste landlords and their 'goondas' and private armies in the villages.

Sweepers and Scavengers

Scheduled Castes include many castes who perform useful duties for society. Among them the Chuhras (sweepers) are most readily identified as 'Untouchables.' They are known by different names in different states: Koli and Daggis in Himachal Pradesh, Chuhra and Chamar in Punjab, Mahar and Mang in Maharashtra, Holeya and Madiga in Karnataka and Malla and Madiga in Andhra Pradesh.

When Ambedkar wanted the 'Untouchables' to give up filthy occupations because they were degrading, Gandhiji tried to reform the method of work and exhorted the sweepers not to give up their 'noble' profession. Gandhiji tried to reform the lavatory system. A number of commissions and study groups were set up to study the living and working conditions of the sweepers both at the centre and in different States. But they all ended up in the trivialities and sentimental nonsense. According to many members of the commissions, the main problem was the 'headloads,' the buckets or baskets used to carry night soil on head. The reform suggested was to replace the buckets with wheel-barrows. The recommendations made by different commissions were regularly referred to the local bodies who could not implement them for want of funds. The government, for political reasons, chose not to interfere in these matters, with the result that the cities and towns continue to be filthy and the sweepers continue to be the most backward and despised section of society.

Sweepers of the Punjab were the most restless people. Whenever opportunity presented itself, they renounced Hindu religion and embraced a religion which guaranteed better status. They embraced Islam and later on Sikhism in large numbers. The story of their conversion to Christianity is worth noting. Once a sweeper in Sialkot decided to become a Christian, the missionary, not sure of the consequences, hesitatingly baptised him. This trickle of conversion soon developed into a flood. Thousands of sweepers, much to the surprise of the Christian missionaries and the British rulers flocked to the Churches and missions and embraced Christianity. The conversion to Christianity brought about significant changes in them. They became different persons, bold, self-confident and in some cases, very religious. They regained their manhood and made advancement in different fields. Christian missionaries devoted much time, money and labour to uplift these most down-trodden people and many teachers, doctors, nurses, soldiers, lawyers, jurists and religious leaders came from these new Christians. No other religion had done so much for the poor sweeper community in the history of India.

The Indian government has paid only scant attention towards the upliftment of the sweeper community. Hindus, true to the Gandhian teaching, do not want them to leave this occupation, and their own leaders have developed a vested interest in their backwardness. They do not want them to give up this occupation and take to other occupations. The self appointed leaders are also exploiting their own people. Mechanisation could help improve their working condition but precious little has been done in this regard during the last thirty five years. The Reports of the four Commissions are gathering dust in the Home and Health Departments of Central and State Governments.

Untouchables and Nation Building

It is the sweat and labour of the 'Untouchables' which has made India into a great and beautiful nation. All the great highways, magnificant buildings, fine muslin for which India became famous, products of iron and steel, beautiful cloth of different varieties, carpets and saddles, swords and sheaths, baskets and shoes were made by the lowly 'Untouchables' of India. Among them were born the famous saint poet Valmiki and Tiruvalluvar, Kabir and Ravidas, Sunita the Arhat and the Jain philosopher Hari Bal. They have also produced warriors, poets, thinkers, artisans, artists, musicians, singers, judges, administrators, statesman, writers, political leaders, actors and scientists. In contemporary India, Dr. B.R. Ambedkar was the outstanding leader, jurist, writer and religious leader, who, as a leader of the 'Untouchables' and administrator, contributed a great deal to the field of education and framing the Constitution, resolving Hindu Muslim conflict, and helping the minorities. He has left an indelible mark on the history of India and given a new direction to the social movement. He awakened the most oppressed, the most neglected and exploited masses of the sub-continent. Among the political leaders and administrators Babu Jagjivan Ram has few equals. Wherever he worked he acquitted himself gloriously and falsified the age-old belief that the 'Untouchables' lack in intelligence and efficiency.

Rome, it has been said, was destroyed by its practice of slavery. India, it would not be wrong to say, lost her freedom and destroyed everything noble in it by the caste system and the practice of untouchability. India has made progress in scientific field and also in agriculture. Many industries have grown and many tall and arrogant buildings decorate our cities. But it cannot be said about the virtues and qualities which really make a nation strong. Hinduism, with its caste system and untouchability, is responsible for many of the weaknesses of Indian society. Unless caste and untouchability are rooted out, our progress will be like a mansion raised on dung hill. Building a strong India calls for drastic measures not kid-glove treatment. If we do not destroy caste and untouchability, they will destroy the whole nation. No nation can make itself great by keeping one-fifth of its people in poverty, ignorance and deprivation.

Dalit Institutions

Contrary to the general belief, the 'Untouchables' are seriously thinking and making efforts to stand on their own feet. With the sudden death of Dr. Ambedkar in December 1956, they felt orphaned, but soon recovered from the shock. Dr. Ambedkar was dead but the institutions founded by him are active. The Buddhist Movement, the Republican Party, the Samata Sainik Dal and the People's Education Society, are all active organisations. The Dalit movement, deriving its inspiration from the teachings and thoughts of Dr. Ambedkar, has produced many writers, poets, thinkers and artists. Militant organisations like the Dalit Panthers are also growing and learning through trial and error. Young men in many parts in India have organised themselves into local units to carry out the message of Dr. Ambedkar.

Politically the 'Untouchables' are weak. However, they have become aware of their strength. Even though they do not have a political party and a charismatic leader like Ambedkar to guide them, they are learning to use political power for the advancement of their community and to put up resistance in a united manner, whenever occasion demands. Ambedkarians have entered all political organisations and are influencing the decisions of the government. No government or political party can today afford to ignore them.

Dr. Ambedkar founded the Independent Labour Party in 1936. It was the first political party for the 'Untouchables.' It was renamed in 1942 as the Scheduled Caste Federation and in 1957 the Republican Party of India was founded. Like all other parties in India, the Republican Party also got split into many factions. But the masses and some sensible leaders are fast realising that it is in their own interest that they form a strong organisation of Scheduled Castes, Backward Classes and minorities. In spite of many failures, efforts to make it a strong party are afoot. The Buddhist movement is also attracting a large number of people in spite of obstacles from the government and the Hindu majority. There is much room for growth of smaller organisations in all parts of India and literature in different languages is growing which gives expression to the aspirations of the people.

5
The Untouchables to Dalit Transition

The Untouchables

The Untouchables consist of the fifth group within the Hindu caste system. Actually, the *varna* order is composed of four castes, and the Untouchables are the outcastes. They are one of the groups composing the Dalits. The others are the Scheduled Castes, Scheduled Tribes and *Shudras*. *Shudras* are compiling the fourth caste, who are mostly labourers. Scheduled Castes and Tribes are defined by the government act of 1935. Scheduled Castes and Scheduled Tribes are parts of groups within castes, races or tribes, which appear to correspond to the classes of persons formerly known as the 'Depressed Classes'. They are listed in the constitution in order to facilitate the arrangement of the quota system. Lastly, the Dalits arrived on the scene by the unification of all of the mentioned downtrodden groups; the Untouchables, the Scheduled Castes, the Scheduled Tribes and the *Shudras*.

The Untouchables are dishonoured; politically, religiously and socially isolated; economically exploited. The relations of the Untouchables with the affiliates of the *chaturvarna* is arranged and defined by the notions of pollution and purity and karma.[1] They are considered as the Untouchables, because of being perceived as impure and less human. The purity notion applies to the higher classes; whereas the Untouchables are polluting by birth and perpetually dirty. The Untouchables had a right to touch neither any member of upper classes nor their staff, because they were regarded as spoiling the cleanness of superior ranks. The cleanness remark is not only to indicate spiritual purity but also the physical hygiene. They do not have any social relations with upper classes. They live in the places they are shown and cannot move anywhere else other than the

Untouchable zone, they cannot share public places and they are relegated to contaminating tasks, ignominious jobs as cleaning, sewage cleaning, farm cultivating or cremating. Trade was banned for them. Hence they are not allowed to enter schools, temples; cannot claim land even though it is legally theirs, the foodstuff they cook cannot be consumed, they are not permitted to touch the water tanks in common usage and even cannot wear shoes in the presence of upper caste members. They have no access to health services, non-toxic water, public parks; public offices even have no access to *dharmshalas*, which is a kind of hotel.

> The natural plague that could be taken as a Divine fiat against the oppressors mainly targets, in fact, the broken and crushed ones of the earth. Thus, it is Dalits' water that turns to blood, Dalits' houses that are swamped with frogs, Dalits' grounds that are crawling with gnats, Dalits' foodstuffs that are infested with flies, Dalits' livestock that are dying with disease, Dalits' bodies that are festering with boils, Dalits' huts that are destroyed with thunder and hail, Dalits' fields that are destroyed by locust, Dalits' living areas that are covered in darkness, and Dalits' firstborn — and every born — son and daughter who are felled by death.[2]

The Untouchables are alleged to be so tainted that they ought to keep at a distance from upper caste affiliates. Yet their shadows are supposed to be to the same extent polluting. Without Brahmans, of course, we might think there could be no Untouchables, since only those who considered themselves 'gods on earth' might be arrogant enough to believe that the mere touch of another human being brought defilement.[3] Before the Untouchables arrive to a public place, in some districts they had to inform the others about their Untouchability.

> By 400 A.D. the Chinese traveller Fa-Hein described a world in which the Chandalas (Untouchables) are named 'evil men', and dwell apart from others. If they enter a town or market, they sound a piece of wood in order to

separate themselves, so that men knowing who they are, avoid coming in contact with them.[4]

When an Untouchable touches an affiliate of a higher *varna*, then the touched has to clean her/him self, and sometimes she/he has to be purified via religious appeals. From their touch, to their shadow and sound the Untouchables were deemed to be totally dirtying. Moreover, it was an offence to break rules and to contact with a higher caste person, so any act of disrespect had a punishment with the utmost rigour in turn.[5] In disgracing Untouchables, Clarke found out an irony. According to Clarke, while on one hand the upper caste members do not pay any attention to the Untouchables and even do not consider them human, on the other hand they need them, which is because they consolidate their stature and power over the bodies of the Untouchables. They are elevated and powerful but they keep this power by the backwardness and subjugatedness of the Untouchables.[6]

Due to the censuses held regularly in every decade, it is known that the percentage of the Untouchables were always around 20% of the total population. Among the Untouchable communities of India, Mahars are the most crowded community and they are followed by Chamhars and Mangs. The Mahar segment of the Untouchables regard themselves as the descendants of original inhabitants of India, the real owners of the soil of India, who were oppressed and enslaved by the Aryan invaders. Those ideas were voiced by Dr. B.R. Ambedkar, the leader of the Dalit movement.

The Untouchables are the weariest, most loathed and the most miserable people that history can witness.[7] They were even deprived of the right to pray to a Hindu deity; which has always been a high caste privilege.[8] The Dalits meet the priest only on very special days of life, like birth, marriage and death. In those religious ceremonies, the priest gave them information about the relationship between the divinity and the people. Even though the priest treated them as part of his religion, he gives the information because it is a piece of the ceremony, but not to teach the people the religion or to incorporate them.[9] The

Brahmins were not seeking to create a rigid uniformity in their religious community. Rather, they were following a discriminating and elitist route. One of the ancient religious Hindu texts, the Dharam Sutra states that:

> If a Shudra listens to a recitation of the Vedas, his ears shall be filled with melted tin. If he recites Vedic texts, his tongue shall be cut out. He who tells religious law to a Shudra and he who teaches him religious observances, he indeed together with that Shudra sinks into the darkness of the hell called Hsamvritta.[10]

The aforementioned hymn in Rig Veda portrays four castes as different fractions of the supreme creator Brahma. Within this stanza, Untouchables are not mentioned as any element of their idol. This connotes religiously, Untouchables do not signify any spiritual meaning, and thus they are less eminent than the other castes as parts of the Brahma. This is the religious explanation of why Untouchables are left overdue, why they are not considered as a part of ordinary life and as a piece of the general public and why they are dejected. The frustration which is their fate is the result of the unpropitious social environment born out of the Hindu social order which is so deadly inimical to their progress.[11]

Untouchables do not have right to study, right to be cured, right to possess assets, they do not have the right to live where they like, can not shop among upper Varna members and the list of bans on them continues ever since. They were surrounded within the borders drawn by superior castes and forced to be servants. The *Manusmriti* (Laws of Manu) says '*No Cha shudraya matim dadyad*' which means 'do not allow the lower classes to learn'. They live quite different from the other Indians, they are different from the way they are nourished to the languages they speak, the rituals they practice. Their right to education is very limited. Either they cannot enter schools or gathered in one separate class, in diverse parts of India, or in some places Untouchables even can not study. Experiences of an Untouchable child are described as follows:

> As a child, Rajkumar was often told that he was not welcome at the government school. 'My teachers said an education was wasted on a Chamar' he said, referring to those traditionally relegated to skinning animals, one of the most degrading tasks in Hinduism. 'Why do you come to school? You should be sweeping the roads,' they said. They told us to go to the fields to collect fodder for their cattle. Forced to sit in the back of the class and beaten for even minor infractions, few of the children from the caste group known as Untouchables, or Dalits, stayed in school long enough to learn to read and write. Rajkumar, 33, was one of the few Dalits to graduate from his school, and one of the rare few in his village to ever go on to college.[12]

This prohibition prevents the Untouchables from becoming skilled at professions. The lines of work for the Untouchables are drawn by the social mechanism consequently the Untouchables are backward cumulatively. For the reason that the jobs they can work in are limited around cheap-labour vocations, the economic and accordingly social conditions of Untouchables are miserable. Untouchables are socially conspicuous, economically vulnerable.[13] The severe poverty they live in brings a number of problems. Whether Untouchables were disgraced keenly to be exploited economicallys worth noting. Because, Untouchables were subjected to a kind of discrimination as racism, a hidden apartheid, such as their circumstances are awfully akin to blacks tarnished to be Negroes and exploited by the rest. Actually, Untouchables were kind of economic slaves as well, as far as they were forced to only engage with degrading jobs, and dispossessed from countless indispensable rights, even from right to faith. Indians prefer to praise themselves stating that slavery never existed in the history of Indian civilization; and the Untouchability institution is less harmful than slavery.[14]

Still there is a paradox. The Untouchables are 'Untouchables' due to religious vindications of Hinduism, but on the other hand, the Untouchables can not even enter the temples to pray. This paradox makes religious explanation about the Untouchable section of Hindu class formation invalid. From this point of view, caste system of India seems not to be a religious but an economic categorization. As a result, it is not wrong to seek other reasons, than religious motives, of substandard situation of the Untouchables.

The Dalits

The history of India has largely ignored the Dalits. They claim to be the real inhabitants of the ancient cities Mohanjodaro and Harappa until the Aryan invasion in 1500 BC, but then they escaped into the forests and tried to preserve their culture there. The invaders enslaved them, when they were caught. Eventually they became the 'Untouchables'.[15] The foreign influence in India, especially the British manipulation, was existent since seventeenth century. The idea of India's independence was spreading around twentieth century. The double struggle for liberty was rolled into one, where the *varna* members were eager to overthrow the foreign administration in order to get the control back, establish a self rule and to consolidate the traditional Indian system; but on the other hand, there were lower classes and outcastes, who were not propagating against the foreign government. For the Untouchables, the British were the enemy of the enemy. Still best from the two bad options was the British administration, because at least the British unfasten the Untouchables out of some bans by providing those people particular basic rights. While on one hand the British policies regarding elevation of low castes were in accordance with humanitarian sentiments, on the other hand there was a secret agenda, which was to make the lower castes look up to the British for protection[16] and to facilitate the divide and rule policy via inflaming the caste tensions. Actually, the British were not acting as the great crusaders, but instead they were like the champions of the social reforms in India, in the eyes of the Dalits. However, at the same time it was the British escalating the bans on Dalits to enter the Hindu temples and using the *Manusmriti* while formulating the civil code, because it was the key to consolidate the social control. So, the British rule was largely by proxy.

Nicholas B. Dirks says that under colonialism, caste was appropriated, and in many respects reinvented, by the British.[17]

The oppressed classes were no more naive towards the old social caste system, but rather enthusiastic to be involved within the political, social and economic routine as any other associates of the society. In fact, Untouchables were aware of themselves and insurgent towards the structure, which oppresses them since nineteenth century. As the time passed by, the way they expressed their complaints about their social, economic, political and religious positing shifted and found its last form by appearance of Dr. Ambedkar. Around ideas of elevating rank, entire suppressed, concealed people assembled for settling own shared target. Gokhale describes the Dalit movement as the unity of purpose and action among the lower castes and the Untouchables.[18] Those people included the Untouchables as well as many other clients of diverse despondent groups. For this reason the Dalit does not signify a caste, a definite class or a group of people. The Untouchable and the Dalit terms cannot be used interchangeably. It is rather an all-encompassing brand. It covers all poor, unfortunate, displaced, disadvantaged people of India, so it is a common denominator summing up the Untouchables and other downhearted Indians.

Dalit means the oppressed and it comes from the Marathi language,[19] the language of Maharashtra, where the Ambedkar Movement was born. The poetic term Dalit, which reflects the consciousness of disgraced Indian people to eliminate the historical injustices and discrimination, is quite a new one. In fact, there is no class or caste namely Dalit. In earlier times, they were known as "Untouchables" and "outcaste" inhabitants. They were predestined to occupy with jobs that did not bestow them sufficient economic returns. Moreover, they did not have any say in governance. Such groups were pre-literate, and they lacked the political and educational skills that would have allowed them to engage directly in the new modes of formal and organized political activity that were coming to dominate political life there towards the end of the century.[20] Among numerous labels to define them; depressed class, Untouchables, exteriors, *atee shudras*, broken men, *avarn*, *antyevasin*, *asura*, *nisada*, *chandala*, *raksasa*, *dasysa*, *dasa*, *panchama*, *damai*, *asprishya*, non-Hindu, protestant Hindu, non-conformist Hindus, downtrodden, *antyaja* and *harijan*, are the most common terms in addition to Dalit, which has a political connotation and marks the struggle of them against the *varna* order.[21]

Harijans

The word *harijan* was coined by Gandhiji due to its meaning 'people of god'. But this term was rejected by Ambedkar, as far as that still had a separating denotation. All the names other than Dalit have degrading nuance and in year 1919, British Administration changed these terms into Depressed Classes or Scheduled Castes and Tribes. In different parts of India, the Untouchables are called with different titles. Most of these terms are known to be expressions of hatred towards the Untouchables and other low layers of the Indian social hierarchy. Still, the people degraded by the traditional Hindu order abhorred Brahmans the same way, because of being made serfs eternally. This mentioned detestation and impressions of the *Varna* system was reflected by the language and many proverbs were created. Among numerous sayings the following proverbs exemplify how upper castes were seen by the lower: "Give the *bhat* the verandah and he will take the whole house"; "There are three bloodsuckers/butchers in this world: the bug, the flea and the Brahman"; "Set a Brahman to kill a snake"; "Bribes to a clerk, gifts to a priest"; "A cat that will not lap milk and a Brahman who refuses a bribe"; "Brahmans are made to eat"; *Bhavaiyans* to play and sing"; Kolis to commit robbery"; and "widows to mourn".[22]

Chronologically, they were recognized with the term Untouchable and outcaste. 'Depressed class' and 'scheduled caste' were the phrases offered by the British, and the second expression 'scheduled caste' has a legal connotation. The term 'scheduled caste' came out by the Government Act of 1935. They were 'scheduled', because the constitution put schedules listing the names of the Untouchables.[23] According to the censuses held since 1941, the percentages of the Scheduled Castes were also recorded and it is seen that their proportion to the total population had never been so low, and this percentage rose every year. In the year 1941, 13.49% of the Indians were the Scheduled Castes; this means out of 295,808,722 Indians 39,920,807 were the Scheduled Caste members. The climb of this percentage was recorded by regular censuses and as a result it was found that in 1951, 14.40%, in 1961 14.67%, in 1971 14.60%, in 1981 15.47% in 1991 16.48%.[24] As for the 2004 census results of India, concerning Maharashtra state, which is the centre of the Dalit Movement, there are 77,800,000 Hindus, 12,000,000 Muslims, 5,838,000 Buddhists, 1,058,000 Christians, 1,300,000 Jainists, 980.000 Scheduled Castes and 850,000 Scheduled Tribes.[25]

Then Mahatma Gandhi pronounced the new term *Harijan*, meaning children of God. Dr. Ambedkar rejected Gandhi's expression, in view of the fact that the Untouchables found the newly proposed word still debasing and statically underlining the inequality of the social structure. *Harijan* word did not offer any change in the situation of the Untouchables or did not present a new identity, but simply in a populist manner aimed to keep lower classes under control by showing them that governing ranks did not abhor them. In a way the label by Gandhi mentioned lower castes being external pieces of the Indian societal order, thus essentially did not incorporate lower castes to the system. The lower ranks of Indian society disliked its patronizing tone and rejected the strategy of reliance on higher caste noblesse oblige with which it is associated.[26] He used 'protestant Hindu' phrase. Finally, the term Dalit was invented to signify struggle of deprived communities. None of the words used instead of Dalit before had such an inspiring and exciting effect. The word Dalit was activating, reviving, revolutionizing to all demoralized Indians. The Dalit idiom feels a denial of pollution, karma, and justified caste hierarchy.[27] Hence, the term Dalit became acceptable for all opponents of Indian caste system.

Gaining of Political Mileage by Dalits

For a low caste or Untouchable, being a Dalit is gaining political identity, as far as their mission of destroying the caste system, making downtrodden classes apparent in India; obtaining basic human rights, having a say in governance, being able to rise in social and economic areas. Dalit is the group once known as 'Untouchable' that languishes beneath the caste system.[28] The word Dalit signifies their anger, their protest, anti-caste objectives and political awakening of depresses classes of Hindu caste society. The term Dalit has become appositive, assertive expression of pride in Untouchable heritage and a rejection of oppression.[29] Not only political, but the Dalit word also provides a cultural identity to underprivileged Indians, because it denotes the other fanatic opponent of Brahman class, who are considered being Aryans. The Aryan invaders are believed to have destroyed the Indus Valley civilization, displace the native Indians, and establish a new culture within Indian lands. This new culture was imposed as the superior, the high class culture, where the local culture was oppressed and brought about as the inferior one. This is why Dalit is just the opposite of Aryan and Brahman culture. Dalit term indicates the modification of Hindu social system, besides that, it also expresses the resurgence expectation of those, who have been exploited since this ancient system was established. The term Dalit eliminates the negative meanings of all other expressions labeling Untouchables and brings a self-expression with the resistive eloquence.

The term Dalit, expressing the politically awakened Untouchables, is raised from the root *dal*. The Sanskrit verb *dal* means to break, to split, to open, to go down and crash. Dalit is the adjective form of the verb *dal*. We find this word *dal* in the prestigious *Oxford Sanskrit English Dictionary*, edition, 1964, edited by the world - famous Sanskrit scholar, Sir Monier Williams. The word Dalit is existent in diverse Indian languages, including the Dravidian. According to the dictionary, Dalit means burst, split, scattered, dispersed, broken, torn as under, destroyed, crushed.[30] The same root '*dal*' is present in other Indo-European languages as well. For instance in English, 'dal' or 'tal' means 'cut'; then 'dale' means 'valley' and 'tale' means a piece of life to tell. In German 'thal' is tailor, one who cuts. The same root is present in Hebrew, perhaps by coincidence. In Hebrew, 'dal' means poor or weak. The contemporary meaning of Dalit is believed to be used by the nineteenth century Marathi social reformer Mahatma Jyotirbao Phule. Phule used it to express the brokenness of the outcastes and the Untouchables as victims of Indian caste society.

To give a definition, Dalit represents the politically, socially and economically exploited, distinguished and victimized Indians. This word symbolizes the awakening of the entire oppressed Indians, be it the Untouchables, *Shudras*, Scheduled Castes and Classes and any others, especially due to treatment prospected by Hindu traditions. It is a rebel counter to traditional Hindu caste system, inequitable social order and economic exploitation of groups. Since the first flames of this uprising one more point changed, which is about religion.

In early times, victims of the long-established order criticized the classification, blamed upper castes and particularly the Brahmans, but not the Hinduism. For instance, Chokamela, one of the Untouchable saints is known by his avowals mostly disapprove of the Untouchability association of the Indian social body. He dislikes the situation of being Untouchable, he rebels against upper castes, and he warns people about not minding the bans on the Untouchables. The literature on Chokamela has no signs of his opponent posture towards Hinduism. Nonetheless, Hinduism became one of the controversial themes of this argument. The wounded people of India decided to heal themselves by getting rid of the source of the problem, which was marked as Hinduism. At the last resort a huge number of Dalit associates converted from Hinduism.

Teltumbde explains the darkness of the information concerning the efforts waged by the oppressed classes in addition to place and orientation of Untouchability institution within the traditional Indian social structure.

> The mythologized history of India does not provide many clues to the direct rebellions of the oppressed masses against their oppression. But it is inconceivable that they did not take place at all over a long period of two millennia that nibbled at their existence every moment with a divine contrivance called caste. The extraordinary

> success of this contrivance of social stratification is as much attributable to its own design that effectively obviated coalescence of the oppressed castes and facilitated establishment and maintenance of the ideological hegemony as to its purported divine origination. None could ordinarily raise a question as it meant incurring divine wrath and consequent ruination of the prospects of getting a better birth in their next life. Thus, the caste system held society in a metaphysical engagement and at the same time in physical alienation with itself.[31]

The new constructed identity, Dalit, was used and popularised by Dr. Ambedkar and Dalit Panthers by early 1930s. However, the earliest use of this term goes back to Mahatma Phule, who pronounced the word Dalit to imply all depressed Indians. We also know that a newspaper was published for lower ranks of Indian castes. The name was "Dalit Bandhu", which means friends of Dalits.[32]

All through the present study, the Untouchable word will maintain to describe the lowest strata of *varna*. As for the word Dalit; it provides the label for the revolutionary Indians who are composed of both the Untouchables, outcastes and also some *varna* members who face hardships of old social classification.

Initiation of The Dalit Movement

Even though the awakening of the oppressed people began around eighteenth century, emergence of conscious and vociferous Untouchable opposition to the social values and religious hierarchies of Hindu society[33] leading to social reform movements became visible by the second half of the nineteenth century. So the Dalit movement in the familiar sense of organised resistance of the ex-Untouchables to caste oppression may not be traced beyond colonial times.[34] Still this does not mean that the struggle of low and out castes did not exist in early times. In his article, Teltumbde utters that the history of this struggle is as old as the caste itself. However, by the Dalit movement, where the Mahars of the Maharashtra state were the backbone of the mentioned movement, this struggle took a more organized path with a well-settled political sight and a decisive purpose. Dr. Babasaheb Ambedkar the leader of the Dalit Movement, was from the Maharashtra state, as well. The first signs of arousing iconoclasm were noted by an official of UK, Mr. Cradock, the settlement Commissioner of Naghpur District in year 1900 was noted as follows:

> Mahars will not remain for years downtrodden and are already pushing themselves from the state of degradation. They have established a school of their own community. He at present lacks education and self respect, but these will come, and the day may not be far distant when a Mahar will be found among the ranks of the native magistry (Report of the Land Revenue Settlement of Naghpur District, 1900).[35]

The anti-Brahmanical movement stimulated especially by the appearance of Jotirbao Phule, besides Shahu Chhatrapati. In his book, Omvedt warns readers of not considering the movement in isolation but in the context of the general colonial situation and the efforts of Indians to respond to it.[36] Actually, not only the non- Brahman but also the Brahman political evolution and motion gained pace by the presence of the colonial rule.

Modernization Movements

The challenges by the West carried Indians to think about development, reform and elevating India to the level of colonial power ruling herself. However, Omvedt stresses that, such considerations were prompting the requests and interests of elites, upper classes. That is why they did not opt for a "social revolution" but for "modernization", revitalization of the old society.[37] They offered initially a well-industrialized India, thus the first step for modernization was providing modern technology, modern training and education for western style production. This is especially done to avoid the answer that Weber gives for the question 'why capitalism could not develop in Middle East'. For Weber, it was because of the Asiatic mode of production.

Thus, it can be deducted that, after the arrival of the British in India, modern technology and development entered India.

In Middle Eastern states, after the penetration of colonial powers, the agricultural production gains speed, not the modern production systems. However, India chose to boost industrial development. The aim was to adopt capitalism in India on behalf of modernization. If they boosted agriculture, they believed they could neither develop capitalism nor modernisation. As a result, Indian elite wanted to launch capitalism in their state. The Marxian view explains why Indian elites asked for capitalism. It is because; the capitalism is a form of 'class society' to Marxists. Class society is the traditional social structure of India. Caste, in short, represents a differentiated form of 'symbolic capital'.[38] Thus, capitalism fits the social structure of India. The resistance of Indian elite against the colonial power was not to protect Indian labour against the exploiting power, but to establish their own economy and modern industrial systems; to become liberated in means of government; and to upgrade both political and economic existence of Indian elite. Albeit in their confrontation against colonialism, they were not after protecting the rights or liberating the labour power, the serf people namely *Shudras* or the Untouchables. Because, with the old social system, the lower classes served ostensible 'elites' as a compulsory role. The Shudras and the Untouchables served the elite, but in turn they were not paid. It was a religious role, to serve the upper castes. But by the rise of capitalism, labour could become a piece of the economic relations and in turn producers had to pay for the services provided by the people they previously ignored. Moreover, adopting capitalism brings adopting European values as well. Accordingly, many other reforms were executed relating to women's position within Indian society. The education opportunities for women recovered in addition to banning the mourning of widow women. There are some other reforms beginning with education; which still were the improvement offered for elites of Indian society.

Nationalism

The nationalism raised against colonial power was not an all encompassing one, but rather enveloped only the minority who recognized themselves with the Aryan identity. The nationalism mentioned by them was a nationalism of upper caste people only. They adopted the 'Aryan theory of race', which had the implication of identifying them ethnically with their British conquerors rather than the majority of their fellow countrymen, which traced civilization in India from the Aryan conquest, and which gave a new pseudo-scientific justification for the caste hierarchy.[39]

Hence, the revolution they pushed cannot be considered as a social revolution. It was barely to improve the position of high caste members before the colonial rule. The entire population of India was not taken into consideration. Still the majority of the Indian population was composed of those ignored people, as members of lower layers of the caste system: *Shudras*. Even though this was a discriminative revitalization movement, numerous scholars regard it as a very precious step towards evolution of old, traditional and colonized India. For these scholars, at least an impulse was recorded for any revolution. Because the demands for social revolution from lower layers of the society heard just after the elite effort for modernization. Phule voiced the forgotten people of India first. He articulated that the modernization movements going on in India had to become a social revolution to break the walls of the caste system and make India a genuinely developed one with equal social lines. For him, to achieve a real improvement, initially the dominance of a particular class had to be defeated. To defeat the domination was only possible by changing the traditional order, as far as the so-called 'elite' is the construction of the ancient Hindu social system.

A series of reforms were required in lines of caste to weed out the colonial rule and make India a developed power in the region. However, priestly Brahmans were not to agree with the idea to make amendments in ancient Hindu hierarchical organism or to challenge Brahmanic values. Some fanatic Hindu upper castes have committed brutal massacres toward the Dalits, who desire betterment in their social position. On one hand, the oppressed people of India, creating the majority, were seeking social reforms; nevertheless on the other hand, The National Congress was rigid about the issue of excluding social revolution heading from the agenda. In spite of this, the 'social revolution' notion had already entered the National Congress and was strong enough to set off breaks within the Congress.

Moderates and Extremists

Mainly, two groups came into view: Moderates and Extremists. The British rule in India brought a nationalism fashion in India. However, echoes of nationalism diversified as the aforementioned two groups. One group was after improving India via using the British as a stepping-stone and for the other group the British rule was completely an interference to Indian affairs, and India was being abused by them. The desire for change and new social formation was what Moderate wing of National Congress sought. The Moderates were aspiring for more Europeanised institutions and educational system, more equality, justice, law and liberty breezing into India. Gokhale was leading the Moderates and Mohammad Ali Jinnah was within lines of moderates.

Alternatively to the Moderates, the Extremists were rigidly rejecting any of the changes and opposing against the entire Europeanistic values, because they were afraid of damaging the Brahmanical instructions. The prominent leader of the extremist view is Bal Gangadhar Tilak, who a journalist was, distributing ideas about revitalization of free India based on Maratha traditions and recognized as one of the architects of free India. According to this standpoint, independence is the principal requirement for a nation. Any measure should be used without hesitation in order to achieve it. Tilak expressed this view by his famed sentenced which was sloganized "*Swaraj* is my birth right and I shall have it". The extremists were after *swaraj* and moderates were after *swadeshi* that these words connoted respectively independence or self-rule and self-reliance. Unavoidably the extremists were also after modernization, yet the innovations they were planning to propose were framed in Hindu instructions. To modernize the ancient route was not an easy task, certainly. Particularly, Tilak and other extremists were opposed to destructive institutions and practices as the *varna* order, the Untouchability, *Sati*, childmarriage, etc. On one side, they did not want to destruct their primeval path, thus the innovations had to be carried out with the utmost care. In fact, it seemed almost impossible to modernize the existing system, thus new ideologies were required.[40] Like Gandhi later, Tilak believed in non-cooperation with British rule; but not in non-violence. On the contrary it is known that he took direct action.[41]

The aforementioned theory concerning the Aryan race was the first conjecture extremists embraced. According to the theory, namely The Aryan Invasion Theory (AIT), semi-agrarian Western people conquered India in 1500 BC. They forced indigenous people to move, and settled in the places emptied by native inhabitants. German linguist Max Mueller provided this new theory. He settled this theory while a group of scientists including Mueller were considering a comparative study of Western and Sanskritic languages. As the parallell nature of European and Indian grammars was discovered Mueller adopted the theory. The Aryans, are considered to be the upper castes of the Varna system, and non-Aryans are *Shudras* and outcastes. Thus, by this theory Indian elite had a chance to claim ancient superiority and now they had an evidence of their dissimilarity with masses. They tried to convince the rest about their relation with the existing imperialist power, the British. There is a problem with political use of this theory. The theory only proves the relativity among the languages, but does not make any references to the contemporary Indian elites and their physical, racial commons together with Europeans. The research was not a study on genetics, but on linguistics. Moreover, there is not a clear-cut physical division among Brahmans and *Shudras*. Aryans are mostly considered to be fair skinned, but still the majority are dark skinned. Thus, Mueller's theory is misused. Their aim was to constitute a new, superior and modern culture with the so-called Aryan background. The new national sentiment was sought among racist scheme. However, because this new nationalism understanding was not an all encompassing one, it created domestic struggles, rather than strengthening India against exterior foes. The Western identity only underlined the borders among castes. Inevitably, this racist trend created radical opponents, even among the lines of Brahmans and Kshatriyas. Radicalization caused avalanche of abhorrence on Brahmanic traditions and Hinduism, and Jotirbao Phule began organizing "non-Aryan"s against this system.

Jotiba Govind Phule

> The Greatest Shudra of Modern India, who made the lower classes of Hindus conscious of their slavery to the higher classes and who preached the gospel that for India social democracy was more vital than independence from foreign rule.[42]

Sarkar asserts that, it was Phule, who first pronounced the anti-Brahman affection in Maharashtra, with his book *Ghulamgiri* (1872), and his organization, the *Satyashodak Samaj* (1873) emphasizing the need to save the "lower classes from the hypocritical Brahmans and their opportunistic scriptures.[43]

One of the foremost social reformers of India and an important social thinker of 19th century, Phule was born to a *mali* caste, family of gardeners, in Phoona. He forfeited his life for Human liberation to the deprived segments of Indian public. For this reason, he initiated the *Satyashodak Samaj* movement, meaning the truth seeking movement, to obtain a non-Brahmin order and to release depressed classes from Brahmanical dominance. His most famed work namely 'Slavery', which is '*Gulamgiri*' in Hindi language, was published in 1872. He is best known with his struggle towards the inequalities of Indian society, ignorance and slavery. He mobilized the backward classes in order to discard the humiliating and degrading social structure and to bring equal and just social order that does neither include discriminative classification nor leave women behind because he desired a welfare society. It is believed that the first person to coin the word Dalit is Phule since he is considered to be the initiator of the modern anti- Brahmin movement.[44]

According to biographies written about him, Phule read a book of Thomas Paine namely *Rights of Man*, which familiarized him with the ideas of rights, equality, unity, solidarity, justice, and social transformation. One other event that triggered his motivation about social change is about one of his experiences. It is known that Phule was dishonoured and embarrassed due to his caste in a marriage ceremony of a friend by superior caste members. This event sounded Phule about the social hierarchy and he sharply decided to make contributions to the betterment of Indian society.

Phule took measures to be disposed of the Brahmanical domination and to engage women in social sphere. Jotirba Govind Phule is branded to be the first Indian initiating the education of women. It is known that he opened a library for the usage of the Untouchable children, two orphanages of Brahman widows and a school of non-Brahman girls. He put emphasis on intellectuality and education, especially the education right of downtrodden children and women, thus he demanded free education for all inhabitants of India likewise the technological and scientific development, launching human rights, economic independence, brotherhood, equality, removal of mediators, Brahmins in religion and many similar constructive factors for a fair society. To realize his aims he established the *Satyashodhak Samaj* on September 24, 1873. This institutions establishment was highly related with the inspirations from Sant Kabir. *Satyashodhak Samaj* aimed to seek truth, highlight the importance of human rights, remind Indian society that all humans are equal by birth and what elevates their level are their own equalities, this is why the *Samaj* made vital contributions in education of lower castes and also girls, for instance they established a school for making a priest for non-Brahmin students, which was unheard of till then. Mahatma Phule exempted poor and downtrodden children from payment of education fees.[45] Still the welfare issue was important because improving the standards of *shudras* and the Untouchables was the imperative of the *Samaj*. *Samaj* depreciated the magnitude of notions like rebirth, penance, and such rituals of Hinduism and Indian tradition that was believed to add value to or remove it from people. Thus, *Satyashodhak Samaj* was completely opposed to Brahmanical elitism. The *Samaj* asserted the essential of saving lower castes and outcastes from Brahmanical dominance. The notions of equality, brotherhood and non-requirement of the middlemen in religious matters were the great ideals of *Satyashodhak Samaj*. Phule also disliked the prominence and even the existence of priests and clerics that points the highest caste of Brahmans. Actually

Phule and his followers apprehended that, the existing social and resulting systems of Hinduism must at least be changed or totally disintegrate to save the Untouchables from their disgraced standing within the ranking.

Because Phule and his institution Samaj were after education since they believed it to be the most precious standard to lift a society up, attempts began to expand education. The education system proposed by supporters of Phule was to be under control of the government, to make it fair. Principally the Samaj underlined the importance of primary education, so supported the idea to make it compulsory. By the year 1882, Mahatma Phule submitted a presentation to Sir William Hunter, the Chairman of the Education Commission, in which he sought compulsory primary education. Moreover, the education of women was particularly underscored below this title. The education curriculum had to be defined well according to Samaj principles, in a way that this system had to be useful in daily life, help people to find jobs, to join in the routine production and economy to better conditions. It was decided to incorporate occupational lectures in the system. The leading professional skill was agriculture and one of the goals was to load agricultural knowledge to the teachers to spread this competence. One other feature of teachers proposed by the Samaj was to select them out of low castes to create a fair educational system.

Phule and his supporters initiated a campaign to overthrow landlords and moneylenders, who prevented economic improvement of farmers and led to injustice. Among his countless efforts, allowing the Untouchables to fetch water from public wells is an important step. The pureness issue for the upper classes was a kind of taboo, and this restriction caused the depressed classes to be affected of pollution, lack of hygiene and influenced easily by epidemic diseases. They even were faced with thirst. Samaj devotees gave a hand for the orphans by constructing orphanages and food centres to feed children. As a challenge towards Hindu traditions, Samaj did not hesitate to criticize Vedas the religious books and the religious customs, branded those rituals misleading, made exertion to prevent widow infanticides, opened Maternity Homes to save the widowed women, even women of upper castes and encouraged widow re-marriages.

Mahatma Phule also made contributions to literature. Presumably, his writings were drawing the attentions to the inequalities of Indian society, fight among Brahmins and non-Brahmins, cruelty of ignorance and peculiar religious customs.

References

1. Balkrishna G. Gokhale, *Theravada Buddhism and Modernization:* Anagarika Dhammapala and B.R. Ambedkar, *Journal of Asian and African Studies*, (February 99, Vol. 34, Issue 1 pp. 271.
2. Clarke, *op. cit.*
3. Wolpert, *op. cit.*, pp. 128-29.
4. Joshi, *op. cit.*, pp. 5-6.
5. Wolpert, *op. cit.*, p. 16.
6. Clarke, *op. cit.*
7. http://www.ambedkar.org, B.R. Ambedkar, *Frustration.*
8. Sagarika Ghose, The Dalit in India: Caste and Social Class, *Social Research*, (Spring 2003).
9. Kancha Ilaiah, *Why I Am Not a Hindu: A Sudra Critique of Hindutva Philosophy, Culture and Political Economy*, (Calcutta: SAMYA, 2002) p. 21.
10. Joshi, *op. cit.*, p. 1.
11. http://www/ambedkar.org, B.R. Ambedkar, *Frustration.*
12. Martha Ann Overland, In India Almost Everyone Wants to Be Special, *Chronicle of Higher Education*, 2-13-2004.
13. Joshi, *op. cit.*, p. 6.
14. http://www/ambedkar.org, B.R. Ambedkar, *Which is Worse? : Slavery or Untouchability?*
15. Jagdish Parikh, The Dalits of India, *East Island Journal*, 10410406, (Winter 92/93, Vol. 8, Issue 1).
16. Srinivas, *op. cit.*, p. 532.

17. Nicholas B. Dirks, The Original Caste: Power, History and Hierarchy in South Asia in McKim Marriott (ed.) *India Through Hindu Categories,* (New Delhi: Sage Publications, 1990), p. 61.
18. Balkrishna G. Gokhale, *Theravada Buddhism and Modernization: Anagarika Dhammapala and B.R. Ambedkar, Journal of Asian & African Studies,* (February 99, Vol. 34, Issue 1) p. 271.
19. Soykut, *Dinler Tarihi Perspektifinden Hindistan Kokenli Dinler ve Ideolojik Catismalar,* p. 98.
20. Rosalind O'Hanlon, Maratha History as Polemic: Low Caste Ideology and Political Debate in Late Nineteenth Century Western India, *Modern Asian Studies,* (Vol. 17, No. 1, 1983) p. 6.
21. Joshi, *op. cit.*
22. Omvedt, *op. cit.,* pp. 71-2.
23. Makhan Jha (ed.), *Scheduled Castes Today,* (New Delhi: M D Publications Pvt. Ltd., 1997) p. 2.
24. *Ibid.,* p. 3.
25. Soykut, *op. cit.,* pp. 111-2.
26. Joshi, *op. cit.,* p. 4.
27. Eleanor Zelliot, *From Untouchable to Dalit: Essays on the Ambedkar Movement,* (New Delhi: Manohar, 1992) p. 267.
28. Uttar Chaos, *Economist,* 8-30-2003.
29. Joshi, *op. cit.,* p. 3.
30. http://www/ambedkar.org/News/WhatIs.htm.
31. http://www/ambedkar.org, Anand Teltumbde, *Theorising The Dalit Movement:* A Viewpoint.
32. Atul Chandra Pradha, *The Emergence of the Depressed Classes,* (Bhubaneswar: Bookland International, 1986) p. 125.
33. Joshi, *op. cit.,* p. 25.
34. http://www/ambedkar.org, Anand Teltumbde, *Theorising The Dalit Movement:* A Viewpoint.
35. Joshi, *op. cit.,* p. 23.
36. Omvedt, *op. cit.,* p. 98.
37. *Ibid.,* p. 99.

38. David West Rudner, *Caste and Capitalism in Colonial* India: *The Nattukottai Chettairs* (Berkeley: University of California Press, 1994) p. 213.
39. Omvedt, *op. cit.*, p. 99.
40. Omvedt, *op. cit.*, p. 102.
41. Lamb, *op. cit.*, p. 76.
42. http://www/ambedkar.org, *Essays on Untouchables and Untouchability: Religious.*
43. Sarkar, *op. cit.*, p. 57.
44. Felix S.J. Raj, Religion and Dalit Identity: The Research for Equality and Dignity, *The Statesman,* (Calcutta, May 25, 2001).
45. http://www/ambedkar.org/jamanadas/TilakGandhi.htm.

6

The Leadership of Bhimrao Ambedkar

During his lifetime, Dr. B.R. Ambedkar (1891-1956) played three roles: that of a caste leader, that of an Untouchable[1] spokesman, and that of national statesman. In his first leadership role, he was guide, guru and decision maker for his own caste, the Mahars of Maharashtra, from the mid-1920's until his death.[2] From the early 1930s onwards he was the chief spokesman of the Untouchables in the eyes of the Government of India, the Untouchable leader who had to be dealt with from the viewpoint of the Indian National Congress, and the individual most responsible for India's policies of compensatory discrimination toward the Scheduled Castes. In his third role, he spoke on all phases of India's development, worked on problems of labour and law as a member of the Government, and even put aside some of his own theories to help create a viable, generally accepted Constitution.

Here we will study the first of these perspectives, that of Ambedkar as *Babasaheb,* an affectionate term of respect used by the Mahars. This is patently unfair to Ambedkar, who never saw himself as merely a caste leader and who only once called a conference or founded an institution that was meant for Mahars alone.[3] However, Ambedkar's first and chief support was from his own caste, and this massive support is what enabled him to work effectively in larger circles. A narrow approach which examined how he led and why his caste responded to him with such devotion may point towards an understanding of leadership among other inarticulate, low-status groups in a changing society. Also, a close look at the Mahars at the time Ambedkar rose to leadership among them may point to the factors which produce readiness for change among a depressed people.

Ambedkar's Image

We will look first at myths, legends and heroes, those all-important cultural images which any sub-group must deny or change if they are to challenge a dominant culture. Ambedkar's very presence created a new image. He appeared at a time of incipient changes among the Mahars. Building on a movement which had just begun, Ambedkar designed, over the years, an ideology and a programme which counteracted negative self-images, made use of Mahar virtues, and urged the Mahar toward every channel open to participation in a modernizing democratizing India. In the end he left the caste with new images and legends, and with a new history as past and present Buddhists. In the words of an older Mahar, "He took us to the stars". A stanza from a recent poem is not as sophisticated as much current Buddhist writing, but it reveals the awesome place Ambedkar holds in the hearts of his people and the innovation he represents :

Lord Bheema[4]

The Emancipator-Spartacus

The Philosopher-Socrates

The Law-giver-Aristotle

The Orator-Demosthenes

The Samson of Intellect

The Nation's Architect

The New-epoch Builder

Lincoln-Lenin-Ambedkar

Mahar of Origin and Heroism

The Mahar myths of origin, as do those of other Untouchable castes, reflect the idea that an innocent, misunderstood or mistaken action caused their untouchability. Unlike many other myths, however, they concern not occupation[5] but the eating of forbidden food. A common myth was a story of four new-born brothers who were asked by their mother how they would treat her after she died. Three brothers said they would worship her; the fourth said he would bear her inside him just as she had borne him, and he, of course, was the ancestor of the carrion-eating Mahar. Even a later myth stresses this sin: Mahars were demoted to untouchability in the seventeenth century by the Peshwa because they ate anything they could find during the Mahadurga famine.[6] A Marathi proverb links them with despised outsiders because of this fault: "The Kanarese is a cheat, the Telugu is a thief, the Mahar is an eater of forbidden food."[7]

Traditional Occupations of Mahars

The eating of carrion was perhaps an inevitable consequence of a traditional duty of the Mahar as village servant, that of dragging carcasses out of the village. He had one other duty which was polluting in nature, that of bringing fuel to the burning grounds. None of his other ordained tasks were inherently polluting. He maintained the village wall and guarded the gate, carried messages and tax moneys, cared for the horses of passing government officials, made public announcements for the villagers, tracked thieves, testified to true boundaries in land disputes. Mahars who inherited this post received *baluta,* gifts in kind, along with the artisans of the village, but also received a small parcel of land as hereditary due, *watan* land. They could claim fifty-two traditional rights, such as the shrouds of the dead, the hides of the carcasses, the privilege of begging for food, certain small amounts of money or grain for ritual duties at rites of passage or festival times. The number of these perquisites is traditional; not all persisted into the modern age. Degrading though they seem to be, the fifty-two rights had meaning for the pre-modern Mahar. While the origin myths deal with the reason for the untouchability, the heroic myths tell stories of the securing of these rights.

The most important Mahar legend is that of its hero, Amrutnak (the *nak* ending indicates a Mahar name). A modern poetic version begins "Great, great is the nation where the Mahar is recognized as a brave man ..."[8] and proceeds with considerable delicacy to tell this story: Amrutnak was soldier-courtier at the court of the Muslim king of Bidar. When the queen was missing after an attack on the royal hunting camp, he volunteered to go in search of her, but first handed the King a small box. After many brave adventures, he brought the Queen back to a grateful court. The King, however, began to worry about the days the Queen had been alone with the handsome Amrutnak! He was told to open the small box, and its contents told him that Amrutnak had made the ultimate sacrifice to insure the Queen's chastity. Amrutnak refused a *jagir* for his service; instead he asked for fifty-two rights for his people, the Mahars.

This theme of sacrifice, trustworthiness and caste loyalty is also stressed in numerous legends of Mahars offering themselves as sacrifices for the foundations of great buildings in return for privileges for their people, or for the fifty-two evidently hard-won rights.

Chokhamela, the Mahar Saint

Chokhamela, a thirteenth-fourteenth century *bhakti* saint-poet, invoked the law of karma to explain his low birth, stating in two poems, "this impurity is the fruit of our past", *(Abhanga* 4). But he passionately protested his birth in another: "If you had to give me this birth, why did you give me birth at all?" *(Abhanga* 6). In one poignant poem, Chokhamela told the story of his being turned away from the temple and beaten by the priests for daring to wear the garland of Vithoba, the God of the bhaktas at Pandharpur.

There is discontent in the songs of this medieval Mahar saint, there is protest of the very idea of a polluting caste, but the overriding feeling is one of joy in devotion to God. "Chokha is uncouth, but his devotion is not uncouth. Why judge him by his exterior?"[9] Although he was acknowledged as one of the saint-poets in the *bhakti* pantheon, he was fully involved in Mahar village duties.

Early Mahar Leaders

This is unpromising material for a modern protest movement. There is bravery, sacrifice, loyalty, piety, but all subservient to outside divine or human forces. The obvious duty of a caste reformer is to call for an end to eating carrion, and this the early Mahar leaders did, loudly and clearly through the first decades of the twentieth century. There is also a possibility for a more positive call to a self-respect in the figure of

Chokhamela. The Gazetteers of the Marathi-speaking districts report many Mahars involved in the *bhakti* sect and some of these called themselves *Chokhamelas* rather than give their caste name, Mahar. A pre-Ambedkar reformer from the Nagpur area, Kisan Fagoji Bansode, made great use of the fact that the Mahars had produced a saint to try to induce self-respect. He started Chokhamela libraries and a Chokhamela hostel, went to Pandharpur to collect Chokhamela's poems, and presented the figure of the saint as a hero in one of his poems:

> Why do you endure curses?
>
> Chokha went into the temple resolutely.
>
> Why do you, ashamed, stay far off ?[10]

In analogous movements, Chamars of the North called themselves Raidasis or Ravidasis after their shoemaker saint and Chamars of the Chattisgarh area were urged toward unity and new status as Satnamis.[11]

Two theories of origin were used by early Mahar leaders to stimulate caste pride, that of the Mahar as the original inhabitant of Maharashtra, "Lords of the Earth" brought low by the Aryans, and that of the Mahar as former Kshatriya, a man of proud warrior race. Neither seems to be part of the "legendry" of the pre-modern Mahar; both were common to many Untouchable castes as they began to strive for self-respect and higher status. The Lord of the Earth theory was potentially powerful since many nineteenth century British writers had derived the name Maharashtra from "Mahar" plus "rashtra" (country) and since some Mahar duties, such as the defining of land boundaries, could be used to substantiate the idea of previous ownership. The census as late as 1931 illustrates the use of this sort of claim in its recording of "Ad-Dharm" in Punjab and United Provinces,[12] and "Adi-Dravida" in Madras[13] as a substitute name for Untouchable castes. Such a movement was begun in Maharashtra by several leaders. Kisan Fagoji Bansode not only "went from door to door in the Mahar areas of Nagpur preaching self-respect among people who felt they were being punished for previous sin"[14] but also told the Mahars they had been former rulers of the land. Gopal Baba Walangkar, a retired Mahar soldier, drew up a petition for readmission of Untouchables into the army around 1890 in the name of the Anarya Doshparikarakham at Dapoli (the Non-Aryan group for the removal of wrongs).

Walangkar's petition is the first documentary evidence of the Mahar movement,[15] and as such its consideration of the question of origin is important. The initial claim to pre-Aryan status is quickly passed over in favour of the Mahars as former Kshatriyas, brought low by the Peshwa in the eighteenth century, a claim reinforced by the Mahars' army record of long and faithful service. But even this claim is superseded by a denial of the importance of origins: the Marathas were Turks; the Chitpavan Brahmans were Barbary Jews; and the high castes of South India were mixed Australian-Semitic non-Aryan African Negroes! What matters is that "God made man the highest of beings and does not make man high or low by differences in eating or outward cleanliness.... We have begun to realize our proper rights of humanity." For humanity, Walangkar uses the simple but potent Marathi word *manuski,* of mankind.

Ambedkar and the Mythic Past

B.R. Ambedkar returned to India in 1923 after nearly ten years of study in the United State and England. Thirty years after Walangkar's beginning, twenty years after Bansode's first conference, he began his work. He was a highly educated man; his degrees, B.A., M.A., Ph.D., M.Sc., D.Sc., Barrister-at-Law are sung in a sort of incantation in one of the Mahar songs about him. He was a highly political person, practical and pragmatic. Still, for personal as well as public reasons, he had to come to terms with the Mahar myths.

The classic myth of origin, the innocent eating of beef, could be discarded as irrational and irrelevant, as it had been by earlier reformers. The eating carrion had to be attacked, and here Ambedkar combined a simple "don't" with a broader view. At a large conference of the Depressed Classes at Mahad in 1927, he asked his audience to take a vow not to eat carrion, and to abandon the *watan* system that bound them to village rights and village duties. He also asked for two resolutions, one calling upon caste Hindus to bury their own dead animals, and another calling upon the Government to prohibit, by law, the eating of carrion.

The claiming of Kshatriya status was open to Ambedkar, and supported by the fact that his father and grandfather had been soldiers in the Bombay army. However, in Maharashtra, the clean caste of Marathas were still battling to be considered Kshatriya instead of Shudra and it would have been of little use for Mahars, even if one believed in the efficacy of a new *varna* status, to make this claim. Instead of telling the Mahars that they had once belonged to the warrior caste, Ambedkar urged them to be militant now: "Goats, not lions, are sacrificed" is one of his sayings many remember. And while he was a member of the Viceroy's executive council during the Second World War, Ambedkar aided in the creation of the Mahar regiment which allowed thousands of Mahars to enter the army in a unit which acknowledged their military worth with its very name.[16]

Identification as former "Lords of the Land", the pre-Aryan inhabitants of India, might have not only unified the Mahars but linked them with the important movements of untouchables in the North and South. But in his student days at Columbia, Ambedkar had written a thesis claiming that Indian culture and the Indian people are basically homogenous,[17] and he never departed from this belief. It may be that his American experience made him wary of a separation based on racial difference. It may be that his father's devout Hindusim, which included membership in the Kabir Panth, and his own interest in the dominant Sanskritic culture urged him toward a solution more identified with India's proudest traditions.

The figure of Chokhamela was attractive, and Ambedkar did dedicate one of his books to "Nandnar, Ravidas and Chokhamela, three renowned saints who were born among the untouchables who by their piety and virtue won the esteem of all."[18] But the "Cult of Vithoba"[19] offered spiritual, not social equality.

Ambedkar did not present the Mahars with a new identity, that of former Buddhists broken in the battle with Brahmans before fourth century A.D., until 1948. He did not leave the Mahars with a new religion correlated with that past identity until 1956, the year of his death. What he did do, was present the Mahars with a new Amrutnak in his own person, a hero who won rights for them, but who did not have to castrate himself to show his absolute loyalty to his sovereign. The rights were political, not tied in with traditional duty, and they were the rights of all Indians in a democratic system. Ambedkar was seen as a saviour, as a giver of rights, as one who sacrificed for his people. No one referred to him as an Amrutnak, but they sang :

> He was a great scholar of India,
> But he had no rest.
> He gave up all his comforts
> To serve his people.[20]

And Ambedkar himself, in his conversion speech in 1956, urged his people to become Buddhists without fear: "I am the one who got rights in the first place, and I will be able to get them again. At least for the present, you should continue to have faith in me."[21]

Ambedkar's Image and the Mahar Stereotype

The image of Ambedkar as it is so often depicted in the homes of the Buddhists and in statues in the railway towns of Maharashtra[22] is almost always as a westernized man, complete with a coat, shirt, tie, shoes, fountain pen and usually a book [representing the Constitution]. The portrait or statue shows a man serious, determined and proud. The personality which Ambedkar presented with that elitist image was arrogant, caustic, aggressive, never violent but rarely polite. To realize the impact of this figure, one must place it alongside the stereotype of the Mahar.

An unknown poet of the ex-soldier Walangkar's period [the 1890s] wrote a bitter poem about his fellow Mahars :

> Their houses are outside the village; there are lice in their women's hair; naked children play in the rubbish; they eat carrion.

> The faces of the Untouchables have a humble look; there is no learning among them; they know the names of the village goddesses and the demon gods but not the name of Brahma.[23]

The Gazetteer writers of the same period were no more flattering. In Kolhapur the Mahars were "darker than Kunbis, with gaunt cheeks, irregular features, a dreamy expression and flat noses," while in Sholapur they were "tall, strong, muscular and dark, with regular features and low unintelligent foreheads."[24] The general image given of the Mahar is that which is applied to depressed groups everywhere: poor, dirty, fond of drink, and of loose morals. Added to this is a suggestion that in spite of their humble lot, the Mahar was "hated and feared", or hot-tempered. One Gazetteer notes that "maharjatica" (of the Mahar caste) is a proverbial term for a cruel man.[25]

Another Marathi proverb, *jethe gao tethe maharwada,* means "Wherever there is a village, there is a Maharwada" (living quarters outside the village proper for the Mahar), and is literally true. Mahars constitute about nine per cent of the Marathi-speaking population, and are found in every village of the Marathi-speaking area. The implication of the proverb, however, is "There's a black sheep in every flock", or "Nothing in life is perfect", or to use an uncouth American proverb of disparagement, "There's a nigger in the woodpile".

Ambedkar had no need to identify himself by dress or speech with the village Mahar. He was a Mahar and no other choice was open to him. His identity of one of the educated elite, however, could be reinforced by clothes and manner. In 1918 a Professor in the University of London recommended him for his extraordinary practical ability, adding: "his character is rather Scotch-American, though in appearance he is a fat Indian".[26] Mohandas Karamchand Gandhi met him in 1932, but "Till I went to England, I did not know that he was a Harijan. I thought he was some Brahman who took deep interest in Harijans and therefore talked intemperately".[27] Toward the end of his life, when Ambedkar did wear Indian dress, a rather romantic American writer described him as "handsome", "jet-eyed", and looking like "a serious bespectacled Roman Senator in his immaculate white Indian robes".[28]

An Untouchable whose character was seen as tough Scotch-American, who could pass for a Brahman on close inspection, who created the image of a Roman Senator, was of more use to the Mahars as a symbol of achievement than one who could be identified with the poor and humble Mahar. While Gandhi's saint-peasant garb reinforced the identity with the Indian masses he sought, Ambedkar's western dress and his independent critical temperament underlined the new identity he sought for the Mahar. Unconsciously but very effectively, Ambedkar brought together a rough iconoclastic *maharjatika* image, an arrogant elite stance, and the kind of "incendiary, explosive, inspiring" protest Maharashtra had seen earlier in such Brahman nationalists as Lokamanya Tilak and Vishnu Krishna Chiplunkar.[29]

Ambedkar's Guiding Principles

In his battle to gain rights for his people, to lift the Untouchables to a status equal to the higher castes of India, Ambedkar used many techniques, many tactics. In the religious field, he at first encouraged attempts to join in religious festivals, to enter temples, to perform marriages with Vedic rites. Later he called the caste to a conference on conversion and asked them to leave the fold of Hinduism. For twenty years, following that decision in 1936, Ambedkar played with the possibilities of entering Islam, Sikhism, Christianity or any one of India's numerous sects within Hinduism. The final decision was to convert to Buddhism, which meant literally to revive a religion long dead in India.

In the political field, Ambedkar at first supported special representation for the Depressed Classes, then joint electorates with Hindus, then separate electorates, and toward the end of his life denied the workability of the reserved seats for the Scheduled Castes for which he had spent so much time and energy. Ambedkar's varying approaches in the religious and political fields, however, reflect the shifting opportunities and the changing political demands around him. There is a remarkable consistency in his total view. From his work and from his own voluminous writings, have emerged the following list of his guiding principles :

(1) The Untouchables should revolt because they are slaves, and slavery is inherently inhuman. There is no racial difference that marks them off from caste Hindus. If Hindu religious scripture ordains the practice of untouchability, those scriptures should be rejected.

(2) Only by acknowledging their slavery, by admitting their inferior position, could Untouchables unify and press for change. Only by Governmental acknowledgement of their deprivation as a class and the correction of that injustice by special treatment on a caste basis could equality eventually be reached.

(3) Only Untouchables could understand their own condition and needs; hence only Untouchables themselves should lead Untouchable movements.

(4) Education and politics are the chief means to equality: education, so that the Untouchable will be able to participate in society on an equal plane; political agitation and participation, so that Untouchables can secure their rights and redress their economic and social grievances by law and political policy.

(5) Untouchables are totally Indian. No foreign ideology, no foreign religion could help them achieve equality as Indians. India must be free before they are totally free, but their battle for freedom must never be subservient to other demands.

(6) Only as some Untouchables become elite can the whole group be raised. Only if ability and ambition enable some Untouchables to be at the top of the pinnacle can the mass below realize its own potential.

The Mahar in the Early Twentieth Century

The most striking difference between the Mahars and most other Untouchable castes is that their hereditary occupation did not carry over into the modern world. No one could say in 1923, as Thomas Coats did one hundred years earlier, that "although considered outcaste (the Mahars) have great weight and are of great importance as members of the community."[30] New methods of administration and communication had cut away much of the power of village officials in general, and the Mahar as "inferior village servant" was left with only the most mundane of his village tasks. The 1921 Census indicates that only thirteen per cent of the employed Mahars were in traditional occupations. The Untouchable Mang's rope and basketry work was still viable, and a third of the Mang workforce together with over half of the shoe and leather working Chambhars were still in traditional occupations.[31]

Although the majority of Mahars were probably still tied to the village as agricultural labor, it is clear that even at the time of the early Gazetteers in the 1880s a number had moved into economic independence. State public works, domestic service to Europeans, the mill industry, ammunition factories, and especially the railroad offered new opportunities to the Mahar. No Gazetteer gives statistics, but the Khandesh writer of 1880 is explicit in reporting the nature of new occupations and their social consequences :

> Of late between landlords and village Mahars complaints and feuds have grown very common .... the railway has done much for the Mahars. They make excellent gangmen, and some of them, gathering capital as petty contractors and moneylenders, show much independence and manage their business without the help of any high caste clerks. Of late, too, they have begun to send their boys to school.[32]

The link between the non-traditional Mahar and the early social movement is clear. Walangkar's 1890 petition failed to reintroduce the army channel for upward mobility among the Mahars (indeed, his fellow army pensioners refused to sign it and it never was presented to the British), but there were still retired soldiers in the 1920s taking part in conferences and the temple and water *satyagrahas*. Kisan Fagoji Bansode found a receptive audience for his social concerns among the mill workers of Nagpur. His counterpart in Pune, Shivram Janba Kamble, was a butler in the Masonic Hall. A number of Ambedkar's early followers worked in the Port Trust of Bombay, and it is not a coincidence that many of the early conferences were held in small towns along the various branches of the railroad, where enclaves of Mahar railway workers formed a group ready for social change that would match their new economic status.

Economic changes, as Khandesh Gazetteer indicates, led directly into educational interests. There are records of the Mahars founding schools or hostels in Nagpur, Pune, Ahmadnagar and Amraoti (where Mahar village service had been placed on a cash basis and was no longer on the traditional *baluta* and *watan* basis). It was in response to the initiative among the Mahars that Vithal Ramji Shinde, a Maratha and the most important of the caste Hindu reformers, began his Depressed Class Mission in Pune in 1906, creating an organization that was to educate thousands of Untouchables.[33] Government schools now, in contrast to the mid-nineteenth century,[34] also admitted Untouchables, although it often involved their being placed on a veranda or in separate seating arrangements. The Mahar male literacy rate climbed from 1 in 1000 to 23 in 1000 between 1901 and 1921. The 2.3 per cent literacy rate, however, must be seen in terms of actual educated Mahars. Of the half a million on the Bombay side of the Marathi-'speaking area, there were nearly five thousand male and three thousand female Mahars who were literate.[35] Of these, 288 were literate in English, and only one, B.R. Ambedkar, was a college graduate.

In economic and educational terms, then, there was at least a small group of Mahars ready for a social change that would remedy their traditional low status. An intangible factor must be added to the tangible facts—that of a legitimization of such a social change by society. It has been suggested in this context[36] that there must be approval by some elements of the elite before a mass movement gathers momentum. Criticism of the caste system and disapproval of the practice of untouchability may be found in many parts of India during this period, but in the Marathi-speaking area there seems to have been an unusual amount of radical criticism which was divorced from any program of action. Keshavsut, the first modern poet, mourned that the glory of some rested on the degradation of the Mahar.[37] R.G. Bhandarkar, Maharashtra's finest Sanskrit scholar, wrote that a great deal of intelligence was being wasted by depriving the Mahar of education.[38] Gopal Ganesh Agarkar influenced many by his totally rational approach to society's problems.[39] The most striking instance of radical thought unconnected with social action may be seen in the 1915 encounter of Gandhi with Hari Narayan Apte, the first great Marathi novelist. Gandhi attended a meeting of the Servants of India Society in Poona and heard their plans to try to arouse the Untouchables to a full realization of the injustice of their position. He told the group, "I am afraid you will make Harijans rise in rebellion against society." Apte told him, "Yes, let there be a rebellion. That is just what I want."[40] Not many Brahmans wanted rebellion, but the creative fringe of the Brahman elite legitimized change without creating the channels which would enable the educated Untouchable to enter a new status, somewhere above his uneducated brethren. There seems to be a vacuum between thought and program waiting to be filed. For instance, it was Ambedkar himself in the late 1920s who saw to it that the second college graduate in the Mahar community secured a post as Deputy Collector,[41] the first Untouchable in India to hold such a high post in the administration.

Ambedkar's Leadership: The Southborough Testimony and its Ramifications

In 1919, during a brief period in India between segments of his overseas education, Ambedkar testified to the Southborough Committee, the group gathering information to determine the franchise for the Montagu-Chelmsford reforms. It was his first political move, and it reveals graphically the difference between Ambedkar and other Mahar leaders as well as leaders of Untouchables in other parts of India. He spoke for no group, only as the college graduate among the Untouchables of Bombay province. His testimony was lengthy, sophisticated, passionate, but never beyond the bounds of a lawyer's plea. He fit his proposals into a total plan for the election procedures in the province for all groups, asking only that "the hardships and disabilities entailed by the social system should not be reproduced and perpetuated in political institutions."[42]

Attempts to influence government policies were not new to the Mahars. Shivram Janba Kamble, the Masonic Hall butler in Pune, had a talent for letter writing and petition which he often employed. His finest effort was a 1910 appeal to the government for employment opportunities for the Depressed Classes "in the lowest grades of the Public Service, in the ranks of Police Sepoys and of Soldiers in the Indian Army." One passage of the appeal reveals considerable sophistication and prophetic judgement :

> And it is most encouraging to know that the Honorable House of Commons ... is composed, to some extent, of the representatives of the lower strata of English society, the workingmen, who, only a quarter of a century ago, were regarded as but Mahars and Paryas by the more educated and affluent classes of their nation.[43]

Kisan Fagoji Bansode, on the eastern edge of Maharashtra, also worked political interest into his messages to the Mahars. A summary of his preaching would read: do not eat carrion, do not drink, spread education, acquire citizenship, organize, press for appointments on local governing bodies, "create among caste Hindus a feeling that the downtrodden should be uplifted", do not become Christians.[44] Bansode was actually brought before Edwin Montagu during the Montagu-Chelmsford tour of 1917, together with an Amraoti Mahar, G.A. Gawai, who had studied up to matriculation, and Montagu recorded in his diary that he was struck "by their extraordinary intelligence", although "one did not speak English."[45] Kamble and Bansode were able and gifted leaders, but neither a butler nor a non-English speaker was equipped to deal with the new political opportunities of the Montagu-Chelmsford reforms.

Mahars had also been called to two conferences in the period of the Montagu-Chelmsford reform tour to express their political desires. However, both conferences were called by caste Hindus, and the resolutions of the conferences reflected the political position of those men. Shinde's Depressed Classes Mission Society held a meeting endorsing the Congress-League Scheme for self-rule and called upon the Congress to resolve that the disabilities of the Depressed Classes be removed. Congress passed such a resolution, its first statement on untouchability, in almost identical language. Another organization, led by Non-Brahman Marathas who feared devolution of British power lest it bring back Brahman rule, held a conference a few weeks later at which its Depressed Class attenders denied support to the Congress-League plan.[46] Untouchables in Madras, who were at this time perhaps even more politicized than the Mahars, followed the lead of the Non-Brahmans in that province and refused to appear before the Franchise Committee because of the objectionable statements of some of the committee's Brahman members.

Ambedkar's use of the public platform of the Governmental Commission, then, independently and confidently, fully supportive of any extension of democracy to India, was in stark contrast to that of other Untouchables. He was not bound to the Non-Brahman movement; his English was fully equal to the situation; he believed in the political process and was only anxious that the Depressed Classes share in it according to their numbers and needs.

Ambedkar asked for nine elected representatives from the Depressed Classes in a Bombay Legislative Council of 100, and for one of those to be chosen by the group to serve on the Central Legislative Council in Delhi. He claimed that the Depressed Classes were entitled to this representation because there was no "like-mindedness" and no "endosmosis" between Touchables and Untouchables and hence Touchables could not represent Untouchables. The Depressed Classes were "slaves", "dehumanized", and so "socialized as never to complain", and they must have communal representation "in such numbers as will enable them to claim redress", and under a franchise "so low as to educate into political life as many Untouchables as possible".

The final decision on franchise was to give the Depressed Classes one nominated member on the Bombay Legislative Council.[47] Ambedkar, undeterred, came back from his second period in London to testify, whenever possible, on matters pertaining both to the Depressed Classes and to his interests as an educated man. He spoke to the Royal Commission on Indian Currency and Finance, to the University Reforms Commission, and, of course, to the Simon Commission, at which time he served on its Provincial Committee to hear evidence as well.

This method of political action resulted in two long-term gains, although it was rarely immediately effective. One was the creation of the Starte Committee, a group designated by the Bombay Legislative Council (of which Ambedkar was now a nominated member) to hear testimony on the needs of the Depressed Classes. The Starte report, issued in 1930,[48] represents the most thorough-going inquiry into the Depressed Class condition and the most far-reaching recommendations of its time. Its recommendations on Depressed Classes scholarships and reserved places in education and in government offices, and on the creation of a special government official to look after the interests of the Depressed Classes and Tribes became, in time, official governmental policy. Its report clearly represents Ambedkar's ideas. Ambedkar's firm grasp of the British method of commission and committee methods of determining change brought the needs of the Untouchables into the purview of the Government more effectively than the Mahar could have dreamed of ten years earlier.

A second result of Ambedkar's articulate use of the parliamentary process was his selection as one of the two Depressed Class members for the Round Table Conferences in London in 1930-1932.[49] Ambedkar's sophisticated testimony to government bodies was probably not known to the village Mahar; however, his selection by the British to meet politicians and princes in London to determine the future of India was known to even the most humble Mahar in the remotest village. Other matters of a more political nature were to stem from the Round Table Conferences, and it was here that Ambedkar came into the direct conflict with Gandhi over the issue of special representation for the Depressed Classes. But the immediate importance of the Round Table Conferences to the Mahar movement was that Ambedkar had indeed taken their needs into the highest circle of power.

Ambedkar's Leadership: The Mahad Conferences

S. Natarajan, an astute historian of social reform, wrote that "in 1930, by a process of repeated conferences the depressed classes were led into the camp of Dr. B.R. Ambedkar".[50] This is something of an exaggeration, but it is certain that thousands of the Depressed Classes in the Marathi-speaking area saw and heard Ambedkar at perhaps a dozen large and innumerable small conferences from 1924 on. Mahars had been calling conferences since 1903, usually under the Mahar name, or participating in the Depressed Classes conferences associated with the Non-Brahmans or caste-Hindu reformers. Ambedkar's conferences held in the name of all the Depressed Classes, were never associated with any other group, and at least twice formed resolutions calling for permanent organization. The Depressed Classes Institute was formed after the Barshi conference of 1924. The Scheduled Castes Federation took shape at the Nagpur conference of 1942. The conferences that were seen as the beginning of the Mahar awakening, however, were those held at Mahad, a small town in Kolaba district in, 1927.

Mahad was not only the most dramatic of the Ambedkar conferences, but also shows his pattern of organization. These factors can be seen at Mahad and also in much of Ambedkar's other work: a call by local leaders; organizational work by "new" Mahars, those freed from village dependency, and publicity in Ambedkar's newspaper; caste Hindus used as associates and legitimizers but not as decision makers or leaders; the presentation of new ideas in direct passionate speech or vivid action; mass action channeled toward some legal or political goal.

Surendranath Tipnis, the chairman of the Mahad municipal government, a follower of the reformer Gopal Krishna Agarkar and a caste-Hindu acquaintance of Ambedkar, announced the Kolaba District Depressed Classes Conference for March 1927. For weeks preceding the Conference, a former Mahar military man, Subhedar Savadkar, and other local Mahars travelled from village to village mobilizing the Untouchables. Keer reports that 10,000 people arrived from almost all the districts of Bombay,[51] and while this may be an exaggeration, Mahars from Nasik and Pune did come in large numbers to Mahad. In his Presidential address, Ambedkar reminded the Mahars of their former opportunities in the army (many recruits had come from the Kolaba and Ratnagiri districts) and of the treachery of the British in closing this door on them. He urged the Mahars to agitate against the ban on recruitment and to seek self-help, self-respect and self-knowledge.

The Subjects Committee of the Conference met that night, and decided to test a new government provision opening public places to all castes. The target was the Chowdar Tank, a large body of water in the Brahman area of Mahad. Ambedkar had not urged this, but it was he who led the procession to the Tank on the following day, stopped and first drank water. A rumour spread through Mahad that the Untouchables were going on to the Vireshwar Temple, and a group of "caste Hindu rowdies" attacked the Conference delegates. Ambedkar urged restraint on the part of the delegates and convinced the Hindus that a temple entry was not planned. Five of the attackers were sentenced to four months imprisonment and the Chowdar Tank was ceremoniously purified by Mahad residents.

Ambedkar, back in Bombay, called for a return to Mahad on 25 and 26 December 1927: "The question whether we belong to the Hindu religion or not is to be decided by us once for all". As the date neared, some residents of Mahad filed a suit against Ambedkar and three others and secured an injunction temporarily prohibiting their use of the Tank. Nevertheless the Conference met, and Ambedkar's address this time condemned the inequality of Hinduism. At night, the *Manusmriti,* the ancient law book which sanctified differential treatment of low castes, was ceremoniously burned.[52] Rather than follow up this dramatic gesture with another satyagraha to the Tank, Ambedkar heeded the court injunction and asked the Conference to postpone its action. A procession went round the tank but did not "pollute" the water. The Conference ended with Ambedkar's address, his first, to a special group of 3000 Untouchable women, in which he asked them to dress well, educate their children, and to combat drunkenness by not feeding their husbands if they had been drinking. Ambedkar won the suit for the use of Chowdar Tank water after a three-year battle in the lower courts.

Thus, although the Mahars were ready for militancy, Ambedkar much preferred a fight in the courts to a battle in the streets. Mass action produced unity and courage, but unless gains were legalized and protected, the masses could do little. This belief can be seen in Ambedkar's role in temple satyagrahas that followed the Mahad effort. In 1927 in Amraoti, in 1929 in Pune and 1930-35 in Nasik,there were ever larger temple entry movements. The Nasik satyagraha involved thousands of Untouchables in a five-year fruitless attempt to enter the Kala Ram temple in that pilgrimage town. Although Ambedkar was seen as the inspiration of these temple entry attempts, and his name was shouted by the marchers as they moved toward the closed temple doors, he was not the initial planner of any but the Nasik effort, nor was he the chief on-the-spot leader of any. Ambedkar's role was to give courage and a sense of protection. He saw the satyagrahas, however, as necessary efforts to unify the Untouchables and make them conscious of their lack of rights. He had no faith in the Gandhian idea of a "change of heart", and indeed neither Gandhi nor the Congress approved of these non-violent efforts to adapt the Gandhian method to their needs.

Ambedkar called off the Nasik satyagraha in 1935, choosing a railway town near Nasik for his announcement, and stating at the same time that he would leave Hinduism since it offered no sign of yielding equality either to plea or mass protest. At this juncture, the devout Kisan Fagoji Bansode of Nagpur, who had introduced Ambedkar to Nagpur Mahars in 1926 as an accomplished leader, left Ambedkar's fold. The movement, however, did not split. Mahars from the eastern side of Maharashtra had not been through the emotional mass action protests of those on the west, but they remained loyal to him. Perhaps the lack of an immediate alternative religion in place of Hinduism, perhaps the fact that Ambedkar did not seek a public show of support until a conference in 1942 in Kamti, near Nagpur, allowed a slow acceptance of a radical idea to permeate the caste.

The Satyagraha method was used only three more times on a large scale in Ambedkar's lifetime: once in 1938 to support an Anti-Khoti legislative bill; once in 1946 to back up Ambedkar's demands for separate electorates; and once in 1953 for land in the Marathwada area, a movement Ambedkar did not initiate but did help by mediating toward a stisfactory conclusion. He did, however, bequeath the satyagraha technique to his people, and in contemporary India, filled with satyagrahas for all causes, mass demonstration technique is no longer used sparingly.

Ambedkar's Leadership: Politics and Education

The success and failure of Ambedkar's political parties and his work as a national leader are well known, and there is no need to detail them here.[53] What is dealt with, very briefly, is the nature of that success and the reasons for failure. Ambedkar's three political parties, the Independent Labour Party of 1936, the Scheduled Castes Federation of 1942 and the Republican Party of 1956, were all attempts to join Untouchables to larger groups or in a solid mass to seek political power. The very success of the Independent Labour Party in the 1937 elections, in which it won 14 of the 18 seats uncontested, pointed to its limitations: fourteen legislators can do little in a political body of 100. The Scheduled Castes Federation attacked the problem in a new way: its chief aim was to secure separate electorates which would allow Untouchable representatives to enter political bodies without seeking caste Hindu support. Its election failure was nearly total, due in Bombay and Madras province, at least, to caste Hindu votes.[54] A third approach was tried with the Republican Party, which was to unite all the dispossessed, but which has remained a Scheduled Caste body. Ambedkar, obviously, never found a way to use the roughly ten per cent of the vote which he could command to secure political power. Nor did he have the organizational technique to unite groups in which the local leadership was not already committed to him or to his policy. He was a statesman, not a party boss. His success, then, was to leave large groups thoroughly politicized. Their vote and their few elected representatives have protest value, and when the dominant party is weak they have a massive committed vote to swing toward that party in return for recognition of their needs and some political favours.

Ambedkar's Educational Institutions

Ambedkar's educational institutions have little to do with politics, save that mock elections and mock parliaments that are held in these institutions encourage the students to consider political matters. Moreover, like the political parties, they provide a way for the educated Mahar, now Buddhist, to work for his people rather than finding his own way into the elite. The educational institutions also indicate the unique quality of Ambedkar's leadership. There are now educated Untouchables all over India. Only in Maharashtra do they run a system of colleges. Beginning with the establishment of Siddharth College of Arts and Sciences in Bombay in 1945, Ambedkar's People's Education Society now supervises colleges of law and commerce in Bombay, Milind College in Aurangabad, Dr. Ambedkar College in the satyagraha town of Mahad [and twenty-eight other institutions]. Nagpur Buddhists have established their own Ambedkar College [and other institutions have sprung up all over Maharashtra]. The system is open to all, but is obviously a comfortable haven for the Scheduled Caste student. And it has pioneered in ways that reflect Ambedkar's broad vision: Siddharth College was the first to offer courses in Sociology in Bombay; Milind was the first college in the backward area of Marathwada, formerly in Hyderabad State. Ambedkar not only talked about the necessity of producing members of the elite, he enabled the production of the elite untouchable, many of them committed to the service of their people.

Another result of this stress on education, on being linked to the mass even though achieving elite status, may be seen in the vast body of Dalit (oppressed) Literature.[55] We know of no other Untouchable group which has produced literature considered seriously on the literary scene. [The neighbouring Dalits of Gujarat and Karnataka are now writing serious literature.] Beginning with Shankarrao Kharat's stories of his father as a Mahar village servant,[56] the Mahars have continually produced literature, chiefly poetry and short stories. These writers do not honour Ambedkar as "Saviour", they are far too sophisticated and much too conscious of continued humiliation. But they were clearly set free by Ambedkar's work among their fathers to declare their bitterness and their despair in eloquent literary forms [and all acknowledge their debt to Ambedkar].

Ambedkar's Leadership: The Completion of Myth

In the last ten years of his life, after decades of pragmatic political work and in the midst of national recognition of his statesmanship, Ambedkar returned to the need to create a new legend, a new history, a new identity for his people. In 1948 he published *The Untouchables* in which he argued that they had been "Broken Men", fragments of defeated tribes which were barely tolerated outside the villages of settled tribesmen, analogous to the Fuidhars of Ireland and the Alltudes of Wales in early days. The Broken Men were not absorbed in India, as they were in Europe, because they were Buddhists who clung to their religion and to their beef-eating in the face of Brahman hatred. Untouchability was born in India around A.D. 400, out of the struggle for supremacy between Buddhism and Brahmanism "which has so completely moulded the history of India and the study of which is so woefully neglected by students of Indian history".[57] Here was an explanation which rationally explained untouchability, which identified the Untouchables with one of the mainstreams of Indian thought, and which even offered reasons for the separate dwelling areas and the eating of forbidden food by the Untouchable.

Ambedkar's own religious interests had leaned toward Buddhism for many years. His early heroes were the Buddha, Kabir and Mahatma Phule, all religious reformers who advocated castelessness. When he moved from a cement chaul to a home in a Brahman area of Bombay in 1934, he named the house Rajgriha, the place of the first Buddhist Council. His first college took the personal name of the Buddha, Siddhartha. But Buddhism was not a viable religion to offer his people until the emergence of an independent India which used the Buddhist wheel and Asokan pillar as its symbols and was newly conscious of its Buddhist neighbours, Ceylon and Burma.[58]

Two months before his death in December 1956, Ambedkar went to Nagpur, which he called the home of the Nagas, an ancient Buddhist people, and again, using local leadership and his own impassioned oratory and example, set the Mahars on a new path. The Nagpur newspapers called the scene of mass conversion "a new Pandharpur",[59] thus evoking images of Chokhamela and the Bhakti movement. In Bombay, ten days after Ambedkar's death, another mass conversion was held, and by the time of the 1961 Census, eighty per cent of the Mahars, locality by locality, had announced their new identity. Small enclaves of Untouchables outside Maharashtra held their own conversion ceremonies, adding half a million Buddhists to the 2,789, 501 in the Maharashtra area. They were left without organization, without a *sangha* and without recognition from caste Hindus that any change in status had taken place, but with a new psychological freedom.

A recent popular article on the current problems of the Untouchables ends with this tribute to Ambedkar's image.

The Harijans today are leaderless. What they need is an Ambedkar rather than a Gandhi because the long tale of their persecution at the hands of Caste Hindus even after Independence has shown that there is going to be no change of heart among the latter through mere gentle persuasion. It is unrealistic to talk of "solutions" for the woes of Harijans but, if there is one, it must surely lie in exploring the limit less possibilities of organized resistance to discrimination within the framework of non-violence....But only an Ambedkar can galvanize the community into action. As things are, no such liberator is in sight.[60]

It is unlikely that there will be another Ambedkar. Any Untouchable leader today would compete with a dozen others who are his equal in education, in articulateness, in grasp of the political and social situation. What may happen is that those things which are in large part a legacy from Ambedkar: a sense of self-respect, opportunities for education and employment in high places, organization on the basis of local leadership for large goals, a militant claim to human rights, a tie between the new elite and the still-suffering masses, a sense of belonging completely to a rich Indian religious heritage—all these potentially creative factors may continually produce new, smaller movements. India's depressed minority has as much dynamism as any such people's movement today, and it has more legalized governmental help. It is possible that India may solve her discrimination problem before the West finds a solution to its own.

The American Experience of Ambedkar

Very few of India's leaders have been educated in America. In the British period, England and, to a lesser extent, France and Germany were the focal points for overseas study. Even today, when Indian students flock to America, their education is generally in the field of technology or science, and they do not enter politics. As far as we know, only three men well known in public life have been thoroughly exposed to an American experience: Jaya Prakash Narayan; the late Chief Minister of the Punjab, S. Pratap Singh Kairon; and Dr. B.R. Ambedkar. As an American, one inevitably wonders what effect his country has had on the lives and thinking of these men.

It is clear that J.P. Narayan's direct contact with American poverty during the Depression era and with American radical thinkers somewhat influenced the development of his socialist attitudes. It is possible that Kairon learned some of his expertise with mass politics during his stay in America. In the case of Dr. Ambedkar, the influence seems to be chiefly in developing his commitment to a pragmatic, flexible democratic system. Ambedkar spent three years from 1913 to 1916 at Columbia University in New York City. There is little material on his political thought from the pre-1913 period with which to compare his post-1916 writings, but even so it is evident that the American experience did influence the thought and action of this unusually gifted and innovative son of Bharat.

B.R. Ambedkar entered the Graduate School in Columbia University in 1913 after graduating from Elphinstone College in Bombay. His patron was Sayajirao Gaikwad, Maharaja of Baroda, who was distinguished for his financial support of reform measures, and had already assisted Ambedkar in securing his college education. Gaikwad sanctioned a stipend for Ambedkar's study in America through the Baroda State Education Department, though it is not known who suggested that Ambedkar should go to America for higher studies. However, Ambedkar was 23 at the time and he seems to have been intellectually mature, with his interests already established. From the time of Jotiba Phule, there has been a sense of appreciation among the leaders of Non-Brahman Movement for America's effort to create an egalitarian democracy. Ambedkar was aware of this, and it is quite possible that he himself decided to go to America.

As a student at Columbia, Ambedkar explored as widely as possible the economic and social aspects of American development. He took an enormous number of courses ranging from the economics of American railways to American history, auditing what he could not take for credit. He seems to have exposed himself to as many of the top-ranking professors at Columbia as he could, whatever their field. Columbia at this time was in its Golden Age, and the list of men with whom Ambedkar studied represents a catalog of important early twentieth century American thinkers. John Dewey, James Shotwell, Edwin Seligman, James Harvey Robinson, Franklin Giddings, and Alexander Goldenweiser were all men of great importance in the development of American thought, and probably nowhere else could Ambedkar have received such a broad and deep exposure to an optimistic, expansive, pragmatic body of knowledge.

Interestingly enough, Ambedkar's own original research at Columbia was concerned with Indian themes. In his primary field of economics, under the guidance of Edwin Seligman, he wrote a dissertation for his Ph.D. on 'The Evolution of Provincial Finance in British India' (published in 1925 by P.S. King and Company, London). His thesis was critical of the imperial British system and its harmful effect on Indian development. The other major publication coming out of the Columbia experience was a paper on "Castes in India, Their Mechanism, Genesis and Development", which was first presented at a seminar in Anthropology with Alexander Goldenweiser and published in May 1917 in *The Indian Antiquary.* Both studies make it clear that although Ambedkar was gaining all he could from his educational opportunity in America, his attention was centered on using that knowledge to analyze the Indian situation.

Ambedkar's paper on caste was not a diatribe against the iniquities of the caste system but rather an effort to present a theory of the development of the system. His two main points are significant. First, there was a basic, unified Indian culture. He wrote, "Ethnically all peoples are heterogeneous. It is the unity of culture that is the basis of homogeneity. Taking this for granted, we can say that there is no country that can rival the Indian peninsula with respect to the unity of its culture". Second, he denied that caste stratification arose through racial, colour or occupational factors. He stated that the caste system grew through a process by which other groups imitated the endogamy of the Brahman priest caste. There is no development of a theory of untouchability in the paper; that was to come late in Ambedkar's life. These two premises, however, remained constant in his thought. His later theory of the development of untouchability and his work for the eradication of untouchability were based on these theories, namely, that Indian culture was basically unified and basically valuable, and that caste inequalities were a social development without a racial origin.

It is difficult to say what influence the study of anthropology and sociology under Goldenweiser and others at Columbia had on Ambedkar. Certainly he felt such systematic study of society was valuable, for he instituted a Department of Sociology at Siddharth College in Bombay at a time when Sociological study was not usually offered in Indian colleges. Also, the sociological vocabulary lingered, and perhaps some of the concepts behind the American jargon. Shortly after returning to India, Ambedkar testified to the Southborough Committee on Franchise, the group which was preparing the election procedure for the Montagu-Chelmsford Reforms instituted in 1921. Ambedkar's lengthy testimony before this body stressed the lack of "endosmosis" or "like-mindedness" between Touchable and Untouchable—phrases evidently borrowed from American social analysis. Ambedkar's solution was to educate and politicize the disadvantaged group into full use of popular assemblies so that the new political institutions would not continue the "hardships and disabilities entailed by the social system". Ambedkar may have observed the ethnic groups in New York, the Irish, Italians and Jews, gaining political power through unified political pressure. The early twentieth century American dream of social and political equality in the great melting pot was apparent in both academic circles and the New York life during Ambedkar's stay at Columbia University. Both Ambedkar's study and experience would have encouraged him to look beneath cultural differences for a basic national cultural unity and to look to the political process as the way in which different groups attained their proper place on the national scene.

A direct comparison between the Negroes of America and the Untouchables of India does not appear in Ambedkar's writings. This is natural, since Ambedkar denied that there was a racial basis for untouchability. In contrast to the leaders of almost all other Untouchable movements, he refused to claim that Untouchables were "Adi-Dravida", (the first Dravidians), or " Ad-Dharm", (the first religion, i.e. pre-Aryan), but stressed that they were of the same racial background as other Indians. His observation of the obvious racial differences between Negro and white Americans, and the segregation based on race in America may have heightened his belief that the Untouchables' way to equality lay in asking for political and educational privilege because of social discrimination, not because of a separate racial background.

Ambedkar's understanding of the American situation was quite sophisticated. Jotiba Phule, as early as 1873, had dedicated his book *Gulamgiri* (slavery) to "the good people of the United States... for their sublime, disinterested and self-sacrificing devotion in the cause of Negro Slavery." But Ambedkar noted the political expediency of Lincoln's action in freeing the slaves. In his criticism of Mahatma Gandhi in *What Congress and Gandhi have Done to the Untouchables* (2nd edition published by Thacker and Company in 1942), he compared Gandhi and Abraham Lincoln, stating that both were concerned with freeing the depressed groups in their countries for the political compulsion of preserving national unity. This view of Lincoln's Emancipation Proclamation now has currency among American Blacks, who no longer view the freeing of the slaves as "disinterested and self-sacrificing". Although Ambedkar did not identify with the American Negro in words, he understood their position well enough to anticipate their criticism of Lincoln. Ambedkar's understanding of the reformer as politician was based on bitter experience, but it also reflects his grasp of comparative history. He did not borrow wholesale from the American experience, but he used his knowledge of American culture to analyze his own country's social situation.

Although the study of economics was Ambedkar's major interest in both the United States and in London, there was little scope for him to take action in this field in his public life in India. His stance was basically socialist, but he did not align himself with any socialist party except for specific election alliances. He admired a number of economic measures taken by the Soviet Union to reform their economy, and at one time advocated state control of the land. But, at the same time, he criticized the political system of the Soviet Union, and he was not a Marxist. The theory that history was the result of economic forces held little meaning for him.

If Ambedkar had succeeded in becoming head of the Planning Commission (and it is probable that this was his wish), he might have developed some of his socialist ideas within the context of democracy. His chief economic measures, however, were limited to those taken while he was Member for Labour in the Viceroy's Executive Council in the years before Independence. While holding the Labour portfolio, he instituted a Tripartite Labour Conference to consider such matters as a Joint Labour Management Committee and an Employment Exchange, and he attempted to institute social security measures for industrial workers. In these matters, both American and British policies offered some guidelines.

It is in the basis of Ambedkar's politics that American influence seems strongest. Behind all of Ambedkar's seeming separatism—separate political parties for the backward classes, special reservation of seats in political assemblies and in government jobs - there was a strong, unwavering belief in the power of democratic institutions to bring about social equality. India's case might demand special techniques not found in the West, but Ambedkar's basic faith was in representative political bodies. It may be too much to say that Ambedkar's American experience created this belief, but it is clear that it strengthened it. John Dewey's philosophy especially was meaningful to Ambedkar, for it offered encouragement that educated and politically aware peoples could work out their own political destiny in a pragmatic way, pruning the useless and preserving the useful in their societies. In his *Annihilation of Caste,* Ambedkar quotes John Dewey, "who was my teacher, and to whom I owe so much". "Every society gets encumbered with what is trivial, with dead wood from the past, and with what is positively perverse. As a society becomes more enlightened, it realizes that it is responsible not to conserve and transmit the whole of its existing achievements, but only such as make for a better future society".

Ambedkar's methods were directly related to Indian conditions. The ideology behind those methods was closely associated with optimistic, pragmatic American democracy, which preached (although it did not always practice) equality, no barriers to upward mobility, the use of machinery to produce leisure, and an attitude of respect for every individual.

Ambedkar's first political party, the Independent Labour Party founded in 1936, took its name from British politics. Two things, however, prevented Ambedkar's identification with British parties: the colonial presence of the British in India, and the preference of British liberals for Gandhi and his non-violent direct action campaigns for independence over Ambedkar and the slow parliamentary path. It also seems likely that American optimism, and the lack of an obvious class system in America, met a natural response in Ambedkar.

Ambedkar's American contacts did not end when he left Columbia University in June 1916, although one must admit they became minimal. He continued to correspond with Edwin Seligman, his teacher in Economics at Columbia, and occasionally recommended Indian students to Seligman. In 1930, Ambedkar wrote an article for the Columbia alumni magazine which reveals quite a sentimental attachment: "The best friends I have had in my life were some of my classmates at Columbia and my great professors, John Dewey, James Shotwell, Edwin Seligman and James Harvey Robinson." In 1952, Ambedkar went back to Columbia to receive an honorary degree of Doctor of Laws and it is clear that this recognition of his work meant much to him. It was in this period of the early 1950s that Ambedkar was publicly critical of India's foreign policy of non-alignment, which seemed to him to cut India off from American contacts.

Mrs. Savita Ambedkar tells a touching story of Ambedkar happily imitating John Dewey's distinctive classroom mannerisms - thirty years after Ambedkar sat in Dewey's classes. It is impossible to find in Ambedkar's life story any hint of a living guru or a personality which dominated him, but here at least is a suggestion that he was fond of both Dewey the philosopher and Dewey the man.

The other story concerns a letter of recommendation written about Ambedkar by Edward Cannon, Professor of Political Economy in the University of London, to the head of Sydenham

College, where Ambedkar applied for a teaching position in 1918. Professor Cannon wrote: "I don't know anything about Ambedkar except that he came to do a thesis and attacked it and me in a way which showed he had quite extraordinary practical ability... I rather wonder if he is a pure Indian; his character is rather Scotch-American". There is absolutely no doubt that Ambedkar was pure Indian, and no one who knew his background and the history of his caste would assign any other nationality to him. But this depiction of his character as "Scotch-American" rather delights me. Ambedkar's pragmatism, his wide-ranging intellectual interests, his realistic approach to social matters, his uncompromising attitude toward those he felt were his opponents — all these factors make his character and work very understandable to an American. Even his bitterness can be understood by an American who has seen social injustice at work in the midst of American democracy. We can conclude by saying that American influence on Ambedkar really counted for very little, it is more likely that in those early years in America his own natural proclivities and interests found a healthy soil for growth and the experience served chiefly to strengthen him in his lifelong battle for dignity and equality for his people.

References

1. Untouchable is the word used by Ambedkar himself for those castes lowest in the Hindu scale of pollution. The early governmental term was Depressed Classes; this was replaced by Scheduled Castes in 1935 when these castes were placed on a schedule as qualifying for special rights. Gandhi's name for the Untouchables, Harijan, dates from his 1933-34 campaign against untouchability, and is in general usage except among Ambedkar's followers. All those who have converted to Buddhism use the term Buddhist and reject all other nomenclature, including their original caste names. All these terms and specific names of Untouchable castes as well have been used in this study according to time period and group usage. [Dalit—downtrodden— has become the most acceptable term in the 1980s.]
2. Other groups of Untouchables, chiefly in urban areas, followed Ambedkar as closely as the Mahars did from the 1940s on.

See Owen M. Lynch, *The Politics of Untouchability* (New York and London: Columbia University Press, 1969), and the same author's article, "Dr. B.R. Ambedkar — Myth and Charisma", in J. Michael Mahar ed., *The Untouchable in Contemporary India* (Tucson: University of Arizona, 1972), pp. 97-112, for a study of the Jatavs of Agra.

3. Only the conference in 1936 called to determine the matter of conversion was announced as a Mahar conference. Ambedkar held that each caste must determine its religious destiny by itself.

   For a broader look at Ambedkar's total work, see Dhananjay Keer, *Dr. Ambedkar: Life and Mission* (Bombay: Popular Prakashan, 1962, rev. ed.). Recent studies, all Ph.D. dissertations and all by non-Mahars, include: Daya Ram Jatava, *Social Philosophy of B.R. Ambedkar* and *Political Philosophy of B.R. Ambedkar* (both published in Agra: Phoenix Publishing Agency, 1965); A.M. Rajasekharia, *B.R. Ambedkar: The Politics of Emancipation* (Bombay: Sindhu Publications, 1971); and W.N. Kuber, *Ambedkar: A Critical Study* (New Delhi: People's Publishing House, 1973). [See the Bibliography on Ambedkar for newer works]

4. C.M. Wagh, "Lord Beema", in *Thoughts on Ambedkar,* compiled by Hoti Lal Nim (Agra: Siddharth Educational and Cultural Society, 1969), pp. 10-11. "Beema", a shortened form of Ambedkar's first name, Bhimrao, links Ambedkar with Bhima, "the terrible", the strongest of the Pandhava brothers in the epic *Mahabharata.*

5. A Bhangi (scavanger) myth claims that Bhangis are the descendants of a Brahman sage who carried away and buried a dog that died in a Brahman assembly. See *Gazetteer of Baroda State,* Vol. 1 (Bombay, 1923), p. 222. A Chambhar myth traces their descent from a son of Shiva, who incurred his father's wrath by making a pair of shoes from his own skin to present to the God. As punishment he was damned to be a cobbler for life. *Gazetteer of the Bombay Presidency: Kolhapur,* Vol. XXIV (Bombay, 1886), p. 109. There are many Mahar origin myths, but none refers to Mahar traditional duties.

6. A number of myths trace the Mahar fall from grace to the time of the Peshwas, chief ministers of the Marathi kingdom. The Peshwas were Chitpavan Brahmans, and are remembered as having introduced especially limiting strictures on Mahars,

such as carrying pots for their spittle and brooms to erase their footsteps from the road.

7. Quoted in Alexander Robertson, *The Mahar Folk* (Calcutta: Y.M.C.A. Publishing House and Oxford University Press, 1938), p. 22,

8. C.B. Khaimode published his poetic version of the Amrutnak legend, as told him years earlier by an older Mahar, in 1961 (Pradna Publishing Company). This version has been translated by D.K. Bholay for Robert J. Miller's article, "Button, Button .... Great Tradition, Little Tradition, Whose Tradition?", *Anthropological Quarterly,* 39, 1, 1961, pp. 26-41. Another loyalty-castration story is told in Robertson, *The Mahar Folk,* pp. 72-3. [See "The Folklore of the Brave" in this volume.]

9. This line is from Iravati Karve's "On the Road: A Maharashtrian Pilgrimage", *Journal of Asian Studies,* XXII: 1 (1962), p. 21. All other quotations were translated from *Cokhamela Abhang Gatha* (Bombay: Balkrishna Lakshman Pathak, 1950) with the help of B.S. Shindc and Mrs. Hemant Fanse.

10. *Pradip* (Nagpur: Sahrao Bansode, 1958).

11. See Lawrence A. Babb, "The Satnamis — Political Involvement of a Religious Movement", in *The Untouchables in Contemporary India, (op. cit.)* pp. 143-51.

12. In the Panjab, 400,000 Depressed Classes, chiefly Chamars and Churas, registered themselves as "Ad-Dharmi" (first religion) in the 1931 Census" in an organized effort to claim special status. [See Mark Juergensmeyer, *Religion as Social Vision* (Berkeley: University of California Press, 1982).]

13. Rao Bahadur M.C. Rajah, an Untouchable leader from Madras, made a strong case for the Untouchable as 'Adi-Dravida" (first or original Dravidian) in his book *The Oppressed Hindus* (Madras: The Huxley Press, 1925). The use of the term in the Census was at the request of the Depressed Classes.

14. Interview with S.V. Dahat of Nagpur, a knowledgeable informant on Bansode's life and the Mahar movement in the Vidarbha area.

15. A handwritten copy of Walangkar's petition in Marathi is in the Khairmode collection of Ambedkar materials at the Bombay University Library.

16. See Major General S.P.P. Thorat, *The Regimental History of the Mahar MG Regiment.* (Dehra Dun: The Army Press, 1954). The regiment was never limited to Mahars, but enlists many along with caste Hindus and still bears the Mahar name.
17. Ambedkar's seminar paper was published as "Castes in India – Their Mechanism, Genesis and Development" in *The Indian Antiquary,* XLVI, 1917, pp. 81-95.
18. *The Untouchables* (New Delhi: Amrit Book Co., 1948).
19. See G.A. Deleury, *The Cult of Vithoba* (Pune: The Deccan College Post Graduate and Research Institute, 1960) for the fullest description in English of this important Maharashtrian sect.
20. "Song of Baba", poet unknown. This unpublished song is among the many collected by Russ Geyer, a Carleton student in Pune in 1970.
21. The Buddhist conversion speech of 15 October 1956, was published in *Prabhuddha Bharat,* 27 October 1956, in Marathi. The translation is with the help of Mrs. Rekha Damle. [The rights he refers to here are those allowed by Government for Hindu Untouchables.]
22. Pressure from the Republican Party has resulted in a life-size statue placed at the Northwest corner of Parliament House Compound. A copy of the Constitution is in one of Ambedkar's hands; the forefinger of the other points at Parliament.
23. These stanzas are from a long poem in Marathi which was attached to the handwritten Marathi petition of Gopal Baba Walangkar. The internal signature is ' 'Pandit Kondiram", whose name I have not found in any other connection. The transaction was made with the help of Pramod Kale.
24. *Gazetteer of the Bombay Presidency: Kolhapur,* Vol. XXIV (Bombay, 1886), p. 112 and *Sholapur,* Vol. XX (Bombay. 1884).
25. The Sholapur Gazetteer reports the use of the term *maharjatica.* The protagonist of Vijay Tendulknr's new and controversial Marathi play, an amoral, hot-tempered iconoclast, describes himself as "a Mahar although born a Brahman". See *SakharamBinder,* translated by Shanta Shahane and Kumud Mehta (Delhi: Hind Pocket Books, 1973).
26. Government File, Education Department, No. 65-1-1918, pp. 237-38. Bombay Archives.
27. Mahadeo Desai, *The Diary of Mahadeo Desai* (Ahmedabad: Navajivan Publishing House, 1953), p. 52.

28. Blake Clark, "The Victory of an Untouchable", *The Reader's Digest* (March 1950), p. 110.
29. The words in quotation marks were applied to Chiplunkar by Stanley A. Wolpert in *Tilak and Gokhale: Revolution and Reform in the Making of Modern India (Berkeley:* University of California Press, 1962), p. 10.
30. Thomas Coats, "Account of the Present State of the Township of Lony" *Transactions of the Literary Society of Bombay,* Vol. Ill, 1823, reprinted 1877, p. 210.
31. *Census of India,* 1921. Vol. VIII: *Bombay Presidency,* Part II — Tables, (Bombay, 1922), p. 363.
32. *Gazetteer of the Bombay Presidency: Khandesh,* Vol XII (Bombay, 1880), p. 116.
33. V.R. Shinde, *The Theistic Directory* (Bombay: Depressed Classes Mission, 1912), pp. 61-2. Although Shinde's educational work was most important in term of numbers, it was the reformist attitude of two Maratha princes, the Gaikwad of Baroda and the Maharaja of Kolhapur, which prompted them to aid Ambedkar in securing his education.
34. A Mahar boy in Dharwar had petitioned for admission to a government school in 1856 and been turned down on the basis of caste. See Syed Nurullah and J.P. Naik, *History of Education in India* (Bombay: Macmillan, 1951), pp. 421-22.
35. *Census of India,* 1921. Vol. VIII: *Bombay Presidency,* Part I, pp. 140-41, and Part n, p. 121.
36. "The Nineteenth Century Background of the Mahar and Non-Brahman Movements in Maharashtra". *The Indian Economic and Social History Review,* VII:3 (1970) pp. 397-415.
37. Keshavsut's poem, "The First Question of the Untouchable Boy", has been translated by Prabhakar Machwe in his short biography, *Keshavsut* (New Delhi: Sahitya Akademi, 1966), pp. 45-6.
38. R.G. Bhandarkar, *Collected Works,* Vol. II, edited by Narayan Bapuji Utgitkar (Pune: Bhandarkar Oriental Research Institute, 1928), p. 491.
39. See R.S. Markhandikar, "G.G. Agarkar - A Study in Radical Liberalism, 1856-1895" *Modern Review,* 118, December 1965, pp. 518-23. Many of the reformers who encouraged Bansode and worked with Ambedkar in the twentieth century were followers of Agarkar's school of thought.

40. Mahadeo Desai, *op.cit.*, pp. 52-3. (The word *Harijan* is used anachronistically here; Gandhi did not coin the term until 1933.)

41. M.K. Jadhav, who had been educated in V.R. Shinde's schools, took a B.A. in Sanskrit from New Poona College in 1925, twelve years after Ambedkar secured his B.A. from Elphinstone College. Ambedkar is given credit for his appointment as Deputy Collector in Bijapur District in 1928.

42. *The Reforms Committee* (Franchise: Lord Southborough, Chairman). Evidence taken before the Reforms Committee, Vol II (Calcutta, 1919), pp. 729-39.

43. The petition is reproduced in *The Life of Shivram Janba Kamble* by H.N. Navalkar(Pune: S.J. Kamble, 1930), pp. 142-47. The petition is in English, the biography in Marathi.

44. Copies of the resolutions of early conferences of the Mahars in the Nagpur area and their resolutions are in the possession of Bansode's son, Shamrao Bansode of Nagpur. Bansode was generally Secretary of these conferences. Other early material is in the extensive collection of Vasant Moon in Nagpur.

45. Edwin S. Montagu, *An Indian Diary* (London: William Heinemann, 1930), p. 306. Montague does not record the names: these are given in N.R. Shende, *Ga, A. Gawai: Vyakti and Karya* (life and work), (Amraoti: Prabhakar Pandurang Bhatkar, 1963), pp. 32-33.

46. Ambedkar discusses both references in *What Congress and Gandhi Have Done to the Untouchables* (Bombay: Thacker and Co., 1946, 2nd ed.), pp. 14-18.

47. D.D. Gholap, a Mahar from Satara and the editor of Ambedkar's first newspaper, *Muknayak,* was selected for this seat. Later two nominated representatives were allowed, and Ambedkar and P.O. Solanki, a Gujarati Untouchable and associate of Ambedkar, served from 1928 to 1930.

48. See Bombay (Presidency) Depressed Classes and Aboriginal Tribes Committee. *Report* (Bombay, 1930). O.H.B. Starte, Chairman.

49. Rao Bahadur Rettamalle Srinivasan, the leader of the Depressed Classes within the Madras Legislative Council, was the other Depressed Classes delegate to the Round Table Conference. He seems to have been a less important leader than M.C. Rajah, who was then a member of the Indian Legislative Assembly. Evidently the Madras movement

was factionalized, and Rajan and Srinivasan did not work together.

50. S. Natarajan, *A Century of Social Reform in India* (Bombay: Asia Publishing House, 1962, 2nd ed.), p. 140.

51. My account, of the Mahad is compounded from Dhananjay Keer, *Dr. Ambedkar: Life and Mission,* pp. 69-76; 97-105, and interviews with Surendranath Tipnis and other Mahad veterans.

52. A radical Brahman, G.N. Sahasrabuddhe, a long-time associate of Ambedkar, moved the resolution to burn *the Manusmriti.* B.S. Dhotre, a retired Mahar primary school teacher, told me that Ambedkar had read the *Manusmriti* with a pandit in the months before the Conference and had asked Dhotre to copy out those portions of it which dealt with punishment for the disobedient Shudra. [These portions were burned.]

53. See any of the volumes in footnotes 3 of my "Learning the Use of Political Means — the Mahars of Maharashtra" in Rajni Kothari ed., *Caste in Indian Politics* (New Delhi: Orient Longmans, 1970) [And in this volume].

54. It was Ambedkar's claim that the vote count showed Scheduled Caste support, but that caste Hindu votes swung the election against the Party.

55. See the Special Issue on Dalit Literature of the *Times Weekly,* 25 November, 1973. The issue also discussed the new Dalit Panther group. [See also my articles in this volume.]

56. Three of Shankarrao Kharat's stories have been translated in Robert Miller and Pramod Kale, "The Burden on the Head is Always There", in J. Michael Mahar ed., *The Untouchables in Contemporary India,* pp. 317-59.

57. B.R. Ambedkar, *The Untouchables,* p. 155.

58. Ambedkar visited Ceylon and Burma in 1950 and 1954 respectively. He evidently hoped for continued contact with Buddhist countries.

59. *Nagpur Times,* 15 October, 1957.

60. K.R. Sundar Rajan, "Harijans: The Great Betrayal — 200 killed every year by Caste Hindus", *The Illustrated Weekly,* XCIV, 30, 30 September, 1973, p. 11.

7
The Mahars of Maharashtra Religious and Political Uprising

Among all the Scheduled Castes in India, the Mahars of Maharashtra have used political means most consistently and unitedly in their attempt to better their condition. The term "political means" covers both early efforts of scattered groups to secure governmental benefits and representation on legislative and political bodies, and later more direct efforts in the form of political parties that secured representation of their special interest, agitated for constitutional guarantees, and created for themselves a firm electoral base. This study attempts to describe the process by which the Mahars, operating under conditions of social degradation, perceive the potency of politics as a means of ameliorating their social condition.[1] Our concern, however, is not so much to evaluate the extent to which they achieved these ends but rather to identify and describe the manner in which a community like this participates in the political process for the improvement of their social conditions, in turn acquires political skills and capabilities and develops behaviours and responses favourable to their assimilation in the broader political culture of the nation.

Mahar Population and Distribution

Mahars and Buddhists account for about nine per cent of the present-day population of Maharashtra. The two next largest Scheduled Castes in Maharashtra are smaller in comparison: Mangs, 1.8 per cent and Chambhars, 1.3 per cent. The total Scheduled Caste population including those who converted to Buddhism constitutes 12.68 percent of the State population of Maharashtra, somewhat lower than the nearly 15 per cent average for India as a whole.[2]

Mahars are found in almost every village of Maharashtra, and are always in a minority. Their quarters, called the *maharwada,* are set apart, usually east of the village proper. A Marathi proverb, *jethe goo tethe maharwada* (wherever there is a village, there is a *maharwada),* underlines their prevalence and also their low status, since it is used idiomatically to mean the same as the English proverb, "There's a black sheep in every flock".[3] A contemporary anthropologist, Irawati Karve, found the Mahars, and not the dominant agricultural caste of Marathas, the most thoroughly widespread caste of Maharashtra and ended an essay on "Mahars and Maharashtra" with the statement of a Mahar minor village official on the border between Marathi and Hindi-speaking peoples, *jethaparayant mahar pochle tithaparayant maharashtra* (as far as the Mahars have gone, there is Maharashtra).[4]

A theory held by some scholars and writers is that the Mahars are the original inhabitants of Maharashtra. One of the old names used for them, *dharnicheput* (sons of the soil) as well as some of their traditional village duties—the arbitration of boundary disputes and the care of the village goddess Mariai — suggest that they may at one time have owned the land. At least one early Mahar leader, Kisan Fagoji Bansode of Nagpur, spoke of pre-Aryan land ownership to try to build the pride and spirit of the Mahars, but the most important Mahar leader in this country, Dr. B.R. Ambedkar, did not exploit this belief.[5]

Traditional Occupations of Mahars

The traditional place of the Mahar in the village community was as a *balutedar* or *watandar,* a village servant whose duty was to the village and whose recompense *(baluta* or gifts in kind, and *watan* or land) came from the village. The Mahar's hereditary duty may, in former times, have involved membership of the village governing body when the village servants, including the *patil* (headman, usually a Maratha) and the *kulkarni* (accountant, usually a Brahman), sat as a panchayat.[6] The Mahar *balutedar's* duties included arbitrating in boundary disputes, acting as the village watchman, mending the village wall, serving as guide and messenger to government servants, calling landowners to pay land revenue at the village *chaudi* (village hall), sweeping the village roads, escorting the government treasury, tracking thieves, carrying death notice and messages to other villages, bringing fuel to the cremation ground, and removing the carcasses of dead cattle from the village. The Mahar also had fixed duties in religious matters, including the kindling of the first *Holi* festival fire from which other fires were lit and guarding the shrine of goddess Mariai which was in the *maharwada*. Recompense given by the village for these duties included not only grain and the skins of the dead cattle, but a small amount of land known as *watan* and a host of other perquisites legendarily numbering fifty-two. The Mahars not required for *balutedar* work (in recent decades at least, they have worked in turn) did agricultural labour, their own *watan* lands being insufficient to support them. This set of duties holds for the Konkan (coastal) and Desh (plains) areas of Maharashtra; in the Vidarbha region to the east, where a looser social structure prevailed, some Mahars were also weavers, tradesmen, and *malguzars* (village revenue collectors).

The Mahar's duties were performed in the context of his untouchability; his touch was polluting and he did not come into direct contact with a caste Hindu or enter a caste Hindu home. The temple, the school, the village well were closed to him. Some restrictions in clothing, ornaments, metal household wares and the observance of ceremonies seem to have been enforced. The Mahar role in the village festivals was clearly specified and generally, though not always, indicative of his inferior status. The Mahar practice of eating the carrion beef, an early target of the Mahar reformers, was the justification, in the mind of the caste Hindu, for his untouchability.

The Mahar *balutedar* duties gave him a widely held reputation for cleverness and curiosity and fairly close association with caste Hindus and government officials in spite of the polluting consequences of his touch and, in some areas, even his shadow. Many of his duties are those of Untouchable castes in other areas, but some appear to be unique to the Mahar. The curious position of the village Mahar, inferior and yet responsible in a way beyond that of servants, is seen in the 1845 description of R.N. Gooddine: "[The Mahar is] the watchman and guardian of the village and the living chronicler of its concerns", to which R.D. Choksey adds, "He, it appears, was acquainted with everybody's affairs, and his evidence was required in every dispute."[7] C.B. Agarwal, in *The Harijans in Rebellion,* writes, "In cases of [land] dispute, his decision was willingly accepted by both the parties. The Mahar, therefore, played the part of a witness and judge simultaneously".[8] But, interesting as it is, there are few factors in the Mahar village position which are indicative of castewise unity. The inter-village contact of Mahars in *tamasha* and *jalsa* (traveling village entertainment and singing groups) may have created channels for the communication of new ideas, but the ideas and the impulse for organization came from non-village factors.

With the advent of British rule, other opportunities for work were opened to the Mahar, his traditional role being such that he was both free and pressed to take whatever new vocation presented itself. While the other Untouchable castes in Maharashtra had tasks which carried over into modern life, the Chambhar leather and shoe work quite successfully and the Mang basket and rope-making with less financial success, the Mahar position as an 'inferior village servant' (a British term) lost significance with new methods of communication, justice and government. The post office, the courts, and the police replaced the Mahar as messenger, arbitrator of land disputes, and watchman. The system of *balutedar* work itself could not expand to care for increasing numbers of Mahars. Work on the docks, the railways and the roads, in textile mills, and in government industries such as ammunition factories[9] became the outlets for Mahar labour, from the 1860s on.[10] Although Mahars evidently did not flock to the cities in as greater numbers as did other castes (even now the percentage of urban Mahars including Buddhists is lower than the urban percentage for Maharashtra as a whole[11]), the railway centres and the mill towns, as well as Bombay, Pune and Nagpur, became the loci for a new Mahar push for education and improved social status. Major consequences followed such exposure. Stimulated through contact with city relatives or to the travelling Mahar propagandists and entertainers, the Mahars remaining in the village began to discard both duties and caste practices that were associated with their low status: the dragging out of carcasses and the subsequent eating of carrion, begging for food, wearing the clothes of the dead. Eventually, under Dr. Ambedkar's leadership, the *watan balutedar* system itself was attacked.[12]

Mahar Military Service

While the new economic opportunities presented to the Mahars undoubtedly encouraged a movement up from their inferior position, another factor that contributed both to their economic and social progress and to their caste spirit derived from the Mahar military service. Even before the arrival of the British, the Mahars had an outlet from traditional work in the time of Shivaji as guards in the hill forts and soldiers in the artillery. It is fairly clear that they had their own units in the later armies of the Peshwas. But it is from the records of their service in the armies of the British that the Mahars draw the contention that they are a martial race. A military monument at Koregaon near Pune serves as a focal point in the legend of Mahar heroism, and a number of Mahar gatherings have been held at its foot. The Koregaon pillar commemorates the soldiers of the British Army who fell during an 1818 battle with the Peshwa's forces. Of the 49 names of the 2nd/lst regiment recorded there, twenty-two are Mahar, or *Parwari,* as army Mahars were known then (identifiable by the *nak* ending of the names a designation used for Mahars into the early years of this century), sixteen are Maratha, eight Rajput and other Hindu, two Muslim and one probably Indian Jewish.[13]

Though their record of military service dates back to the pre-British period and may lend some plausibility to their claim to the status of a martial group, it was their entry into the British army which proved significant for the subsequent history of the Mahar movement. It is important to gauge this significance. It consists not in any automatic elevation in the social hierarchy through military service, which indeed is ruled out in a hierarchical system governed by considerations of ascriptive status and ritual purity. It rather consists in the fact that military service at such an early date exposed them to British institutions much before the dissemination of western culture took place on a large scale. Such an exposure socialized them sufficiently early to the new political order so that when new opportunities and alternatives became available, they were found prepared to use them more effectively than those groups which did not have this experience.

Dr. Ambedkar, probably basing his belief on the army experience of his ancestors on both sides for several generations, attributed the beginning of the Untouchables' movement almost solely to their contact with the British Army :

> Until the advent of British, the Untouchables were content to remain Untouchables. It was destiny preordained by the Hindu God and enforced by the Hindu State.... Fortunately or unfortunately, the East India Company needed soldiers for their army in India and it could find none but the Untouchables .... In the army of the East India Company there prevailed the system of compulsory education for Indian soldiers and their children, both male and female. The education received by the Untouchables in the army ... gave them a new vision and a new value. They became conscious that the low esteem in which they had been held was not an inescapable destiny but was a stigma imposed on their personality by the cunning contrivances of the priest. They felt the shame of it as they never did before and were determined to get rid of it.[14]

With the abolition of the old Presidency armies in 1893 and the establishment of units on a class basis, together with the increased recruitment from the northern martial races, the Mahars were denied further recruitment in the army. Ambedkar's father was of the last generation to be able to use this channel of financial security and social prestige. Two documents, one from the late nineteenth century and the other from the early twentieth, illustrate the importance of army service to the Mahars. These were clearly the beginnings of their efforts to induce government to intervene on their behalf, and their questioning of their traditional inferior status.

In 1894, Gopal Baba Walangkar, a Konkani military man, drew up a petition in Marathi requesting re-acceptance of Untouchables into army ranks, but secured little support from his less audacious caste fellows.[15] The petition was never translated into English or presented to the British, but it serves as a document for Mahar attitudes of the time. Sent from the *Anarya Doshpariharakham* at Dapoli (Non-Aryan Group for the Removal of Wrongs at Dapoli, an army pensioners' center in Ratnagiri), the petition speaks for Parwari (Mahar), Mochi (Chambhar) and Mang peoples who have served loyally in the past in both the army and domestic service. It makes the claim that the Untouchables were former Kshatriyas, demoted by the Peshwa at the time of the Mahadurgadevi famine in 1676 for eating whatever they could find to save their lives. Because of education in the army, they have begun to read the religious books of the Hindus and to question the behaviour, thoughts and the ancestry of the caste Hindus. A challenge was issued by the author of the petition several years earlier, asking what religious scriptures proved that these people were low and what remedies there were in Hinduism that would remove this lowness. The writer claimed that "none of the caste-proud or their priests" have proved the Untouchables' lowness. Examples of the bravery of both Untouchable soldiers and domestics are given, and a plea made that Untouchables should be recruited in the army, police and civil administration in accordance with the promise made by Queen Victoria after the Mutiny.[16]

Memorandum of Requests of Mahars

The Mahars of Pune, a large army camp centre, found themselves better organized and with a spokesman, Shivram Janba Kamble, who was eloquent in English. Ten years after Walangkar's effort, a memorandum was sent to the Governor of Bombay on behalf of fifteen hundred Mahars in the Deccan (the Desh area) and Konkan. The reply from the Poona Collector's office indicated that he could do nothing about their requests: admission to the lower grades of public service, removal of restrictions in public schools, permission to join the police and the Indian Army. A longer and more sophisticated document was sent in 1910 by the Conference of Deccan Mahars, with Subhedar (Captain) Bahadur Gangaram Krishnajee as president and the same Shivram Janba Kamble as secretary to the Earl of Crewe, Secretary of State for India, asking for employment in the lowest grades of the public service, in the ranks of police sepoys and of soldiers in the Indian Army.[17] The petition appealed for consideration for Mahars on the grounds of former service, English justice and human worth. The authors claim, "Our people [have] been employed in the Indian Army from the very commencement of the British Raj in our country, and they have risen to the highest positions by their valour and good conduct," and list the names of 107 Mahar officers (Jamadars, Subhedars and Subhedar Majors) in the infantry, rifles and marines as proof. Several strong pleas on the grounds of British morality were made including this one :

> And it is most encouraging to know that the Honourable House of Commons, as constituted in these times, is composed, to some extent, of the workingmen, who, only a quarter of a century ago, were regarded as but Mahars and Paryas by the more educated and affluent classes of their nation. If the Brahmanical castes and the Muhammadans have been given the full rights of British citizenship, we must be given the same.
>
> The petition held up to the British "the noble part which Japan played in the elevation of its outcastes".

There seems to be no record of an answer to the 1910 Petition. Mahars enlisted in labour units of the army in World War I and toward the end of the War, the 11th Mahars was raised but shortly disbanded. During World War II the need for troops plus the presence of Dr. Ambedkar in the Viceroy's cabinet resulted in the raising of a Mahar regiment, now known as the Mahar Machine Gun Regiment.[18] In spite of the lack of immediate response to the Petition, it was important in setting a pattern for future Mahar petitions and protests to the government. The appeal is in terms of the rights of citizens; there is no attempt to invoke Kshatriya status as proof of worth as there was in the 1894 petition, nor does any other major twentieth century Mahar document attempt to manipulate the varna system in order to claim a higher status.[19]

The 1910 petition made little mention of religion. The British were reminded that Mahars as Christian converts had attained a high status in the professions and that "the kindly touch of the Christian religion elevates the Mahar at once and forever socially as well as politically". But aside from expressing the view that "the abomination of caste, which sins both against God and Man, has no authority in the Vedas," reinforced by a quotation from Max Muller, the petitioners dealt with the matter of their condition in political and social not religious terms.

There is also considerable evidence that Mahars freed from traditional village services saw a need to try to adopt a Hinduism more sophisticated than that offered by village gods. A poem, probably by a Mahar, attached to the handwritten copy of the 1894 petition depicts the hardships and the bad habits of Untouchables in rough and direct language, and includes the complaint :

> Our religious names are Satvi, Jarvai, Mesai, Vetal, Mhasa, Bahiri, Bhadvi, Mariai. We do not know Brahman, Vishnu, Mahesh, Krishnarai, Rukhamai, Ram, Sita, Lakshman.

Many of the military Mahars joined the Kabir and Ramanandi panths, the sects which stressed equality. The fact that many Mahars of the Bawani sub-sect in Vidarbha joined the Mahanubhav *panth* may be related to their high status in the Mahar caste itself and to the greater economic freedom in their area, which permitted Mahars to be weavers, traders and shopkeepers. Were the Mahars to have continued an effort to relate to Hinduism on a higher level than village status allowed, they had a natural channel in the person of their own saint, Chokhamela, a fourteenth century poet-saint. Chokhamela's *abhangas* (songs) are still sung by pilgrims of the *warkari* cult on pilgrimage to Vithoba's temple at Pandharpur.[20]

Chokhamela Reforms Society

There seems to have been a beginning toward using the name Chokhamela as a caste name, building temples in his honor, naming groups and institutions after him, much in the same way that the Chamars of Uttar Pradesh have used the name of their saint, Ravidas, in an attempt to gain status.[21] The resolutions of the Chokhamela Reform Society meeting at Ramtek, a pilgrimage center near Nagpur, in 1923, illustrate the methods of this approach:

Approachaes: (1) a temple should be built where Untouchables as orthodox Hindus can have equal rights in weddings and thread ceremonies along with Brahmans, Kshatriyas and Vaishyas; (2) there should be religious education to bring about the unity of the Hindu people; (3) upper class people should help educate the so-called Untouchables, and government should give concessions to the upper-classes to encourage them.[22] But even such a document dealing primarily with religion includes a recognition of the importance of education and a hint at the necessity of governmental help if change is actually to come.

There are numerous scattered efforts to create specific Mahar institutions within Hinduism, to join a reforming caste Hindu organization or to adopt higher caste ritual practices *(Sanskritization,* in M.N. Srinivas' useful term) throughout the first third of the twentieth century. As examples: Gopal Baba Walangkar, author of the 1894 army petition, encouraged the replacement of Brahman *joshis* who cast wedding horoscopes, one of the few duties performed by Brahman priests for Mahars, with Mahar *joshis.* Kisan Fagoji Bansode of the Nagpur area and G.A. Gawai of Amravati, both important Mahar social reformers and spokesmen for increased participation in a higher form of Hinduism, joined the Prarthana Samaj in 1910. Vithoba Raoji Sant Pande built a separate bathing place for Mahars at Ramtek near Nagpur around 1914 and "placed the whole community under a deep obligation".[23] In the late 1920s, Mahars in the Bombay area attempted to participate in the public worship of Ganpati at Dadar started performing weddings in accordance with "vedic rites", and at least on one occasion donned the symbol of the high caste Hindu, the sacred thread.

Mahars Claiming of Religious Rights

The most vigorous efforts by Mahars and other Untouchables to claim religious rights as the equal of the caste Hindus were three temple entry attempts: an abortive temple-entry satyagraha at Amravati in 1927; a lengthy, somewhat violent (several Untouchables ended up in the hospital) attempt of Untouchables together with several caste Hindu reformers in 1929-30 to climb Pune's holy hill, Parvati; and a five-year long satyagraha at Kala Ram Temple in Nasik, ending in 1935, which served to unify and organize the Mahars and won them sympathy in England during the negotiations of the Round Table Conference in 1930-32, but did not open the doors of the temple to Untouchables.

In 1935 Dr. Ambedkar, by then the recognized leader of the Mahars, announced his decision to leave Hinduism. A conference of Mahars, called in Bombay the following year, took a similar decision for the caste as a whole. From that date onward, there is no record of any organized attempt by Mahars to participate in Hindu ritual activities. The energy and sense of unity stimulated by the temple entry attempts could be turned to political and educational matters without losing momentum.

The nineteenth century claim that the Mahar was of Kshatriya status was dropped in the twentieth century, replaced by the claim that the Mahar was of worth simply as a human being. The fact that the Maratha was also involved in a battle for Kshatriya status at this time rather pre-empted this action. But more important than this is the fact that their goal—re-entry into the army, places in the police force and civil services - required dealing with the British on western terms. The Mahar military past was now no longer employed as a ground for higher varna claims, but as a source of discontent with their economic and social status, and of a mystique of militancy used by the Mahar reformers to break down the apathy and sense of inferiority of the traditional Mahar.

The claim to religious rights lost ground as the consciousness of the importance of education and political power, articulated by the western-educated Ambedkar, increased. Further, the experience of failure of religion-centred activity prepared Mahars to reject Hinduism altogether. The figure of Chokhamela remained as a source of caste pride rather than a stimulant to claiming a place of worth in the Hindu hierarchy. They now increasingly came to rely on the opening of new avenues for rising in status in a new stratificatory system that was beginning to be established with the advent of formal education and change in traditional occupational system.

Ambedkar's letter to the leader of the Nasik satyagraha in 1934 proposes the new way upward for the Mahar. He suggests that the satyagraha should be stopped :

> I would advise the Depressed Classes to insist upon a complete overhauling of Hindu Society and Hindu theology before they consent to become an integral part of Hindu Society. I started temple entry satyagraha only because I felt that that was the best way of energizing the Depressed Classes and making them conscious of their position. As I believe I have achieved that, therefore I have no more use for temple entry. I want the Depressed Classes to concentrate their energy and resources on politics and education.[24]

As against this Kisan Fagoji Bansode, 1879-1946, a labour leader, newspaper editor, social worker and a poet of the Nagpur area, persisted with the approach of the Mahar claim to religious worth. Bansode went almost all the way with Ambedkar in social and political matters, but retained the belief that progress could be made within Hinduism. A poem illustrates his attitude, as militant as Ambedkar's, but couched in religious terms :

> Why do you endure curses?
>
> Choka went into the temple resolutely,
>
> Why do you, ashamed, stay far off?
>
> You are the descendants of Choka,
>
> Why do you fear to enter the temple?
>
> Brace yourself like a wrestler, come,
>
> together let us conquer pollution.[25]

Respected as Kisan Fagoji Bansode was in the Vidarbha area, the Mahars there followed Ambedkar perhaps even more enthusiastically than their caste fellows elsewhere.

The factors that led to the Mahar social awakening -military service and other contacts with British; employment opportunities outside the village patterns; the beginnings of education, provided at first by caste Hindu reformers and Christian missions and from the 1920s onward at least, in part, by their own efforts; a latent caste spirit stimulated by reminders of their military past and the religious worth of Chokhamela; and a highly educated leader, Dr. Ambedkar, capable of forming them into a political force — equipped them for the use of political means toward a modern goal of social equality.

Political Means: Right to Reinstatement in Army

The petitions to Government for reinstatement in the army represent the first Mahar attempt to use what I have broadly defined as political means to gain their goals—at that time a modest goal of economic opportunity. The increased democratization of British rule in India after World War I offered a chance to engage in political activity on a larger scale. Two Mahars, G.A. Gawai of Amravati, and B.R. Ambedkar, offered testimony to the Franchise Committee (Southborough) which was gathering material for the implementation of the Montagu-Chelmsford Reforms. Gawai spoke on behalf of the Depressed India Association, requesting separate electorate for an enlarged and more responsible provincial assembly.[26] Ambedkar's testimony, making the same basic point, filled ten closely printed pages and initiated what can only be called the Ambedkar Era among the Mahars.

B.R. Ambedkar, a Mahar from a Ratnagiri army family, appeared on the political scene for the first time in 1919, when he was called to testify to the Southborough Committee. The Mahar community had exhibited an early interest in political means, exemplified by the petitions and the Depressed India Association begun in 1916, which G.A. Gawai represented. Ambedkar, highly educated and with a dedication to western parliamentary democracy, was able to guide this political awareness into far more effective channels. His education both enabled him to speak in modern political terms and won him the respect and admiration of his caste. By the time the Southborough Committee hearings took place, Ambedkar was a graduate of Elphinstone College, had spent three years at Columbia University and one year at the London School of Economics. His higher education was made possible by the financial support of the Gaikwad of Baroda.[27] He returned to India in 1917 and was a professor at Sydenham College at the time of the Southborough Committee meetings. Later he resumed his London studies with the help of the Maharaja of Kolhapur[28] as well as his own savings, secured a D.Sc. from London University and was called to the Bar in 1923. His degrees indicated an accomplishment rare for an Indian, almost incredible for an Untouchable. The Mahar reaction is shown by a song about Ambedkar, part of an enormous Mahar-Buddhist-Ambedkar song literature, that begins by listing his degrees: B.A., M.A., Ph.D., D.Sc., Bar-at-Law, in a sort of incantation.

In response to a question, Ambedkar told the Southborough Committee that there was, among the Depressed Classes of Bombay State, one B.A. (himself), six or seven matriculates, and about twenty-five men who had passed the sixth or seventh standard and who consequently would be literate in English. Gawai's testimony to the Committee in the Central Provinces added three or four matriculates to this number among the Untouchables in his area. Ambedkar did not see the lack of education among his people as a bar to political participation, but pleaded that the franchise for the Depressed Classes should be "so low as to educate into political life as many Untouchables as possible".

Ambedkar's testimony informed the Committee, in words that reflected his Columbia courses with John Dewey and Franklin Giddings, that India's social divisions on the basis of "lack of like-mindedness and endosmosis", were not Hindu, Mohammadan, Christian, Parsi, Jew, etc., but Touchable Hindu, Untouchable Hindu, Mohammadan, Christian, Parsi, Jew, etc. In a statement that ranged far beyond demands for the Depressed Classes, he urged joint electorates with reserved seats for Mohammadans, lest communal representation sharpen the angularity of the division between Hindus and Muslims, and low-pitched franchise for the Marathas, which would serve that large community better than reserved seats or separate electorates in allowing them a voice free from Brahman domination. But he argued that Untouchables, whom he characterized as "slaves", "dehumanized", and "socialized as never to complain", must have communal representation since "untouchability constitutes a definite set of interests which the

Untouchable alone can speak for", and representation "in such numbers as will enable them to claim redress".

Of the Legislative Council of Bombay Presidency's proposed 100 members, he suggested that the Untouchables be allowed nine representatives, eight for their percentage of the population and one from among the nine to be elected by them to the Imperial Legislative Council. He stigmatized the Congress followers as "political radicals and social Tories", and summarized his position in these words: "British rule in India was meant to provide equal opportunity for all, and... in transferring a large share of the power to popular assemblies, arrangements should be made whereby the hardships and disabilities entailed by the social system should not be reproduced and perpetuated in political institutions."[29]

Ambedkar's first public political plea in 1919 resulted in failure. The Southborough Committee, ignoring Ambedkar, Gawai and a number of caste Hindus from Bombay, including Vithal Ramji Shinde, V.J. Patel, R.P. Paranjpye and M.M. Joshi, who urged direct representation of the Depressed Classes, gave them one nominated representative in the Bombay Legislative Assembly. The first man selected for representation was D.D. Gholap, a Mahar from Satara who had been in charge of Ambedkar's paper, *Muknayak*. Following the Muddiman Committee report on the working of the Montagu-Chelmsford Reforms in 1925, which among many other matters contained an admonition on the need to correct the Depressed Class status, another nominated Untouchable representative was added to the Bombay Legislative Council, and Ambedkar was named to this seat in 1926.

The presence of two Untouchables on the Bombay Legislative Council probably had little effect on the nature of its laws. A resolution was passed in 1923 urging that all public places and institutions maintained by public funds be open to Untouchables, and an attempt to put teeth in the resolution was made in 1926 by advising the Government not to grant money to municipalities which did not observe the rule. But these resolutions were the work of S.K. Bole, a caste Hindu reformer from the Bhandari community. Early bills presented by the Depressed Class representatives, but not passed, pertained to education for Untouchables, and that the Mahar/ *watan* land be made *ryotwari,* and hence eligible for sale, a strike at the bonds of the *balutedar* system.

The Mahad Conferences

In the decade between the sessions of the Southborough Committee and those of the Simon Commission in 1928, which provided the next opportunity for Untouchables to plead for direct representation, a great deal of organizational and educational work went on in the Mahar community. In the pre-Ambedkar era, Shivram Janba Kamble had organized conferences as early as 1903; the Depressed India Association was formed in Nagpur (and continued to function in the 1920s, but without Ambedkar's cooperation); and four conferences were held in Bombay in 1917-18, some under caste Hindu leadership, all concerned with the Untouchables and their increased political importance in the coming Reforms.[30] Ambedkar's first full-scale conference seems to have been in March 1920, at Mangaon in Kolhapur, a princely state whose ruler, Shahu Maharaj, had been active in the non-Brahman movement of the Marathas and in education for backward classes, including Untouchables. Ambedkar also spoke at the first all-India conference convened by Untouchables at Nagpur later in 1920, before his return to England. At Nagpur, he persuaded all Mahar sub-castes, at that time endogamous groups, to eat together, although not all Untouchable castes were prepared to interdine.[31] Ambedkar also propounded a theory at Nagpur, which has held for the subsequent Mahar political movement, that the caste Hindu could not know the mind of the Untouchable, and hence could not lead him. He criticized Vithal Ramji Shinde, the most active of the caste Hindu workers among Untouchables, for suggesting that Untouchable representatives should be selected by members of the Legislative Council rather than by the Government or institutions of the Untouchables themselves.[32] Direct representation was their goal; if that was not possible, then a neutral British government or their own organized groups should select members, not a largely caste-Hindu body.

Ambedkar presided over or spoke at a number of conferences in the Maharashtra area after his return from

England in 1923, but the Mahars themselves date their political awakening from a conference held in 1927 at Mahad, a town in Kolaba district south of Bombay. As is true of most conferences and organizations of the Untouchables in the 1920s and 1930s, caste Hindus played a part in this event. A C.K.P. (Chandraseniya Kayastha Prabhu),[33] supporter of Ambedkar, S.G. Tipnis, the then head of the chity council of Mahad, invited Ambedkar to hold a conference of the Depressed Classes there. The venue of the conference was a field belonging to a Muslim outside the town. At the meeting, evidently without previous planning, a decision was reached to test the 1923 resolution of the Bombay Legislative Council, which had been confirmed by the Mahad city council, that all public places should be open to Untouchables. The conference attenders marched to Chowdar tank, a large pond on the outskirts of the town in a caste Hindu area. Leaders of the procession then stopped and drank water, attempting a symbolic fulfillment of the law, but a rumour had spread through Mahad that the Untouchables were going on to the Vireshwar Temple to attempt entry, and the procession and conference ended in an attack.

The caste Hindus purified the tank and the Untouchables planned another demonstration. At the second conference, held later in the year, a copy of *Manusmriti,* the ancient law book which symbolized Hindu injustice to the Untouchables, was ceremoniously burned, but a second satyagraha for water did not take place. The district magistrate appeared with an injunction, based on a suit initiated by caste Hindus on the ground that the tank was private property. Ambedkar evidently preferred to fight in the courts rather than on the streets, and persuaded the conference members to disperse. The legal struggle ended ten years later, with the judgement in favour of Ambedkar.

The Mahad satyagraha failed to achieve its specific purpose at the time, but was successful as a rallying point for the internal reform of the Depressed Classes, the public expression of their grievances, and the stimulation of a sense of unity. The resolutions of Mahad conferences express the mood of the 1920s. The first conference "appealed to the caste Hindus to help the Untouchables secure their civic rights, to employ them in services, offer food to Untouchable students, and bury their dead animals themselves". The government was requested to pass laws prohibiting Untouchables from eating carrion, enforcing prohibition, providing free and compulsory education, and making the Bole Resolution of 1923 effective. Ambedkar addressed a meeting of the Depressed Class women urging them to dress well, not to observe caste restrictions in dress or ornaments, to be clean, not to feed husbands or sons if they were drunkards, and to send their children to school.[34]

The large numbers of Untouchables at the Mahad conferences, the unsuccessful but dramatic satyagraha at Chowdar Tank, and the burning of *Manusmriti,* which is remembered even today by Mahar and caste Hindu alike, made the Mahad conferences a legend in Mahar history. Its anniversary was celebrated as "Independence Day" thirteen years later.[35]

As the Mahar political movement gathered momentum, the non-Brahman movement, with which it was partially identified, died away, or rather took a new form as its leaders were slowly absorbed into the Congress. The two movements had some things in common: both groups had grievances against the Brahmans; both looked back on the nineteenth century figure of Jotirao Phule as a prophet;[36] such non-Brahman leaders as Shahu Maharaj and Keshavrao Jedhe knew Ambedkar and attended Untouchable conferences. But the caste difference between the two groups and their social situations—the Marathas were a land-owning dominant caste, the Mahars a nearly landless minority—worked against any real cooperative effort between them. Although the Mahar grievances were voiced chiefly against the Brahman, the Mahar village protests in the form of quitting *balutedar* duties or claiming some form of social equality increased, and the village boycott directed by the non-Brahman castes proved an effective weapon against the Untouchables. The inability of a leader like Ambedkar to accept a subordinate role in a caste Hindu organization also mitigated against cooperation. Just as the Justice Party in Madras failed to include significant numbers of Untouchables, the non-

Brahman movement in Maharashtra could not make common cause with the Untouchables.

Simon Commission's Impact

The reaction of the Depressed Classes to the Simon Commission's tour of India was far different from that of the Congress or the moderates. Eighteen Depressed Classes associations testified willingly to the Commission, sixteen of them asking for separate electorates for Untouchables. While his students walked out of his class at Government Law College in protest, Ambedkar told the Commission that the Untouchables were relieved of anxiety because the Simon Commission did not include an Indian, since such a nominee could not be truly representative of all groups. However, he did not renew his 1919 request for separate electorates. Adult franchise and reserved seats, up to 22 in all in a Bombay Assembly of 140 (15 according to their numbers plus seven as weightage to insure their rights), would satisfy him and the organization he spoke for, the Bahishkrit Hitakarini Sabha (Depressed Class Association).[37] He also requested guarantees for the Depressed Classes, as did an appeal from the Central provinces Depressed Class Association, signed by fives Mahars (including Kisan Fagoji Bansode), two Chamars, one Mang and one Bhangi, which expressed a similar view of rights and privileges in even stronger and more distrustful language.

Demands and Requests: This group requested: (1) an increase in the government power of veto for protection of the minority, (2) separate representation not only in legislatures, but all public bodies including universities in proportion to their numerical strength, (3) posts in government service for Depressed Class members, with minimum qualifications required, (4) representation in the cabinet dependent only upon Depressed Class votes, (5) special grants for education, (6) no application of a bill affecting the Depressed Classes if three-fourths of the community opposed it.[38] Both the Vidarbha and the Bombay demands reflect the feeling of the need for education (2.9 per cent of the Mahars were literate, according to the 1931 Census), the need for government jobs (Ambedkar pointed out that there was not one Depressed Class clerk in government service), and a desire for the Depressed Classes not only to participate in all public bodies but to be able to control any legislation affecting them.

Ambedkar's Political Rise

Ambedkar's nomination to the 1930 Round Table Conference called to discuss India's future constitution was an acknowledgement of the leadership he had gained, and the very fact of this participation extended his fame to every corner of Maharashtra and beyond. For Ambedkar, his and Dewan Bahadur R. Srinivasan's nomination meant "that the Untouchables were regarded not merely as a separate element from the Hindus but also of such importance as to have the right to be consulted in the framing of a constitution for India".[39] Subhas Chandra Bose voiced another interpretation of Ambedkar's political rise: "In 1930 and after, Dr. Ambedkar has had leadership thrust upon him by a benign British Government, because his services were necessary to embarrass the nationalist leaders".[40] However, Ambedkar, on his own terms, identified himself with nationalism, if not with the nationalists. Before the first Round Table Conference held in August 1930, Ambedkar said at Nagpur :

> I agree with the Congressmen that no country is good enough to rule over another. But I must also take the liberty to tell them point-blank that the proposition does not end there and that it is equally true that no class is good enough to rule over another class.

He added, "It is only in a Swaraj constitution that you stand any chance of getting the political power into your own hands without which you cannot bring salvation to your people",[41] but he found it necessary to continue to press for political safeguards for the Depressed Classes while the British continued to rule India, not trusting that those who put independence above social reform would allow the Untouchables equality.

Demand for Separate Electorates

At this Nagpur conference, shortly before he left for London, Ambedkar stated that he would be satisfied with joint electorates provided that there was adult franchise and reserved seats. Earlier, in 1919, he had asked for separate electorates, as did Jains, Marathas, Lingayats, Marwaris and a number of other groups in a sort of separate electorate fever, but in 1928, before the Simon Commission, he reversed his position. There he used the argument against separate electorates which Gandhi was later to use against him - that this would result in increased disunity. This ambivalence seems to show that Ambedkar's goal was direct, effective representation; the method of achieving that goal varied with the circumstances. At the Round Table Conference, however, he reversed himself on the matter of electorates again. Perhaps under a sense of representing all Depressed Classes, most of whom wanted separate electorates, perhaps because communal electorates for Muslims seemed to be guaranteed, perhaps because Gandhi would not even concede that reserved seats for Untouchables were necessary, Ambedkar came out strongly for separate electorates for the Depressed Classes and held his position through the three Round Table sessions. From this time on, "separate electorates" was the battle-cry of the Untouchables under Ambedkar's leadership until Independence.

Ambedkar's Criticism of Congress and Gandhi

At the second Round Table Conference, the only one Mahatma Gandhi attended, Ambedkar's attitude toward Gandhi hardened. At the time of the temple road satyagraha at Vaikam in Travancore, in 1924-25, Ambedkar had referred to Gandhi critically but not without respect. He felt that Gandhi did not give as much importance to the removal of Untouchability as he did to the propagation of Khadi and Hindu-Muslim unity. "If he did, he would insist on the removal of untouchability as a precondition for voting in Congress". But he concluded, "When no one else comes near us, even Mahatma Gandhi's sympathy is of no little importance".[42] Later, at the 1930 Nagpur conference, Ambedkar referred to Gandhi's moral influence in the struggle for Untouchables' rights. However, an unproductive meeting between the two and the confrontation in London in 1931, where Gandhi denied the recognition of the Depressed Classes as a minority and hence eligible for political safeguards, made Ambedkar bitterly critical.

After the third Round Table Conference, the General Secretary of the Depressed Classes Institute, S.N. Shivatarkar, a Chambhar, wrote in Ambedkar's paper, *Janata,* a criticism of the Congress and Gandhi that reflects the feeling on Ambedkar's side :

> In spite of the fact that the removal of the untouchability has been included in the constructive programme of the Congress, practically nothing has been done so far by the body to achieve that object, and in our fights against untouchability at Mahad and Nasik most of the local Congress leaders have been our bitter opponents.
>
> Gandhiji was prepared to concede [at the Round Table Conference] on behalf of the Congress special claims of the Mohammedans and the Sikhs including their demand for separate representation on "historic grounds", but he was not willing even to concede reserved seats in general electorates to the depressed classes, although he knew, at least he ought to have known what sort of treatment they would get, should they be thrown at the mercies of the caste Hindus.
>
> The greatest presumption on Gandhi's part at the Round Table Conference was that he claimed that he represented the depressed classes and not Dr. Ambedkar.... Leadership cannot be imposed, it must be accepted by those on whose behalf it is claimed. Congress is now dissecting the community of untouchables by playing one section of that community against the other.[43]

The *Free Press Journal* reported in 1931 that "a large section which embraces the vast majority of the Depressed Classes community", under the leadership of "P. Balu, B.J. Deorukhakar and Mr. Patel", repudiated Ambedkar's position on separate electorates and special representation and declared, their faith in the Congress and Mahatma Gandhi.[44] There are indications, however, that Ambedkar's active supporters were more numerous. When Ambedkar returned from the second Round Table Conference, 114 Depressed Classes associations of Bombay city and the Presidency presented addresses of welcome. The Muslim leader, Shaukat Ali, and Ambedkar came back on the same boat and addressed crowds of Muslims and Depressed Class members from the same platform. When Gandhi had returned a month earlier, Shivatarkar had organized for a black flag demonstration. A free-for-all ensued between Congress supporters and some 8,000 Depressed Class demonstrators.[45]

The Poona Pact

Gandhi's fast against separate electorates, which had been granted to the Depressed Classes by the Communal Award of 1932, brought Ambedkar and a number of caste Hindus to Pune, where Gandhi was imprisoned in Yervada jail, to negotiate an agreement that would somehow satisfy the Depressed Classes and yet allow Gandhi to end the fast. The Poona Pact of 1932 which resulted gave the Depressed Classes a greater number of representatives in provincial legislatures, 148 seats in place of the 71 allowed by the Communal Award. But a system of primary elections in which only the Depressed Classes were to vote, to be followed by the general election in which caste Hindus and Untouchables would vote together, took the place of the double vote, one in a separate electorate and one in the joint constituency, which the Communal Award had already provided. Both sides were later unhappy with the Poona Pact, the caste Hindus because they felt their own representation lessened, and the Depressed Classes because the double elections for their candidates seemed expensive and cumbersome, and not a proper substitute for a separate electorate. Nor did the long and arduous campaign against untouchability which Gandhi undertook after his release from prison or the establishment of the Harijan Sevak Sangh win over Ambedkar. Ambedkar was named on the Board of the Harijan Sevak Sangh, but resigned when he felt his views were not being considered.[46] One way of explaining the conflict between Ambedkar and Gandhi, perhaps an oversimplification, is to say that Ambedkar saw advancement for the Untouchables in terms of using political means to achieve social and economic equality with the highest classes in a modern society, while Gandhi held to a more traditional concept of Varna system, cleansed of untouchability, in which Untouchables would be Shudras and their unclean work made honourable.

One outcome of the Poona Pact, however, was to bring Ambedkar to the limelight again, adding to his fame and giving his leadership more of an all-India stature. An Englishman said of him in 1932: "I think we may accept Dr. Ambedkar as the most important leader and accredited spokesman of the depressed classes. None of the local leaders have either his education, forensic ability, or pugnacity, and his recent conduct during Mr. Gandhi's fast, the extraordinarily favourable agreement which he exacted from Hindu negotiators, reveal him as a political tactician of quality".[47] Ambedkar's chief rival for the Depressed Class leadership, Rao Bahadur M.C. Rajah of Madras, was also involved in political action. Rajah, the first nominated member from the Depressed Classes on the Central Legislative Assembly, also instituted Depressed Class conferences, testified to the Simon Commission, and had some following among the Mahars of Vidarbha as well as in South India. He and Dr. B.S. Moonje of the Hindu Mahasabha brought forward a compromise plan allowing reserved seats in a general constituency for the Depressed Classes in 1932 before the Poona Pact was signed, but although M.C. Rajah was present at the Poona Pact negotiations, he was eclipsed in importance by Ambedkar.[48]

Formation of the Independant Labour Party

As the 1937 elections for provincial legislatures under the new Constitution approached, Ambedkar gave the political movement a specific focus by establishing the Independent Labour Party. According to a news release issued in August 1936,[49] he had been persuaded by friends to form a party with a broader base than the Depressed Classes alone, and a party modelled on the English Labour Party came into being. The program of the new party was "mainly to advance the welfare of the labouring classes", and contained little direct mention of what were, by then, called the Scheduled Castes. Socialist in flavour, the party accepted "the principle of State management and State ownership of industry whenever it may become necessary in the interests of the people". Aid to agriculturists through land mortgage banks, cooperatives and marketing societies; technical education and the promotion of new industries; reform of the *khot, talukdari* and *watan* tenant systems; free and compulsory primary education; and a pledge to bring about a fair mixture of castes in the administration were planks in the platform. The executive committee of the party included many of the caste Hindus who had worked with Ambedkar in social affairs for the previous ten years.

Elections of 1937

In the elections of 1937, the party won ten of the fifteen reserved seats for the Scheduled Castes and three general seats in the Bombay Legislative Assembly, and three of Central Provinces and Berar's reserved seats.

The list of candidates reveals something of the nature of the Mahar political movement in the 1930s. The majority of tickets were given to Mahars, although there were at least two candidates from other Untouchable castes, a Mang and a Gujarati Scheduled Caste man. Two of the caste Hindus elected were C.K.P.; one was a Brahman. Candidates such as R.R. Bhole (Pune) and D.G. Jadhav (Khandesh) represented the new college-trained generation of Mahars; others such as B.K. Gaikwad (Nasik), had less formal education but a history of work in the various Mahar satyagrahas and conferences.

The absence of Chambhars, the wealthiest, ritually highest group among the Scheduled Castes in Maharashtra, is striking. The secretary of Ambedkar's Depressed Classes Association had been a Chambhar and the secretary of the coming Scheduled Castes Federation was to be a Chambhar, P.N. Rajbhoj, yet the caste as a whole did not follow Ambedkar. Chambhars had already achieved some degree of economic advancement with their leather work, while the Mangs were the most educationally and economically backward of the three groups, but neither Chambhars nor Mangs could see a Mahar leader as their salvation. Ambedkar seems to have attempted to win these castes over, frequently appearing at Chambhar or Mang meetings. He gave a detailed reply to criticism raised at a Chambhar conference in 1939[50] and devoted space in *Janata* in 1941 to a long letter from a Mang accusing him of being only a Mahar leader,[51] but by this time the Mahar conversion announcement had further alienated other castes. Neither group was active to a large degree in the Independent Labour Party or its successor, the Scheduled Castes Federation. Nor was the attempt to make the Independent Labour Party a working class party successful. Caste Hindu labour was not ready for Untouchable leadership, nor could the identification of the Congress with Independence be overcome.

During its short lifetime, from 1937 until 1939, when the Congress ministries resigned, the Independent Labour Party functioned with vigour but without much effect in the Congress-dominated Bombay legislature. Ambedkar protested at the minimum salary proposed for ministers, which he felt was impractical idealism. The I.L.P. members also protested against the use of the word *Harijan,* which the Untouchables felt was patronizing, in a proposed Local Boards Act - the Wardha Scheme of Education; and increased powers of the city police in matters other than riots. The education of Scheduled Caste students, the problems of Scheduled Caste teachers, the lack of adequate water supplies for Untouchables, and the need to abolish the *watan* system were raised at various times. The Harijan Temple Entry Bill passed evidently without comment by the I.L.P. members, although orthodox Hindus protested outside the Council House.

In two matters the I.L.P. participated in extra-parliamentary ways to add strength to their parliamentary voice. There was a march of peasants in Bombay in 1938 to protest againt *khoti,* a land tenure system in Ratnagiri against which Ambedkar had introduced a bill. Also in 1938, the I.L.P. joined the Communists in calling a one-day strike to protest aginst the Industrial Disputes Act, which Ambedkar declared ought to be called "The Workers Civil Liberties Suspension Act".[52] The Khoti Abolition Bill was not passed; the Industrial Act was.

With the conversion announcement in 1935, the establishment of a political party in 1936, and considerable success in the 1937 elections, the shift from attempting to gain status in matters of religion to organizing for political activity was nearly complete. Ambedkar considered but rejected various possibilities of converting to a religion that offered political as well as social advantages—Sikhism or Islam. The announcement of intent to convert was followed by a twenty-year hiatus, culminating in conversion to Buddhism, a religion that offered release from Hindu concepts of caste and a high moral standard but had no political overtones. Lloyd and

Susanne Rudolph's general statement that as the processes of democratic politics began to reach the mass electorate, the aims of caste associations changed, and "instead of demanding temple entry and prestigious caste names and histories in the census, the association began to press for places in the new administrative and educational institutions and for political representation",[53] can be applied to the Mahars. Their political movement overrode efforts to claim religious rights, failed in its attempts to present class or labour, and took on much of the nature of a caste association functioning in the political arena.

A note by a Harijan Sevak Sangh research worker indicates the depth of the political awakening and some of its consequences on the local level :

> Harijan leaders, especially those belonging to Dr. Ambedkar's party, have become fully conscious of their civic rights and encourage their followers to assert them. But as this is done in a somewhat defiant manner and no attempt is made for persuading the caste-Hindus or to secure the cooperation of the Harijan Sevak Sangh, often there arise as a result severe conflicts, boycotts, and even be labouring of Harijans by Hindu villagers.[54]

The next step of the Scheduled Castes associated with Ambedkar was a move further in the direction of separation from caste Hindu society. In July 1942, the All India Depressed Classes Conference was held at Nagpur. The meetings were attended, according to Dhananjay Keer, by 70,000 people,[55] with representatives from Bengal, Bombay, Punjab, the Central Provinces and Berar, the United Provinces and with N. Shivraj from Madras as the President, but Mahars undoubtedly predominated. The first resolution of this Conference condemned the proposals of His Majesty's government regarding the constitutional changes brought to India by Sir Stafford Cripps as a betrayal of the interests of the Scheduled Castes and a breach of the assurances given to them that a constitution would not be imposed upon them without their consent. Further resolutions restated the demands that had been part of Scheduled Caste political activity in some form since the earliest days of the movement, funds for primary and advanced education for the Scheduled Castes, representation in the public services and all legislative bodies, and separate electorates. After long and mature deliberation", the conference came "to the conclusion that a radical change must be made in the village system, now prevalent in India and which is the parent of all the ills from which the Scheduled Castes are suffering for many centuries at the hands of the Hindus". The resolution continued to ask for a constitutional provision for transfer of the Scheduled Castes to separate Scheduled Caste villages, "away from and independent of Hindu villages". The last resolution established a political party for the purpose of carrying on the political movement of the Scheduled Castes, to be called the Scheduled Castes Federation.[56]

It is difficult to say how much the separate village resolution reflected the mind of the village Mahar, and how much it indicated an attempt by Ambedkar[57] to establish the desperate seriousness of Scheduled Caste demands. It was made at a time when the Muslim League's demand for Pakistan was of great concern to both the Congress and the British, and when the early Cripps proposals seemed to overlook the problems of the Scheduled Castes in their anxiety to heal the Hindu-Muslim rift and carry on the war. The demand for separate villages was ignored by the British as was the demand for separate electorates, although at least in the case of the latter there was a longstanding and widespread opinion among the Scheduled Castes that separate electorates were necessary for them to be truly represented in the legislatures.

The 1945 elections for the Provincial Legislatures saw the newly established Scheduled Castes Federation utterly defeated. Ambedkar's official position as Labour Member in the Viceroy's Executive Council prevented him from taking an active part in the party organization, which may have been a factor in the defeat. He himself produced official election figures for the Cabinet Mission, which showed that in the primary elections, in which the Scheduled Castes alone voted, the Scheduled Castes Federation had received a larger percentage of votes than the Congress had done in Madras, Bombay and the Central

Provinces.[58] He also offered proof that, in each province, the majority of Scheduled Caste votes had gone to non-Congress candidates.[59] There had been some violence in Nagpur and Bombay at the time of the elections, and Ambedkar charged terrorism and intimidation as well as open hostility on the part of returning and polling officials as reasons for the election defeat.[60] But Sir Stafford Cripps felt that it was not possible, "even had we decided to do so, to arrange for Dr. Ambedkar's organization to have any special right of election of the Constituent Assembly. It had failed in the elections and we could not artificially restore its position".[61]

Satyagrahas and Demonstrations

Ambedkar resorted to extra-parliamentary action to press the demand for recognition, and the Scheduled Castes conducted large-scale satyagrahas for separate electorates before state legislatures at Pune, Nagpur, Lucknow and Kanpur in 1946. The satyagraha and demonstration methods of political activity had been sparingly used in the Mahar movement. The Mahar satyagraha for water; the full-scale temple Satyagrahas, one at Pavarti in Pune without Ambedkar's aid and one at Nasik with his early approval and later disinterest; the peasant march against Khoti and the one-day strike protesting against the Industrial Disputes Bill are the chief examples, and the Scheduled Castes together with caste Hindus participated in all of them. Petitions, attempts to secure favourable legislation and occasionally battles in the courts were preferred to satyagraha when the issue concerned British law and administration. The comparatively small numbers of the Scheduled Castes and their dependent position in the village made demonstrations vis-a-vis caste Hindus a dangerous and not very effective weapon. On the eve of Independence and even thereafter, the method of extra parliamentary demonstration became more widely used, probably both because of the increasing political awareness of the Mahars and the change in the nature of the governmental adversary.

The 1946 Satyagrahas were conducted solely by the Scheduled Castes demonstrating for separate electorates and recognition of their demands by those planning for Indian Independence. The failure of all other methods, including numerous memoranda to the concerned bodies for Scheduled Caste demands; a book of Ambedkar entitled *What Congress and Gandhi have Done to the Untouchables,* which stressed the necessity for considering the Scheduled Castes as a separate element in Hindu society, and a fruitless trip to London by Ambedkar, evidently prompted the use of the demonstration method.

The phenomenon of "separatism" which marked the political movement under Ambedkar from 1939 until Independence was strong enough even before the formation of the Scheduled Castes Federation for M.R. Jayakar, a Bombay political figure and judge, to write to his fellow-moderate, Tej Bahadur Sapru, in April 1941: "The depressed classes, under Ambedkar's guidance, are becoming more conscious of their separateness and not of their unity with Hinduism and perhaps in a short time a cry will go up for Maharstan".[62] Undoubtedly separatism was stimulated by the demands of the Muslims for Pakistan. It may also have been a macrocosm of what has been noticed on the village scale when the Scheduled Castes' attempts to gain status are defeated. F.G. Bailey writes of the Boad Outcastes of a village in Orissa, "They are moving out of the social structure of the village ....They cannot rise within the existing ritual and political structure of the village ... they are showing the first signs of becoming a separate village community".[63] But both on the village and national level, separatism requires an outside force to relate to, if any gains are to be made. For the Boad Outcastes, it was the Congress government; for the Mahars, it was the British. With the advent of Independence, separatism as a political device lost its value.

The situation changed for the Scheduled Castes with the coming of Independence. Replacing the British Raj was the Congress Government, committed by its long association with Gandhi to the removal of untouchability. The triple prongs of a British government willing to engage in social reform when it did not endanger its position, an Indian elite which accepted the necessity of correcting ancient injustice, and a Scheduled Caste political movement which articulated specific needs had resulted in considerable legislation. The Congress Government continued to add legal prohibitions of untouchability, ameliorative economic and educational benefits, and reservations in public bodies and governmental posts. Lelah Dushkin wrote in 1957, "Probably nowhere in the world is so large a lower-class minority granted so much favourable special treatment by the government as are the Depressed Classes of India today".[64] The actual function of the political party under Ambedkar's leadership from Independence until 1956 was to see that the special treatment provisions were properly used, that the discrimination and injustice still practised was brought to public attention, and that the seats reserved for the Scheduled Castes in legislatures were filled by men under obligation to speak for Scheduled Caste interests, although its platform was far broader than this.

The early years of Independence found Ambedkar in a position from which he was able to operate constructively and cooperatively. He had won a seat in the Constituent Assembly from Bengal in 1946, and later, after Partition, from Bombay. He was named Chairman of the drafting committee for the Constitution, which meant he was responsible for guiding it through the Assembly, and was included by Nehru as Law Minister in the first cabinet, one that "contained a strikingly careful selection of representatives of communities and regions - far more so than any later governments".[65] And Ambedkar responded with words which indicated separatism was a thing of the past. In a public meeting at which he was presented a golden replica of the draft copy of the Indian Constitution by the Scheduled Castes Federation in Bombay, he told his audience to place the country above their community to avoid "our independence being put into jeopardy". The Scheduled Castes, he said, should forget the narrow outlook of the past and think of the wider interest as a whole; they should forget past differences with the Congress and other political parties. Cooperation, although not federation with any other organization, should be the goal.[66]

Elections 1952

The era of cooperation ended in the fall of 1951, just before India's first general elections. Ambedkar resigned from the cabinet primarily because of lack of Congress support for the

Hindu Code Bill, for which he as Law Minister was responsible, but also because he felt he had little voice in the cabinet, and because, he charged, the old oppression of the Scheduled Castes still existed. Nehru's foreign policy had cost India its friends, and the official position on Kashmir caused an unnecessary impasse, he stated. Ambedkar participated in the 1952 elections not as a friend of the administration, but as a bitter opponent.

Scheduled Castes Federation in Elections 1952

The Scheduled Castes Federation entered the elections as one of a few parties with previous election experience. In its platform, the Federation pledged that it would insist on reservations subject to minimum qualifications, so long as the Backward Classes, Scheduled Castes and Scheduled Tribes "are not able to find their place in the Civil and Military services of the country". Otherwise, the party's statements dealt with larger issues. Expansion of production, birth control, cooperative or collective farming, the need to partition Kashmir, the abandonment of neutralist foreign policies in favour of cooperation with the parliamentary democracies, the abolition of prohibition, the nationalization of insurance, the formation of linguistic provinces — all were approved by the party.[67]

In the elections of 1951-52, the Scheduled Castes Federation lost badly. In Bombay state, four candidates contested seats for the Lok Sabha; only one, P.N. Rajbhoj, standing from Sholapur, was successful. Ambedkar was defeated by his long-time Chambhar opponent, N.S. Kajrolkar, in the Bombay (North) constituency.[68] The Federation had put up thirty-eight candidates for the Bombay Legislative Assembly, its ambition going beyond the twenty-seven seats reserved for the Scheduled Castes. With the exception of B.C. Kamble, standing from the Chinchpokli-Lower Parel-Love Grove constituency in Bombay, all lost.

Before the election,"at one stage there was an attempt to invite Dr. Ambedkar to stand on a Congress ticket. According to S.K. Paul, the Congress had kept a seat vacant for Dr. Ambedkar until the last moment, till it came to be known that his party entered into an electoral alliance with the Socialist Party".[69] The Congress had not read Ambedkar rightly. Even in the days of the Constituent Assembly and the first cabinet,

Ambedkar had advised the Scheduled Caste Federation to preserve its independence, and his resignation from the cabinet was not likely to change that position.

The alliance with the Socialist Party, which was the logical group for the Scheduled Castes Federation with its socialistic platform to cooperate with, was not a happy experience for either group. In a study of the elections, Venkatarangaiya reports that some Socialists felt the alliance with the Scheduled Castes Federation had been injurious. Middle class resentment was increased because of the alliance of the federation with the Peasants and Workers Party in some parts of the state and also because of alleged attacks by the Federation leaders on Gandhi.[70] In another report, Venkatarangaiya adds that Ambedkar's proposal to include Bombay in Maharashtra cost him and the Socialists the Gujrati vote.[71] Ambedkar himself said he was "at a loss to understand the defeat" ,[72] The facts that the proportion of votes per candidate was higher for the Federation than for any other party but the Congress; that the Scheduled Castes Federation had tripled its 1946 vote, which the Congress did not quite do; and broadened its area of influence, winning twelve seats in the Legislative Assemblies of six states (Hyderabad, Madras, Pepsu, Bombay, Himachal Pradesh), did not relieve the general gloom. Hugh Tinker writes, "The most disappointed candidates were those of the Scheduled Castes Federation....The great majority of these "reserved" seats went to the nominees of Congress: non-entities for the most part, but returned by the magic name of Nehru".[73]

Bhandara by Elections: In 1954, Ambedkar and his 1952 running partner, Ashok Mehta, contested the by-election in Bhandara, a district near Nagpur. Mehta, running on the Socialist Party ticket for the general seat, won; Ambedkar, as a Scheduled Castes Federation candidate for the reserved seat, lost. The factors in the loss of the Bhandara by-election seem to be the failure of those voting for Mehta to also support Ambedkar; the alienation of caste Hindus by Ambedkar's bitter denunciation of Nehru, the Congress, and Gandhian policies; the thorough coverage of the area by a high powered group of Congress leaders; and possibly the defection of G.M. Thaware, a Mahar leader who had broken with Ambedkar and joined Congress before his death in 1952.

Reasons for defeat: The chief reason, however, for the Scheduled Castes Federation defeat was that they had nowhere to go with their political power. The Federation constituency was limited to a minority by the factors of caste. In the 1937 election, the reserved seats in Bombay had evidently been left to the Scheduled Castes at the time of voting; votes recorded for these seats were in most cases considerably fewer than votes recorded for general seats. In the following elections, this factor does not seem to have held. With the coming of Independence and the Partition, separate electorates became a psychological impossibility both for the Muslims and Scheduled Castes, and the occupant of the reserved seat was to be determined by the general vote. Ambedkar evidently realized the necessity of both winning the reserved seats and using the votes from that limited number of seats in a larger alliance. In 1948 he told an Uttar Pradesh Scheduled Castes Conference, according to a newspaper report, that political power was the key to all social progress and that the Scheduled Castes could achieve salvation only if they captured political power by organizing themselves into a third party and holding the balance of power between the Congress and the Socialists.[74] The 1952 election alliance with the Socialist Party was evidently an attempt to use this strategy, but the overwhelming victory of the Congress made it clear that they were not equal political groupings and hence balance to power could not be held this way.

The Republican Party: Formations Performance: In 1956 Ambedkar made an attempt to transform the Scheduled Castes Federation into a party which would speak for all the "dispossessed", the Scheduled Castes, Scheduled Tribes and Backward Classes. The move to create the Republican Party came about the same time as the Conversion to Buddhism in Nagpur on 14-15 October 1956. Both were efforts to take the Scheduled Castes out of untouchability and into a larger group, one religious and the other political.[75] Both trace back in origin to decisions made twenty years earlier when the Mahar conference in 1936 in Bombay opted out of Hinduism and the Independent Labour Party was founded. And in spite of Dr. Ambedkar's intentions, both movements have been largely confined to the Mahars and other groups which had been involved in political activities under his leadership. Dr. Ambedkar died on 6 December 1956, two months after setting the conversion movement and the idea of a new political party in action and without making plans the development of either.

The Republican Party was not formally organized until October 1957, and the elections earlier in the year were fought by the Scheduled Castes Federation under its old name and with its old personnel. The factor which entered into the election was not the Buddhist conversion, but the battle-cry for a linguistic state of Maharashtra. The Scheduled Castes Federation campaigned in the elections under the banner of the Samyukta Maharashtra Samiti (United Maharashtra Committee).[76] In the spirit of unity engendered by linguistic state feeling, plus the careful allotment of tickets, the Federation won nineteen places in the state Legislative Assembly (counting those won in later by-elections), and six in the Lok Sabha. The lesson learned by the Party in the election was that no harm seemed to come from cooperating with other parties, even the Communists hitherto avoided because they did not come in Ambedkar's category of groups committed to parliamentary democracy, and that a statewide issue helped the constituents to forget caste.

The next elections reinforced the need of the Party both for issues that identified them with the larger electorate and for control of the number of candidates in each constituency. Without either, the Party lost the 1962 elections to the Congress, winning only three seats in the Maharashtra Legislative Assembly and none in the Lok Sabha from that state.[77]

The figures on winning candidates from the Republican Party in the 1962 elections conceal the Party's strength in Maharashtra. In actual number of votes, the Party is second to the Congress with 11.66 per cent of the total, twice as much as the nearest opposition party.[78] At the local level, the

Republican Party has a strong voice in a number of Maharashtrian urban centres, particularly in Vidarbha and in the railroad towns. In Zilla Parishad elections the Party gained at least one seat in twelve of twenty-five districts, a better record than the Communist Party's, or the Jan Singh's. In Amravati district, the Republican Party ran a number of caste Hindu candidates and won, defeating the Congress by twenty-three to twenty-one seats.[79] But even the victories make it clear that only when the solid Mahar strength behind the Republican Party can be combined with a larger issue or with other groups in election alliances can the Party show that strength in the polling results.

In addition to the problem of alliances, the Republican Party faced the difficulty of splits in the Party leadership. A group led by B.C. Kamble, a Bombay lawyer, and some other generally young and well-educated men pulled away from the party dominated by B.K. Gaikwad, Ambedkar's long-time associate, in 1959 and contested the 1961-62 elections separately, adding to the disastrous results for the Party as a whole. In Bombay city itself, the Kamble group put up 21 candidates for the municipal elections, the R. D. Bhandare group ran twenty candidates. A chart showing seats contested and won by the Scheduled Castes Federation over a period of four municipal elections suggests the effect of the split:[80]

The Scheduled Castes Federation

Year	*Seats Contested*	*Seats won*
1948	9	7
1952	11	5
1957	14	12
1961	41	6

While the Kamble split now seems confined to Bombay city, a new rift has come with Bhandare's expulsion from the Party. The factionalism that was kept more or less in order during Ambedkar's lifetime has now come to visible ruptures, and the ensuing competition for leadership may cut into the Mahar political unity severely. Still another problem affecting the political leadership is that most educated Mahars and Buddhists enter government service, one of the few ways up economically that are open to the Scheduled Castes, which effectively places them beyond political activity.

Faced with the inconsequential representation in the legislatures, the Party seems to be turning more to extra-parliamentary methods, as perhaps are other opposition parties also, to press its demands. Two massive land satyagrahas have been held, one in 1954 in the Marathwada area of Maharashtra, the second in 1959 around Nasik, Jalgaon, Dhulia, and Ahmednagar, evidently with some result in the distribution of wasteland to the landless. Silent marches in a number of cities in 1964 called attention to the harassment of Buddhists in a Maharashtrian village, where a personal quarrel had erupted on a caste basis, ending in public insult of Buddhist women. A large but scarcely publicized satyagraha was held in Uttar Pradesh and Maharashtra and a few areas in other states in December 1965 and January 1966 in which the party claims 300,000 satyagrahis participated. A conference between B.K. Gaikwad, Barrister B.D. Khobragade and B.P. Maurya, leaders of the Republican Party, and Congress leaders, including the Prime Minister, ended the satyagraha, which had filled the Maharashtrian jails.

Charter of Demands 1966

The Charter of Demands for which the demonstration took place details the present aims of the Republican Party : (1) a portrait of Dr. Ambedkar as "Father of the Indian Constitution" in the central hall of Parliament,[81] (2) the nation's land given to the tiller, (3) idle and wasteland given to landless labour, (4) adequate distribution of grain and control over rising prices, (5) improvement of the situation of slum dwellers, (6) full implementation of the Minimum Wages Act of 1948, (7) extension of Scheduled Caste privileges to the Scheduled Caste members who have embraced Buddhism,[82] (8) the ceasing of harassment of the Depressed Classes, (9) full justice under the Untouchability Offences Act, and (10) reservation in services for the Scheduled Castes and Scheduled Tribes completed by 1970.[83]

Since that large satyagraha, two smaller demonstrations have been organized. A *morcha* (protest procession) of 5,000 men and women marched to the Council House in Bombay on 13 July 1965 "to protest against the single member constituency on behalf of the Republican Party".[84] Also in July, Republican Party members joined other Opposition parties in "anti-starvation" protest, chiefly in Satara and Kolhapur,[85] calling off the agitation only when the Kashmir trouble erupted.

In the 1967 elections, the Republican Party again faced the problem of alliances. The Buddhist diversion lessened the number of reserved seats in Maharashtra. The Republican Party repudiated the concept of reserved seats, however, as had the Scheduled Castes Federation in 1955, a pragmatic decision based on the inability of a minority group to determine the outcome of the vote. A way out of the dilemma is an agreement on the distribution of tickets at the top level. This fact, plus the liberal record of the Congress under the leadership of Yeshwantrao Chavan in Maharashtra, seem to have led to an attempt at an entente with Congress in that state. A press interview with the Republican Party President, B.K. Gaikwad, in the summer of 1966 indicated that the Republican Party might cooperate with the Congress in Maharashtra, trading its support for a suggested fifty Assembly and fifteen Lok Sabha seats, a number far above those previously reserved for the Scheduled Caste. The alliance would be minimal, and the Republican Party candidates would contest seats under their own banner: "The Republican Party would prefer annihilation to contesting the elections on the Congress ticket".[86] Whether the Congress will agree to an alliance so favourable to the Republicans; whether Mahars and Buddhists will vote according to plan, forgetting the twenty years of belief that the Congress is the arch enemy; whether Republicans yoked to the Congress can retain independence in the legislatures - these are questions to be answered in time.

References

*First published in Ranjit Kothari ed., Kothari., *Caste in Indian Politicts* (New Delhi: Orient Longmans; 1970, reprinted in 1986). Minor corrections and deletions have been made. The use of the world Mahar in this essay is by no means a indication that Dr. Ambedkar's influence was limited to one caste, but an attempt to analyze how he was able to infuence one group. For another caste, see Owen Lynch.

1. The political movement which the Mahars have dominated has never been confined exclusively to their caste and from 1936 has included non-Marathi speaking groups. Since 1956, a majority of the Mahars have converted to Buddhism and no longer use the caste name. Nevertheless, in the interests of a workable title, and to bring into relief the substance of the movement we are about to consider, I have used the present title.

2. Scheduled Caste Census figures are from *Census of India, 1961*, Volume X, Maharashtra, Part V-A, by B.A. Kulkarni (Delhi: Government of India, 1964), p. 29. Buddhist figures are from the same Volume, p. 31.

   The term, Scheduled Caste, came into use with the Government of India Act of 1935, previously the terms Untouchable and Depressed Class were generally used. Mahatma Gandhi's term Harijan which gained currency around 1933 is unacceptable to the Mahars.

3. Alexander Robertson, *The Mahar Folk* (Calcutta: Y.M.C.A. Publishing House and Oxford University Press, 1938), p. 1.

4. Irawati Karve, *Partpurti* (Fulfilment) (Pune: R.J. Deshmukh, 1951), p. 81; in Marathi. This and other translations have been made with the help, at various times, of Rekha Damle, M.D. Panchbhai, Lalita Khambadkone, D.R. Maheshkar, S.D. Gaikwad, and Pramod Kale, but I am to be charged for any inaccuracies in the final version.

5. Dr. Ambedkar, asked if he were a pre-Aryan during the question period after his report to the Simon Commission, said, "Well, I do not know. That is a view." *Indian Statutory Commission,* Vol. XVI (London: H.M.S.O., 1930), p. 54.

   In his book, *Who Were the Shudras* (Bombay: Thacker & Co., 1946), Ambedkar claimed the Shudras of Indo-Aryan society were Kshatriyas, but that the Shudras of today are unrelated to the ancient Shudras. In *The Untouchables* (New Delhi: Amrit Book Co., 1948), he denied a racial origin for untouchability and proposed the theory that the Untouchables were "Broken Men" who, in contrast to "Settled Tribesmen", did not give up Buddhism when Brahmanism triumphed in India.

6. A.S. Alteker, *History of Village Communities in Western India* (Madras: Oxford University Press, 1927), p. 43.

7. R.D. Choksey, *Economic History of Bombay, Deccan and Karnataka*— 1818-68 (Pune: R.D. Choksey, 1945), pp. 66-7.

8. C.B. Agarwal, *The Harijans in Rebellion* (Bombay: Taraporevala and Sons, 1934), p. 7.
9. The British seem to have employed large number of Mahars in their ammunition factories, and the towns in which these factories are situated today seem to have a disproportionately large number of Mahar residents. Harold Mann's *Land and Labour in a Deccan Village* (Bombay: Oxford University Press, 1917) offers some witnesses to this and also suggests that village Mahars within cycling distance of some plant were factory employees. In the village he studied were ten Mahar *watandar* families, too many for the necessary watan duties. Of the 30 Mahar men in the village, 24 were employed at the Kirkee ammunition factory.
10. One of the few available dates for the beginning of Mahar urbanization is found in Morris David Morris, The *Emergence of an Industrial Labour Force in India* (Berkeley and Los Angeles: University of California Press, 1965), p. 73n: "One would probably be safe to suggest as a first approximation from the census data that before 1864 untouchables were much less likely to move to Bombay than other groups and that afterwards they tended to move in at a slightly more rapid rate than all other groups combined, at least until 1921".
11. The 1961 Census indicates that 13.81 per cent of Mahars and 20.8 per cent of Buddhists in contrast to 28.22 per cent of Maharashtra's general population is urban. Mahar and general percentages form *Census of India* 1961, Vol. X, Maharashtra, Part V-A: 32-3. Buddhist percentage taken from figures in *Census of India,* Paper No. 1 of 1963, 1961 Census - Religion (Delhi: Government of India, 1963), p. 24.
12. In a paper entitled "Social Condition of the Mahar in Poona and Vicinity", read at the Association for Asian Studies, New York, April 1966, Robert J. Miller said, "I ... emphasize the readiness of the Mahar ultimately to follow leaders who attacked the system *as a whole*.... The most renowned leader of them, B.R. Ambedkar, proposed a breaking of the link with the system at its only point of strong connection with the village Mahars — abolition of the status of hereditary servant".
13. Sir Patrick Cadell, *History of the Bombay Army* (London: Longmans, Green and Co., 1938) pp. 154-55.

14. B.R. Ambedkar, *What Congress and Gandhi have Done to the Untouchables*, 2nd ed. (Bombay: Thacker and Co. Ltd., 1946), p. 189.

15. Vithal Ramji Shinde, *Majhya Athvani va Anubhav* (My Memories and Experiences) (Poona: R.B. Andre, Shri Lekhan Wacan Bhandar, 1958), p. 214; in Marathi.

16. A handwritten copy of the petition is in the C.B. Khairmoday collection of materials on Ambedkar and the Mahars now in the University of Bombay Library.

17. The memoranda and the 1904 reply are reproduced in English in the Marathi biography of *Shivram Janba Kamble* by H.N. Navalkar (Pune: S.J. Kamble, 1930), pp. 157-64,166-68.

18. A military history of the Mahars may be found in *The Regimental History of the Mahar MG (Machine Gun) Regiment* by Major General S.P.O. Thorat (Dehra Dun: The Army Press, 1954). Photographs show a replica of the Koregaon pillar and the word "Koregaon" on the cap badge of the Mahar Regiment from 1942 until Independence.

19. The Somwanshi sub-caste of Mahars may have made some effort to identify themselves with the Rajputs, and G.M. Thaware, a Nagpur Mahar leader, made the claim, "The Scheduled Castes formerly belonged to a class of Warriors and from the Indian History these classes and specially the Mahar community rose to a high position in Shivaji's Raj" in a letter to Gandhi. *Gandhiji's Letters Re: Untouchables* by G.M. Thaware (Nagpur: L.P. Meshram and M.G. Dongre, c. 1941), p. 52. Nevertheless, the emphasis on Kshatriya status has been a minor part of the Mahar movement. For contrast, see the history of the Jatava caste of of Chamars in Agra in Owen M. Lynch's "The Politics of Untouchability", a paper read at the Conference on Social Structure and Social Change in India, 3-5 June 1965. [Now a book: Owen M. Lynch, *The Politics of Untouchability* (Now York and London: Columbia University Press, 1969.)]

20. For a historical and contemporary account of the Bhakti religion centered at Pandharpur, see G.A. Deleurey, S.J., *The Cult of Vithoba* (Pune: Deccan College, 1960).

21. See Bernard S. Cohn, "The Changing Status of a Depressed Caste", in McKim Marriot ed., *Village India,* 4th impression (Chicago: University of Chicago Press, 1960), pp. 53-77. Ravidas is also honoured by the Chambhars of Maharashtra.

22. A copy of the resolutions of the Chokhamela Sudharak Mandal in Marathi is in the possession of Vasan t Moon of Nagpur [who maintains an extensive library of research materials on Dalit movements.]
23. From the minutes of the Loyal Mahar Sabha, in English, in the possession of Vasant Moon of Nagpur. A separate ghat was also built for Mahars at Nasik on the Godavari river, but I have no information on its date.
24. Letter to B.K. Gaikwad, 3 March 1934.
25. Kisan Fagoji Bansode, *Pradip,* edited by Shamrao Bansode (Nagpur: Jagruit Prakashan, ca. 1958), p. 48, in Marathi. Choka is an abbreviation of the name of the Mahar poet-saint Chokhamela.
26. (Franchise) Evidence Taken Before the Reforms Committee, Vol. I (Calcutta: Government of India, 1919), pp. 723-25.
27. The support of Ambedkar's education was one of the many gestures toward reform made by Maharaja Sayajirao Gaekwad of Baroda, who had encouraged the education of Untouchables in his own state. In return for the financial aid, Ambedkar was to give ten years service in Baroda State. He actually gave only a few months service at two different times, claiming the treatment he received in the Baroda offices and the lack of suitable housing available for an Untouchable made it impossible to stay.
28. Shahu Maharaj of Kolhapur was an important figure in the Non-Brahman movement. He established a hostel for Untouchables in Kolhapur around 1908 and was in close contact with Ambedkar until his death in 1922.
29. *The Reform Committee,* Vol. II. pp. 729-39.
30. One conference was held under caste Hindu leadership to rally Untouchable support for the Congress-League scheme; the conference in turn asked for a Congress resolution for the removal of the disabilities of the Depressed Classes. The second conference was held later in 1917 under Non-Brahman Party leadership to counteract the pledged support of the first conference to the Congress-League scheme. A third conference was held in 1918 under the leadership of Subhedar Ganpatrao Govind Rokde, probably a Mahar, demanding separate electorates. A fourth conference was held by V.R. Shinde's Depressed Classes Mission and produced an All-India Anti-Untouchability Manifesto.

31. Dhananjay Keer, *Dr. Ambedkar, Life and Mission* (Bombay: Popular Prakashan, 2nd edition 1962), p. 43.
32. C.B. Khairmode, *Dr. Bhimrao Ramji Ambedkar,* Vol. I (Bombay: Y.B. Ambedkar, 1952); p. 267; in Marathi.
33. The C.K.Ps. are among the "advanced castes" of Maharashtra. In Ambedkar's circle of caste Hindu supporters and friends, the majority were from this community. A possible reason is that they were, in certain situations, in competition with the Brahmans.
34. Dhananjay Keer, *op.cit.,* pp. 70-1, 104-05.
35. *Times of India,* Bombay: 21 March 1940 [a picture book on the Mahad satyagraha, with Marathi test, has recently appeared].
36. Jotiba Phule, 1827-90, began the Satya Shodhak Samaj (Truth-seeking society) in 1873. Its objects were "to redeem the Shudras and Atishudras (Untouchables) from the influence of Brahmanical scriptures ... to teach them their human rights, and to liberate them from mental religious slavery". Dhananjay Kecr, *Mahatma Jotirao Phooley—Father of Our Social Revolution* (Bombay: Popular Prakashan, 1964), p. 126. Phule belonged to the Mali caste, an agricultural community ranked with the Marathas. He was the first Hindu to conduct schools for the Untouchables. Ambedkar considered him one of his three *gurus,* along with the Buddha and Kabir, and Phule's picture is often found in Mahar institutions.
37. *Indian Statutory Commission,* Vol. XVI, pp. 27-37. Dr. Ambedkar was also a member of the Provincial Committee in Bombay. His report in that capacity appears in Vol. Ill of the Indian Statutory Commission. The Bahishkrit Hitakarini Sabha was an organization founded by Ambedkar in 1924 to work for the social and economic betterment of the Depressed Classes.
38. Petition to the Indian Statutory Commission from the Central Provinces Depressed Classes Association, Nagpur, 24 February 1929; privately printed.
39. B.R. Ambedkar, *What Congress and Gandhi...,* pp. 40-1. Srinivasan was a member of the Depressed Classes from Madras who seems to have faded out of the political picture after the Round Table Conferences.
40. Subhas Chandra Bose, *The Indian Struggle,* Part II — *Netaji's Life and Writings,* 1920-34 (Calcutta, Thacker, Spink and Co., 1948), p. 40.

41. "All India Depressed Classes Conference", Nripendra Nath Mitra ed., *The Indian Annual Register,* Vol. II (Calcutta: Annual Register Office, 1930), pp. 367-74.
42. C.B. Khairmode, *Dr. Bhimrao Ramji Ambedkar,* Vol. II, pp. 117-18; in Marathi.
43. *Janata, 9* January 1932, Bombay; in Marathi.
44. *Free Press Journal,* 11 October, 1931, Bombay.
45. Dhananjay Keer, *Dr. Ambedkar...,* pp. 191-93.
46. B.R. Ambedkar, *What Congress and Gandhi...,* pp. 134-40.
47. John Coalman, in a speech before the East India Association, published in *Asiatic Review,* Vol. XXIX, No. 97C (London: January 1933), pp. 46-7.
48. M.C. Rajah and Dr. Ambedkar joined forces only in 1942, when they protested together against the lack of provision for separate electorates for the Scheduled Castes in the Cripps Proposals. *Times of India,* 1 April 1942, Bombay.
49. *Times of India,* 15 August 1936, Bombay.
50. *Bombay Chronicle,* 4 July 1939. The Chambhar criticism is not available. Ambedkar replied that "he had no ambition for the Mahars, in fact would do everything in his power to liquidate it as a community though he would want them to progress as human beings". He accused the Congress of playing a political game, giving as an example: "Although it was the Mahars who fought for right of entrance in the Police Training School at Nasik it was all non-Mahars who were admitted". *Janata,* 14 June 1941, Bombay, in Marathi. The letter from "the first educated Mang in the Nizam's state". D.N. Kamble, makes the following requests: (1) Mahars must consider Mangs as equals, (2) promising Mang young men should have a chance to go forward, (3) Mahars must not obstruct Mang processions, (4) Mahars must not take *watandari* rights from Mangs, (5) Ambedkar must give as much concern to the Improvement of Mangs as to Mahars. Ambedkar replied that he had successfully encouraged inter-caste dining, that the Mahar hostels were open to all, that the Independent Labour Party considered quality, not caste, and warned the Mangs against taking the way of Congress.
52. Ambedkar's lengthy testimony is in the *Bombay Legislative Assembly Debates,* Vol. IV, Part I, pp. 1330-59.
53. Lloyd and Susanne H. Rudolph, "The Political Role «f India's Caste Associations", *Pacific Affairs,* Vol. XXXIII, No. I, March 1960, p. 7.

54. Vamanrao A. Bhatt, *The Harijans of Maharashtra* (Delhi: All India Harijan Sevak Sangh, 1941), pp. 16-17.
55. Dhananjay Keer, *Dr. Ambedkar...*, p. 348.
56. *Report of the Depressed Class Conference* (Nagpur. G.T. Meshram, 1942).
57. As early as 1926, Ambedkar had suggested at a meeting in Jejuri that Untouchables seek land for colonization: Keer, p. 63. In 1929 at a conference in Ratnagiri District at Chiplun, Ambedkar said he would try to secure land for cultivation in Sind and in Indorc State for Untouchables: Keer, p. 127. A reccommendation of the State Committee, of which Ambedkar was a member, stated: "we also consider it possible that some of the Depressed Classes would take up land in Sind if a suitable scheme could be worked out by the Barrage Revenue authorities in consultation with the Backward Classes officer". *Report of the Depressed Classes and Aboriginal Tribes Committee,* Bombay Presidency (Bombay: Governmental Central Press, 1930), p. 42.
58. A copy of his chart is in C.B. Khairmoday's collection of Ambedkar materials in the Bombay University Library.
59. B .R. Ambedkar, *What Congress and Gandhi...*, pp. 378-86. The charts are not entirely convincing.
60. B.R. Ambedkar, *The Cabinet Mission and the Untouchables* (Bombay: privately printed, no date).
61. Anil Chandra Banerjee and Dakshina Rajan Bose, *The Cabinet Mission in India* (Calcutta: A. Mukherjee, 1946), p. 108.
62. Jayakar to Sapru, 7 April 1941, Letter J 65 in the Sapru Collection, National Library, Calcutta.
63. F.G. Bailey, *Caste and the Economic Frontier* (Manchester: Manchester University Press, 1957), pp. 224-26.
64. Lelah Dushkin,' "The Policy of the Indian National Congress Toward the Depressed Classes — An Historical Study", Unpublished M.A. thesis. University of Pennsylvania, 1957. Dushkin has also discussed Scheduled Caste policy in a series of three articles in *The Economic Weekly,* 28 October, 4 and 18 November 1961, Bombay. See also Dushkin's "Scheduled Caste Politics" in J. Michael Mahar ed.., *The Untouchables in Contemporary India* (Tucson: University of Arizona Press, 1972).

65. W.H. Morris-Jones, *The Government and Politics of India* (London: Hutchinson University Library, 1964), p. 87.
66. *Times of India,* 12 January 1950, Bombay.
67. *Asian Guide to the First Eelections* (Bombay: Asia Publishing House, 1951), pp. 191-93.
68. It is probable that Ambedkar was defeated by caste Hindu votes. The Scheduled Castes Federation with 16.92 per cent of the electorate in the Bombay North constituency got 17.27 per cent of the valid votes. M. Venkatarangaiya, *The General Election in the City of Bombay* (Bombay: Vora and Co., 1953), p. 40.
69. *Ibid.,* p. 40.
70. M. Venkatarangaiya, "Bombay City", In *Reports on the Indian General Elections, 1951-52.* by S.K. Kogekar and Richard L. Park (Bombay: Popular Book Depot, 1956), pp. 66-7.
71. M. Venkatarangaiya, *The General Election...,* p. 146.
72. M. Venkatarangaiya, in Kogekar and Park, *op. cit.,* p. 65.
73. Hugh Tinker, *India and Pakistan - A Political Analysis* (New York: Frederick A. Praeger, 1962), p. 55.
74. A.P.I. news release, 27 April, 1948.
75. For a fuller discussion, see "Buddhism and Politics in Maharashtra" by Eleanor Zelliot, in Donald Eugene Smith ed., *Religion and Politics in South Asia* (Princeton: Princeton University Press, 1966); [and in this volume].
76. Ambedkar had reluctantly given the party permission to align with the Samyukta Maharashtra Samiti in the fall of 1956. He had been an early supporter of the idea, publishing a defense of *Maharashtra as a Linguistic Province* (Bombay: Thacker and Co.), in 1948. Later he feared the possible "nationalism" of large linguistic states, and the rule of the numerically dominant caste (in Maharashtra, Marathas, not Brahmans), and recommended that Maharashtra be divided into four states. *Thoughts on Linguistic States,* privately printed in 1955.
77. The number was later reduced to two. D.P. Meshram was declared unqualified, as a Buddhist, to hold a reserved seat after a legal battle that reached the Supreme Court. The Republican Party in Uttar Pradesh, allied with the Muslims in some areas in 1962, had more success, winning three Lok Sabha and nine Legislative Assembly seats in that election.

78. *Report on the 3rd General Elections in India,* Vol. II, Statistical (New Delhi: Indian Election Commission, n.d.), pp. 12-13.

79. A discussion of the Zilla Parishad elections in Maharashtra is available in Barbara J. Ravenell's "The Scheduled Castes and Panchayati Raj", unpublished M.A. thesis, University of Chicago, 1965, pp. 102-04. The Amravati figures are from the *Times of India, 6* June 1962, Bombay.

80. B.A.V. Sharmaand R.T. Jangam, *The Bombay Municipal Corporation—An Election Study* (Bombay: Popular Book Depot, 1963), p. 54.

81. This demand indicates the need of Untouchables for recognition of their place in Indian history, represented by the contributions of Dr. Ambedkar. Allied to it are attempts to enhance the prestige of Buddhism, such as the proposal of Maharashtrian Republicans that the Buddha's birth-date be a public holiday. *Maharashtra Legislative Assembly Debates,* Vol. I, No. 30, 18 August 1960.

82. In Maharashtra,' "The State Government has from 1st May 1960 extended all concessions and facilities available to Scheduled Castes also to the Scheduled Caste converts to Buddhism except the statutory concessions under the Constitution and certain special schemes for the removal of untouchability, etc. which cannot by their very nature apply to non-Hindus". Government Resolution Education and Social Welfare Department, SCW 2260, 6 July 1960. *Census of India 1961,* Vol. X, Part IV-A, p. 31. In other states and in matters pertaining to the Central Government, converts to Buddhism lose their privileges fin 1990, Buddhists were included in Central Government reservations.]

83. *The Charter of Demands* (New Delhi, Dada Sahib B.K. Gaikwad, B.P. Maurya and B.D. Khobragade for the Republican Party of India, 1964).

84. *Danik Maratha,* 1 3 July 1965, Bombay; in Maralhi.

85. *Maharashtra Times,* 21 and 22 August 1965, Bombay; in Marathi.

86. *Maharashtra Times,* 28 May 1966, Bombay; in Marathi.

8

The Mahar Battle for Religious and Political Rights

The key figure in the Buddhist conversion movement and in the political history of the Mahars is Dr. Bhimrao Ramji Ambedkar, a Mahar who was born in 1891 and who died on 6 December 1956, two months after the initial conversion ceremony. A catalyst of aggressive forces within the Mahar community already pushing upward, an innovator of new techniques for rising, and a symbol of achievement for many untouchables outside the Mahar caste as well as within, Dr. Ambedkar still dominates both the conversion movement and the political activities of the Republican Party. The history of the movement and of the Party can be written only in terms of his life.

Famous Mahar Leaders of Pre-Ambedkar Times

Prior to Ambedkar's first public statement on the political rights of the Depressed Classes in 1919, the Mahars' attempts to raise their social and economic status were made through claims to recognition of worth within the Hindu religion, and use of British-created economic opportunities. Four of the best-known Mahar leaders in the pre-Ambedkar era illustrate the use of both paths. Gopal Swami Yagavkar, a saint whose *samadhi* (grave) is still venerated by both Mahars and caste Hindus, was a paymaster in the British Army. Gopal Baba Walangkar, also a soldier in the British army, wrote an essay showing that the Vedas did not support untouchability.[6] Kisan Fagoji Bansode, from the Vidharba region, collected the songs of Chokhamela, the Mahar saint in the Pandharpur pantheon, wrote Chokhamela's biography, and joined the Prarthana Samaj.[7] Shivram Janba Kamble, a butler in a British club in Pune, directed an unsuccessful satyagraha at Parvati, Pune's holy hill.

Shivram Janba Kamble was the chief author of a petition written in 1910 which pleaded for the re-establishment of Mahar enlistment in the army. The document, which seems to have been ignored by the British government, illustrates both the consciousness of low position and the aspirations of the Mahar of that time :

> We, the Mahar inhabitants of India, residing in the Bombay Presidency, have experienced the vitalizing influence of the general awakening of our Indian People, and long to participate in the new privileges which have been granted by our illustrious Emperor.... We do not aspire to high political privileges and positions, since we are not educationally qualified for them, but humbly seek employment in the lowest grades of the public service, in the ranks of police sepoys and soldiers in the Indian army .... We have been excluded from the military service entirely, for reasons unknown to us.... If the other castes of the Hindus should object to our enlistment in the same regiments with them...we would request that separate regiments of our people might be created, or separate companies of our people might be attached to Muhammadan regiments .... The kindly touch of the Christian religion elevates the Mahar at once and forever socially as well as politically, and shall not the magic power of British law and British justice produce the same effect upon us, even as followers of our own ancestral faith?[8]

Eight years later, more "new privileges" were to come to the Indian people as the British raj attempted to broaden the representative base of its power. The opportunity to testify to the Southborough (Franchise) Committee, which prepared a report to be used in the Montagu-Chelmsford reforms, coincided with the arrival on the scene of a Mahar who was well educated enough to "aspire to high political privileges". Dr. Ambedkar, himself from a Mahar army family and the second high school graduate among the Mahars, had returned in 1917 from three years of education in America (M.A., Ph.D., Columbia University), and one year in England, made possible by the liberal Gaikwad of Baroda as part of his program of educating the lower castes. One of the two Untouchable witnesses, the other also a Mahar,[9] Dr. Ambedkar used the opportunity to outline a complete franchise system for Bombay Presidency. But his main plea was for direct representation of the Depressed Classes in the Bombay legislative council in proportion to their population, through their own electorate separate from that of the caste Hindus. His testimony gave a gloomy picture of the state of the Untouchable in 1919 :

> Socio-religious disabilities have dehumanized the untouchable ... The untouchables are so socialized as never to complain of their low estate .... The exact description of the treatment cannot be attempted. The word untouchable is an epitome of their ills and sufferings. Not only has untouchability arrested the growth of their personality but it comes in the way of their material well-being. It has also deprived them of certain civil rights.... The principal modes of acquiring wealth are trade, industry or service. The untouchables can engage in none of these because of their untouchability.... In the whole Bombay Presidency there [are] one B.A. [himself] and six or seven matriculates among the depressed classes.[10]

In Ambedkar's testimony were various elements which were to recur again and again throughout his career; some of these bear a relationship to the final conversion to Buddhism. He emphasized the need of the Untouchable for self-respect; the reality of the division between caste Hindu and Depressed Class, which had to be acknowledged if any justice was to be done; the belief that the Brahman's "deep ingrained ethnocentrism has prevented a reconstruction of Hindu society and stood in the way of a revision of vested rights for the common good"; distrust of Congress as a group composed of social conservatives; the representation of Untouchables by Untouchables, because caste Hindus, however sympathetic, could not properly represent their wants and grievances; and the need for political power and political education for the Depressed Classes. Ambedkar appeared before the Southborough Committee in the hope that the coming transfer of some power to popular assemblies would include direct representation of the Depressed Classes so that "the hardships and disabilities entailed by the social system should not be reproduced and perpetuated in political institutions". His plea was ignored by the Southborough

Committee, which in its final report gave one nominated seat (Ambedkar had asked for nine elected seats) to the Depressed Classes in the Bombay Presidency. But Ambedkar was to continue to use every opportunity which presented itself to attempt to secure political power for the Depressed Classes.

Another trip to England, financed by the Gaikwad of Baroda and also the Maharaja of Kolhapur, an active figure in the Non-Brahman movement, gave Ambedkar the additional qualifications of barrister-at-law and M.Sc. and D.Sc. (Economics) from the London School of Economics and Political Science. After his return, he gave some attention to the process of improving the Untouchables' status by the traditional means of emulating the religious practices of the higher castes, but there was ambivalence in his attitude toward Hinduism. In an early editorial in *Muknayak* (The Voice of the Dumb), his first newspaper started in 1920, he wrote: "We are not yet ready to give an answer to the question of whether the Untouchables should have a temple of their own or attempt to enter the Hindu temple".[11] On a few occasions, Ambedkar made some attempt to enter; physically or symbolically, the Hindu temples. The right to participate in the public Ganpati festival was secured; on at least one occasion, Ambedkar and his followers donned the sacred thread symbolizing rebirth worn by the three higher castes; an abortive attempt to enter the temple at Amravati was followed in 1930 by a large-scale satyagraha at the Kala Ram temple in Nasik.

Even the Nasik satyagraha may have been more of a social device than a battle for religious rights, for in 1934 Ambedkar himself wrote to the Nasik leader, Bhaurao Gaikwad, that the proposed renewal of the attempt (still unsuccessful) to gain entrance to the temple should be stopped altogether.

> I did not launch the temple entry movement because I wanted the Depressed Classes to become worshippers of idols which they were prevented from worshipping or because I believed that temple entry would make them equal members in and an integral part of Hindu society. So far as this aspect of the case is concerned, I would advise the depressed classes to insist upon a complete overhauling of

Hindu society and Hindu theology before they consent to become an integral part of Hindu society. I started temple entry satyagraha only because I felt that that was the best way of energizing the Depressed Classes and making them conscious of their position. As I believe I have achieved that, therefore I have no more use for temple entry. I want the Depressed Classes to concentrate their energy and resources on politics and education".[12]

But if he did not stress the need for the Untouchables to become "an integral part of Hinduism", Ambedkar did insist that Untouchables should look and act like the highest of caste Hindus. In his newspapers and at innumerable conferences he enjoined: stop the traditional Mahar work of dragging the dead cattle out of the villages and the practice of eating carrion; dress well; don't drink; don't beg; get educated and send your children to school; be self-respecting. In 1942 when recalling the progress made during twenty years of work, Ambedkar's references were not only to political gains but also to the process of self-purification of those practices which "justified" the untouchability of the Untouchable. The Scheduled Caste man, he declared, has stopped eating dead animals, observing meaningless Hindu customs, and now had the privilege of sending representatives to the legislature.[13] On another occasion in the same year he congratulated his audience on its political awareness (75,000 people had attended the public meeting), good progress in education, and entry into the police and the army. However, "the greatest progress that we have made is to be found among our women folk. Here you see in this conference these 20 to 25 thousand women present. See their dress, observe their manners, mark their speech. Can any one say that they are Untouchable women"?[14]

Demand for Separate Electorates

While the process of purifying and modernizing was going on within the caste, Ambedkar had further opportunities to bring Untouchables' grievances and demands before the British government. The emphasis on the Depressed Classes as a separate element in Indian society was intensified, and Ambedkar increasingly urged constitutional arrangements which would accentuate this separateness. The demand for joint electorates with adult franchise before the Simon Commission in 1928 gave way to insistence on separate electorates at the Round Table Conference in 1930, probably in the light of the Muslim minority's demands. Ambedkar argued that the Depressed Classes "must be regarded as a distinct and independent minority.... We cannot be deemed part of the Hindu community".[15] This was later softened, however, to a plea for the Depressed Classes to be called "Protestant Hindus" or "non-caste Hindus".[16]

For Dr. Ambedkar, the selection of two Depressed Class members (Rao Bahadur R. Srinivasan from Madras and himself) as delegates to the first Round Table Conference in 1930 was in itself recognition of the right of the Depressed Classes to be considered a separate element on the Indian political scene, and he felt the Conference acknowledged that as a fact. At the second Round Table Conference in 1931, however, Mahatma Gandhi was also present, representing the Congress and speaking strongly against the idea of the Untouchables as a separate entity in Indian society. In Gandhi's mind, separate electorates might allow Dr. Ambedkar himself to "mount to power and position but nothing good will accrue to the 'Untouchables'."[17]

The conflict at the Round Table Conference over who represented the Untouchables and whether they were or were not a separate group was heightened a year later when the Communal Award was announced. In an attempt to meet both the demands of Ambedkar and Gandhi, the British government announced that Depressed Class members were to have a double vote: one in the general electorate, the other in a special electorate only for Depressed Class voters. Gandhi, confined in the Yervada Jail in Pune, went on a fast[18] to protest this decision on the ground that it would be harmful for the Depressed Classes and would vivisect and disrupt Hinduism, would serve neither as penance for caste Hindus nor as a remedy for the degradation the Depressed Classes had groaned under for centuries.[19] Gandhi claimed the Depressed Classes question was predominantly a religious matter. Ambedkar regarded political power as vital for the Untouchables' progress; direct election of Depressed Class members to legislatures, without the possibility of caste Hindu votes determining the outcome, was essential. He had by that time no interest and little faith in the Depressed Classes' full assimilation into Hinduism.

Gandhi's fast unto death against separate electorates placed his life in Ambedkar's hands. Ambedkar agreed to the Poona Pact, capitulating on the matter of separate electorates at the price of an increased number of reserved seats for Untouchables in legislative bodies, and Gandhi gave up his fast.

Conflict with Gandhi

The conflict with Gandhi had been foreshadowed in a speech given by Ambedkar in Nagpur in 1920 in which he criticized V.R. Shinde, organizer of the pioneering Depressed Class Mission and a Maratha by caste, for suggesting that the representatives of the Untouchables should be selected by the members of the legislative council, not by government or by Untouchable institutions. Dr. Ambedkar's objection was that since the caste Hindu could not know the mind of the Untouchable therefore caste Hindu organizations for the uplift of the Depressed Classes should be opposed.[20] Ambedkar considered Gandhi an enemy of the Untouchables from the time of the Round Table Conference until Gandhi's death in 1948.

The conflict between the two men can be defined in several ways: Ambedkar's insistence on the rights of the Depressed Classes versus Gandhi's stress upon the duty of the caste Hindus to do penance; Ambedkar's complete rejection of caste versus Gandhi's defense of *chaturvarna* (the idealized four-caste system with no untouchability) as necessary to Hinduism; Ambedkar's rational democratic liberalism versus Gandhi's appeals to traditional modes of thought; and the inevitable clash between the aggressive demands of a minority group leader and the slower, broader-based and somewhat paternalistic extension of rights by the majority group reformer.

Ambedkar was critical of the British government in India, but he was of the school which demanded social reforms before political reforms, and he preferred British raj to a "Hindu raj" in which the Untouchables would not have established rights. A few years after the Poona Pact he took two steps, one religious and one political, which underlined his position as the leader of a group independent of Hinduism and Independent of the Congress. Criticism of Hinduism became a flat rejection in 1935 at a conference at Yeola (near Nasik), when Ambedkar stated: "I was born in the Hindu religion; but I will not die in the Hindu religion".[21]

A conference of Mahars which met next year in Bombay resolved to leave Hinduism, to stop participating in worship and festivals. The reaction to this announcement among the Mahars beyond the reach of the conference is hard to judge; certainly any attempt to stress religious practices as a way toward a higher social status was abandoned. But it is doubtful that disbelief in the efficacy of prayers and vows to the Hindu gods suddenly descended, and such Hindu rituals as were used for weddings and other ceremonies undoubtedly continued. The reaction to the announcement among caste Hindus was vigorous and almost totally critical. The reaction of other religions was to offer hospitality to Dr. Ambedkar and the Depressed Classes without question. Muslims, Sikhs and Buddhists sought him out. Christians, not convinced of the appropriateness of mass conversion, expressed great interest but maintained a little distance.

The Conversion

The conversion announcement was made without reference to any religion. Dr. Ambedkar seemed to be inclined toward Sikhism, explaining later that "conversion to Islam or Christianity would denationalize the Depressed Classes".[22] But after several interactions with the Sikhs, including the building of a college in Bombay by Sikhs as expression of goodwill towards the Scheduled Castes, Dr. Ambedkar let the issue of conversion lapse, probably because he felt that the reserved seats won for the Depressed Classes might have to be sacrificed by conversion to Sikhism. In 1946, when Dr. Ambedkar was asked by a Christian minister why his first choice had been Islam rather than Christianity, which was the strongest rumour of that time, he said that it was not easy to uproot humanity. The Untouchables were willing to stay where they were provided they had political safeguards, and there was no agreement among them as to where to go.[23]

In 1936, the same year the Mahar conference resolved to abandon Hinduism, Dr. Ambedkar founded the Independent Labour Party to fight the Congress in the elections to be held in 1937. The Independent Labour Party issued a platform quite broad in scope, mildly socialistic, with only incidental mention of the Depressed Classes. One section urged legislation to prevent social reformers from being outcasted by the orthodox and to penalize terrorism or boycotts used to prevent individuals or classes from exercising their rights. Another plank was the demand for facilities for higher education and foreign education for communities which were educationally backward. A third asked for modernization of *watan,* the village system that gave land rights for traditional services from its village servants, which Ambedkar considered detrimental to the progress of the Mahars. A few caste Hindus were influential in the party, and its general program was to rectify the injustices suffered by any underprivileged group. In the 1937 elections, the Independent Labour Party scored considerable success, winning 16 of the 18 seats contested, including 3 general and 10 reserved seats out of 15 in the Bombay state legislature, and 3 reserved seats in the Central Provinces and Berar.

In 1942, along with increasing pressure for separate electorates, Ambedkar turned the Independent Labour Party into the Scheduled Castes Federation, making a direct appeal to the Scheduled Castes to win power through unity. A large meeting at Nagpur brought together delegates from Bombay, the Central Provinces and Berar (who were for the most part Mahars), and also from Madras, Bengal, Punjab and the United Provinces. The first article of the new party's constitution read: "The object of the All-India Scheduled Castes Federation is the attainment by the Scheduled Castes of a status as a distinct and separate element in the national life of India and to obtain for them their political, economic and social rights to which they are entitled by reason of their needs, their numbers and their importance."[24]

This would have been the strategic time, with many Congressmen in jail, for the development of a strong all-India organization that might have welded the Scheduled Castes into the force Ambedkar dreamt of. But Ambedkar was the Labour Member of the Viceroy's Executive Council and was hampered by that official post from large-scale political activity. His own temperament also prevented him from using the war years to build his organization, as M.A. Jinnah did with the Muslim League. Dhananjay Keer has written in what seems an accurate judgement :

> Ambedkar did not try to organize his political party on modern lines. He had no taste for individual organization. There were no regular annual conferences or general meetings of the organizations with which he was connected. Where and when he sat was the venue of conference and the time of decision.... When he wanted his people to assemble under his banner, he simply gave them a clarion call and the organization sprang up like the crop in the rainy season. In the summer there would be nothing in the field, the banner resting in his study corner and the people at home.[25]

Resolutions, petitions, memoranda, large-scale satyagrahas at provincial legislatures in Pune, Nagpur, Kanpur and Lucknow, and a flying visit to England in 1946, all failed to bring British recognition of what Ambedkar felt were the rights of the Scheduled Castes to a separate electorate. Independence in 1947 brought partition and with it the end of the question of separate electorates for the Muslims, and for the Scheduled Castes too. And with Independence came the surprising and gracious gesture, in view of his outspoken criticism of the Congress, Gandhi and Nehru, of Ambedkar's appointment to the Constitution drafting committee, then to the committee chairmanship and to Nehru's first cabinet as law minister.

The proposed "Constitution of the United States of India" which Ambedkar published in *States and Minorities* in March 1947, before his appointment, is quite different from the actual draft Constitution he defended before the Constituent Assembly in November 1948. Gone is the provision for agriculture as a state industry, which Ambedkar regarded as the only solution to the problems of the Scheduled Castes, the great majority of whom were agricultural labourers.[26] Gone also were the provisions for separate electorates and separate villages for the Scheduled Castes. Similar in both documents are anti-untouchability clauses, an officer to look after "minority affairs", representation of the Scheduled Castes in Legislature and the services, and special governmental responsibility for the education of the Scheduled Castes. The Constitution, of course, is the reflection of the thinking of Congress leaders of the time, not only a product of Ambedkar's mind. Actually, his main contributions to the Constitution may have been in the general fields of stressing centralized government and a unitary judiciary, plus his skill in guiding the draft Constitution through the Constituent Assembly.

Ambedkar became known as the draftsman or author of the Constitution, but his efforts to get the Hindu Code Bill as a whole through Parliament, an achievement he desired even more, failed. He resigned in 1951, chiefly over the failure of the cabinet to support the Bill. Out of the cabinet, Ambedkar faced two election defeats and increased illness in the final years of his life. But the last two public acts of his life, the Buddhist conversion and the founding of the Republican Party, are not symptoms of failures or renewed expressions of separatism.

Refuge in the Buddha

The conversion to Buddhism in October 1956, which came just before Dr. Ambedkar's death, was the result of personal conviction as well as a conscious effort to lay down a way his people could follow after his death. Dr. Ambedkar's own path to Buddhism cannot be entirely correlated with his political life. His interest began when a Bombay teacher, K.A. Keluskar, gave him a copy of the life of Buddha in 1908, on the occasion of his passing his matriculation examination, an incident which is part of the religious lore of the Buddhists today. Sometime in the 1920s he corresponded with Maharshi Shinde, the Maratha reformer of whom he was very critical on other points, about Shinde's interest in Buddhism.[27]

In 1934 the house he had built in the predominantly Brahman Hindu colony in Dadar, Bombay, was named Rajgriha, after the ancient city of the Buddhist kings. The first of the colleges established by his People's Education Society, which began in 1946 in hutments in Bombay, was called Siddharth, Buddha's personal name. In 1948 he republished *The Essence of Buddhism,* first published in 1908, and noted in the introduction that the author, Lakshman Narasu, had battled not only against caste but also against British high-handedness. And in the same year he published his own book, *The Untouchables,* with its thesis that the Untouchables had been Buddhists, degraded and banished from the villages because they had held fast to their Buddhism when others returned to Brahmanism. As early as 1951 he urged his followers to convert to Buddhism, and that year he began writing the "Bible", *The Buddha and His Dharma,* a secular, rational, social interpretation of Buddhism, which he felt was needed to bring Buddhism to the masses.

The conversion actually came twenty-one years after the initial announcement that the Scheduled Castes should leave Hinduism. It has been called a "political stunt" by many, but it makes little political sense except as a unifying force for the Mahars, who probably would have remained cohesive in any case, or as a corollary to the Republican Party then being formed, an effort to weld the Scheduled Castes, Scheduled Tribes and Backward Classes into a powerful political group. It is fairly certain that most of Dr. Ambedkar's political lieutenants were against conversion, thinking that it might result in the loss of hard-won rights to reserved seats and reserved government jobs and serve no positive political purpose. But Dr. Ambedkar's leadership of the Scheduled Castes Federation and of the Mahars was unchallengeable, and the day of conversion found the political leaders as well as the masses, mostly Mahars, dressed in white and assembled in Nagpur, ready to become Buddhists.

Reasons for Conversion

There seem to have been two main purposes for the conversion in the mind of Dr. Ambedkar: (1) the rejection of Hinduism and in consequence the status of untouchability;

(2) the establishment of a religion which would serve as a bulwark against communism and to which all Indians could eventually turn. The first purpose is illustrated by the stories of his ill-treatment as an Untouchable which Dr. Ambedkar related during the *diksha* speech, and by the references to Hindu practices in *six* of the twenty-two oaths used during the ceremony. The oaths, in Marathi, are used at each conversion ceremony. They proclaim belief in the Buddhist way of life, but also such statements as: "I will not regard Brahma, Vishnu and Mahesh as Gods nor will I worship them"; and "I embrace today the Buddha Dhamma discarding the Hindu religion which is detrimental to the emancipation of human beings and which believes in inequality and regards human beings other than the Brahmans as lowborn".[28]

The second purpose is illustrated by an address on "Buddha and Karl Marx" delivered by Ambedkar at the World Fellowship of Buddhists meetings at Kathmandu shortly after his conversion. In this address he regarded Buddhism as a substitute for communism: "If we can become one-tenth as enlightened as the Buddha was, we can bring about the same result by the methods of love, of just and good will".[29] As early as 1950, Dr. Ambedkar wrote in the *Maha Bodhi Journal:* "Some of those who believe that only the acceptance of the gospel of Buddha can save the Hindus are filled with sorrow because they do not see much prospect of the return or revival of Buddhism. I do not share this pessimism".[30] He felt that not only all the suppressed and the downtrodden but also all those who felt there was something wrong with Hinduism would turn to Buddhism, much as the masses in the Roman Empire had turned to Christianity for "mental and moral relief". At the time of conversion, he told his people that they must be honourable, respectable, responsible Buddhists, and if they could accomplish this, "We will save our country".[31]

The first of these purposes seems, from the standpoint of those who converted, well served. The conversion was accompanied by the throwing out of the Hindu gods from the *maharwada,* the Mahar quarter of the village, sometimes quite unceremoniously and with obvious intent to defy the caste

Hindus, in other places immersed in rivers or tanks or buried more courteously. The palanquin of the village goddess, usually kept by the Mahars, was given over to the keeping of the caste Hindus. Along with the break with Hindu religion went an intensification of the process of abandoning ritual duties or work traditionally given to the Mahar as part of his service to the village. The conversion encouraged the Mahars to make the last break with any village duty that defined their low position and this action, more than actually conversion, brought some reprisals from caste Hindus. Even now, newspaper reports tell almost monthly of violence in some villages where Mahars (or Buddhists) refuse to do village sanitation work, refuse to carry petromax lamps on their heads for weddings, or refuse to do road work without cash payment in advance.

The conversion seems also to have been successful in removing from the Mahar himself any vestige of a feeling of inferiority. Buddhists often say that they experienced a sudden sense of release, a psychological freedom. A Brahman teacher who was at Siddharth College in 1956 reported that his Buddhist (formerly Mahar) students not only threw out their gods and goddesses but also were noticeably filled with a new spirit of self-confidence. A sociologist who spent several months in 1962 surveying the situation of Untouchables in villages stated: "The Buddhists are still in a gallant mood. They haven't cooled down yet".[32]

The conversion continues the "purifying process" that has been part of the movement all along, a "Pali-ization" rather than a "Sanskritization" of practices, to use the Buddhist equivalent for M.N. Srinivas's useful word for the emulation of high caste practices.[33] A part of the conversion ceremony, and of any Buddhist occasion, is the taking of the Panch Sila in Pali - five moral affirmations which announce the intent to avoid doing harm to any living being, to refrain from taking what is not given, to refrain from sexual misconduct, to refrain from wrong speech, and to refrain from intoxicating liquor and drugs. The vow to refrain from alcohol is particularly important in the Indian context. The Buddhists themselves and some observers (not all) say that there has been a decrease in drinking among the converts. Community pressure is not infrequently used to bring an indulging Buddhist into line. Since the conversion there have also been increased efforts to secure education, particularly in the villages, this again an intensification of a process of awakening that can be traced back to 1890 in some areas.[34]

The social significance of Buddhism is that it has become the culmination of the process begun years before, denying the doctrine of untouchability, attempting to remove any low caste characteristics that separated the Untouchables from caste Hindus, and cutting any ritual or economic ties that reinforced the low position of the Untouchable. The adoption of the name "Buddhist" is not an escape for the Untouchable; it is now a synonym for Mahar or Untouchable. But it gives the Mahar a sense of freedom, of progress, of change from Hinduism without a lessening of his Indianness. While the Buddhist today claims Buddhist tradition and Buddhist history as his heritage, he rejects any implication that Buddhism is part of Hinduism.

The Buddhist is also caught in a situation in which he rejects the idea of his untouchability and yet does not reject the benefits conferred upon Untouchables by government, which he feels Dr. Ambedkar won for him and which are recompense for the ill-treatment of the past. Some Buddhists would prefer to cut all links, helpful and unhelpful, with their former status; most do not see why they should lose benefits which attempt to correct former injustice, economic and educational, because they themselves reject social injustice by conversion. Many have hopes that the problem will be resolved for their children, who will be "true Buddhists" without caste.

The Republican Party

Plans for the Republican Party, and the name indicates Ambedkar's hope for a broader base than the Scheduled Castes, were not completely formulated before his death. Correspondence with Rammanohar Lohia of the Socialist Party, and letters written to P.K. Atre and S.M. Joshi, leaders of the Maharashtra opposition to the Congress, just before his death (but not mailed), are evidence of a hope for some new sort of alliance. Although he gave permission in the autumn of 1956 for the Scheduled Castes Federation to join the Samyukta Maharashtra Samiti, a group of all opposition parties which successfully pressed for a Marathi-speaking Maharashtra as a separate state, he made no long-range plans for the operation of a new allied party. When the manifesto of the Republican Party appeared, after his death, it expressed interest in cooperating with the organizations of the Backward Classes and the Scheduled Tribes, which it considered lacking in political consciousness. It also expressed hope for the emergence of all-India party in opposition to the Congress, of which it could be a unit, but no more specific foundation for a new force was laid.

In Maharashtra, the Republican Party members are Buddhists;[35] Buddhists are republicans. The number of Congress Buddhists can be counted on the fingers of one hand. Ostensibly, the leaders of the Republican Party are the leaders of the Buddhist movement. But there is another group of religious leaders who are apart from politics. The writers of the dozens of pamphlets on Buddhist ceremonies and doctrine, the pilgrims to Bodh Gaya and Sarnath, the young men who learn enough Pali to lead *wandana* (prayer) and conduct wedding, naming and funeral ceremonies, the thinkers, the warriors, are usually apolitical. There is an effort to create a new religious culture that is unrelated to the political field.

Dr. Ambedkar's hope that the Republican Party would be a more broadly based political group than the Scheduled Castes Federation has not been fulfilled. In the 1962 election, the Republican Party captured 3 seats in Maharashtra legislative assembly (in contrast to 9 during the Samyukta Maharashtra Samiti period), 8 seats in the Uttar Pradesh assembly (due to a Republican-Muslim alliance that was temporary), and 3 seats in the Lok Sabha from Uttar Pradesh. It lost the 5 state assembly seats it had won in 1957 in Punjab, and the Lok Sabha seats it had formerly held from Madras, Mysore, Gujarat and Maharashtra.

In Maharashtra, the same factor that accounts for the strength of the Party (it claims to be second in strength, after the Congress) imposes corresponding limitations. The solid bedrock support of the Mahars or Buddhists provides a powerful base, and in certain favourable situations (railroad towns, mill towns, areas where the Buddhists are 15 per cent of the population or more) a significant number of elected places in local governing bodies have gone to the Party. But the support is limited by the number of Buddhists, since the identification of the Party with the Buddhists defines its constituency. Historically, the Republican Party and its predecessor, the Scheduled Castes Federation, have been related in one way or another with almost every other political group on either the national or local scene—an inevitable consequence of being too small to stand alone and too united to be of no consequence. What direction the Party will go now to gain electoral strength is unrelated to the fact of the Buddhist conversion.

Because of its program, the natural alliance for the Republicans would be a socialist party. But the Socialist Party Scheduled Castes Federation alliance of the first general elections in 1952 was not an entirely happy experience. The Federation felt it had not received promised support. In the Bhandara by-election in 1954 the Socialist leader, Ashok Mehta, was elected to the general seat; the running mate, Dr. Ambedkar, lost the reserved seat. For their part, the Socialists felt that the Mahars could be counted on to vote for the Mahars, but not necessarily other party-endorsed candidates. Some Socialists were unhappy about the party's outspoken criticism of Gandhi and Nehru; some felt uncomfortable with the social status of the Federation's members. A recent invitation from the Samyukta Socialist Party to the Republican Party to join its alliance was turned down on the grounds that the Socialists were concerned only with economic matters and the problems of the Scheduled Castes and Buddhists demanded action on more than one front.

The Scheduled Castes Federation joined forces with the communists only once, in the Samyukta Maharashtra Samiti,[36] along with every other opposition party in Maharashtra. There is an assumption among some Buddhists and some political observers that the natural political direction of the Untouchables is toward communism. Windmiller and Overstreet note the small number of Untouchables (three) among the 139 delegates to the Communist Party of India Congress in 1943, and add: "It is interesting to note the number of Untouchables was so small, for this oppressed class would seem to be a rich source of recruits for this party" .[37] Some Buddhists themselves say that except for Dr. Ambedkar, who was always critical of the Communist Party, and for the Buddhist conversion, the Mahars would be communists.

The theory that the Untouchable would inevitably be drawn to communism is not substantiated by the American counterpart of the Indian situation; few Negroes have found the Communist Party an acceptable home. In India, support for the Communists comes from Untouchable castes only in Andhra and Kerala. In other states they are by and large Congressite or Republican. The attraction of communism for the middle-class unemployed youth is not found to any significant degree among the Mahars or Buddhists. The educated Buddhist at the moment finds unemployment no problem because his numbers are not yet great enough to fill the reserved government jobs available to him, and hence he is not as subject to the frustration of unemployment or as open to radical theories. Added to this is the fact that all Ambedkar's influence was on the side of parliamentary democracy. He was never attracted to communism, either in his years abroad or in India. The Communist Party in Bombay was for him "a bunch of Brahman boys".[38]

For Ambedkar, and for many Republican leaders, theoretical communism is synonymous with economic justice. In his last speech on Buddhism, given in 1956, at Kathmandu, Dr. Ambedkar said that Buddhism contained all of communism's economic and egalitarian benefits without violent methods. If the push for education produces Buddhists ready for white-collar jobs in such numbers that reservations no longer provide them, or if the communists find a way to organize the vast depressed army of agricultural labourers, the Buddhists may become more interested, or the Republican Party itself may find reason for common cause.

The most effective political alliance of the Buddhists today [1966] is with the Muslims in Uttar Pradesh. Three of the eight Republican Party MLAs and one of the three MPs are Muslims. Although that grouping has brought election results, it is limited to UP. There is some cooperation and undertaking between Buddhists and Muslims in daily life. The Buddhists do not feel any economic or social competition with the Muslims, do not feel that the Muslims regard them as Untouchables. In cities and small towns, the Muslim localities often neighbour those of the Buddhists. Buddhist functions may be held in Muslim institutions more easily than in caste Hindu buildings. Dr. Ambedkar understood the mind of the Muslim minority well enough to produce the prophetic *Thoughts on Pakistan* in 1940, a book which delineated all the reasons why the Muslims were part of India and should not want a separate state but declared that the mental attitude of nationhood was stronger than race, language or habits, and that therefore Pakistan was inevitable. However, many Buddhists today do not differ from the normal caste Hindu feeling about Pakistan or Kashmir, and many hold the same stereotype of the Muslim as a militant person whose first loyalty is outside India. It does not seem likely that localized political cooperation in some parts of U.P. and in a few Maharashtrian cities will spread.

Temporary alliances with conservative parties such as the Jana Sangh in local elections are not unknown, but the primarily high caste constituency and conservative economic platform of the Jana Sangh, plus Dr. Ambedkar's warning against right-wing parties, make extensive cooperation unlikely. Thirty years of anti-Congress teaching would make it difficult for the Republican Party to cooperate closely with the Congress, although there have been a few arrangements made at high levels for voting support. Rumours persist that this, or that, leader, or indeed the whole party, will go over to the Congress. But at this time, any leader transferring his allegiance from the Republican Party to the Congress loses the support of his own people in gaining a reserved seat or a cabinet post.

In addition to the problem of limited constituency and unsatisfactory alliances, the Republican Party is troubled by a split which occurred in 1959 ostensibly over the issue of communism (continued alliance with the Samiti, in which the Communist Party was very active), but more probably over the question of leadership. Republicans in Maharashtra are still divided into two hostile groups, although the power of the new faction is waning. A recent split in Bombay adds a third faction in that area. There is in spite of the general unit and cohesion of the Buddhists, much quarreling over leadership and much local factionalism. Both the split and the leadership rivalry reflect the fact that the party has had no one clear leader since the death of Dr. Ambedkar; his long-time associate, B.K. (Dadasaheb) Gaikwad of Nasik, comes the nearest and commands general respect, but not total obedience. A number of Buddhists remark on the political situation with considerable bitterness: "Each man is a little Ambedkar". "It is like brothers quarreling over their inheritance".

Two other factors affect the leadership of the party. One is the almost irresistible temptation to a man from a low economic status to make secure his new-found position at the expense of a larger ideal, an affliction that hampered the effectiveness of the Justice Party at an earlier date in South India. The other is in the fact that the way up for a Buddhist or a Scheduled Caste man is through government service. Position in private industry, teaching posts in secondary school or college, or a small business of his own, are either very difficult for the Buddhist to secure or of less economic advantage than a government job. This governmental path upward effectively removes most of the educated, concerned Buddhists from direct political activity.

One effect of both the Buddhist conversion and the work of the Republican Party has been to link those who have progressed economically and socially with those still backward, thus limiting the tendency of those in the upper strata to cut themselves off from their past and to form a new urban caste, neither high nor Untouchable.[39] Although many Mahars do "pass", the sense of identity and pride in the community is still strong, giving the whole caste a feeling of moving upward as individuals within the group improve their position or gain recognition for worth.

According Respect for Ambedkar

The figure of Dr. Ambedkar, dominating both Buddhism and the Republican Party, is the key to the direction of both movements. The respect accorded him borders on devotion, both for village Buddhists and for the educated. Not only is there a photograph or painting of Dr. Ambedkar in almost every home and at every meeting, both religious and political, but his very name has become a symbol. The Indian nationalist cry, *Jai Hind,* has been transformed into *Jai Bhim* (for *Bhimrao* Ramji Ambedkar), with *Jai Buddh* added at religious occasions. On Buddhist invitations the traditional Hindu salutation *Saprem Namaskar* becomes *Saprem Jai Bhim.* Occasionally in political meetings the term *Bhim Raj* will be used to replace the Hindu term for the ideal government, *Ram Raj.* A great body of songs has grown up with Ambedkar's life and teachings as their theme, and singing parties in many areas celebrate the lives of Ambedkar and Lord Buddha.

The devotion to Dr. Ambedkar would seem to assume the nature of a cult, except that its entire direction is to lead the Buddhist into the westernized, educated, secular world. The photographs of Dr. Ambedkar more often than not show him in a blue pinstripe business suit surrounded by books, and even those pictures which portray him as a Boddhisatva in a yellow robe look somehow very western. Often pictures showing him with the late President Rajendra Prasad or the late Prime Minister Jawaharlal Nehru are prized, as if to say: "We too share in the leadership of our country". The recent Republican Party satyagraha included, along with demands for land, slum clearance, justice to the Untouchable and implementation of the Minimum Wages Act, a demand that a portrait of Dr. B.R. Ambedkar, "The Father of the Indian Constitution", be placed in the central hall of Parliament. [In 1989, Ambedkar's portrait was unveiled in the central hall of Parliament House.] In his delineation of the values established by the advanced castes and adopted by low castes in the hope of raising their status, Richard Lambert adds a new idea to the usual list of cleanliness, literacy, economic or political power - the value or sharing in and contributing to the mainstream of cultural accomplishment.[40]

It is largely through Dr. Ambedkar as a national figure that the Buddhists claim this achievement.

The figure of Dr. Ambedkar and what he stands for identifies the nature of both the Buddhist movement and the Republican Party: A push upward, independent of caste Hindu groups, towards modern, democratic and often material values, a movement that rejects traditional Hinduism but clings tightly to its Indian-ness. Those groups which have joined the movement have a sense of self-respect, a feeling of unity, an ambition for higher social and economic status, and a political awareness which may yet aid significantly in the solution of India's age-old problem of untouchability.

Notes

1. Census of India, Paper No. 1 of 1963, 1963 Census—Religion (New Delhi, 1963). The figures are minimal because some Scheduled Caste members who have participated in a conversion ceremony still list themselves as Hindus in order to claim government benefits reserved for Scheduled Castes.
2. A note on nomenclature: four terms are used to describe the same group: Untouchable, Depressed Class, Scheduled Caste, Harijan. The word Untouchable is used freely among the Untouchables themselves. Those Untouchables who are influenced by Gandhi's organization, the Harijan Seva Sangh, and most caste Hindus use the term Harijan (people of God). Its use by an Untouchable indicates that he is of the Congress, not one of Dr. Ambedkar's followers. Depressed Class was the term used widely until Scheduled Castes came into currency in 1935, according to the schedule prepared under the Government of India Act. The term neo-Buddhists, generally used for the converts, is unacceptable to them. They call themselves, simply, Buddhists.
3. Madras has some history of lingering Buddhist influence. N. Shivraj, president of the Scheduled Castes Federation and later the Republican Party, called himself a Buddhist, as did his father. Nevertheless, there has been no major conversion movement to Buddhism in the Madras area.
4. The Independent Labour Party, founded by Dr. Ambedkar in 1936, became the Scheduled Castes Federation in 1942, and

that group in turn took the name, the Republican Party, in 1957. The leadership and the program, allowing for time change and loss of caste Hindu supporters of Dr. Ambedkar in Bombay when the party took on a direct Scheduled Caste relationship in 1942, has remained much the same.

5. Scheduled Caste privileges include some economic aid in housing and small industry, scholarships at both state and central government level at all stages of education, reservation of 12½ per cent of all posts in government service. For a discussion of the effect of conversion on Scheduled Caste privileges see Donald E. Smith, *India as a Secular State* (Princeton: Princeton University Press, 1963), pp. 322-26.

6. Gopal Baba Walangkar also made some effort to deny Brahman superiority. He formed a group of *Mahar* to perform the astrological services that normally were the prerogative of the Brahman *joshi*. The fixing of the proper astrological time for ceremonies was the only service generally performed for the Mahar by the Brahman priest. It is said that Dr. Ambedkar greatly admired Walangkar for his independent spirit.

7. Kisan Fagoji Bansode is the only one of the group without a British connection. Although attracted to Ambedkar, he remained attached to Hinduism and was critical of the announcement of conversion in 1935.

8. The full document is quoted in H.N. Navalkar, *The Life of Shivram Janba Kamble and Brief History of the Poona Parvati Satyagraha* (Pune: S.J. Kamble, 1930), pp. 142-57.

9. G.A. Gawai of Amravati, who reported to the committee from the Central Provinces and Berar.

10. *Evidence taken before the Reforms Committee (Franchise)*, Vol. 2 (Calcutta: Government of India, 1919), pp. 729-39.

11. Cangdeo Bhavanrao Khairmode, *Dr. Bhimrao Ramji Ambedkar*, Vol. 1 (Bombay: Yeshwantrao Ambedkar, 1952). p. 266 (in Marathi). This sentence, and other translations from the Marathi, were made with the help of D.R. Maheshkar and Mrs. Y.B. Damle.

12. A typed copy of the letter dated 3 March 1934, in English, is in the Khairmode files at the University of Bombay Library.

13. *Times of India*, 27 April 1942, reporting Dr. Ambedkar's speech on the occasion of his fiftieth birthday.

14. *Report of Depressed Class Conferences, Nagpur Sessions* (Nagpur: G.T. Meshram, 1942), pp. 28-9.
15. *Indian Statutory Commission,* Vol. 16, "Selections from Memoranda and Oral Evidence by Non-officials (Part I) (London, 1930), p. 54.
16. "Supplementary Memorandum on the Claims of the Depressed Classes for Special Representation, submitted to the Round Table Conference by Dr. Bhimrao R. Ambedkar and Rao Bahadur R. Srinivasan," 4 November 1931. Quoted in B.R. Ambedkar, *What Congress and Gandhi have Done to the Untouchables* (Bombay: Thacker & Co., Ltd., 1946), pp. 315-17.
17. Quoted; in *ibid.,* p. 71.
18. *The Epic Fast* is the title of Pyarelal's book (Ahmedabad: Navjivan, 1932) describing Gandhi's 1932 fast in Yeravda Jail against the principle of separate electorates.
19. Gandhi's letter to Sir S. Hoare, 11 March 1932, quoted in *ibid.,* pp. 99-103.
20. Dhananjay Keer, *Dr. Ambedkar, Life and Mission* (Bombay: Popular Prakashan, second ed., 1962), pp. 42-3.
21. Shankaro Kharat, *Asprishyanca Muktisangram* (The Battle of the Untouchables for Freedom) (Pune: Shri Joshi and M.D. Lokhande, n.d.), in Marathi, p. 204.
22. *Times of India, 24* July 1936, quoted in Keer, *op.cit.,* 278.
23. *Jai Bheem, 25* December 1946, Madras. Typed copy in the files of Nanak Chand Rattu, New Delhi. The interview, originally in the *Globe,* was with the Rev. Gordon Livingston.
24. *Constitution of the All-India Scheduled Castes Federation,* printed in *Report of Depressed Class Conferences* (Nagpur: G.T. Meshram, 1942).
25. Keer, *op.cit.,* 477.
26. Dr. Ambedkar did make such a proposal to the drafting committee, but dropped it when it received little support. G.A. Austin, "Tryst With Destiny: The Indian Constituent Assembly and the Framing of the Indian Constitution", D.Phil. thesis, Oxford University. I am grateful to Mr. Austin for some of my ideas about Dr. Ambedkar and the Constitution, although he is not responsible for my interpretation; [Sec Granville Austin, *The Indian Constitution: Cornerstone of a Nation* (Bombay: Oxford University Press, 1972).]

27. Principal M.P. Mangudkar of Shri Shahu Mandir Mahavidyalaya, Punc, reports seeing these letters among the Shinde papers. Principal Mangudkar's discussion of Dr. Ambedkar's pragmatic philosophy has been of great help to me.

28. The Twenty-two Oaths are printed in English in a leaflet entitled *Dhamma Deeksha,* published by the Buddhist Society of India, Ambedkar Bhavan, New Delhi.

29. The speech, given on 20 November, 1956, at the fourth Conference of the World Fellowship of Buddhists at Kathmandu, has been published in a pamphlet, *Buddha and Karl Marx (Nagpur:* M.D. Panchbhai).

30. *The Maha Bodhi,* Vol. 58, April-May, 1950.

31. From the Marathi speech of Dr. Ambedkar on October 1956 in Nagpur, as published in *Prabuddh Bharat,* 27 October 1956.

32. Dr. M.G. Kulkarni of the Gokhale Institute of Politics and Economics, Pune, has made available to me his reports on surveys of villages in Buldana and Nasik districts in 1962. I have quoted only his personal remark, but his detailed knowledge of the village situation has added to my understanding of present conditions.

33. The term was first used by Dr. Srinivas in *Religion and Society Among the Coorgs of South India* (Oxford: Oxford University Press, 1952), p. 30, and is detailed in "A Note of Sanskritization and Westernization", first published in the *Journal of Asian Studies* and now reprinted in *Caste in Modern India* (Bombay: Asia Publishing House, 1962).

34. Since the Buddhists are no longer counted as Scheduled Castes, no figures on their literacy, are available. *The Census of India,* 1961, Vol. 10, Maharashtra, Part V-A, "Scheduled Castes and Scheduled Tribes in Maharashtra — Tables", (Delhi: 1964), does give figures on literacy and education for those who registered themselves Mahars. The Mahar literacy rate in 1961 was 15.69 per cent, compared to 29.82 per cent as a general figure for Maharashtra, and was considerably lower than that for the Chambhars, another Scheduled Caste group primarily found in cities. However, among those Scheduled Caste individuals who have matriculated or gone on for higher education, the Mahars predominate. It is a general belief in Maharashtra that the Mahars' (and Buddhists') eagerness for education surpasses that of all but the highest castes.

35. The Buddhist who wishes to contest a reserved seat must register himself as a Mahar. A recent Supreme Court decision deprived D.P. Meshram of Nagpur of his seat in the Maharashtra legislative assembly on the grounds that his activities in the Buddhist religion proved him a Buddhist, and as such not eligible for the reserved seat. The decision was generally approved by Buddhists, since it underwrote their conviction that they are no longer Hindus. The Republican Party's inability to win a majority of the reserved seats from Congress candidates, in any case, has caused them to ask for non-renewal of reservations on the state and national level in legislative bodies.
36. The Communists' hope that perhaps the Samiti had "laid the basis of healing the great split between the democratic movement and the Untouchable masses, led by the late Dr. Ambedkar", has remained unfulfilled. Quoted from B.T. Ranadive, "Maharashtra Election Review", *New Age,* July 1957, p. 15, in Selig Harrison, *India, The Most Dangerous Decades* (Madras: Oxford University Press), pp. 192-93.
37. Gene D. Overstreet and Marshall Windmiller, *Communism in India* (Barkeley: University of California Press, 1959), p. 358. The recent dismal record of the Communists in Maharashtra is perhaps the major factor behind Untouchable disinterest.
38. From an interview with Dr. Ambedkar quoted in Harrison, *op.cit.,* p. 191.
39. Harold R. Issacs has described this situation in terms of the educated ex-Untouchables who "do not quite get *nowwhere,* but neither do they get *somewhere*". See India's *Ex-Untouchables* (New York: John Day Co., 1965).
40. R.D. Lambert, "Untouchability as a Social Problem: Theory and Research", *Sociological Bulletin,* Vol. 7, No. 1, March 1958, Bombay.

9
Untouchability: The Ambedkar-Gandhi Vision

Gandhi's Harijans

As far as their standpoints towards the Untouchability problem of India were distinct, Mahatma Gandhi and Dr. Ambedkar were political rivals. Actually, Gandhiji was concerned with the idea of freeing India from the British dominion and ignored the Untouchables, but paid effort only to silence them. He was neither willing to demolish the traditional Hindu social order nor bestow the Depressed Classes separate representation in the Congress. On the other side, Dr. Ambedkar was the voice of the Untouchables in the Indian political scène. Ambedkar expressed the wishes of the Untouchables that can be concisely listed as basic Human Rights and political representation.

The term coined by Gandhi, *harijan* to define Dalits, was not accepted by the Dalits, since this word still had a denotation of exclusion. Actually, as Omvedt believes that Gandhi did not mobilize the lower castes and the Untouchables into a well-organized national movement; but the middle class, the bourgeois and upper-caste Indians. They were already controlled by the Congress Party. This conservative consolidation of the Indian national movement has left the masses of the population still immersed in poverty and caste degradation.[1]

The Congress Party was an elite organisation, dominated by Brahman professionals in addition to some upper class merchants. Those people were totally different from the rest of the Indian society by even clothing and language, so they were separated from the masses. Still Gandhi was aware of the fact that, integration of masses into the movement was vital.

In order to close this gap, the Party opened auxiliary branches in towns and villages of India. However, this did not work. Omvedt explains this due to the reality that the problem was not reaching the masses. The problem was the feeling of disturbance of the elite by the integration of masses. Mahatma Gandhi took some measures on behalf of the Untouchables, on his own. One of them was Temple Entry Movement, in which Gandhi declared that he would fast unto death if the trustees of certain temples do not open to the Untouchables.

The anti-caste non-Brahman movement was there since nineteenth century, but the question was brought to issues like temple-entrance allowances, thus Dalits raised their case as preferring the British rule to Brahman one. By 1920s, low and outcastes supported the non-cooperation movement of Gandhi. The symbol of entire Indian people, including downtrodden classes was Gandhi, in this resistance. But then they, the lower classes, shifted from the Congress lines and attacked the landlords by developing their own movement. Omvedt names it as the inability of Gandhi; he could prevent the deepening radicalism between classes and gather them under the common interest. The Dalits interpreted the independence movement as throwing off both the British and the Brahman rule including dominance of landlords.[2]

There is another view explaining that Dr. Ambedkar neither found the term *harijan*, coined by Gandhi, friendly; nor found Mahatma Gandhi in cooperation with them in the case. As far as Gandhi's fast unto death in order to prevent granting Dalits a separate electorate as Muslims, Christians and Sikhs. Gandhi wanted to prevent Untouchables obtaining such rights because in the eyes of Gandhi, the Congress was representing all Indians, where Dalits were no exceptions. Mahatma Gandhi dedicated his life to Hindu-Muslim unity and believed that a separate electorate would bring the Untouchables a distinct nationhood sentiment, which would pave the way to a distinct state and thus to the disintegration of India.[3] One of the principles of Mahatma Gandhi was *sarva dharma sambhava* meaning equality of all religions. Even though the Depressed Classes were deprived of the right to worship, they were considered as Hindus, so they were not benefiting from this understanding of Great Soul. In the eyes of Gandhiji, the Untouchables were factionists, who were breaking the unity among Hindus. Ironically, Dr. Ambedkar owed the same wave length with Gandhi on this issue; he was also a supporter of unity within India and disintegration was the last thing he would desire. Dr. Ambedkar was an opponent to the politics of both Hindu elites and Muslims; because that would break India up. Ambedkar was not willing to divide India and establish a separate *Buddhistan*, rather he wanted a united Indian nation and he cared for the equality within Indian nation. This is why he called for a public conversion.

Ambedkar pointed a problem, which was the general belief that Congress represents all, including Dalits. In one of his writings namely 'What Congress and Gandhi Have Done to the Untouchables' Dr. Ambedkar avows that politics in India has two main facets, which can be indicated as foreign politics and constitutional politics. The foreign politics of India deals with India's freedom exertion from British Imperialism. As for the constitutional politics, Dr. Ambedkar implies the consideration of free India's constitution. These two aspects of Indian politics commonly failed to differentiate, and this could be seen easily by observing the foreigners, who were interested in Indian political affairs. Those foreigners became adherents of the Congress and ignored the parties representing Muslims, non-Brahmins, Dalits. In the eyes of the foreigners, the Congress represented all. For Dr. Ambedkar, the foreigners only saw the solidarity maintained under Congress during the independence struggle against the British colonialism, and they missed the constitutional politics of India. Ambedkar stated that this failure was a result of the position of the Untouchables. The Untouchables left the Congress propaganda unchallenged and maintained silence. The Congress represented all against the common case against the British rule in India. However, as for the constitutional politics, the bases of parties was differentiated. Under constitutional terms, Gandhi's party, Congress did not maintain the sufficient space for the Untouchables. The Congress was engaged with the idea of fighting for freedom, but still this does not ensure that its aim was to constitute democracy in India. While pursuing freedom, the Congress left the Untouchables behind. The Congress was not trying to free the Untouchables, from the social, economic and political cage that they were put in. Ambedkar stresse that most of the notions were fallacious and misleading. For instance there was a distinction between the freedom of a country and the freedom of the people in the country. The freedom of a nation was the focus, nevertheless the nation, which was a unit politically, was divided into classes, socially and people of a class were not promised the same freedom.

Ambedkar's Views on the Ruler and the Ruled Pattern

The parliamentary democracy in India has problems. In principle, parliamentary democracy promises equality, freedom in return of some duties. To ensure this, a system is formed where people are voiced in legislature, the decisions taken by the legislature are enforced by the executive and justice controls the legality of the operations under legislature and executive. Still this system does not function well in India. Normally, equal adult suffrage is a *sine qua non* of parliamentary democracies. Nonetheless, the political system in India has failed to assure to the masses the right to liberty, property or the pursuit of happiness, consequently wrong ideology and wrong organisation from the beginning, as Ambedkar articulates. The wrong ideology is omitting the social and economic democracy. Those two are missed, because liberty swallowed equality in India. Typically, in organisation of democracies there are two main groups, rulers and the ruled. The rulers spring out among the lines of ruled and become rulers. This is not the case in India. The rulers are fixed and the ruled people never take place among rulers. This indicates that government of people is never formed in India. Ambedkar counts seven universal reasons for this situation, and he conveys those points as threats towards democracy.

First is, all through the history, there has always been a struggle of power between rulers and the ruled. Secondly, rulers find it easy to dominate over ruled by the status prestige and power they hold. The third is, neither the regular elections nor the equal adult suffrage prevents preceding rulers to reach the rank they held, but they keep it. The fourth is, the ruled has a constant belief that they will always remain as the ruled and the present rulers are the natural leaders, who are going to linger as leaders for ever. The fifth thing is the incompatibility of a governing class with democracy, there should not be a governing class, but people elected among ruled should be rulers for a certain period. Sixthly, a constitution offering an adult suffrage is not adequate to make self-government and democracy real. The important thing is to capture the power of the preceding governing class to keep the power to govern. The last point is, in some countries bearing parliamentary democracy, adult suffrage is not sufficient to incorporate the masses to the governance, but also other factors are needed. So, the Congress did not remove the governing class, rather Congress left it as a governing body for ever. By leaving the down classes aside from the political system, the governing body made itself invincible. So the Congress fought for the freedom of the governing class, according to Ambedkar. Moreover, the freedom fight of Congress was not to create a free and democratic India, but to restore the ancient social, political and economic systems once again.

Ambedkar marks that the ruling class in India is definite and they are the Brahmins, even though from outside people think that it is decided via elections. Brahmins are the ruling class by birth as far as they are considered to be *Bhudevas*, which means gods on earth. High or less, majority of the Hindus gather under the belief that a Brahmin is regarded sacred. It is a well established ancient belief. In earlier times Brahmins were immune to punishement, even if they committed a murder, due to their sacredness. Besides having natural governing leaders, the second challenge to the system is the controversy between the Congress and the Untouchables, because of the Congress Untouchables remained an unattached component of India's national, religious, social, economic and political life. The Congress is dominated by the Hindus. The Untouchables are Hindus in territorial sense, as inhabitants of Hindustan, but not in religious sense. The Untouchables are deprived of hearing the holy texts, entering the temples, going to the same places of pilgrimage and reputing the same totems sacred. So, Untouchables and Hindus are not participating in the same prayer. They are isolated from each other to the maximum and even the shadow of an Untouchable never intersects with a Hindu's. According to Dr. Ambedkar, even though they are Hindu's, still they are distinct from each other.

Ambedkar's Perception on Uniting Social Groups

Ambedkar strictly opposes the idea uniting social groups under religious terms and he asserts that, if it was a true path to define social groups, then there would be a united European society, with no Italians Germans, British, etc. Still, religions do not coincide with social groups in India, like in the example of Sikhs and the Untouchables, because the only difference among them is faith, but they are socially united because they marry each other, they live in the same places and even while a son of a family is a Sikh the other may be a Hindu. However, for instance Untouchables do not dine with Brahmins. Ambedkar concludes that Hinduism and social unity are incompatible and Hinduism is the greatest obstacle to Hindu unity.

Separate Social Group Issue: Ambedkar accuses the Congress of not accepting the Untouchables as a separate body. By considering the Untouchables as affiliates of the same social unit they belong, they keep the Untouchables under their domination. When they accept that they are separate from Hindus, then they will have to share governmental positions with the Untouchables. A separation between two groups brings political recognition question. When the Untouchables are recognized, then also constitutional safeguards will be needed to protect them against the autocracy of genuine Hindus, as maintained by Dr. Ambedkar. In framing the constitution of the European constitutions, social groups are not taken into account; however, in India it is compulsory. This is because these groups in India are anti-social. Some of the groups in the mentioned lands are non-social, but non-social nature of a social group does not make it essential to be recognized in the constitution. The castes are antisocial in India. Especially the relation among four castes and the Untouchables is anti-social.

When the Untouchables are not recognized in the constitution, then they will be deprived of relentless amount of human rights; from travelling in the same compartment with members of any caste to wearing jewellery or bearing land. This is why the Untouchables need constitutional safeguards. The mentioned safeguards were listed by the Untouchables in Resolutions passed by the Working Committee of the All-India Scheduled Castes Federation in Appendix XI as (i) Guaranteed minimum representation in the Legislature; (ii) guaranteed minimum representation in the Executive and (iii) guaranteed minimum representation in the Public Services.[4] Ambedkar demarcated the aims of those guarantees as to prevent the Untouchables being pressured by the Hindu majority. Ambedkar does not find the optimist claims of the Congress members accurate.

The Congress alleges that the institution of Untouchability vanishes, so no need to give the Untouchables a different status than Hindus. While on one side Dr. Ambedkar hopes it to be true, on the other he wants to guarantee the destruction of this institution by constitutional terms. Moreover, the view of Ambedkar about the Untouchability vanishing is slightly different from the view of the Congress. As a touch-me-not-ism, Untouchability vanishes, but they are still socially segregated. What is vanishing is only one aspect of Untouchability, for Ambedkar. The Untouchability is not only a religious but also an economic system. This system allows upper castes to exploit Untouchables. Thus, it makes hard for *varna* affiliates to be disposed of such economic comfort.

Still, providing separate electorates for the Untouchables is also not a solution for Ambedkar. Even though, by the separate electorates the Untouchables would be able to send own representors to the parliament, as far as Hindus vote for Hindus and Untouchables vote for Untouchables, a social unity cannot be obtained. Ambedkar utters that; such a situation would not make Untouchables happy. They are after a social unity and an atmosphere of independence in all terms of economy, political and social, at the same time.

Gandhi and Ambedkar: A Study in Leadership

The Constituent Assembly of independent India passed a provision legally abolishing untouchability on 29 November 1948, nine months after the death of Mahatma Gandhi. As the measure was approved, the house resounded with cries of *Mahatma Gandhi Ki Jai-victory* to Mahatma Gandhi—a tribute to Gandhi's thirty-year effort to remove the practice of untouchability from Indian society. Present at that session of the Constituent Assembly as chairman of the drafting committee for the constitution was Dr. B.R. Ambedkar, an Untouchable. Three years before, he had ended his book *What Congress and Gandhi Have Done to the Untouchables* with the bitter words, "The Untouchables . . . have ground to say: 'Good God! Is this man Gandhi our Saviour?'"

The irony of the moment was lost on those present—a legalistic measure was taken in the name of Gandhi who had no use for legalism, coupled with the lack of recognition for Ambedkar, the Untouchable who had drafted the measure and who had bitterly fought Gandhi to secure legalistic solutions to the problem of untouchability. The amalgamation of the two approaches to the problem in that moment, however, does symbolize India's continuing attempt to synthesize the ways of Gandhi and Ambedkar in efforts to remove the stigma of untouchability from democratic national life.

Both Mohandas K. Gandhi and Bhimrao Ramji Ambedkar are known, to different groups, as the "saviour of the Untouchables". Gandhi was a caste Hindu, the "Father of Independence" who is said to have spoken and written more on untouchability than on any other subject. Gandhi publicly put the abolition of untouchability, along with Hindu-Muslim unity, as the essential prerequisite for India's true independence. He also made popular the term "Harijan" (children of God) for the Untouchables. Ambedkar was the most highly educated Untouchable in India, recognized by many as the Untouchables' chief spokesman, the founder of a political party for Untouchables, and the moving spirit behind organizations, schools, and colleges established for their uplift. One of Ambedkar's final acts was the initiation of a Buddhist conversion movement that ultimately attracted more than 3 million Untouchable adherents. On the day after Ambedkar's death, Nehru described him as "a symbol of the revolt against all the oppressive features of Hindu society" *(New York Times,* 6 December 1956).

Despite their common concern, Ambedkar and Gandhi were often at odds in their programs for the abolition of untouchability. In 1932 Gandhi thwarted Ambedkar's attempt to gain political concessions from the British, concessions that Ambedkar believed to be essential for the Untouchables' progress. Ambedkar retaliated by criticizing Gandhi more harshly than he did the orthodox Hindus who upheld untouchability as a religious essential. The conflict between these leaders is examined below in terms of their ideological differences and the different solutions which they advocated for the resolution of one of India's major social problems.

Gandhi may be described as a dominant group leader working for a national goal who was concerned, both from a moral standpoint and from a realization of the need for unity, about injustices to a low status group within the nation. Ambedkar's correlative role was that of the militant leader of a politically conscious segment of the same depressed group. Seen in this light, the conflict between these two men has some parallels with certain aspects of the Black Power movement versus "White Liberals" in America of the 1960s.

The Indian situation, however, included several unique elements in that the leadership of the majority and minority groups represented, in simplistic terms, idealistic Hindu traditionalism and Western-influenced modernism. The Indian scene was also marked by a society-wide hierarchical system of social groups justified by religion; by the presence of other vocal minorities, especially that of the Muslims; and by the administrative power of still another group, the British government in India.

This study is concerned with the interaction of Gandhi and Ambedkar in the Indian milieu, more specifically with Ambedkar's standpoint of Gandhi's policies and actions. Although a view from Ambedkar's standpoint of Gandhi's efforts to eradicate untouchability distorts the Mahatma's role in Indian history, this perspective, taken together with the abundance of literature on Gandhi, reveals a lesser known aspect of the Untouchables' role in contemporary India.

Before discussing Gandhi's actions and Ambedkar's reactions to them, it would be well to look at the background and ideology of each of them. Gandhi's statements on untouchability have been collected in several small volumes: *Caste Must Go; All are Equal in the Eyes of God; None High: None Low; The Bleeding Wound!; My Soul's Agony; My Var-nashrama Dharma; The Removal of Untouchability,* and others, which draw chiefly from his two newspapers, *Young India* and *Harijan.* Descriptions of his work, which sometimes included private asides as well as public pronouncements, have been written by his close associates about the Vaikam Satyagraha, his experiences at the Round Table Conference in London, his Communal Award fast[3] and the 1930s anti-untouchability campaign. Material on Gandhi has been taken from these works and the two other sympathetic but frank accounts of Tendulkar,[5] and Desai.[6]

Ambedkar's underlying beliefs and aims have been derived from his writings on caste,[7] his testimony to various British commissions, biographies in English[8] and Marathi,[9] and other observations of his life.

Mohandas Karamchand Gandhi (1869-1948)

At the beginning of his autobiography Gandhi identifies his caste as Bania (merchant) and states that for three generations his forefathers had not practiced the caste occupation, but had served as prime ministers in several princely states of the Kathiawad peninsula (now Gujarat). This was, and is, an essentially conservative region in its adherence to traditional patterns of social relations. Hindu and Jain merchant groups constitute an influential segment of the population. Vaishya, or Bania, castes are third in the traditional four-fold division of Hindu society, included with Brahman and Kshatriya among the twice-born. However, in Gujarat, probably more than in any other part of India, Banias are without peer in wealth, influence and piety. They tend toward orthodoxy. Gandhi's *jati,* the Modh Banias, outcasted him in 1888 upon hearing of his proposed trip to London for higher studies, and evidently never rescinded the proscription.

Gandhi's autobiography, which covers his life up to 1921, when he was fifty-two, contains only a few references to

Untouchables or untouchability. The most striking reference is the story of his insistence on the admission of an Untouchable family to the *ashram* he had established near Ahmedabad in 1915. At the time of his assumption of leadership of the Indian National Congress in 1920, Gandhi made what seemed to be his first strong public statement on untouchability. They reflect his dual role as Mahatma and politician in Indian life, already apparent at that time. As politician, Gandhi said: "Swaraj is as unattainable without the removal of the sin of untouchability as it is without Hindu-Muslim unity" *(Young India,* 29 December 1920). As Mahatma Gandhi said: "I do not want to be reborn. But if I have to be reborn, I should be born an Untouchable...." *(Young India,* 27 April 1921). As both Mahatma and politician, Gandhi sought to weave the divergent interests in India into a unified opposition to the British, at the same time trying to pursue a course of reform without rending the social fabric of Indian society. In Dalton's words, "Indian society saw Gandhi, and Gandhi regarded himself, as occupying the peculiar position of a figure above the discord around him, and uniquely capable of harmonizing it".[10]

Gandhi inherited the Congress position on untouchability first recorded in a resolution in 1917 which urged "upon the people of India the necessity, justice, and righteousness of removing all disabilities imposed upon the Depressed Classes".[11] The Congress resolution seems to have been made in response to a meeting of the Depressed Classes in Bombay earlier in 1917 which asked for such a resolution, in almost the same wording, in exchange for support of the 1916 Congress-Muslim League constitutional scheme.[12] Gandhi's contribution to the position was to personalize it. Volunteers for the Non-cooperation Campaign in 1921 signed a pledge which placed responsibility on the individual: "As a Hindu I believe in the justice and necessity of removing the evil of untouchability and shall on all possible occasions seek personal contact with and endeavor to render service to the submerged classes".[13] This emphasis on the caste Hindu's obligations to the Untouchables remained a major tenet of Gandhi's teaching.

Gandhi's statements on the evil of untouchability were unequivocal from the first, although his views regarding other caste-based practices changed and grew less orthodox, with the years. In 1920 he voiced moderate opposition to social intercourse between castes which some reformers advocated: "Interdrinking, interdining, intermarrying ... are not essential for the promotion of the spirit of democracy" (*Young India,* 8 December 1920). Twenty-six years later, he said, "If I had my way I would persuade all caste Hindu girls coming under my influence to select Harijan husbands" (*Harijan,* 7 July 1946). Underlying Gandhi's change in attitude toward social practices was an unchanging belief in *varnashramadharma,* the divinely ordained division of society into four groups defined according to duty: Brahman, Kshatriya, Vaishya, Shudra. Although Gandhi castigated the contemporary Indian caste system with its superior and inferior divisions, he held to the end a belief in the traditional ordering of society for the preservation of harmony and the growth of the soul, and with it, traditional duties. "The Law of Varna prescribes that a person should, for his living, follow the lawful occupation of his forefathers", but with the understanding that all occupations are equally honorable: "A scavenger has the same status as a *Brahmin"* (*Young India,* 17 November 1927).

According to Gandhi, untouchability had no part in this divine ordering—the treatment of castes below the Shudra level as unclean was not only inhumane, but harmful to Hinduism. Gandhi described it at various times as a curse, an excresence on Hinduism, a poison, a snake, a canker, a hydra-headed monster, a great blot, a device of Satan, a hideous untruth, Dyerism and O'Dyerism, and the bar sinister. An Untouchable, wrote Gandhi, "should be regarded as a *Shudra* because there is no warrant for belief in a fifth caste" (*Young India,* 23 April 1925). While Shudras were created to serve the other three castes, their work was honorable. All varnas possess equality of status, but not equality of opportunity. "One born a scavenger must earn his livelihood by being a scavenger, and then do whatever else he likes. For a scavenger is as worthy of his hire as a lawyer or your President. That, according to me, is Hinduism" (*Harijan,* 6 March 1937).

Other early reformers, including Vivekananda and Dayanand Saraswati, espoused a similar conception of the ideal society as one composed of equal, harmoniously integrated Varnas. The belief that untouchability was a perversion of true Hinduism, and a view of the Untouchable as one deserving of Shudra status, was acceptable even to such an orthodox Hindu leader as B.G. Tilak. Shortly before Gandhi's assumption of leadership in the Congress, Tilak wrote, "It is a sin against God to say that a person is untouchable, who is not so to God Himself. . . . Hinduism absorbed the Shudras, can it not also absorb the untouchables?"[14]

With his gift for symbolism, Gandhi selected the Bhangi, a scavenger caste of North India, to represent the problem of untouchability. Gandhi's abhorrence of untouchability, and his association of such practices with the sweeper caste, appear rooted in childhood experience. Although not mentioned in his autobiography, Gandhi's reactions to his family's sweeper at the age of twelve are recorded in an article that he wrote in *Young India,* 21 April 1921.

A scavenger named Uka, an "untouchable", used to attend our house for cleaning latrines. Often I would ask my mother why it was wrong to touch him. If I accidentally touched Uka, I was asked to perform ablutions, and though I naturally obeyed, it was not without smilingly protesting that it should be so. I was a very dutiful and obedient child, and so far as it was consistent with respect for parents, I often had tussles with them on this matter. I told my mother that she was entirely wrong in considering contact with Uka as sinful.

Uka remained the symbol for Untouchables in Gandhi's mind. Scavenging and the Bhangi figure prominently in many of Gandhi's pronouncements and actions. He himself cleared a dirty latrine at the Calcutta Congress of 1901 and records it in his autobiography. He often used the metaphor of the mother's cleansing work for her child as a counterpart to the Bhangi's work for society. Sanitation work at Gandhi's ashrams was done by all members as a means for demonstrating the honorable nature of these essential duties. In later years Gandhi sometimes stayed in suitably cleaned Bhangi colonies. During the last days of his life, Gandhi even declared: "would rejoice to think that we had a sweeper girl of a stout heart, incorruptible and of crystal purity to be our first President... assisted in the discharge of her duties by a person like Pandit Nehru".[15]

Although Gandhi was not the first to cry out against untouchability, he was the most prominent caste Hindu to proclaim that it was harmful to Hinduism, to make its removal a personal responsibility of the caste Hindu, to keep it before the public eye with passionate oratory and vivid imagery, and to found an organization for service to Untouchables. Perhaps as important as his ideology and his pronouncements was his personal example, from the beginning, of touching the Untouchable.

Bhimrao Ramji Ambedkar (1891-1956)

Ambedkar came from Western India, as did Gandhi, and was a London-trained barrister, as was Gandhi, but his caste, social background, and intellectual environment were very different. He was a Mahar, the largest Untouchable caste in the area now called Maharashtra, where this group constitutes about 10 per cent of the population. The Mahars were, in British administrative parlance, "inferior village servants", whose traditional duties involved the maintenance of streets, walls and cremation grounds, carrying messages, hauling away dead cattle, and similar menial and polluting tasks. However, the Mahars were not responsible for the cleaning of latrines or the removal of night soil. This work was and is done by Bhangis from North India and by Gujarati Untouchable migrants. During the nineteenth and early twentieth centuries, a substantial number of Mahars removed themselves from their traditional village servant role.

The establishment of British rule in Bombay Presidency provided Mahars with the opportunity for service in the army, employment in cotton mills, ammunition factories, railroads, dockyards, construction work, and as servants in British homes. The 1921 Census records that only 13.5 per cent of the Mahar working force of nearly 300,000 were employed in their traditional occupation even though most Mahars maintained strong ties with their ancestral village. The emergence of Mahar leaders and a new spirit of militancy in the nineteenth century was due in large measure to the influence of education acquired in the army[16] and in domestic service. In the twentieth century, leaders also emerged from the ranks of primary school teachers. Early efforts to legitimize Mahar claims to higher status were based on the assertion that their ancestors were of the Kshatriya varna (warrior class), a claim not uncommon among Untouchables elsewhere in India. This claim was advanced in petitions submitted to the British in the 1890s to protest the closing of Mahar enlistment in the army. Although army recruitment of Mahars was stopped at about the time of Ambedkar's birth in 1891, his father and grandfather served in the army, and his early education and environment were those of a child in army cantonment schools and pensioned soldiers' colonies. Despite this background, Ambedkar differed from previous Mahar leaders in that he never claimed high caste status for Untouchables, since such claims implied an acceptance of upper caste superiority, nor did he invoke another common claim-that Untouchables were pre-Aryan, the original settlers of the land. While Untouchables in Madras and the Punjab were to base their demands for separate political status on a claim to pre-Aryan origin, Ambedkar argued that the Untouchables' position in Indian society was of social, not racial, origin and therefore subject to change.

Ambedkar's views as to the origin of untouchability are presented in *The Untouchables* published in 1948, late in his political career. According to the account presented here, untouchability originated in the practices of separation and denigration imposed on those who remained Buddhists during an earlier period of renascent Hinduism. Despite the repressive role attributed to Hindus, Ambedkar's attitude toward Hinduism remained ambivalent for much of his life. In the early 1920s he participated in efforts at "Sanskritization" in which Untouchables imitated high caste religious ritual. But he soon found that the performance of Vedic style weddings, the donning of the sacred thread, and similar efforts to emulate upper caste ritual practice had little effect on the attitudes of others. Such innovations were dropped in the 1930s. However, from 1927 to

1935 Ambedkar helped organize campaigns to force the opening of Hindu temples to Untouchables. This also proved to be ineffective and in 1935 Ambedkar decided to reject all claims to Hinduism and to convert to another religion. At about this time, he presented in *The Annihilation of Caste* a list of reforms for Hinduism that appear naive and legalistic, based on abstractions rather than possibilities. The cardinal reforms listed were: there should be one standard book of the Hindu religion, acceptable to all Hindus; priests should receive their office not by heredity but by state examination; priests should be limited in number by law and should be subject to disciplinary action by the state.[17] Ambedkar's final resolution of the Untouchables' religious dilemma was adopted in 1956 when he converted to Buddhism in an attempt to link the Untouchables to the greatness of India's past while denying the contemporary concept of caste. This solution was in keeping with Ambedkar's pride in India's culture, a theme that appears intermittently throughout his writings, and his admiration of such religious reformers as the Buddha, Kabir, and Mahatma Phule.

Although Ambedkar experienced discrimination and humiliation during his youth, the Maharashtrian atmosphere of reform allowed him exceptional opportunities for education and later for leadership. As a bright Untouchable boy, and later as an educated, militant Untouchable leader, he was aided by caste Hindu reformers. The Gaikwad of Baroda, whose financial contributions to reformers and educators in Bombay Presidency were of considerable consequence, gave Ambedkar a stipend during his college days as part of the Baroda policy of educating Untouchables. Later the Gaikwad helped Ambedkar to go abroad for further education, and he obtained an M.A. and Ph.D. from Columbia University in New York, a D.Sc. from London University, and entrance to the Bar from Grey's Inn, London. Ambedkar returned to Bombay in 1923 to begin his organizational work among Untouchables, and soon came into close association with caste Hindus who encouraged his leadership. Many of his closest associates were high caste Hindus and they formed his intellectual circle at a time when there was no other Mahar who shared his intellectual interests. Caste Hindus also worked on the staff of Ambedkar's newspapers and labour unions, formed an inter-dining group of which he was president, taught in his educational establishments, and in 1936 they helped form his first political party, the Independent Labour Party. It was a Brahman, G.N. Sahasrabudhe, who backed Ambedkar in one of his most dramatic rejections of Hindu orthodoxy, the burning of the ancient law book, *Manusmriti,* in 1927 as a protest against traditional caste restrictions.

Ambedkar, therefore, did not find Gandhi's condemnation of untouchability radical; he was in close touch with reformers who not only condemned untouchability, but the Varna concept of caste as well, and who accepted his leadership in determining solutions to the problem. Not only as a highly educated Untouchable to whom pity was anathema, but also as a Maharashtrian reformer, Ambedkar found Gandhi's general ideology unappealing. Ram Joshi's later evaluation of the Maharashtrian urban intelligentsia's attitude toward Gandhian reform describes the milieu in which Ambedkar worked :

> They disdained Gandhi's traditional outlook and modes of behaviour .... They considered his philosophy outdated and rejected his programme, which was based primarily on a concern for the rural masses .... In any case, they had no interest in a ... drab reform programme which could neither stimulate their intellect nor excite them to revolutionary action.[18]

Ambedkar's programs were intended to integrate the Untouchable into Indian society in modern, not traditional ways, and on as high a level as possible. This goal stood in marked contrast to Gandhi's "Ideal Bhangi" *(Harijan,* 23 November 1936) who would continue to do sanitation work even though his status would equal that of a Brahman. Ambedkar's ideal for the depressed was "to raise their educational standard so that they may know their own conditions, have aspirations to rise to the level of the highest Hindu and be in a position to use political power as a means to that end".[19] Both reformers had a vision of equality, but for Ambedkar, equality meant not equal status of the *Varnas,* but equal social, political, and economic opportunity for all. Ambedkar planned his programs to bring the Untouchable from a state of "dehumanization" and "slavery" into one of equality through the use of modern methods based on education and the exercise of legal and political rights. At the same time, Ambedkar's modernizing ideology was tempered in practice by a clear perception of the tenacity of caste and tradition. He sought to awaken in the Untouchables an awareness of their debased condition and the common interests that would promote the unity needed for the development of effective organizations and mass action. For such reasons, Ambedkar advocated a separatist policy accentuating caste distinctions as an initial stage in creating a society in which identities would be unimportant.

Ambedkar's commitment to education as a major means for Untouchable advancement led him to initiate in the 1920s a program for the creation of hostels for Untouchable students. This effort resulted in the development of a system of colleges organized by the People's Education Society, founded by Ambedkar in 1945. While Ambedkar exhorted numerous conferences of Untouchables to expand their educational opportunities at every level, much of his own effort was aimed at producing highly educated men, capable of raising the image of the Untouchable through their ability to function at the highest level of Indian urban society. He also advocated the abandonment of customs and practices associated with the stereotype of the Untouchable, including the consumption of alcohol and carrion beef. Ambedkar's pronouncements on the need to live clean and moral lives sound very much like Gandhi's. However, Ambedkar's vision of the Untouchable's future role went far beyond that of Gandhi, or indeed that of any other Untouchable leader.

Ambedkar's political policies were developed in the light of India's democratizing political reforms. During his lifetime Ambedkar saw the representation of Untouchables in the Bombay provincial Legislative Council grow from one appointed member (granted in 1921 by the Montagu-Chelmsford reforms) to full-fledged elected representation based on a system of reserved seats. Achievements of this kind, founded on "protective discrimination" and western forms of government, supported Ambedkar's contention that political power must be assured to the Untouchable minority even if separatism was fostered by the granting of such power. This view, coupled with Ambedkar's firm belief in the power of representative political bodies to correct social and economic injustice, underlies many of the issues that arose between Ambedkar and Gandhi. Ambedkar's adaptation of western concepts to the Indian scene is also reflected in the terms he used to justify Untouchable political rights: democracy, fraternity, and liberty. In his Marathi speeches, Ambedkar conveyed the implication of these concepts in a single word, *manuski,* that was readily understood by the most illiterate Mahar villager. Although *manuski's* literal meaning is "human-ness", it serves to evoke feelings of self-respect and human attitudes towards one's fellow men.

In 1946, Gandhi said, "I myself have become a Harijan by choice" *(Harijan,* 9 June 1946). Ambedkar had no choice. His actions were moulded not only by his own personal background and achievements, and the Maharashtrian thinking of his day, but also by his status as an Untouchable. The Untouchable caste he came from had begun social and political movements before he assumed a position of leadership. His contribution was to raise these attempts to a level of such effectiveness that the caste could achieve en masse a religious conversion, build a political party, and greatly increase its participation in education at all levels. Beyond his own caste, Ambedkar helped to shape the vast program of legal rights and safeguards for Untouchables which India developed. He directly influenced some other Untouchable castes through his conversion movement and his political parties, and indirectly affected many more. In his own person, as lawyer, writer, statesman, constitutionalist, he was an example to all India of what an Untouchable could become.

The Vaikam Satyagraha

The Vaikam Satyagraha of 1924-25 in Tranvancore state offered Gandhi his first opportunity to act publicly on behalf of Untouchables and produced Ambedkar's first public comment on Gandhian methods. Gandhi was not the initiator of the campaign to remove the prohibition against Untouchables' use of the roadway passing the temple at Vaikam, but he was in contact with campaign leadership and visited the area during the second year of the satyagraha to negotiate with temple and state officials.[20] The satyagraha for the use of the road was begun by several South Indian caste Hindus, a Syrian Orthodox Christian, and some followers of Sri Narayana Guru, the spiritual leader of a large and comparatively well-to-do Depressed Caste, the Ilavas. Although undoubtedly patterned after the Gandhian satyagraha method and supported by many Gandhians, the satyagraha was also an outgrowth to the Ilavas' own movement to gain political and religious rights. It came in the wake of the Ilavas' 1918 appeal to the Travancore government for the opening of state temples to all Hindus and their 1921 threat to convert in a body to Christianity.

Gandhi's negotiation with a Nambudiri Brahman trustee of the Vaikam temple at the time of the satyagraha, faithfully recorded by his secretary Mahadev Desai[21] shows something of the temper of the orthodox at the time as well as Gandhi's method of persuasion :

> Gandhiji: Is it fair to exclude a whole section of Hindus, because of their supposed lower birth, from public roads which can be used by non-Hindus, by criminals and bad characters, and even by dogs and cattle?
>
> Nambudiri Trustee: But how can it be helped? They are reaping the reward of their karma.
>
> Gandhiji: No doubt they are suffering for their karma by being born as untouchables. But why must you add to the punishment? Are they worse than even criminals and beasts?
>
> Nambudiri Trustee: They must be so, for otherwise God would not condemn them to be born untouchables.
>
> G: But God may punish them. Who are we human beings to take the place of God and add to their punishment?
>
> N: We are instruments. God uses us as His instruments in order to impose on them the punishment that their karma has earned for them.
>
> G: But supposing the Avarnas outside varna, i.e.,

untouchables, said that they were instruments in the hands of God in order to impose afflictions on you? What would you do?

N: Then the Government would stand between them and us and prevent them from doing. Good men would do so. Mahatmaji, we beseech you to prevent Avarnas from depriving us of our old privileges.

After a thorough discussion of the religious authority behind the prohibition against the Untouchables' use of the road, Gandhi made a last proposal: "Would you accept arbitration? You appoint a Pandit on behalf of the Satyagrahis, and the Dewan acts as Umpire. What do you say to that?" No reply was recorded. Although the temple authorities finally capitulated and the road past the temple was open to all (or moved farther away from the temple—the denouncement of the satyagraha is not clear), Untouchables were not allowed to enter the temple until 1936. At that time, coincident with another Ilavas threat to convert to Christianity, Travancore became one of the first states to enact a law opening its state temples to Untouchables.

Although the Vaikam satyagraha represents the only time Gandhi used non-violent direct action on behalf of Untouchables' rights, it foreshadowed many aspects of subsequent Gandhian activity, stress on the orthodox Hindus' inhumane treatment of Untouchables, attempts to secure voluntary lifting of the ban by changing the hearts of caste Hindus, and working within a Hindu framework of ideas. The temple trustees' negative response was also typical of later reactions to Gandhi's policies which often elicited bitter criticism from orthodox Hindus.

Ambedkar referred briefly to the Vaikam satyagraha in a speech that he delivered in 1924 to a provincial conference of the Depressed Classes. It was his first large public meeting after the completion of the London phase of his education, and also the founding meeting of his first organization, the Bahishkrit Hitakarini Sabha (Organization for the Welfare of the Excluded). At this time, however, Ambedkar spoke against conversion to another religion as a means of removing disabilities, and he stressed self-improvement, unity, and organization as the paths to a better life for Untouchables. He used the Vaikam satyagraha with its high caste participants as an example, not of caste Hindu sympathies, but of the political importance of the Untouchable :

> If we remain Hindus as we are, then the Aryan religion will persevere in this country. On the other hand, if we become Muslim, then there well be a predominance of that foreign culture in India. If this were not so, the Brahmans would not have been ready to offer satyagraha for the untouchable class at Vaikam.

Ambedkar's Analysis

The following year the Bombay province Depressed Classes Conference, again with Ambedkar as president, heard Ambedkar present a more detailed analysis of the Vaikam satyagraha, which Gandhi had then joined. The address as a whole was still conciliatory in tone and more emphatic on internal reform than on changing Indian society, but there was no wholehearted support for Gandhi. Although Ambedkar stated that for Untouchables "the most important event in the country today is the satyagraha at Vaikam," he pointed out that after a whole year of protest there had been no result. He next spoke of Gandhi :

> Before Mahatma Gandhi, no politician in this country maintained that it is necessary to remove social injustice here in order to do away with tension and conflict, and that every Indian should consider it his sacred duty to do so.... However, if one looks more closely one finds that there is a slight disharmony... for he does not insist on the removal of untouchability as much as he insists on the propagation of Khaddar [home-spun cloth] or Hindu-Muslim unity. If he had he would have made the removal of untouchability a precondition of voting in the party. Well, be that as it may, when one is spurned by everyone, even the sympathy shown by Mahatma Gandhi is of no little importance.

Ambedkar went on to note that the orthodox Brahmans at Vaikam had used scripture to justify their position to Gandhi :

> This clearly indicates that either we should burn all these scriptures or verify and examine the validity of their rules

regarding untouchability...and if we are unable to prove their falseness or invalidity, we are to suffer untouchability till the end of time! . .. Truly these scriptures are an insult to people. The government should have confiscated them long ago.[22]

Although Ambedkar did not completely reject Gandhi's support until their political battle over Depressed Class political rights in 1931, two remarks in the 1925 address portend his later actions. His scathing comment on Hindu scriptures culminated in a public burning of *Manusmriti* in 1927, and in 1935 Ambedkar announced his vow to leave Hinduism entirely and to convert to some other religion. Ambedkar's complaint that Gandhi had not required an oath of disbelief in untouchability as a precondition for membership in the Congress later turned to a wholesale condemnation of the Congress resolutions on the subject as hypocrisy.

Mahar Satyagraha

Before Ambedkar's rejection of Hinduism in 1935, the Mahars made several attempts to gain religious and social rights by using the Gandhian technique of satyagraha, mass action without violence. A Depressed Classes conference was held in Mahad in 1927. During the course of that conference, a group of several thousand moved en masse to a tank in the Brahman section of the town, where the leaders of the procession stopped and drank water. After the conference, the tank was ritually purified by the townspeople. Later in the year Ambedkar called another conference in Mahad to reiterate the Untouchables' right to use the public water supply. It was at this second conference that the *Manusmriti* was publicly burned. This radical gesture was balanced by Ambedkar's decision to comply with a court injunction prohibiting further satyagraha for water rights. He preferred to fight a ten-year court case, which he won, rather than take to the streets again. In spite of the long delay in the resolution of this issue, the Mahars look upon the Mahad satyagraha as the beginning of their political awakening. The spirit and unity demonstrated in that first mass action became a Mahar legend. Some caste Hindus attended the conferences, but the burning of *Manusmriti* cost Ambedkar the approval of all but the most radical of his caste Hindu supporters.

The second Mahar satyagraha was initiated in 1929 in an attempt to gain entry to the Parvati Temple in Pune. This effort was also conducted in the Gandhian style, but it was approved by Gandhi or the Congress. Untouchables from several castes led by a Mahar from Pune together with some Maratha and Brahman sympathizers joined in a four-month attempt to enter the gates of the complex on Parvati Hill. A song written by a Mahar for the satyagraha related that the marchers climbed the steps to the temple gates shouting the names of Lord Shankar, Shivaji Maharaj, Chokhamela and Dr. Ambedkar.[23] Gandhi's name was not mentioned, but the technique and inspiration for the satyagraha undoubtedly were drawn from Gandhi's teachings. Although Ambedkar's name was shouted by the marchers, he was not present.

The Anti-Untouchability Sub-Committee created by the Congress in March 1929 investigated the satyagraha. The committee, which included the Hindu Mahasabha leader Pandit M.M. Malviya and Jamnalal Bajaj, a Marwari businessman from Wardha who had built a Temple for Untouchables in his home district, expressed their disapproval of the satyagraha and recommended that the Congress should not support it. According to their report,[24] half a dozen temples had already been opened; negotiations with the temple trustees were being upset by the "atmosphere of bitterness and distrust" created by the satyagraha; and the "Bombay untouchable leaders... did not make too much of a fetish of non-violence." The latter criticism is inconsistent with another statement in the report that the Pune satyagraha observed "exemplary non-violence" in the face of attack.

Although there was no direct confrontation between Ambedkar and Gandhi on this issue, the failure of the satyagraha (Parvati Temple was not open to Untouchables until India's independence in 1947) and the lack of Congress support in an action performed according to Gandhian principles increased the distrust on the part of Ambedkar and his followers for the Congress and Gandhi. The last of the Mahar satyagrahas, held from 1930 to 1935 at Nasik, widened the breach.

The Kala Ram Satyagraha

This largest and longest satyagraha effort took place at the Kala Ram Temple in the important pilgrimage center of Nasik. Organized by Ambedkar and the local Mahar leaders, the Kala Ram Satyagraha involved thousands of Untouchables in intermittent efforts to enter the temple and to participate in the annual temple procession. As in the case of the Parvati satyagraha in Pune the attempt was unsuccessful. Here, too, opposition came not only from the orthodox Hindus but also from some local Congressmen. The outcome of the Kala Ram satyagraha, however, was not only further disillusionment with the satyagraha method and the attitude of the Congress, but also a rejection of Hinduism and a strengthening of the separatist political stance then developing among Untouchables.

In 1930, the first year of the Kala Ram satyagraha, Ambedkar appeared before a large conference of the Depressed Classes at Nagpur. Although he had helped to plan and had encouraged the Nasik satyagraha, he barely mentioned the Untouchables' attempt to enter the Kala Ram temple in his presidential address to the conference. Instead, he dwelt on political matters, Ambedkar had just been designated as one of the two Depressed Class representatives at the Round Table Conference to be held in London, and he stated the position he would present to that august body in its deliberation on the future constitution of India. He held that only *swaraj* (independence) would bring the possibility of equality to the Depressed Classes, a position not before stated by an Untouchable leader. Ambedkar's option for independence, however, contained a proviso. He told his audience that while he agreed with Congressmen who said that no country was good enough to rule over another, he intended to tell the Congress "point blank" that the preposition does not end there and that it is equally true that no class is good enough to rule over another class.[25]

In his Nagpur speech, Ambedkar also indicated that he did not intend to press for a separate electorate for Untouchables, one in which they could vote for their candidates independently of the caste Hindu vote. This position differed from the plea for a separate electorate, similar to that won by the Muslims, advocated in 1928-29 by most of the Depressed Class groups in their testimony to the Simon Commission. Ambedkar, however, did ask for guaranteed rights, including "adequate" representation on all elected political bodies. This more moderate stance was still out of line with the Congress position. In 1928 the Nehru plan for government had rejected the idea of specific guaranteed rights for Untouchables at the same time that it abrogated the 1916 Congress-Muslim League agreement assuring communal representation for Muslims.

Round Table Conferences

At the first Round Table Conference, held in 1930, which no Congressman attended because of the Non-Cooperation Movement, Ambedkar altered his moderate goal. Since his plea for adult suffrage had been rejected by the British, and the Muslim demand for separate electorates appeared unalterable, Ambedkar shifted his position and argued for separate electorates for the Depressed Classes for a ten-year period. Consequently, Ambedkar's political stance with regard to the Congress was stiffened considerably prior to his encounter with Gandhi at the second Round Table Conference held in London in 1931.

At the second Round Table Conference, Ambedkar confronted Gandhi, who not only refused to consider separate electorates for the Depressed Classes but also opposed any form of special representation involving reserved seats. The two men had met for the first time in Bombay just before the second Round Table Conference. Ambedkar's caste Hindu friends had arranged the meeting, but it did not lead to any understanding between the two. Ambedkar felt that he had been treated rudely, and Gandhi said later that he had not known Ambedkar was an Untouchable until the London Conference,[26] which implies that he knew little of Ambedkar's work in Bombay. This unsatisfactory meeting, and the basic disagreement between these leaders on the issue of special representation for Untouchables, made negotiation during the Round Table Conference sessions difficult. The situation was exacerbated by

Gandhi's questioning of Ambedkar's bonafides: "I say that it is not a proper claim which is registered by Dr. Ambedkar when he seeks to speak for the whole of the Untouchables of India.... I myself in my own person claim to represent the vast mass of the Untouchables".[27]

After the third Round Table Conference, during which Gandhi was in jail, the British government announced a decision regarding representation which, it was hoped, would effect a compromise between the Congress and Ambedkar. This communal award of 1932 gave the Depressed Classes a double vote, one in a special constituency for a modest number of reserved seats, and another in the general electorate. Gandhi's response to communal award was to enter a "fast unto death" on 20 September 1932. On the first day of the fast, he wrote in a letter to P.N. Rajbhoj, a Chamar Untouchable from Pune :

> My fast has reference only to separate electorates.... I must say that I am not in love with the idea of Statutory reservation. Whilst it is not open to the same objection that separate electorate is, I have not a shadow of doubt that it will prevent the natural growth for the suppressed classes and will remove the incentive to honourable amends from the suppressors. What I am aiming at is a heart understanding between the two, the greatest opportunity of repentance and reparation on the part of the suppressors. I am certain that the movement is ripe for the change of heart among them. I would therefore favour widest possible franchise for the suppressed and establish a convention between the two sections for securing proper election of representatives of the suppressed.[28]

This seems to be the voice of Gandhi speaking as Mahatma. A somewhat more political motive for Gandhi's protest is indicated in the report of a conversation between Gandhi and Sardar Patel a day after the fast began. Gandhi's secretary, Mahadev Desai, recorded Gandhi's comments :

> The possible consequences of separate electorates for Harijans [this must be Desai's editing—the word Harijan was not yet used by Gandhi] fill me with horror. Separate

> electorates for all other communities will still leave room for me to deal with them, but I have no other means to deal with "untouchables". These poor fellows will ask why I who claim to be their friend should offer Satyagraha simply because they were granted some privileges; they would vote separately but vote with me. They do not realize that the separate electorate will create division among Hindus so much that it will lead to bloodshed. "Untouchable" hooligans will make common cause with Muslim hooligans and kill caste-Hindus. Has the British Government no idea of all this? I do not think so.[29]

The British Government's response to Gandhi's fast was to declare that a solution to the representation of the Depressed Classes had to be settled within the Hindu community. Consequently, the man whose leadership of the Depressed Classes was challenged by Gandhi in London became the arbiter of Gandhi's fate. Ambedkar met with various Hindu leaders under ever-increasing tension as Gandhi's condition worsened. Since reserved seats had been unenthusiastically accepted by Gandhi in the period following his confrontation with Ambedkar in London, the issue was a separate electorate, a cause Ambedkar had adopted only the year before. Ambedkar drove a hard bargain, trading a separate electorate for a separate primary election plus a large increase in the number of seats reserved for Untouchables—from the seventy-eight given in the Communal Award to 148 seats.

Yervada/Poona Pact

In the ensuing years, neither caste Hindus nor Depressed Class politicians were happy about this agreement, called the Yervada or Poona Pact. Caste Hindus, particularly in Bengal, felt that reserved seats of the Depressed Classes unduly diminished the number of legislative seats available to Hindus in areas with a large Muslim population. Depressed Class leaders found the primary system to be expensive and unwieldy, and Ambedkar made at least one futile attempt to change it. Some Depressed Class leaders felt that the Congress did not nominate able and truly representative Depressed Class members for reserved seats. Although the Congress never formally approved the Poona Pact, it became, after the provision for a primary election was abandoned, the basis for all future elections.

The Poona Pact in itself accomplished little more than might have emerged from an earlier compromise, but the dramatic circumstances in which it was forged gave a great deal of publicity to Gandhi's concern for the Untouchable and to Ambedkar's leadership. Both men intensified their efforts to eliminate untouchability during the next two decades, each continuing to follow the line of action already established. Gandhi sought to change the heart of the caste Hindus by moral pressure within the framework of Hindu tradition. Ambedkar continued to work in the fields of education and politics in an attempt to gain legal rights for Untouchables in the secular world.

All India Anti-Untouchability League

Among Gandhi's activities was the organization of a group devoted to the removal of untouchability. Formed in Bombay on 30 September 1932, it was first called the All India Anti-Untouchability League. Pandit Madan Mohan Malviya of the Hindu Mahasabha presided at the first meeting; the industrialist Ghanshyamdas Birla was named president, and the secretary was Amritlal B. Thakkar, a social worker who worked among the tribal peoples. Several Untouchables were on the central board, including M.C. Rajah of Madras, who in 1927 became the first Untouchable to serve in the central legislative assembly, Ambedkar, and Rao Bahadur Srinivasan of Madras. The latter was Ambedkar's fellow delegate to the Round Table Conferences.

Harijan Sevak Sangh

The name of Gandhi's organization was soon changed to the Servants of Untouchables Society. This title was then translated into Hindi as the Harijan Sevak Sangh, using the term Harijan (children of God) adopted by Gandhi as a new appellation for the Untouchable. The purpose of the society was to use peaceful persuasion to secure access for the Depressed Classes to all public wells, roads, schools, temples, and cremation grounds. Social reforms such as inter-dining and other caste-based practices were admittedly outside the scope of the new organization. Gandhi toured 12,500 miles over India from

November 1933 to the end of July 1934, to preach against untouchability and to collect funds for the organization.

Although Ambedkar was a member of the first central board, his connection with Gandhi's organization lasted only a few months. While en route to the third Round Table Conference in 1932, Ambedkar wrote a long letter to the organization's secretary, A.B. Thakkar (a letter that Ambedkar claimed went unanswered), stating that he wanted the Anti-Untouchability League to be concerned primarily with civic rights and equal opportunity in economic matters and social intercourse.[30]

Ambedkar's view of the proposed goals of the League proved to be quite different from that of its founders. Ambedkar soon resigned, and other Untouchable members on the board seem to have disappeared quietly from the scene. In its form as the Harijan Sevak Sangh, the new organization was closed to Untouchable leadership. Gandhi defended this policy in response to criticism by explaining that it was an organization for penitents, for the expiation of the guilt of the caste Hindus. For this reason, Untouchables should advise, but were not to be the main actors.[31]

The years immediately after the Poona Pact were Gandhi's most intense period of work for anti-untouchability, but he failed not only to win the support of Ambedkar, but also to conciliate the orthodox Hindus. They took exception to his program and to his personal actions as well. An article vehemently critical of Gandhi for his temple entry campaign and also for his allowing the marriage of his son to a daughter of C. Rajagopalachari, a Madrasi Brahman, appeared in a Bombay journal, *The Indian Mirror* on 5 August 1933. This article included the accusation, expressed in a poem by Professor J. Mangiah, that Gandhi turned "good" Untouchables into malcontents :

Untouchables our folks are good,
Till Gandhi told them they were Gods
Content they were to faith they stood
To Congress lessons now each nods.

Sardar Patel, always the pragmatic advisor, told Gandhi during the Harijan campaign, "Why have you placed yourself between two stones? I keep telling you not to do so. Let the two stones grind each other. Why must you come in between?[32]

While the orthodox resented Gandhi's use of the word Harijan for Untouchables and rejected Gandhi's attempts at persuasion regarding the temple entry issue, educated Untouchables found the word Harijan patronizing and the results of the temple entry campaigns insignificant. Jagjivan Ram, a rising young Untouchable Congress politician from Bihar, described the Harijan Sevak Sangh as being erroneous in conception, faulty in emphasis, and halting in execution.[33] He addressed a spirited protest to Gandhi when Gandhi asked a Christian missionary to pray for the Harijans but not to try to convert them as they did not have "the mind and intelligence to understand what you talked.... Would you preach the Gospel to a cow?" *(Harijan,* 19 December 1936). Gandhi replied that no ill will was intended; for him the cow was a symbol of gentleness and patient suffering.[34] It was clear, though, that in Gandhi's concept of service to the suffering Untouchables, there was little room for the educated, politically conscious Untouchables pressing for civil rights.

Through the mid-1930s Gandhi continued his labours to exorcize the evil of untouchability by an arduous nine-month Harijan tour, a lengthy fast to purify his soul and to call attention to the existence of the plight of untouchability, and attempts to secure temple entry. During the same period Ambedkar moved farther and farther away from the possibility of cooperating with Gandhi's program based on religious reform or with Congress' political measures.

The Conversion Move

In 1935, Ambedkar announced at Yeola, a town in Maharashtra near the site of the earlier struggle for temple entry at Nasik, that although born a Hindu, he would not die a Hindu. The following year, a conference of Mahars held in Bombay city passed a resolution to disassociate themselves from Hinduism by converting to some other religion. Ambedkar's plan provided that each Untouchable caste was to make its own decision. Although the idea was widely discussed among Untouchables in North India and in Travancore in the south, no caste other than the Mahars committed itself to leaving Hinduism en masse. The Mahars, however, did not implement their decision even though Christian, Muslim and Sikh religious leaders announced themselves ready to receive Untouchable converts. Ambedkar's 1935 conversion speech and the Mahar response to it bore every evidence of sincerity, but none of the existing religions satisfied Ambedkar's criteria. Islam and Christianity were evidently disqualified because they were foreign and not Indian in origin. Sikhism was seriously considered, but there was no guarantee that the hard-won political rights of the Untouchables would be continued if they became Sikhs. Although Ambedkar was already attracted to the Buddhist past, there were no effective Buddhist organizations in India and little of the interest in Buddhism that was to appear in post-independence India.

The decision to convert may also have been postponed because of Ambedkar's intense political and administrative activity during the following decade. In 1937, his newly formed Independent Labour Party backed fourteen Scheduled Caste candidates for reserved seats and four caste Hindus for general seats in the Bombay Legislative Assembly. The party won eleven reserved and three general seats. (Two of the defeated candidates had contested seats in the area where the Mahad satyagraha had taken place ten years before.) Although Ambedkar's party was successful in the election, its position as a small minority in a Congress-dominated assembly was very weak. The party was rarely successful in its areas of concern, chiefly labour and agricultural policies. In 1942, Ambedkar reformulated his political plans.

The Scheduled Castes Federation

He formed a new party, the Scheduled Castes Federation, and limited it to Untouchables in the hope of uniting all Untouchables in a new battle for political power. Ambedkar had been selected the same year to serve as the Member for Labour on the Viceroy's Executive Council, a post which gave him considerable power in formulating policy and granting patronage, but kept him from spending much time on party organization. His energies were devoted to administration on the highest governmental level and to writing a series of books on national problems and the position of the Untouchable.

It was during this period of the mid-I940s that Ambedkar launched his most vitriolic attacks on Gandhi. Ambedkar's personal political success, and the recognition accorded him as an able administrator, did little to assuage his anger. Although he recognized that the prospects for the Depressed Classes had been improved through the extension of educational opportunities and the reservation of government jobs, he was acutely conscious of the continuing disabilities that affected most Untouchables. Ambedkar's criticism was not of the orthodox Hindu, whom he had given up years before as hopeless, but of Gandhi and the Congress-those who would inherit political power in the impending withdrawal of British rule.

What Congress and Gandhi Have Done to Untouchables, first published in1945, contains Ambedkar's most impassioned criticism. It is basically a plea for a separate electorate for the Untouchable. Public statements, voting records, and numerous incidents showing the isolation and maltreatment of Untouchables are presented to support the contention that political separation from the Hindus in the electoral system is necessary for the attainment of Untouchable political rights. An indictment of Gandhian philosophy and action is a major theme of the book. The Harijan Sevak Sangh is held to be a political charity, intended to bring Untouchables into the Congress camp. The temple entry campaign is criticized for its lack of success and the turning off and on of this issue to further Congress political interests. The *Varnashramadharma* scheme is described as an unnatural ordering of society, impracticable and inhumane in its allocation of occupations by heredity. Gandhi's idea of ennobling the scavenging profession is viewed as "an outrage and a cruel joke". In many ways Ambedkar's reaction parallels current Black criticism of Lincoln's resolution of the problem of balancing the interest of a depressed minority against the need to foster national unity. According to

Ambedkar, "Mr. Gandhi's attitude is that let Swaraj perish if the cost of it is political freedom of the Untouchables".[35]

However, Ambedkar's words appear to have exerted little influence on the British. The Cripps Cabinet Mission, sent to India in 1946 to arrange the transfer of power to Indian hands, was more influenced by the failure of the Scheduled Castes Federation in the 1946 elections. Consequently, the British provided no special political rights for the Untouchables beyond reserved seats in the legislatures. Ambedkar's response to the Cripps proposal was to launch huge satyagraha demonstrations before the state legislatures at Pune, Nagpur, Lucknow, and in the industrial city of Kanpur from July to October 1946. This effort failed to move the planners of India's future.

After 1947

The creation of Pakistan in 1947 stilled the Muslims' demand for a separate electorate and eliminated the possibility that the Scheduled Castes might obtain such an award. Although Ambedkar's major effort on behalf of his community failed, his role as a national leader was recognized and enhanced by his election to the Constituent Assembly. Initially elected to this body in 1946 through the cooperative efforts of the Scheduled Castes and Muslim League in Bengal, after the partition of Bengal in 1947 he was continued in the same position by the Congress of Bombay — evidently as a gesture of goodwill. In August 1947, Ambedkar was named Law Minister in the first cabinet of independent India, while retaining his position as chairman of the committee responsible for drafting a constitution of the new nation.

The first years following Independence were a period of cooperation between politically conscious Untouchables and Congress Hindus. Ambedkar skilfully piloted the constitution through the Constituent Assembly. In doing so, he relinquished some of his radical ideas, such as the nationalization of agriculture, in order to create a constitution based on consensus. However, the refusal of the Congress leaders to support Ambedkar's Hindu Code Bill led him to resign from the cabinet in 1951. His resignation statement indicated frustration over Nehru's domineering leadership as well as India's treatment of Untouchables.

In the last years of his life Ambedkar devoted himself chiefly to his interest in Buddhism. In the months before his death in 1956 he took two actions based on his belief that separatist action on the part of Untouchables and other dispossessed groups was necessary for their eventual integration. He became a Buddhist on 14 October 1956, setting in motion a conversion movement that was to encompass three million people. He also announced the establishment of the Republican Party, which was to be an instrument of political power for all the dispossessed, including the Scheduled Tribes, as well as the Scheduled Castes. His death left both new movements in the hand of those Untouchables most thoroughly organized by his work - the Mahars of Maharashtra.

Legacies of Leadership

Despite Ambedkar's criticism of Gandhi, and Gandhi's unwillingness to include such men as Ambedkar in the structure of his reform schemes, there were indications that each was conscious of the other's necessary place in any final solution of the problem of untouchability. Ambedkar recounted to reporters on the evening before his conversion to Buddhism that years before he had told Mahatma Gandhi, "I will choose only the least harmful way for the country" *(Nagpur Times,* 14 October 1956). On the other side, there is widespread belief on the part of many Mahars that Gandhi wanted Ambedkar to be Prime Minister. This is supported by a note in the *Illustrated Weekly of India* to the effect that if Gandhi had had this way, "B.R. Ambedkar, lifelong opponent of Gandhism, would have been even at the head of the state" (22 January 1950).

Convergent Paths of Ambedkar and Gandhi

The paths of Gandhi and Ambedkar, while they often diverged, ultimately converged, forcing on the Indian conscience the problem of untouchability as an issue of national concern. Nurullah and Naik reinforce this view in their analysis of the influence exerted by these two men :

> Gandhiji's main work lay among the caste Hindus, and its greatness is to be measured by the extent of change brought

> about in the minds of the caste Hindus. But however painful, it is a fact of history that he did not have a very large following among the Harijans themselves. On the other hand, Dr. Ambedkar was Harijan by birth .. .and therefore was destined to be the leader of these people by virtue of his birth, complete identification with their cause and unequalled capacity .... In a way, his work was complementary to that of Mahatma Gandhi, although owing to differences of approach, he often came in conflict with Gandhiji and the Congress.
>
> The great service of Dr. Ambedkar to the cause is the awakening that he created among the Harijans. He gave them a leadership which they sadly lacked and which was very badly needed. He puts the problem of the Harijans before the country in its true perspective—political, social and economic.[36]

There are no equivalents of either Gandhi or Ambedkar in India today, no famous Mahatma preaching that untouchability is a sin, no statesman-cum-partisan leader serving as an outspoken champion of Untouchables. Although Jagjivan Ram comes nearest to filling this latter role, he is primarily known as an astute politician. In a sense, the viewpoints of Gandhi and Ambedkar were amalgamated in such a way that political and social measures which Ambedkar would have approved are taken in the name of Gandhi. The scene described earlier in the Constituent Assembly illustrates this.

Impact of Protective Discrimination on the Present Status of Untouchables

Although the measure legally abolishing untouchability was adopted with cries of "Victory of Mahatma Gandhi!", Gandhi never advocated legal measures, feeling as he did that all change must come voluntarily from the heart. Yet such was his effect on the Hindu mind that the practice of untouchability is now considered, at least by the educated, as wrong, and uplift of the Untouchable to the level of others as good. In a speech to the Rajya Sabha, Prime Minister Indira Gandhi called for bringing "one of [Gandhi's] near dreams of reality" by giving education, employment, and land ownership to Harijans and ensuring "that people belonging to the Scheduled Castes and Tribes are put in positions of Authority where they can solve their own and others' problems" *(Times of India,* 13 August 1967).

The vast machinery of protective discrimination for the Scheduled Caste was developed chiefly in the 1930s and '40s under the British, and legitimized psychologically by the Gandhian campaigns of the period. The post-Independence government adopted most of these measures and further refined and extended them. Benefits since accorded to Untouchables have included reserved seats in all legislative bodies, the reservation of government jobs, aid to students through the college level, it prizes villagers demonstrating equality, gifts of money for marriages in which one partner is an Untouchable, support for housing projects, and legal machinery for suits against discriminative practices. Such measures reflect the attitudes and policies developed by the leaders and events of the past. They have also inhibited the emergence of a new Mahatma decrying passionately against remaining injustices, or the development of a separatist Untouchable leader capable of building a movement outside the wall of government privilege and patronage. These privileges have also walled off the continuing problems of the Untouchable from the Indian consciousness. Untouchability is news only when a government commission is appointed to investigate some aspect of the problem, or when a particularly dramatic event occurs, such as the burning of forty-two Untouchables in a hut in an east Tanjore district village during landlord-tenant conflicts *(Blitz,* 4 January 1969). Even public expressions of orthodox views are relatively rare as evidenced by the sensational news coverage given in 1969 to the Shankaracharya of Puri's public pronouncements in defense of untouchability.

While Gandhi may be credited with the general atmosphere of concern for the Untouchable expressed in India's official policies, efforts of the kind he most favoured have diminished since his death. A continuation of the Gandhian tradition may be found in several voluntary agencies that maintain hostel and child-care centres for the Depressed Classes and seek to alter attitudes through propaganda. Vinoba Bhave, Gandhi's spiritual heir, initiated a voluntary land redistribution program that benefits some Untouchables through gifts of land to the landless.

Men like N.R. Malkani, a long-time Gandhian worker, have continued to labour for the Bhangi by working on the modernization as well as the humanization of scavenging.[37] However, such efforts have not received widespread financial support from private citizens. "With the advent of freedom, the public response became somewhat cold and people began to argue (rightly or wrongly) that in a welfare state it was the State which should provide all the aid needed by such institutions".[38]

A continuing undercurrent of faith in the varna system appears to guide many social workers and reformers. K.K. Thakkar,[39] suggests that the Shudras should assist the three upper varnas who are credited with doing "constructive work". He tempers this view by advocating that varnas should be assigned on the basis of ability rather than birth. Dr. Pandharinath Prabhu of the Tata Institute of Social Sciences, in discussing caste and class at the seminar on "Casteism and Removal of Un-touchability" in Bombay in 1955, reflected the views of Gandhi and other Hindu religious reformers in his conception of varna: "In fact, the entire Varna System is devised to co-ordinate and assemble the best and the utmost of group welfare, by yoking each section of the group to duties and responsibilities in terms of the efficiency of the specific work and service each of the sections is able to render unto the community life".[40] As in Gandhi's day, this approach has been more concerned with duties than with rights; it has not produced leaders from the ranks of the Untouchables; it has not offset the subtle discrimination felt by the educated Untouchable; it has little influence in most Indian villages where Untouchable living quarters, wells, and temples are still separate from those of caste Hindus.

Ambedkar's influence has also persisted. His ideas on political rights and privileges have been generally accepted by Untouchables. He himself still stands as an example of what an Untouchable can become. As late as the 1960s, the Scheduled Castes were still seeking self-respect by attempting to secure national recognition of his achievements. A "Charter of Demands" presented by the Republican party to the government in 1965 and backed by a satyagraha involving a third of a million people, headed its program with the demand that a portrait of Dr. Ambedkar be placed in the Parliament Building. (A statue of him has now been erected on that site). In 1969, three Swatantra Party Harijans not actually allied with Ambedkar's political movement undertook a fast in Ahmedabad to protest the absence of Dr. Ambedkar's portrait from the Gujarat Legislative Assembly.

In addition to the vital element of self-respect which Ambedkar engendered among Untouchables, his vision of progress though education and politics, rather than the Gandhian vision of a change of heart among caste Hindus, has come to inspire most Scheduled Caste leaders. However, these leaders and their followers are rarely united beyond their own regions. In general, they support the dominant party of the area—the Communist Party in Kerala, the DMK in Madras, the Congress in many provinces. Only in Maharashtra and portions of Uttar Pradesh has Ambedkar's Republican Party commanded any significant number of seats in recent elections.

Ambedkar's view that the problem of the Untouchable is economic, social, and political, as well as religious, widely prevails in India. The Untouchable who enters the modern sector of Indian society as school teacher, factory worker, or government servant, is comparatively free from earlier social disabilities. Even though there may be subtle discrimination in some areas, and a closed door in others, the educated Untouchable functions in a world where a concern with pollution is mitigated by other considerations. However, for the majority of Untouchables, who are landless villagers, the only open road to a higher economic and social status entails leaving the security of their village and somehow obtaining education. Gandhi may have softened the Hindu heart, Ambedkar may have awakened self-respect and interest in politics among Untouchables, but economic dependence upon others continues to restrict the upward movement of the Untouchable.

References

1. Mahadev Desai, *The Epic of Travancore* (Ahmedabad: Navajivan, 1937).

2. M.K. Gandhi, *The Nation's Voice,* edited by C. Rajagopalachari and J.C. Kumarappa (Ahmedabad: Navajivan, 2nd edn., 1947). This is a collection of Gandhi's speeches in England and Mahadev Desai's account of the sojourn—September-December 1931.
3. Pyarelal Nair (Nayyar), *The Epic Fast* (Ahmedabad: Mohanlal Maganlal Bhatt, 1932).
4. Rameshwari Nehru, *Gandhi is My Star* (Patna: Pustakbhandar, 1950).
5. D.G. Tendulkar, *Mahatma: Life of Mohandas Karamchand Gandhi,* Vol. I-VIl, (Bombay:Vithalbhai K. Jhaveri and D.G. Tendulkar, 1952).
6. Mahadev Desai, *The Diary of Mahadev Desai,* trans. from the Gujarati and edited by Valji Gcvind Desai (Ahemadabad: Navajivan, 1953). This is a record of Gandhi's life from 10 March 1932 to 4 September 1932—aperiod of intensive concern with untouchability.
7. B.R. Ambedkar, "Castes in India—Their Mechanism, Genesis and Development," *Indian Antiquary,* XLVI, 1917, pp. SI-95; *Annihilation of Caste, with a Reply to Mahatama Gandhi* (Bombay: Bhusan P. Press, 1936); *What Congress and Gandhi have done to the Untouchables* (Bombay: Thacker, 2nd edn., 1946; first published in 1945); *Who were theShudras?* (Bombay: Thacker, 1947, first published in 1946); *The Untouchables* (New Delhi: Amrit Book Co., 1948; 2nd edn., Lucknow, 1969).
8. Dhananjay Keer, *Dr. Ambedkar: Life and Mission* (Bombay: Popular Prakashan, 1962).
9. C.B. Khairmode, *Dr. Bhimrao Ramji Ambedkar,* Vol. I (Bombay: Y.B. Ambedkar, 1952); Vol. II (Bombay: Bauddhjan Panchyat Samiti; (1958); Vol. III (Bombay: Pratap Prakashan, 1964); Vols. IV and V (Bombay: Dr. Ambedkar Education Society, 1966,1968).
10. Denis Dalton,' "The Gandhian View of Caste and Caste after Gandhi," in Philip Mason ed., *India and Ceylon: Unity and Diversity* (London: Oxford University Press, for the Institute of Race Relations, 1967), p. 170.
11. Quoted in B.R. Ambedkar, 1946, *op. cit.,* p. 1.
12. S. Natarajan, *A Century of Social Reform in India* (Bombay: Asia Publishing House, 2nd edn., 1962), p. 148.
13. Pattabhi Sitaramayya, *The History of the Indian National Congress,* Vol. I (Bombay: Padma Publications, 1946, first published in 1935), p. 226.

14. B.G. Tilak, "The Emancipation of the Untouchable", *The Hindu Missionary,* 42,15 April 1918, (Bombay).
15. Pyarelal Nair (Nayyar), *Mahatma Gandhi: The Last Phase* (Ahmedabad: Navajivan, 1958), p. 228.
16. B.R. Ambedkar, 1946, *op. cit.,* p. 189.
17. B.R. Ambedkar, *The Annihilation of Caste* (Bombay: Bhusan P. Press, 1936).
18. Ram Joshi, "Maharashtra" in Myron Weiner ed., *State Politics in India* (Princeton: Princeton University Press, 1968), pp. 194-95.
19. A.V. Thakkar, *Aboriginals Cry in the Wilderness: Their Education and Representation in Legislature* (Bombay: A.W. Thakkar, Servants of India Society, c. 1945), p. 7.
20. Joan V. Banduvant, *Conquest of Violence: The Gandhian Philosophy of Conflict* (Princeton: Princeton University Press, 1958), pp. 46-52.
21. Desai, 1937, *op. cit.,* pp. 17-21.
22. C.B. Khairmode, *Dr. B.R. Ambedkar,* Vol, *op. cit.,* pp. 117-18.
23. Tulshiram Jamgekar, *Parvativaril satyagrahaca pawada* (Pune, 1930).
24. Indian National Congress; Anti-Untouchability Sub-Committee, *Report of the Work Done by the Anti-Untouchability Sub-Committee,* April-December 1929 (Jamnalal Bajaj, Secretary). Reported in the *Indian Annual Register,* 1929, Part II, pp. 276-80.
25. *Indian Annual Register,* 1930, Part II, p. 369.
26. Mahadev Desai, 1953, *op. cit.,* p. 52.
27. Indian Round Table Conference (Second -1931 London), *Proceedings of the Federal Structure Committee and Minorities Committee* (London: H.M.S.O., 1932), p. 544.
28. Gandhi, *My Soul's Agony* (Ahmedabad: Navajivan, 1932).
29. Desai, 1953, *op. cit.,* p. 301.
30. Ambedkar, 1946, *op. cit.,* pp.134-41.
31. Ambedkar, 1946, *op. cit.,* pp. 142,279-90; Pyarelal, 1958, *op. cit.,* pp. 667-68.
32. Kewal L. Panjabi, *Indomitable Sardar* (Bombay: Bhartiya Vidya Bhavan, 1962), p. 79.

33. Nalin Vilochan Sharma, "A Biography of Jagjivan Ram", in *The Working Man* (Patna: Jagjivan Ram Abhinandan Granth Committee, 1957) p. 107.
34. *Ibid.,* p. 83.
35. Ambedkar, 1946, *op. cit.,* p. 283.
36. Syed Nurullah and J.P. Naik, *History of Education in India* (Bombay: Macmillan, 1951), pp.723-33.
37. N.R. Malkani, *Clean People and Unclean Country* (Delhi: Harijan Sevak Sangh, 1965).
38. P.C. Dave, "Voluntary Organizations and the Welfare of Backward Classes", *Vanyatali,* XIV, pp. 156-64.
39. K.K. Thakkar, in the *Indian Journal of Social Work,* Vol. 17, No. 2, pp. 44-99.
40. Report of "Seminar on Casteism and the Removal of Untouchability", Delhi, 26 September-2 October 1955 (Bombay: Indian Conference of Social Work, 1955), p. 116.

10

Conversion and the Untouchables

Caste system is a type of social stratification found almost exclusively in India. It has existed over several centuries in this country and may be taken as a fundamental unit of social organisation.

Caste is ascriptive and one gets membership in it by birth. It has certain other important attributes. The notions of ritual purity and pollution govern the behaviour of people. There are caste-based occupations specially those which carry high prestige and status and others which carry low status with social stigma. Social interactions in terms of commensal and connubial relationships are often restricted to members of the particular sub-castes. So caste and sometimes sub-caste endogamy is the rule. Differential social relations mark the entire organisation such as hierarchical relationship of superior and inferior (super-ordinate and sub-ordinate).

The Varna System and the Untouchables

The vedic division of social order was based on four *varnas* viz., Brahman, Kshatriya, Vysya and Sudra. The *Varna* order, unlike the caste system, was a loose kind of organization, where membership was acquired on the basis of qualities pertaining to a *varna*.

The Brahmana, Kshatriya, Vysya and Sudra *varna* groups did have occupational attributes. The Brahmanas were identified with priesthood and learning and the Kshatriyas with martial valour. The Vysyas engaged in agriculture and trade while Sudras remained the humble servants of the three upper *varnas*. There is no reference in the vedas to the fifth, or the *panchama-varna,* which later came to be identified as the

Untouchables. Even the occupational attributes of the four *varnas* seem to be fluid and the boundaries of each *varna* remained open. It was not a fixed and rigid social order, although some of the caste attributes were already present in their rudimentary form in the *chaturvarna* organization.

Today the *varna* system has outlived its utility except for providing a broad model for an all India category. The post-vedic period, especially the upanishadic and the puranic, provided fertile grounds for the rigid classification of social groups. Birth became the sole criterion to reckon membership of social groups. Occupational attributes continued and came to be observed more rigidly. According to the laws of Manu, those who transgressed the rules of behaviour pertaining to different groups became out-castes.

From this time onwards presumably it is these outcastes who were lumped together as 'Untouchables' and hence it is justifiable to assume that the outcastes constitute the forefathers of later-day 'Untouchables.' In the post-vedic history of the Indian caste system there is a definite trend for more and more proliferation. Additional features were added on the basis of occupation and diet. The distinction between vegetarian and non-vegetarian was not a rigid one during vedic period. However, consumption of alcohol, and even dealing in it came to be a definite attribute of low caste status.

Fission rather than fusion seems to have played a predominant role throughout. Groups began to demarcate their social boundaries from one another. In all these exercises, the race for higher status continued unabated. Only those who conformed to certain values and preserved certain traits were able to attain higher status in the caste hierarchy. Others were automatically pushed down the caste ladder. In the *chaturvarna* pyramid the Sudra caste occupied the base. The upper castes formed the top of the pyramid.

The Kshatriyas and the Vysyas who came immediately below the Brahmins in that order, enjoyed high status and were entitled for some form of education as determined by the Brahmins. The largest majority of Indian population, the Sudras, were denied any access to education. So also the women of all the four *varnas* were in fact reduced to the status of Sudras.

The Brahmins constituted a negligible minority group of 5-6 per cent of the population. As a minority group it has endeavoured throughout history to keep its boundaries fixed and doors closed to others. As a class of literati they had access to all knowledge and this made them superior to others and put them in an advantageous position over all the others. Added to this, the Brahmins enjoyed the highest ritual purity. The physical and social boundaries were safeguarded by elaborate practices of ritual pollution in relation to time, place and persons. Ritual pollution in relation to certain categories of persons became ascriptive, resulting in unbridgeable physical and social gaps.

Those who belonged to the *panchama-varna* (the fifth caste), variously known as the 'Untouchables,' 'Unapproachables' and the 'Unseeables' though, for all practical purposes, the term 'Untouchable' seems to have subsumed the latter two. The number of people reduced to the status of 'Untouchables' were so enormous that their problems have haunted the conscious souls over the centuries. Many experiments were tried to reduce their misery, sometimes by appealing to exalted metaphysical principles, sometimes by expounding ways and means of elevating human souls.

Beliefs in *Karma* and *punarjanma* (cycles of rebirth based on the merits of one's action during one's life time) never left any scope for lower castes to improve their chances for better life. Leave alone the services of the Brahmin priest, the very sight of the 'Untouchables' was forbidden. Recitation of the sacred texts by the 'Untouchables' was severly punished. The concern for the 'hereafter' over the needs of the 'here' made the office of the priesthood so crucial that everybody remained subservient to the priest, and the awe inspiring power of the Brahmin literally sealed the fate of all castes below the Brahmins and more specifically, 'Outcastes' or the 'Untouchables.'

The powerful and superior position held by the Brahmins

and the privileges stemming therefrom have seldom been questioned and when questioned, have rarely succeeded in checking the Brahmins. This unquestionable Brahmanical superiority, however, did not render Hinduism a unified system. Polytheism coupled with the absence of the feeling of brotherhood has made Hinduism disparate groups with no single centralised religious authority. The customs, traditions, values and practices which emanated from the Hindu system became diversified on the basis of differential social status. Those who had Brahmanical origins were held in high esteem and those who came close to Brahmanical values could claim affinity to their co-caste fellows immediately higher in the caste hierarchy. Those who were at the bottom of the social hierarchy, especially the 'Untouchable' groups who tried this mechanism, however, could not succeed in raising their social status.

The tyranny of the Brahmanical values and caste rigidities have from time to time, given rise to protests and reform movements. Many of these movements used religious idioms and tried to bring about social transformation and change by recruiting people to the new faith from several low caste Hindu and Untouchable groups. Both indigenous as well as those faiths which came from outside recruited people from within the country and tried to make a dent in the caste system. In this study we shall treat these movements from the aspect of their philosophy of conversion.

Buddhism

Conversion as a phenomenon leading to the change of faith is a very old practice in the Indian sub-continent. Buddhism was not primarily concerned with caste or with the practice of untouchability. Its main concern was with the salvation of individual souls. Gautama Buddha was overwhelmed by the theory of Karma, transmigration of souls and priestcraft. After prolonged periods of meditation and withdrawing himself into solitude, he was able to show the path of *Nirvana* through enlightenment. *Nirvana,* unlike Hindu *Mukti,* was to be attained without undergoing the pangs of rebirth. The role of the priest was eliminated. Even god as a supreme being was outside the purview of Buddhist philosophy. It was a religion based on reason and compassion.

Buddha came from a royal background and Buddhism, backed by ruling powers, especially during Asoka's rule reached its zenith both within and outside India. Sri Lanka, South East Asian countries, Burma, Japan and China soon came under the impact of Buddhism. So widespread, it developed secondary features. Buddha became a legendary figure and was elevated to the place of divine being himself. Also structural differences led to the formation of *Hinayana* and *Mahayana* divisions among the Buddhist followers.

In India, Buddhism flourished for a while. It began to combat with Hinduism and for a time it looked as though the entire subcontinent would come under its spell. But long before this could happen, the tables were reversed. Under the Gupta rulers, Hinduism was restored to its original glory. The golden age of Hinduism, as is usually described by the historians, saw the retreat of Buddhism in the land of its birth.

Dr. Ambedkar has put forth a proposition as to the origin of the 'Untouchables.' According to this explanation the 'Untouchables' were broken Kshatriyas who earned their livelihood as watchmen for villages and stayed at the periphery of the villages. The villagers in turn provided them with food and shelter for the services rendered. In the continuous skirmishes which followed between the predatory Bandit groups and the watchmen, the argument goes, the groups were further broken up into 'broken men' of 'floating groups' who were unattached to any group. The fact that they ate beef, and worked in leather, further rendered their position more vulnerable in the caste order and they came to be segregated and discriminated against by the others.

This account given by Dr. Ambedkar has not been subjected to serious analysis. The fact that so far it has not been critically examined, would suggest that historians have not taken it seriously. It is time that historians and others who seriously think of the issue took it up in earnest to explore the truth or otherwise of this proposition. As for Dr. Ambedkar, it was not just a proposition, but a fact beyond doubt. His leaning towards Buddhism and the conviction with which he endorsed Buddhist principles and finally embraced Buddhism at the fag end of his life along with a vast number of followers cannot be treated lightly or as a fad.

Yet all said and done, even a person like Dr. Ambedkar had to reckon with the religious susceptibilities of people as against abstract metaphysical ideas. This suggests the strong hold religion has on society.

Jainism

Alongside Buddhism, Jainism as another form of religion was floated by yet another prince. Unlike Buddhism, Jainism never posed a serious threat to Hinduism and its dominance. Conversion to Jainism admittedly seemed to have been selective from the beginning. It never aspired to become a proselytising faith. Outside India, for example, we see very little of Jainism, except where Jain traders have migrated. Even within India, it remained a faith with a small group of followers who never questioned the caste system or the practice of untouchability.

Like Buddhism, Jainism was also preoccupied with the liberation of the soul. The Hindu notions of Karma and rebirth, and the undue role played by the Brahmin priests to control the religious life of the people seem to be some of the moving factors which motivated Mahavira and his followers to explore new avenues. Jainism surpassed Buddhism in making compassion a cardinal virtue. Non-injury to living beings was an ethical precept accepted both by Buddhism and Jainism. But Jainism carried the principle of Ahimsa or non-violence too far. Orthodox Jains cover their mouth and nose lest small insects get in while breathing and get killed.

These earliest attempts of social and religious reforms give an insight into the nature of Indian society, its religion, and caste stratification. These movements suggest that Indian society has rich literary traditions albeit a near total Brahmanical domination from ancient times. It can be argued that the Brahmanical superiority came from the fact that the minority Brahmin group was able to hold on to its exclusive possession of knowledge and withhold others from getting any access to it.

Customs, traditions and values were initiated by Brahmins. They were made to govern the lives of 'all' Hindus, including the Sudras and the Harijans. The Brahmins interpreted the Hindu laws: the sanctity of marriage, family and caste traditions and male superiority. Brahmins took quick notice of any new demands, be it in the field of religion, caste, education or secularisation, politics or social reform. As a result, many indigenous social movements were led by Brahmins.

Reform Movements

Arya Samaj in Punjab and Brahmo Samaj movement in Bengal were spearheaded by men like Dayananda Saraswathi, Raja Ram Mohan Roy and Tagore. Reform of Hinduism in select ways was attempted by both. Both recruited people from among different castes and tried to bring about changes. These reform movements are still lingering on but never became a counter force to Hinduism.

Education of women was common to both these movements. Sati received special attention of Brahmo Samajists as this was quite common among the upper castes. A call to go back to Vedas and to revive vedic Hinduism were the basic message of Dayananda Saraswathi. The Brahmo Samaj, on the other hand, was willing to share religious values both from inside and outside the country. The *Suddhi* movement introduced by the Arya Samaj tried to reclaim those who had converted to other religions. In fact the *Suddhi* or purification, though it appears to be a revolutionary step, as reformation within Hinduism is at the same time a controversial attempt. The rank and file for example has no common social platform and the social status of the reconverted remains as problematic as ever.

The followers of Arya Samaj and Brahmo Samaj did not repudiate Hinduism. Caste differences and customary practices came under reform, but while the former looked back, the latter tried to modernise and secularise. They did not deal directly with the problems of the 'Untouchables.' The 'Untouchables' by and large, remained in the periphery even in the new scheme of things.

Kabir Panth, Raidasis, Satnamis, all emphasise devotion and truth. Caste discrimination as well as the practice of untouchability do not find much favour with them. In fact, the founders as well as followers of Raidasis and Satnamis belong to 'Untouchable' groups. Reform of habits, like giving up meat eating and alcoholic drinks to improve their social status seem to be central to them.

Devotion and salvation dominate most of the indigenous attempts to bring about reformation within Hinduism. In north India, Kabirpanth gave inspiration to many smaller movements including Sikhism. It is said that Kabir was born of a virgin Brahmin widow, and brought up by Muslim weaver family. He picked up the best of both Hinduism and Islam discarding the bad aspects. Belief in one god, unity of men, truth, love and compassion were the qualities emphasised by Kabir. Kabirpanth which attracted large number of followers ended up in mystifying Kabir leading to distortions and group differences, so that here also Brahmins are given great importance in the Panth and Panth-mathas as against the Sudra and other low-caste adherents.

Sikhism, which is concentrated in Punjab, seems to be one of the most successful religious movements which again combined in itself the best of Hinduism and Islam based on devotion, salvation, deliverance from the chain of death and rebirth to all mankind irrespective of caste, creed and sex. Thus, Sikhism like other indigenous movements repudiated social differentiation based on caste and upheld the ideal of equality.

People from upper castes like Khatris, Jats, artisans and craftsmen accepted Sikhism. People from 'Untouchable' caste groups also embraced the new faith to escape from traditional degradation. However, Sikhism was not able to rise above the narrow loyalties of converts from several castes. The lot of the 'Untouchable' Sikhs is more or less the same as that of their Hindu brethren.

Most of the north Indian movements in Modern times were geared to combine the best of both Hinduism and Islam. Sikhism and Kabirpanth are examples of this, Brahmo Samaj, on the other hand, was willing to include the exemplary features of Christianity. The Arya Samaj movement came as a reaction to conversions to Christianity and Islam. Simultaneously it attempted to rectify the defects of rigidity within Hinduism by giving a call to go back to vedas and to revive vedic Hinduism. However, it was not a movement which devoted to elevate the 'Untouchables,' and how many and how often 'Untouchables' embraced and professed Arya Samaj doctrines remains a speculation. Arya Samaj has not been able to bring about social equality among its adherents. Differential social status and rank persist among its followers.

Of the regional and local movements emanating from the 'Untouchables,' the *Raidasis and the Satnamis* were the most important. They tried to reform themselves on the model of Brahmanical values. Though they lamented the caste system and the practice of untouchability, they could not bring about any radical changes in society. They became new sects within their own communities.

The *Varcaris of Maharashtra*, based on devotion, is again a sectarian organisation which tried to ignore minute caste distinction.

The S.N.D.P. *(Sri Narayana Dharma Paripalana) movement* in Kerala was also based on social and religious reform within the broad framework of Hinduism. Unity of mankind, oneness of god and equality were the oft repeated precepts of their leader, Sri Narayana Guru. By and large this movement remained confined to the Ezhava caste. The Ezhavas have managed to attain a considerable degree of social mobility, especially through the socio-economic programmes and the political involvement initiated by the movement.

Before dealing with Islam and Christianity, the religions which came from outside the country[1] and today constitute two influential minority groups, we would deal with *Veerasaivism*, a Saivite sectarian movement of Karnataka. The movement started in the 12th century AD by Basava, a Saivite Brahmin. Basava rebelled against the vedic rituals of blood sacrifices, degradation of women and caste distinctions. He attacked the Brahmanical values of ritual purity and pollution, preached equality and introduced the notion of dignity of labour.

Basava and his followers too worked within the broad framework of Hinduism. Shiva, one of the Hindu Trinity, was given an exalted place. *Jangamas* replaced the Brahmin priests. The movement had considerable appeal and impact. Large number of people drawn from different social strata, particularly from the lower castes, embraced Veerasaivism. The royal patronage and political positions which Basava enjoyed under Bijjala, the Jain king, greatly assisted spreading the faith.

Today Veerasaivas (or Lingayats) in Karnataka occupy the first place in terms of their numbers. There are several occupational groups among them which occupy distinct places in the caste Hierarchy. For though Basava condemned caste differences and the practice of untouchability, the various groups which converted to Veerasaivism retained their occupational and previous caste status in the new religion. There are for example, Lingayat agriculturists, Lingayat Businessmen, Lingayat Oilmen, Tailor, Potter, Barber and Lingayat Washermen. These groups are as crystalised as Hindu castes. Lingayats also practice untouchability, with reference to the barber caste.

Marriage, and to some extent, interdining is confined mostly to the members of the same sub-caste. Veerasaivism which rebelled against Brahmanical value system and tried to replace them by more humane and universal principles, gradually succumbed to the influence of Hindu caste system. There are castes and sub-castes and hierarchical ranking, some superior and others inferior among the rank and file of Lingayats. Instead of containing the contagion of caste and untouchability Veerasaivas actually lead to their proliferation. The innumerable Veerasaiva Mutts, for example, serve to increase the narrow loyalties and sub-caste differences.

The history of caste system in India is thus replete with movements and counter movements to reform society. In the

Indian context, caste has always been intimately related to religion, because where Hinduism begins and caste ends or vice-versa cannot be easily distinguished. The rules of caste are rules of religion, one buttresses the other and both have sustained one another over centuries. It is futile to talk of Hinduism minus caste system. In this sense, it becomes reasonably clear why many of the indigenous movements, both reformist and protest movements, directed their attention on caste organisation rather than on Hindu religious susceptibilities. A vast majority of them, however, operated within the framework of Hindu religion so that it was easy for them to get a following.

It is only by appealing to the religious susceptibilities of the followers, leaders of certain sectarian movements can achieve success. Arya Samaj, Brahmo Samaj, Sikhism and even Veerasaivism adopted this strategy and converted people to their view point and enrolled them as members of the sect. Their main intention was to bring about certain changes in the caste system and thus to replace an old set of values by a new set. But values die hard. Even the changed values gradually got transformed in the new system and became akin to old values in Hinduism. All the indigeneous movements eagerly extolled the merits of such values.

In spite of condemning Brahmanical values on many fronts, the new movements tacitly accepted the superiority of some of these values. Hence the challenges posed by them were not foreign to the 'native' religion. There were many common points and the people could easily grasp them. Through a process of fission and fusion aspiring people broke away from the parent body and formed new groups with slightly different sets of identity but within the framework of Hindu ideology. Each attempt to reform and change the caste system produced a chain reaction so that Hinduism became more and more elastic to include within itself contradictory forces.

Today in Hinduism there is no single, well organised authority. It is an amorphous mass. In fact, one could argue that it has always been so. Hinduism has always included within its scheme the extremes of ritual purity and pollution, the herbivorous teetotaller and the carnivorous alcoholic compartmentalised into superior and inferior status.

Islam

We shall now turn to analyse the impact of two faiths that came into India from outside. Islam came to India with the Muslim invaders. The predatory desert religion with its religious ideologies of monotheism and brotherhood of mankind had no soft corner for other religions. Its cries of 'Jehad' and its suppression of women, as is evidenced in modern Iran, overran different parts of India for several decades.

From looting the booty, the Muslim invaders established their kingdoms and empires and ruled over the Hindus. The Mughal rule in India was both a period of consolidation of Islamic political power as well as of Muslim religion. Unlike the indigenous reform movements, the Muslims were not interested in appeasing the spirit of casteism and Hinduism. Their intentions were quite clear.

By overt and covert methods, they made the Hindus to embrace Islam. This became very clear by the time Mughal rulers consolidated the empire. Many Hindu rulers in North India were subjugated by the Muslim rulers. Marriage relationships were contracted by the Mugals with converted Rajput royal families. Islamisation in India did not, however, follow a set pattern. Often the conquered people embraced Islam out of fear and to avoid persecution.

Muslim rulers like Hyder Ali and Tipu Sultan of erstwhile Mysore, the Bahamani kingdoms, the Nizam of Hyderabad in south India highlight the conflict caused by the coming of the Islam to India. Violent reaction to Muslim domination can also be seen in the rise of Hindu kingdoms of Vijayanagar, the rise of Shivaji and the rise of Maratha rulers.

Here again the lower castes were the first to react favourably to the conversion movement. The royal patronage enjoyed by the followers of Islam, on the one hand and the rigid stratification which existed in Hindu society, on the other, helped the spread of Islam throughout the country.

Islam has many plus points in contrast to Hindu caste system. Discrimination based on ritual purity and pollution is absent in Islam. Food restrictions are few. There is also a strong sense of brotherhood among the followers of Islam. Religious authority is also strong and more centralised than it is in Hinduism.

There are many occupational groups among Muslims, which do indicate 'differential status and rank. While interdining may be in vogue, inter-marriage among different sub-groups is not frequent. The conflict between the Sunni and Shia sects, for example, and fierce battles which are fought between them for status is common knowledge. One can also observe status distinctions between Arab descendents, upper caste converts and lower caste converts among Muslims. Living amidst the Hindu majority, Muslims in rural India have combined Islamic and Hindu cultural traits. In some areas they also observe some form of untouchability.

One striking phenomenon about the Islam in India is its near absence among the tribal people. The tribal people, given to simple subsistence economy have developed egalitarian social structures among themselves. However, similar ideologies in Islam attract the attention of the tribals. This would suggest that the Muslim leaders did not have an over-all plan of conversion.

The major factor seems to have been the people themselves who were caught under one or the other stress of exploitation and therefore chose to convert to Islam in order to improve the social conditions.

Christianity

Christians, unlike Muslims did not strictly follow their rulers. Christian theology emphasises monotheism and upholds in theory the fatherhood of God and the brotherhood of mankind. The Christian faith which was largely contained within the European continent for a long period, made rapid strides during the colonial period. The maritime powers which gave the western countries lead over others, helped in carrying the messages of Christianity to different parts of the world. The political power which accompanied facilitated the process of conversion.

The strategy adopted by Christian missionaries from the beginning was very different and subtle in contrast to physical force and might exhibited by Islam.

The Christian Church organisation itself is well established, hierarchically structured, and vested with differential religious authority. It could send its missionaries in an organised way to carry the message of Jesus to different people all over the world. The missionaries lived and worked among the potential converts to Christianity. They spread education, rendered medical services and preached the gospel of Christ appealing to the people to see the superior, humanitarian side of Christianity. Love, compassion, appeal and persuasion by the missionaries paid rich dividends to their cause.

The Christian missionaries found a very fertile ground in India. The disunity among the Hindus coupled with the social discontent, accumulated over centuries, provided a favourable atmosphere for the spread of Christianity. If the Brahmins and upper castes embraced Christianity because of its religious ethics or as an escape from the structural constraints within which they were caught, the low castes and the tribals embraced Christianity in groups mainly for improving their social status.

The tribals who were exploited by the Hindus and despised by them were provided with essential educational and medical services, by the missionaries. The sympathetic understanding shown by the Christian missionaries about their day-to-day problems and coming to their rescue and assistance in times of need has had its impact. Many tribal areas in India have come under the impact of Christianity more readily than Hinduism or Islam. The tribal social structure with its egalitarian base did not require changes in accepting Christianity. In many areas the native religious beliefs and practices of the tribals continued hand-in-hand with Christianity. Similarly the low caste Hindus particularly the 'Untouchables' found in Christian teachings a soothing effect and a means of escaping from the depth of degradation in Hindu fold. The educational services of the missionaries opened up new avenues to the 'Untouchables' which were until then, denied to them. This helped them achieve a degree of social betterment.

The Church organisation, the different denominations, and foreign missionaries bringing financial aid attracted different castes to Christianity. Those who converted to Christianity from upper caste background under favourable economic conditions continued to hold their elevated position. Religious conversion did not seriously counteract the caste idiom and behaviour patterns. As a result, social interrelation and social intercourse was restricted to like groups and the narrow loyalties of pre-conversion caste status and rank continued to dominate social life. The upper caste converts tended to appropriate authority and power and to assume leadership in Church hierarchy. It was difficult for the low caste converts to Christianity to scale these formidable barriers and rise within the religious hierarchy. Even at Church services in certain places differential treatment was given to different social groups.

Here we can see the interplay between caste and class and the dominant role they play in society. In the case of upper castes who have better access to economic resources and political power both have tended to fuse, whether the upper castes belonged to Hinduism, Christianity or Islam. On the other hand, the lower castes without access to economic and political power, suffer both from caste distinction and class separation. They cannot overcome the basic handicaps, lower caste status or class restrictions. As long as the elements of caste survive, religious conversion would not remove differential opportunities, though a negligible minority can strive to overcome and reap the benefits of social mobility. Similarly, as long as extreme economic disparity continues, caste and class would tend to re-instate each other.

Social equality is an elusive phenomenon. In the Indian

context it is made more difficult and complicated because of caste stratification and the religious values which buttress them. The late Dr. B.R. Ambedkar who took initiative to revive Buddhism in India is a good example of this. It would sound naive to suggest that Dr. Ambedkar did not know the implications of such religious conversions in the Indian context. For historically every attempt to reform Hinduism or to attack caste system has produced not much positive results. Group conversion should be strengthened by organisation and supporting institutions. Individual conversion is based on personal convictions and leads to change in individual's attitudes. In the case of group conversions, religion is used as a devise, perhaps a force to counter other forces. Ambedkar believed that Buddhism could provide the 'Untouchables' with such a force to better their conditions.

To begin with, Buddhism was an indigenous faith and as such would not be frowned upon by caste Hindus. Dr. Ambedkar had his pet theory of connecting the origins of untouchability to 'broken men' and these people as professing Buddhism. He found personally the philosophy of Buddhism as most satisfactory, since it was based on rationalism and compassion. Further, it would amount to a social and religious reform by reviving one of the world religions. Whether Dr. Ambedkar ever contemplated linking Indian Buddhists with their co-religionists outside and exposing their continued plight before the world community to seek the active sympathy from outside, will always remain at best a speculation. He died too soon after the historic conversion ceremony at Nagpur in 1956.

In post-Ambedkar years, conversion to Buddhism has not been very spectacular. Even those who have embraced Buddhism come from a particular sub-caste among Scheduled Castes and mostly from Maharashtra. Elsewhere in India a few Chamars and others have taken to Buddhism. Moreover religious conversion is seldom matched by required improvement in the secular sphere. Their economic conditions and social surroundings have not substantially changed.

Twenty-two Vows of Dr. Ambedkar

Dr. B.R. Ambedkar prescribed 22 vows to his followers during the historic religious conversion to Buddhism on 15 October 1956 at Deeksha Bhoomi, Nagpur in India. The conversion to Buddhism by 800,000 people was historic because it was the largest religious conversion, the world has ever witnessed. He prescribed these oaths so that there may be complete severance of bond with Hinduism. These 22 vows struck a blow at the roots of Hindu beliefs and practices. These vows could serve as a bulwark to protect Buddhism from confusion and contradictions. These vows could liberate converts from superstitions, wasteful and meaningless rituals, which have led to pauperisation of masses and enrichment of upper castes of Hindus.

The famous 22 vows are :

1. I shall have no faith in Brahma, Vishnu and Mahesh nor shall I worship them.
2. I shall have no faith in Rama and Krishna who are believed to be incarnation of God nor shall I worship them.
3. I shall have no faith in 'Gauri', Ganapati and other gods and goddesses of Hindus nor shall I worship them.
4. I do not believe in the incarnation of God.
5. I do not and shall not believe that Lord Buddha was the incarnation of Vishnu. I believe this to be sheer madness and false propaganda.
6. I shall not perform 'Shraddha' nor shall I give 'pind-dan'.
7. I shall not act in a manner violating the principles and teachings of the Buddha.
8. I shall not allow any ceremonies to be performed by Brahmins.
9. I shall believe in the equality of man.
10. I shall endeavour to establish equality.
11. I shall follow the 'noble eightfold path' of the Buddha.
12. I shall follow the 'paramitas' prescribed by the Buddha.

13. I shall have compassion and loving kindness for all living beings and protect them.
14. I shall not steal.
15. I shall not tell lies.
16. I shall not commit carnal sins.
17. I shall not take intoxicants like liquor, drugs etc.
18. I shall endeavour to follow the noble eightfold path and practise compassion and loving kindness in every day life.
19. I renounce Hinduism which is harmful for humanity and impedes the advancement and development of humanity because it is based on inequality, and adopt Buddhism as my religion.
20. I firmly believe the Dhamma of the Buddha is the only true religion.
21. I believe that I am having a re-birth.
22. I solemnly declare and affirm that I shall hereafter lead my life according to the principles and teachings of the Buddha and his Dhamma.

References

Ambedkar, B.R. 1948. *The Untouchables: Who Were They and Why They Became Untouchables.* New Delhi: Amrit Book Company.

—. 1951. *The Buddha and His Dharma.* Bombay. Siddharth College Publication.

Singh, Harjinder. 1977. ed. *Caste Among Non-Hindus in India:* New Delhi: National Publishing House.

Hutton, J.H. 1961. *Caste in India: Its Nature, Function, and Origins.* Oxford: Oxford University Press.

Lynch, Owen M. 1969. *The Politics of Untouchability Social Mobility and Social Change in a City of India.* New York: Columbia University Press.

Mahar, Michael. J. 1972. ed. *The Untouchables in Contemporary India.* Tucson, Arizona: The University of Arizona Press.

Malik, S.C. 1977. *Dissent Protest and Reform in Indian Civilization.* Simla: Indian Institute of Advanced Studies.

Parvathamma, C. 1972. *Sociological Essays on Veerasaivism.* Bombay: Popular Prakashan.

—. 1973. 'Ambedkar and After: The Position and Future of Indian Scheduled Castes Masses and Classes.' *The Eastern Anthropologist,* 26(3); 221-34.

—. 1977. 'Dissent, Protest and Reform Movements in Indian Civilization-Veerasaivism: A Saivite Sectarian Movement in Protest and Reform in Karnataka.' pp. 188-191 in *Dissent, Protest and Reform in Indian Civilization,* edited by S.C. Malik. Simla: Indian Institute of Advanced Studies.

—. 1980 'The Weaker Sections of Society' The Scheduled Castes of India: Paper presented at XVth Indian Social Conference, Meerut.

Patwardhan, Sunanda 1973. *Change Among India's Harijans,* New Delhi: Orient Longman.

Rao, M.S.A. 1979. *Social Movement in India.* 2 Vols. New Delhi: Manohar Publications.

Srinivas, M.N. 1952. *Religion and Society among the Coorgs of South India.* Bombay: Media Promoters.

Weber, Max. 1958. *The Religion of India.* New York. The Free Press.

11

The spread of Buddhism in India

The rebirth of Buddhism in India is perhaps best represented by two phenomena: the first is the count of 3,250,227 actual Buddhists in the 1961 Census; the second is the use of two Buddhist motifs as official symbols of independent India—the *chakra* or wheel on the Indian flag and the lion capital of an Ashokan pillar.

The census figure of 1961 indicates that in the land of the Buddha's birth less than one per cent of the population is Buddhist; yet this is an enormous increase over the 1951 Indian Census figure of 180,823 Buddhists, most of whom were borderland hill peoples and other Asians living in India. The current count of over three million Buddhists represents a conversion movement begun in 1956, chiefly by Untouchables, 75 per cent of whom belong to the former Mahar caste of Maharashtra.

The use of the wheel and the lion capital by the Indian Government reflects not only its choice as a secular state of "neutral symbols", neither Hindu nor Muslim, but also acknowledges the importance of, and new intellectual interest in, the history of Buddhism in India. The history of the conversion movement and of the intellectuals' rediscovery of Buddhism go back less than 100 years, and they are unrelated—except that renewed interest among intellectuals gave Buddhism the necessary prestige to serve as a base for converts from low status groups seeking a path that would lead to higher status and self-respect.

Spread of Buddhism in India

Buddhism seems to have been a living religion in India from the sixth century B.C. to the twelfth century A.D. There are problems enough sorting out facts from myth in its beginnings and spread, but its decline is even more of a puzzle. Gautam Siddhartha, the Sakya (or Shakya) prince who became the Buddha, was born in that remarkable sixth century B.C. which saw religious genius arise at many points in the great arc from Greece to China that was the civilized world. Buddhism, then, was only one of several heterodox movements in India, all of them a revolt in some way against the brahmanical ritualized orthodoxy of the time. From the beginning, man himself was the focal point of Buddhism. The gods, rituals and whatever caste structure there was at the time were not so much denied as set aside in the emphasis on ethics, morality and the path to Nirvana. Equality in the body of monks, the Sangha, was offered to all, not just to those born in the priestly castes. The elements of humanity, gentleness and freedom from sacrifice and superstition, found in the life and teachings of the Buddha, formed the basis for the renewed interest in Buddhism which appeared in India 2,400 years later.

The spread of Buddhism from the third century on can be seen in its art - those magnificent stupas and caves, some almost untouched by time, other in ruins, in the northwest, the east, the central and the west of India and as far south as Amravati on the river Krishna. The pillar and rock edicts of king Ashoka in the third century B.C. indicate the establishment of Buddhist precept over a great part of the subcontinent. Buddhism was carried through the mountain passes to Central Asia and China and by sea to Ceylon and Southeast Asia. However, even during the latter part of its spread east, and while foreign monks still came to India to gather scriptures and see the holy places, Buddhism as an institutionalized religion was losing ground in India.

Reasons for decline: Many factors entered into its disappearance: destructive invaders — probably White Huns — leveled the Buddhist university of Taxila in the fourth century A.D.; Turkish conquerors, probably Muhammad Bakhtiar Khilji, razed the Buddhist university at Nalanda in the twelfth century. That Buddhism in India was unable to revive these institutions, or to continue after the twelfth century as an organized identifiable religion, can be attributed to its inward decline and to the absorptive power of the most syncretic of religions, Hinduism.

Although we know from its art and scriptures that Buddhism must have had widespread influence in India, it is impossible to determine how many Indians at any time actually considered themselves Buddhists. Brahmanical rites and thought were always powerful, and Hindu daily ritual was undoubtedly practiced throughout India during the Buddhist period. The *Mahabharata,* India's great epic, compiled during the centuries before and after the birth of Christ when Buddhist art flourished, does not mention Buddhism by name. The classical period of Hinduism, from the fourth to the sixth centuries A.D., after which the university at Nalanda was built, produced works which take fleeting notice of Buddhism (the gambler turned Bhikshu, almost a comic figure, in Shudraka's *Little Clay Cart* is an example). Hinduism not only continued, but absorbed many Buddhist practices and ideas. The Buddha was accepted as an avatar of Vishnu, a part of the Hindu pantheon but not widely worshipped, and it is only in this form that he appears after the twelfth century. In the south the colour and warmth of devotional religion, *bhakti,* and the intellectual vitality of the *advaita vedanta,* preached by Shankaracharya in the eighth century, chipped away at the institution of Buddhism on both popular and philosophical levels. Buddhist concepts of non-violence and reverence for life were absorbed into Hindu *ahimsa* and vegetarianism. Hinduism in its varied forms, enriched by Buddhism, dominated India when the Muslim challenge appeared in the twelfth century. It may be that the remaining Buddhists on the periphery of the Hindu heartland - in East Bengal and Sind — became Muslim. But by the twelfth century the life of the great Sangha institutions, Buddhist art, the interpretation of Buddhist thought, even the knowledge of the Buddhist period, became lost to sight.

At the beginning of the nineteenth century, European scholars began the work of translation from Pali, Sanskrit and Tibetan, making possible the study of Indian Buddhism in the West. In 1837 an English official in India, James Prinsep, deciphered the script used on the Ashokan rock and pillar edicts, and recognition of the breadth and benevolence of that Buddhist king's rule came to both Europe and India. Alexander Cunningham, another Englishman, prepared the way for a revival of pilgrimage when he, using the seventh-century Chinese pilgrim Huen-Tsang's travel book as a guide, identified various Buddhist holy places. Many scholars, working in Europe and never coming directly in contact with Indian life, contributed to an increasing knowledge of Indian intelligentsia.

Mahabodhi Society of Calcutta

However, it was Henry Olcott, a less orthodox personality, who most profoundly influenced the rebuilding of Buddhist institutions. Olcott, an American Civil War Colonel and one of the founders of the Theosophical Society, went to Ceylon in 1880 to help what he felt was submerged Buddhism. A young Sinhalese, David Hewavitame, joined the Theosophical Society there and after contact through the Society with Western Buddhist studies and Japanese Buddhism, conceived of a resurgent world Buddhism. Hewavitame became Anagarika Dharmapala (literally, the homeless protector of religion). In 1891, as a Buddhist bhikshu, he went to Bodh Gaya, the place where the Buddha had received enlightenment. He had set in motion an interest in Buddhism which led to the establishment of the Maha Bodhi Society of Calcutta. His focus was not on reinterpretation of the doctrine or on conversion but on securing recognition for Buddhism, its reputation and its still living institutions in Asia, and on restoring its pilgrim centres.

The Buddhas Text Society

From the 1880s onwards, Indian scholarship, stimulated both by European studies in Buddhism and by a pride in Buddhism as part of Indian heritage, produced a steady flow of translations and interpretations, both in English and in some vernacular languages. The Buddhist Text Society was founded in 1892 in Calcutta, and Sarat Chandra Das and Satish Chandra Vidyabhushan (the first person to obtain an M.A. in Pali in 1901) worked under its auspices. In Western India, Dharmananda Kosambi worked both as a scholar and as one personally involved. He lived for a time in both Ceylon and Burma and, besides translating Pali works wrote on Buddhism in Marathi in a way that was both scholarly and persuasive. In South India the new interest in Buddhism seems to have penetrated below the intellectual level to become an interest of some lower caste groups. Buddhist temples started being built fairly early in the twentieth century in their quarters in Madras and in the Kolar Gold fields. In *The Essence of Buddhism*, published in 1907, P. Lakshmi Narasu, a Professor of Physics and Chemistry at Madras Christian College, predicted a popular revival of Buddhism in India. Buddhist themes entered literature and the arts, chiefly through the Tagores in Bengal. A number of reformers considered themselves Buddhists, although this was not accompanied with a concomitant rejection of Hinduism. This kind of interest is exemplified by A.R. Kulkarni, a Nagpur Brahman advocate who became interested in Buddhism as a purifying strand of Hinduism in the 1930s. In the 1940s he actually left his law practice to preach Buddhism, though without any implication of conversion. A few Indians, including some from the Arya Samaj tradition, became Buddhist monks; of these, Rahul Sankrityayan and Anand Kausalyayan combined Hindi literature with the propagation of Buddhism.

By 1947, knowledge and appreciation of the Buddhist period in Indian History had grown to the point where the *chakra* (the wheel of dharma) on the national flag and the lion capital found on an Ashokan pillar as a national emblem were acceptable to almost all Indians. By 1956 interest in Buddhism made the celebration of the 2,500th anniversary of the death of the Buddha an event on a national scale in India. A Buddha Jayanti celebration was observed in Delhi, a film on the life of the Buddha was produced, and a number of books on the Buddhist tradition and Buddhist art were published under Government auspices.

The conversion movement: The year of the 2,500th anniversary of Buddhism in India also saw the beginnings of a conversion movement. The social movement of the Mahar caste, an untouchable caste of Maharashtra, which culminated in conversion, roughly parallels in time the revival of intellectual interest in Buddhism, but it touches that revival chiefly through the figure of its twentieth century leader, Dr. BR Ambedkar. Ambedkar's own life reveals some of the factors that produced the Mahar upward movement. His father and grandfather had already broken away from the traditional position of the Mahar as a village servant by enlisting in the British army. Born into a family already urbanized and educated to some degree, Ambedkar's ability in school brought him to the attention of one of a number of caste Hindu reformers interested in the education of the lower castes—the Gaekwad of Baroda. With the Gaekwad's financial aid and his own stubborn persistence, Ambedkar graduated from Elphinstone College in Bombay, the first B. A. among Untouchables in western India. He went on to secure an M.A. and a Ph.D. from Columbia University in New York, a D.Sc. from London University and was admitted to the Bar from Grey's Inn in London. Returning to India in the early 1920s, he was able to command an interest in education and in political action already present in the Mahar caste, bringing enough unity and organization into that group so that it was ready, almost en masse, to follow him into a political movement and a religious conversion in the mid-1930s.

The independent labour party: 1936 saw two significant developments among that strata of the Untouchables led by Ambedkar. The Independent Labour Party was formed by Ambedkar in Bombay to fight the elections of 1937. Although founded as a general party, it drew its strength from Ambedkar's own large caste. It represented an organized attempt to capture the political power that Ambedkar and other Untouchables had come to feel was necessary to secure their social rights. But while the political movement is important and interesting, it is the movement toward conversion that concerns us here. To gain special political and social privileges as the Muslim minority had and to prove that the Untouchables were a group separate from the caste—Hindu majority and had separate interests, it became essential for the Untouchable to politicize. This political motive was undoubtedly present in the 1930s decision to convert; but the personal need for self-respect was perhaps just as important, if not more so.

Conversion as a way out of the Untouchable status was not new in India. Islam, and more especially Christianity, drew large numbers of their converts from lower castes, and Sikhism in the twentieth century actively encouraged untouchable conversion.

Conversion in South India: Actually, conversion to Buddhism was not unknown, although its numbers in Madras and on the Malabar coast were small. The Madras Buddhists generally declared themselves Hindus, but in Cochin in 1931 the Census Commissioner reported 96 Buddhists, mostly educated Malayali Iluvans, an Untouchable caste, who "disgusted with the social disabilities to which their caste is subjected within the Hindu fold, have become Buddhist converts.... Though their numbers are so few as to be altogether ignored, still, they point to a new tendency". The influence for conversion to Buddhism on the Malabar coast probably came from Ceylon, rather than from the revived intellectual interest in Buddhism in India itself. The Commissioner's comment, however, indicates the same reason for conversion that a few years later affected the Mahars.

In 1935 Ambedkar announced his decision to leave Hinduism, but at that time Buddhism was not seen as a viable alternative for the Mahars. Ambedkar was aware of the increased intellectual interest in Buddhism. He himself had received as an examination prize in 1907 a biography of the Buddha in Marathi from its author, a Bombay school teacher. He had been in correspondence with V.R. Shinde, a social reformer who was interested in Buddhism, and who had founded a wide network of schools and hostels for the Untouchables in the 1920s. Moreover, Ambedkar named his new home in Bombay, built in 1934, Raj Griha, after the Bihar city of the ancient Buddhist kings. But in spite of all this, when he announced that he "would not die a Hindu" in 1935, he was not yet ready to commit himself and his followers to Buddhism.

Ambedkar's Plea to Convert: Ambedkar's personal conversion announcement in 1935 was followed in 1936 by a Mahar conference in Bombay. After an address by Ambedkar, the conference as a whole declared its intention to converting to another religion. Portions of Ambedkar's impassioned plea for conversion form a sort of litany, which in the printed version is lifted out and placed in a poetry format. The passage begins :

Religion is for man; man is not for religion (and continues:)

If you want to gain self-respect, change your religion.

If you want to create a cooperating society, change your religion.

If you want power, change your religion.

If you want equality, change your religion.

If you want independence, change your religion.

If you want to make the world in which you live, happy, change your religion...

The response to Ambedkar's plea to convert was positive, probably because the Untouchable castes in the Bombay area had just gone through some eight years of attempts to participate in Hindu festivals and to enter Hindu temples without success. The 1935 announcement was made near Nasik, and many in Ambedkar's audience had undoubtedly participated in a five-year-long satyagraha (the word is borrowed from Mahatma Gandhi's non-violent technique, but Gandhi did not participate) to enter the famous Kala Ram Temple in Nasik, a pilgrimage city. Efforts to gain education, and efforts to secure political rights such as special representation in legislative bodies, had been fairly successful; however, efforts to claim religious rights had generally ended in failure. The idea of leaving Hinduism met with considerable approval among Ambedkar's own caste in western India and found echoes both in the south and north of India.

After the great conversion announcement of 1935-36, however, there was a hiatus of 20 years before Ambedkar's formal conversion to Buddhism took place. For the first few years, Ambedkar flirted with Islam, Sikhism and Christianity in an attempt to combine a personal need for self-respect, felt by many Untouchable groups, with an astute political move that would allow Untouchables more political power. Ambedkar personally felt Islam and Christianity to be "foreign religions", and his threatened conversion particularly to Islam, seems to have been more in the nature of a weapon to force recognition of the Untouchable needs from Hindus than a genuine interest. Sikhism was an Indian religion, and Ambedkar seems to have most seriously considered this avenue, but as a political expedient it was impractical. The appointment of Ambedkar in 1942 as Labour Member of the Viceroy's Executive Council, the highest position in Government to which any Untouchable had ever risen, and his subsequent place in the Constituent Assembly and in Nehru's first cabinet in independent India, gave such active rein to his political abilities that the religious question, except for his own personal interest, was left in abeyance.

During the time when Ambedkar was most active on the national scene, his personal interest in Buddhism increased. His college, established in 1946, was named Siddharth, the personal name of the Buddha, and a second College founded in 1951 was given the name of Milind, after the Greek king who converted to Buddhism. In 1948 Ambedkar republished P. Lakshmi Narasu's *Essence of Buddhism,* adding his own introduction, and the same year he also published his own study, *The Untouchables,* which theorized that Untouchables had been Buddhists who had been pushed aside from society when they fiercely clung to their religion, while there was a resurgence of Brahmanical Hinduism. In 1950 he visited Ceylon and in the same year began his own compilation of Buddhist scriptures, *The Buddha and His Dhamma,* which was published in 1957. This volume contains his interpretation of Buddhism — rational, moral, ethical and egalitarian, with little attention to contemplation and complete eradication of any mystical or magical elements.

The actual conversion ceremony to Buddhism was held in 1956. Ambedkar by this time was an old man, in Indian terms, and so ill that he died only two months later. He took *diksha* from the oldest Buddhist monk in India before a large audience in Nagpur and set in motion the conversion process that brought over three million Indians into the Buddhist fold in the next few years. Most of the converts are former Mahars of Maharashtra, but small groups of new Buddhists exist in most other states.

Those involved in the intellectual revival of Buddhism in India have not been entirely happy about this actual conversion movement. The Maha Bodhi Society was represented at the Nagpur conversion ceremony and has from time to time carried articles in its journal about the movement (including one by Ambedkar in 1952). Although some Maha Bodhi monks aided in the conversion, several branches are not sympathetic to the conversion process. Nor can they be, since most Maha Bodhi members are caste Hindus whose leadership the new converts have rejected. The Government publication, 2500 *Years of Buddhism,* edited by P.V. Bapat, which appeared in 1956, does not mention the conversion movement in its 1959 reprint. The conversion movement's insistence that Buddhism is separate goes against the general intellectual position found in S. Radhakrishnan's Foreword to the book. He writes, "The Buddha did not feel that he was announcing a new religion. He was born, grew up, and died a Hindu. He was restating with a new emphasis the ancient ideals of the Indo-Aryan civilization".

The Conversion Effect

The newly converted Buddhists from the Untouchable castes cannot accept this position, for their conversion is a denial of their former position in the Indo-Aryan civilization. The conversion "oaths" devised by Ambedkar for the Nagpur ceremony not only contain positive statements about Buddhism such as, "I will follow the Eight-Fold Path of the Lord Buddha; I will have compassion for all living beings and will try to look after them", but include negative statements about Hinduism such as, "I will not regard Brahma, Vishnu and Mahesh as Gods nor will I worship them; I will never get any Samaskar performed by brahmans". This negativism, psychologically necessary to the differing social status of those in the converting group and the intellectual group, prevents any close cooperation.

Those of us who have worked on the Buddhist movement are often asked, both from Indians and Westerns: "It is just a political stunt"; "They aren' t really Buddhists"? Our answers generally take the form of other questions "What possible political advantage does conversion offer"? Conversion to Buddhism immediately cuts off, except in Maharashtra where

Buddhists are counted as "backward classes" deserving of governmental benefits, all those official, political and social privileges afforded by the Government of India to Untouchable castes. Ambedkar's delayed conversion came long after the period of combining the conversion idea with political expediency, and by then reference to conversion as a political threat had lost its significance. Instead, it had reference to the great Asian Buddhist world, the reputation of Buddhism as an important religion both in India and the West and the possibility of Buddhism as a moral force.

The answer to the question of "real Buddhists" seems to be, "What is a 'real' Buddhists"? Buddhism in Tibet, in Ceylon, in Burma, in Nepal, to name only those countries which are close to India, differs greatly, and each country has absorbed local cultural tradition. A Buddhism stressing rationality, morality and equality may be just as scripturally justifiable as any of its more established varieties. And even the place of Ambedkar as a Bodhisattva, a concept which sets the teeth of some Buddhists on edge, is justified by the concepts: "He actually was the bringer of Buddhism to his people". "Even the Buddha himself claimed to be no more than a man; why not a human saviour"?

Life Span of Buddhist Movement

Perhaps a more valid question is, "What will be the lifespan of the current Buddhist movement"? There are signs which may give rise to a prediction that the new Buddhists will return to Hinduism at a somewhat higher level because of their emphasis on education and the purification of their living habits. There is among them the continuation of some Hindu ritual, especially among those who either are so well off economically and educationally that they have been able to integrate into modern, urban Hindu society, or so poorly off economically that they cannot afford to break the links with their Hindu neighbors.

However, there are also signs in the movement that point to the possibility of long-time continuation: the production of song literature, lives of the Buddha and translations of scripture in the vernaculars; the study of Pali, the Buddhist scriptural language, by young Buddhist college students and the teaching of Pali chants to groups at all levels; the celebration of Buddha Jayanti with processions, speeches and drama all in the new tradition; the development of leadership, not so much in the traditional Sangha of monks as among young educated laymen; the presence of some 20 to 25 bhikshus–English, Thai, Tibetan, Japanese, Sinhalese—living or travelling in the centers of the new Buddhism, communicating belief and practice with varying degrees of success to those who call themselves Buddhists; pilgrimages, often by means of free passes by those who work on the railway, to the Buddhist holy places. Wherever it *is* financially or legally possible, Buddhist converts have built small *viharas,* Buddhist temples, or converted old temples into Buddhist centers, where an image of the Buddha (and a picture of Ambedkar) is installed, prayer or *vandana* meetings bhikshus live and the nursery schools or the young men's student groups of the community meet.

Perhaps as important as any of these is a psychological change. Although *Bauddha,* the Marthi word now used for themselves by Buddhist converts in Maharashtra, is generally understood by others as a synonym for Mahar, the convert himself feels a release from the concept of pollution, a new freedom and self-respect.

There are few signs that today's Buddhist movement in India will produce the great art or the profound scriptures of its past days, but there is little doubt that the revival of Buddhism, both in its intellectual and conversion facts, has added a hopeful stress on equality and humanitarian behaviour to the Indian scene.

Reference

For a more scholarly discussion of the pre-Ambedkar Buddhist revival see "The Indian Rediscovery of Buddhism, 1855-1956", in A.K. Narain ed., *Studies in Pali and Buddhism* (New Delhi: D.K. Publishers and Distributors, 1979).

12

Legitimizing the Mahar Movement

The Mahar movement, more than any other Untouchable caste movement to achieve upward mobility, may be seen as Western in its orientation. It is easy to see why: the methods used by the Western-educated Dr. B.R. Ambedkar, the unquestioned leader of the movement, seem modern - governmental petitions and testimony, organized political parties, parliamentary procedures, mass contact through conferences and newspapers. The institutions created by the Mahars can all be named in English: the People's Education Society, the Republican Party, even the Buddhist Society of India. The rhetoric used also seems universal to all low-class movements: claim equality! agitate! educate! There have also been the purely Indian (or purely Maharashtrian) and traditional elements of the movement. This chapter attempts to look from inside the movement, through its own documents, to see in what ways it attempted to legitimize higher status and new functions through religious sanctification or traditional legitimation. It focuses on six moments in time in the eighty-five years of the modern recorded history of the Mahars of Maharashtra.

The first is the 1894 petition of Gopal Baba Walangkar, a retired Mahar British army soldier, whose work is the first written record of new Mahar ambition in the nineteenth century. Its very existence indicates a change in the economic status of the caste, i.e., the fact that some Mahars had left the traditional position of the village servant for non-traditional occupations. The second document repeats the theme of the first: a plea for recruitment into the British army and the lower ranks of administration; it is the 1910 petition to the Government written by Shivram Janba Kamble, a Mahar butler in the Masonic Hall in Pune.

The next three documents are from the period when Ambedkar was the leader. The Mahad Conference of 1927, which is seen by many Mahars as the moment of their mass awakening, was called by Ambedkar after ten years of work through conferences, newspapers and parliamentary action. The conversion speech of 1935 announced Ambedkar's rejection of Hinduism and an end to the Mahar effort to force entrance into the institutions of Hinduism, although conversion to another religion was set aside for twenty years in favour of intense political, educational, and social activity. At the time of the third of Ambedkar's documents, the Buddhist conversion speech of 1956, such unity had been achieved that 75 per cent of the Mahars and a number of small groups outside Maharashtra followed Ambedkar into Buddhism, resulting in three million new Buddhists.

The final documents are current and consist of literature, the poetry and short stories of the Dalit school. This is the writing of the now-educated, highly politicized, still radical Mahar-Buddhist left; it constitutes both a new level of Mahar achievement and restatement of their basic aims.

Ways of Seeking Legitimacy for the Mahar Movement

From the very beginning of the Mahar movement, its leaders seem to have searched for legitimacy for a change in social position in five ways which could be classified as religious, or, more broadly, traditional :

1. Brahmanical approval of new status and function. In the Maharashtrian context, a Brahman must be seen as elite, as cultural and social arbiter, as well as ritual specialist.
2. Societal acknowledgement of a right to a place in religious activities on a level with clean castes.
3. Recognition of religious knowledge and purity of life.
4. Scriptural sanctification.
5. Justification by mythic history.

In examining the six documents, the briefest of notes on the historical context of the material have been added and the ways in which the document illumined the quest for legitimacy in one or another of these five ways have been stressed.

(*a*) The Walangkar Petition

Toward the end of the nineteenth century, recruitment of Untouchables from Maharashtra (Bombay Presidency) into the British army was stopped in favour of a "martial race" (chiefly from the Northwest) pattern of recruitment. For Mahars, who had been employed in the British army for a hundred years, this blocked one of their main paths of social advancement. A retired Mahar Havaldar, Gopalnak Viththalnak Walangkar, known as Gopal Baba, prepared a long petition for re-entry into the army and circulated it among the Untouchable pensioners. They were not ready for such unified action, however, and the petition was never signed and sent to the British Government. A handwritten copy which is bound together with a long poem by Pandit Kondiram, evidently a Mahar religious figure, is in the Khairmode Collection of Ambedkar material in the University of Bombay Library. (Ambedkar was a distant relative of Walangkar's and from the same Mahar army family background.) Newspapers of the 1890s confirm the authenticity of the document and report similar sentiments in Walangkar's public speeches.

Walangkar's main plea for the re-admission of Mahar, Chambhar, and Mang castes (all Marathi-speaking Untouchables) into the army was based on the proven worth of the "anarya" (non-Aryans) as military men. His rhetoric, however, also suggests an interesting pattern of legitimizing devices, and the accompanying poem further develops the Mahar position. Walangkar deals with the five legitimizing points in the following ways :

(i) Brahmanical approval

Although there was high caste criticism of the treatment of Untouchables at this time and even the possibility that a sympathetic Brahman helped Walangkar write his petition, Walangkar's main effort is to question the origin of the high castes, and hence their right to discriminate, rather than to note the approval of the reformers among them. His sweeping judgments reflect a view of India's history as one of great mobility and change: Why should the opinion of the high castes count for so much, asks Walangkar, when the high caste people of the South were originally "Australian-Semitic, non-Aryan and African Negroes"; when the Chitpavans were "Barbary Jews" shipwrecked on the coast who married low caste women and became Brahmans when they became rulers; when the Marathas themselves came to India as Turks? God has sent the British to rule, Walangkar claims, as punishment for these people's persecution of the Untouchable. In the tough language of the nineteenth century Maharashtrian reformers, Walangkar bypasses the need for Brahmanical approval by disparaging Brahmans, a position possible only so long as the British controlled the opportunities wanted.

(ii) Right in religious activities

Walangkar does not concern himself with this. A newspaper report of another of his public protests *(Indu Prakash,* Bombay, 5 May 1890) notes his protest against Untouchables not being allowed to stay in *dharmsalas* (pilgrims' guest houses) but there does not seems to be any protest against Untouchables being debarred from temples and religious processions.

(iii) Recognition of religious knowledge and purity of life

Walangkar notes that even if a group stops eating beef for generations, they are still Untouchables. Sanskritization evidently brought no social reward. The poem attached to Walangkar's petition indicates why Walangkar did not belabour this point. In bitter, reproachful tones it notes the social consequences of the deprivation of the Untouchables: lice in women's hair, children playing in rubbish and dancing in *tamasha* (folk drama), men eating carrion, ignorance, humble faces, knowledge only of the demon gods, immoral *gosavis* (holy men). No claim to higher status on the basis of religious knowledge and purity of life among the masses could be made at this time. Internal reform must come first.

(iv) Scriptural Sanctification

Walangkar asked the Brahmans, his petition states, five years earlier to prove the lowness of the Untouchable by religious scripture and to show how by religious remedies this lowness could be removed, but "none of the caste—proud of their priests upto now, have proved our lowness". The poem of Pandit Kondiram is more radical. It ends starkly: "Burn these brahmanical scriptures".

(v) Mythic History

Walangkar presents two contradictory myths in casual form to underwrite his plea for re-entrance into the army. The name of the group in whose name the petition was written is, in English, the Non-Aryan Group for the Removal of Wrongs. The position that Untouchables were the pre-Aryan peoples of India was accepted by movements in the South *(Adi-Dravida,* the first Dravidians) and in the North *(Ad-Dharm,* first religion). Such a concept legitimizes social protest by assuming that the Aryan conquest, not inherent polluting qualities, reduced the Untouchable to a low status. However, in Maharashtra, this mythic history rationale was little used. Walangkar himself counters his own claim by asserting that the Mahars were former Kshatriyas, demoted during the Great Famine for eating forbidden food. A consistently satisfying mythic-history was not developed in the Mahar movement until Ambedkar's Buddhist conversion speech of 1956 but the need for such a mythic history is apparent at all levels of the Mahar movement.

The Walangkar petition and Pandit Kondiram's accompanying poem cannot be read as evidence of mass Mahar thought. Both were obviously far more radical statements than the majority of Mahars were prepared to make publicly. However, one can draw some general conclusions about the movement from these early protests.

First, Mahar leadership was more concerned about function than about ritual status. The right to have an opportunity to leave the traditional village Mahar duties of watchman, scavenger, message-bearer, etc., demanded that the ruling power provide opportunities to make that move. The right to have a new function, however, did involve legitimizing arguments both to the Government and to fellow Hindus. In the Walangkar petition, we see the Mahar avoiding a claim based on ritual purity to stress the view that high status groups have been low themselves in the past, that change has taken place in many periods of India's past, that the Mahar has just as much a right to change function as have high caste peoples. What is needed is good performance of that function and some sort of legitimizing mythic history to explain present low status and hence allow changes!

Later documents are more concerned with ritual status as the mass of Mahars reaches toward the lifestyle and values of the clean castes. However, this initial view of change in function as basic remains constant. It was the Mahar who had left the village function of, in British legal terms, "inferior village servant", who began the Mahar movement. As the movement progressed, not only did more Mahars enter non-traditional occupations (the mills, dock-work, construction, the railroad), but also those remaining in the village were urged to drop that aspect of their village function which was most polluting — the eating of the carrion beef which it was their duty to drag from the village. The Mahar traditional occupation could not modernize although it could be stripped of polluting elements. It was up to the "new" Mahar, the Mahar who had left the village, to legitimize his new function, and then to try to extend that legitimacy and its consequent higher status image to his brethren still in the village.

Shivram Janba Kamble's Petition of 1910

Kamble's position as butler in the Masonic Hall in Pune illustrates another new Mahar occupation — that of the servant of the British. This kind of service allowed the Mahar to learn English as well as to secure economic independence from village work, and, low as such service seems now, produced a number of Mahar innovators in the past. Kamble's group were those who had become urbanized and worked as semi-skilled labour, as well as a few old retired soldiers of Walangkar's breed. His petition, although it is also a plea for re-admittance into the army and opportunities for service in the lower reaches of Government administration, is far more sophisticated than Walangkar's. It was sent to the Earl of Crewe, Secretary of State for India in London, from the Conference of the Deccan Mahars and may have helped, along with war-time necessity, in the creation of a Mahar labour force as an adjunct to the army during World War I. Looking at the Kamble petition through the same five foci as we did Walangkar's petition indicates that the basic matter of function still predominates (Navalkar, 1930).

(i) Brahmanical Approval

Kamble notes the anti-untouchability stance of several Brahman reformers and political leaders. Here the elite rather than the ritual status of the Brahman is important, but it must be remembered that in the Maharashtrian context, social elite are Brahmans, thus inextricably mixing ritual and social status. Kamble also rests his case on the fact that the British parliament now contains groups who, "only a quarter of a century ago, were regarded as Mahars and Paryas by the more educated and affluent classes of their nation", thus extending the concept of radical change in history from the Indian to the European milieu.

(ii) Right in Religious Activities

Since Kamble's petition is directed very consciously to the British, this element does not enter into the document. Kamble's own activities, however, included a sustained attempt in 1929 to enter Parvati Temple in Pune. This satyagraha failed completely in the face of obdurance and violence. However, Kamble's efforts to force entrance of Untouchables into tea shops in Pune indicated that an attack on this aspect of ritual pollution in the urban areas could be successful.

Kamble's position on these matters cannot be gleaned from the petition. A suggestion that Kamble attempted to use mythic history is in the title of a newspaper that he founded in 1909, *Somwanshiya Mitra,* friend of the Somwanshi is a sub-caste among the Mahars; it also is a major mythological division of Hindus into "the race of the moon" in contrast to "the race of the sun". Kamble used the word Mahar in calling caste conferences as early as 1903 and was far more caste-based in his activities than either Walangkar before him or Ambedkar after him. It seems to me that in his use of *Somwanshiya* he is linking the Mahars to a mythic past, important chiefly to

Rajputs, and hence suggesting a Kshatriya linkage. Kamble worked with a retired Mahar army man in his various campaigns in Pune and he often held meetings at the foot of the Koregaon monument, a pillar erected to commemorate the war heroes during the British defeat of the Peshwa in 1818 which lists many Mahar names. Kambles' stress on the militant Mahar past indicates a basic Kshatriya mythic history.

The Mahad Conferences of 1927

B.R. Ambedkar appeared publicly on the Bombay scene in 1918, when he testified at length to the Southborough Commission. This testimony, however, was mid-point in his advanced education. After graduating from Elphinstone College, he had studied at Columbia University and gone on to England to do a D.Sc. from the London School of Economics and thereafter to enter the Bar. Returning in the early 1920s, he used the same methods as Kamble, conferences and newspapers, to build group unity, served as a legislator (as a nominated Untouchable representative) in the Bombay Assembly, and began to push at a much greater pace the demands for opportunities for employment in the British administration, the schools and the police. The Mahad Conference of 1927 was one of the many he called, but its drawing power and its actions created the numbers and the news which made it a landmark.

The Kolaba District Depressed Classes Conference (note that the name Mahar is not used) met at Mahad, a small town south of Bombay. The site was chosen on the basis of an invitation by the caste Hindu reformer who headed the Municipality and who was a friend of Ambedkar. The speeches and resolutions of the first conference were similar to those of other conferences. After the meeting, several thousands marched to a pond in the high caste area of Mahad and the first to arrive drank the water from the rank. This action incited such violence that the Untouchables had to hastily withdraw for fear of their lives. A second conference was called later the same year to protest against the ritual cleansing that the Mahad pond had undergone, and it was at this meeting that the Mahar path of radical protest was begun and the ancient law book, *Manusmriti,* which condoned untouchability, was burned.

In terms of the five point rubric used previously, the conferences' speeches and actions yield these positions:

A number of Brahmans keen on social reforms and high caste non-Brahmans were among Ambedkar's followers. One had invited Ambedkar to use Mahad as a site for a conference; a Brahman proposed the resolution to condemn the *Manusmriti*. Ambedkar did not ask for Brahmanical sanction for change in any ritualized way. He did, however, use all the support he could muster from the elite for his program, maintaining his hold on the reins of power and delegating certain responsibilities to these radical reformers. In addition, Ambedkar himself appeared as one of the elite; his speech, dress, presence, educational background and aggressive temperament were all similar to those of Maharashtrian Brahman elite. It might be said that by the time of the Mahad Conference, Ambedkar himself had assumed an elite function — as teacher, writer, legislator — without, of course, elite or clean-caste ritual status. Using what radical brahmanical approval was available to him, Ambedkar was beginning to reject any sort of orthodox legitimization. He both served as a source of charisma for his own caste and as an enabling device in governmental circles. Ambedkar's "westernization" could also be called "brahmanization" in a broad cultural sense and this met some ideal goal current among his people, binding them to him.

The Mahad satyagraha was for the right to use the common water tank, but it was the fear of the higher caste population that the Untouchables would enter the temple that had triggered the attack, according to reports. Temple-entry was in the air and the Mahars were soon to make three organized attempts at Amravati, Pune and Nasik. They had already made an unsuccessful attempt to take part in a Ganpati procession in Bombay. Ambedkar was never especially concerned with ritual rights, but it is clear that those who followed him expected that participation in institutionalized Hindu activities would be a consequence of their activities and self-improvement.

Ambedkar did not try to claim that the heterodox religious practices of the Mahars were worthy of respect, nor did he for long encourage Sanskritized religious practices. As a student at Elphinstone College in Bombay he had attempted to study Sanskrit, but objections by the teacher forced him to take Persian as his second language instead. There is no doubt that had he been able to master Sanskrit, he would have added that source of religious knowledge effectively to his own elite image. Deprived of the basic skill, he devoted his energy in encouraging "purity of life" among his followers. At the Mahad conference he asked all those who attended to take a vow to renounce the eating of carrion and reinforced this attempt to remove the basic root of Mahar pollution by asking caste Hindus to bury their own dead cows and the Government to prohibit by law the eating of carrion! He also asked his listeners to "improve the general tone of our demeanour, *re-tone our pronunciations* and revitalise our thoughts". Women in special meetings were asked to dress like caste Hindu women, to send their children to school, not to feed their husbands if they were drunk. Internal attempts at reform, now much stressed by the Mahar movement, fit very well into M.N. Srinivas' rubric of Sanskritization, but note here that the emphasis is on elements which are social rather than ritualistic.

The high point of the second Mahar Conference of 1927 was the ceremonial burning of the *Manusmriti,* an act recalled with shock by caste Hindus even today. Within a few years, Mahatma Gandhi was to challenge anyone to find justification for Untouchability in the scriptures, but the Mahars had already asked the question, had found evidence of scriptural legitimization of their untouchability, and rejected it.

Justification by Mythic History

Ambedkar used neither the pre-Aryan nor the former-Kshatriya myths. Possibly he felt that a pre-Aryan claim would set the Mahars aside as a separate race, and he had seen permanent racial division in America during his student years. As for claiming Kshatriya status, the clean caste Maratha community had fought that battle for years with a much more viable argument of past kings and Rajput linkages. During his Mahad speech, Ambedkar hinted at a time when "we, who are condemned as Untouchables, were much advanced, much ahead in education compared with communities other than the advanced classes. This part of the country was then pulsating with the action and authority of our people" (Keer 1962: 69-70). His reference is not clear but the need for a mythic past, however, is clear, and when Ambedkar had developed a view of the Mahar past which would both explain the caste's low position and justify its current struggle for empowerment, it became a vital part of his message.

The Conversion Speech of 1935

By the mid-thirties, the Mahars had been involved in six years of futile temple-entry struggle; they had also been involved in agitation for political rights which had won them reserved places in the legislature which would insure representation even beyond their numbers. The conversion speech can be seen in two lights: one is the genuine anguish which Ambedkar felt as a Hindu who polluted other Hindus; the other is the glow of political success and the hope that the threat of conversion, which would cut down the numbers of Hindus in the numbers game of separate electorates vis-a-vis Muslims, would act as a catalyst to force Hindus to open up in the religious field from political motives. The mood of the speech is best expressed by a short quotation :

> Because we have the misfortune of calling ourselves Hindus, we are treated thus. If we were members of another Faith, none would dare treat us so. Choose any religion which gives you equality of status and treatment. We shall repair our mistake now. I had the misfortune of being born with the stigma of an Untouchable. However, it is not my fault; but I will not die a Hindu, for this is in my power. (Ambedkar, 1936)

Acknowledgement of Religions Rights: The analysis of the conversion announcement involves only one of the five points, that of the need for an acknowledgment of religious rights. It is this element of legitimization that Ambedkar was trying to force. The religious rights he saw as necessary to underwrite the Mahar claim to equality must be gleaned not only from his speeches but also from his reaction to the responses which followed (The Depressed Classes, 1935).

Although individuals among the Mahar community protested, no Mahar group rejected the idea of conversion. The *Manusmriti* was burned again, this time near Nasik, the site of a five-year temple entry satyagraha. Groups from outside Maharashtra, chiefly in the North and in the Kerala area, picked up the conversion refrain, but Ambedkar did not use this response to organize a massive movement. Caste Hindus also responded. Pandit Madan Mohan Malaviya offered to fund a special ritual "with which all disabilities would go except dinner and marriage". Dr. Kurtakoti, the Sankaracharya of Karwar Math, offered to found a new sect with equal status to other sections of Hinduism. To these overtures, Ambedkar answered with a clear view of what he meant by religious equality: K.K. Sakat, an Untouchable who was an exemplary Hindu, should be elevated to the position of Sankaracharya for a year and so acknowledged by Chitpavan Brahmans; Hinduism should be changed from a "religion of rules" to a "religion of principles", and the necessary changes would involve: (1) one standard book of Hindu religion, (2) no hereditary priesthood, but an examination system open to all, (3) state permits required for priests, (4) a limit by law on the numbers of priests, (5) state supervision of the priest's morals, beliefs and worship. No Hindu, however interested in reform, indeed no realist, could accept these dicta. Hinduism would have to entirely change its character. But Ambedkar's point is that the Mahar here himself claims the right to earn Brahmanhood.

Ambedkar dallied with the Muslims, Christians, Sikhs, Buddhists and Arya Samajists who were interested, for one reason or another, in the possibility of a Mahar conversion to their numbers. For a while, he seemed to lean toward Sikhism, but then dropped the whole idea when it became clear that after conversion they could not carry the new political privileges of the Untouchables into a new religion. The Mahars, however, never again returned to a group movement for Hindu religious rights.

The Buddhist Conversion of 1956

Twenty years after the Mahar Conference on conversion, Ambedkar was at last ready to announce a new religion. An old man, sick with diabetes and with less than two months to live, he took *diksha* (conversion) from the hands of the oldest Buddhist monk in India under the hot October sun in Nagpur. The following day he converted the half-million of his followers who had responded to his call to convert.

Ambedkar had been interested in Buddhism since the early 1930s; by 1956 Buddhism had become not only an intellectual passion but a more viable new religious home for those who found sanction within Hinduism for their new role and function. In Buddhism, Ambedkar had found an Indian, not a foreign, religion which could legitimize the claims of the Mahar. The nature of the Buddhism which he initiated may be seen in his conversion speech; in *The Buddha and His Dharma* (1957), Ambedkar's rationalized life of the Buddha and explanation of his teachings; in the twenty-two "Buddhist Oaths" which constituted part of the conversion ritual; and in the small number of practices Ambedkar was able to develop before his death.

Opting out of Hinduism might seem to obviate the need to legitimize through the five ways used here to analyze all other documents. Looking at the conversion through these lenses, however, does show that the acceptance of Buddhism in some ways tracks closely with previous Mahar efforts.

By choosing Buddhism, Ambedkar leapt over the necessity of eliciting approval. Buddhism itself is egalitarian, and by 1956 Buddhism as a religion was respected although not much practiced in India. The symbols of independent India, the wheel on the flag and the lion pillar, were Buddhist or from Buddhist times. Two important neighbors, Burma and Ceylon, which Ambedkar had visited to experience living Buddhism, were Buddhist countries. Several important scholars, chief among them Dharmanand Kosambi, a Maharashtrian, were doing research on Buddhism and a few Indian intellectuals (Rahul Sankrityayana, Anand Kausalyayan, Kashyap) had become Buddhists out of conviction. Ambedkar stressed the respect in which Buddhism is held in the world in his conversion speech: "Even today, 2500 years afterwards, all the world respects the principles of Buddhism". "Only one name is proclaimed throughout the world, and that name is Buddha".

Ambedkar made it clear that the Buddha's message was equality. "In the Buddhist religion, 75 per cent of the Bhikshus were Brahman; 25 per cent were Shudra and others". Ambedkar did not set in motion a way to develop a Sangha; he actually only began the institutionalization of the conversion. It is as if he made a gift of Buddhism to those who had followed him along the educational and political paths he opened, wiping away the stigma of religious inequality by presenting a way to say with inner certainty, "I am equal; I do not pollute". The Buddhist's Oaths illustrate the way in which Ambedkar combined the rejection of specific Hindu beliefs with an acceptance of Buddhism. The rather crude negative oaths seem to have been essential to inculcate the sense of psychological freedom from pollution that the Mahar had never been able to gain within the confines of Hinduism.

Throughout his conversion speech, Ambedkar told little stories which reinforced all the long years of striving to purify Mahar practices. A Brahman had asked him, "Why do you throw away 500 rupees profit every year from hide, hoof and meat when you are so poor"? and Ambedkar had told him, "You have many dependents. Why don't you remove the dead cattle and get the profit? I myself will give you 500 rupees on top of that". He used another homily to reiterate the need to maintain the dignity of women: In the locality of prostitutes in Bombay, the women rise in the morning and say, "Suleman, bring bread and a plate of minced meat". The Depressed Class sisters do not even get ordinary chumey-bhakri. However, Ambedkar said, they live with dignity; they live piously. The point is clear; the Mahar, now Buddhist, life is to be pure by both Hindu and elite standards. The Buddhist newly converted said Ambedkar, must bring honour to Buddhism, whether he is an educated or an illiterate man.

Ambedkar's conversion speech simplifies Buddhism. It is in no way a scholarly analysis of religious knowledge Mahars would then be expected to exhibit. It must be understood, however, that education had been a major tenet of the movement from its earliest days. In his speech Ambedkar assumes that the Mahar will value education; he refers often to his own school days and his own learning. He states that it is his duty to lead his people "to a stage of full knowledge" and that he is writing a book which will help them to achieve this end. The speech of 1956 stresses good behavior. In the colleges he had established, Ambedkar had instituted departments to teach Pali and it is clear that he expected those who became highly educated to master the source of Buddhist religious knowledge. At this time the emphasis is still on gaining religious knowledge and establishing purity of life, not on securing acknowledgement of those accomplishments.

Obviously the scriptural sanctification required here is in Buddhism. In his speech, Ambedkar talks of an argument with Mahatma Gandhi over *chaturvarna* (four-fold caste hierarchy) in which he asked, "who created the *chaturvarna* and who will end it"? and Gandhi can give no answer. Ambedkar then added that Marxism is not enough to remove suffering. No "scripture" sufficed for Ambedkar save the Buddha's teaching of equality.

Ambedkar had already developed his theory that Untouchables had been Buddhists cast aside as India became re-Hinduized in his book, *The Untouchables: Who were they? and why they became Untouchables*. In his speech at the time of conversion he stated that during the Aryan harassment of the Nag people, Agastya Muni helped one Nag man to escape. "We spring from that man". The Nag people then met Gautam Buddha and "spread the teaching of Bhagwan Buddha all over India". The city of Nagpur was chosen for the conversion because it was the city of the Nags. In his speech, Ambedkar does not fully develop his theory, nor does he belabour this point. In the Mahar mind, however, the idea was quickly assimilated. The Mahar as former Buddhist, persecuted because he had clung to his Buddhism, was now returning to his old faith. Ambedkar had given a fully satisfactory explanation of the low status and a justification for a claim to a respected place in Indian society.

The analysis ought to end here with a note comparing Walangkar's original statement of Mahar aims and Ambedkar's concluding message for his people. The Mahar, now Buddhist, movement is still dynamic, however. Buddhism has not proved to be a panacea. *Bauddh,* in Marathi, means Mahar. As a Buddhist, he has a sense of psychological freedom, a satisfying mythic history, and full rights within a respected world religion. But although many of the old practices of untouchability are gone, the Buddhist still suffers from poverty, from some discrimination, and from the violence which erupts when he oversteps his place in the village. In the last three years the movement has developed another aspect, that of Dalit politics and Dalit literature. Dalit means broken, "reduced to pieces", oppressed or low. It avoids the ritual pollution connotations of the word Untouchable but unmistakably refers to that group.

Dalit Panthers, Dalit Literature

Dalit literature, that is, writing which is considered genuine literature rather than folk-protest poetry and "movement" literature, may be said to have begun in the late 1950s with the short stories of Shankarrao Kharat, who wrote movingly of his childhood as a village Mahar (Miller, 1972). A lawyer and former Vice-Chancellor of Marathwada University, Kharat produced books within the movment: an edition of the letters of Ambedkar, the story of the Buddhist conversion. He also produced short stories which had to be considered as genuine evidence of creativity in the strong Marathi literary tradition. Since that time, a fairly steady flow of short stories and poetry and a series of Buddhist and Dalit Literacy Conferences have resulted in what must be called a significant new school of Marathi writing, that of Dalit Literature. Acknowledgment of the worth of this writing is evidenced in the 25 November 1973 supplement of the *Times Weekly.* Dileep Padgaonkar's introduction to this special issue on Dalit Literature states: "Its immense merit is to have effectively rebelled, in life as in letters, against the middle-class Hindus who have monopolised cultural expression".

Accompanying the tough, realistic, unorthodox literature, a new socio-political movement has surfaced; it was organized in 1972 as the Dalit Panthers. The first of the new Mahar Buddhist writers, Shankarrao Kharat, is not part of this movement, but most of the recently acknowledged young writers are. The Dalit Panthers reject the compromising ways the political party Ambedkar had established came to adopt. Their methods (calling for a boycott of an election, marching on a village where a caste Hindu who raped a Buddhist girl was not brought to justice) are outside normal politics. The Panthers, however, do not reject Ambedkar or Buddhism, and although their loyalty to his teaching, if not his organizations, is mixed with a vague Marxism, they feel the new thrust of his movement.

The rhetoric of the Dalit Panthers returns to the days of Ambedkar's exhortation to his followers to be defiantly strong, even to the time of Walangkar's disparagement of Brahmans, of belief in the possibility of radical change. Ambedkar once told his people, "Become the ruling community", a slogan I have seen painted on the walls of a tiny library built in the 1930s in a Mahar city slum. A pamphlet of the Dalit Panthers states, "We do not want a little place in the Brahman alley. We want the rule of the whole land". The poetry returns to the tough, bitter tone of the Poem of Pandit Kondiram which lay, unpublished, in the personal library of Ambedkar along with the Walangkar petition of 1894. One example is Arun Kamble's *The Life We Live,* translated by Gauri Deshpande in the *Times Weekly Supplement* of 25 November 1973 :

If you were to live the life we live
(them out of you would poems arise).
We: kicked and spat at for
    our piece of bread
You: fetch fulfillment and
    name of the Lord.
We: down-gutter degraders
    of our heritage
You: its sole repository
    descendants of the sage.
We: never have a paisa to scratch our arse
You: the golden cup of offerings in your bank.
Your bodies flame in sandalwood.
Ours you shovel under half-turned-sand.
Wouldn't the world change, and fast,
If you were forced to live at last
This life that's all we've ever had?

Another poem by Kamble, *Speech,* translated by Gauri Deshpande in the same *Times Weekly* supplement, also contrasts the Mahar-Brahman images :

Bone-chewing granpus
at burning ghat
permanent resident
of my own heart
with weight of traditon
behind his back
yells, "sadding bastard, I tell you,
Stutter with our tongue"!
Picking through the vedas buttering his queue
Brahmin teacher at school
bellows, "speak my pure tongue,
whoreson".
Now, you tell me which
speech
am I to tongue?

Here is the defiant Mahar, the Buddhist free from the psychological burden of pollution, bitter about both past and present but still proud of being what he is, and proclaiming both bitterness and pride in the Brahman's own tongue sophisticated literature.

What dimension does the new school of Dalit Literature add to the Mahar movement? What new demands are made and what sorts of legitimation are sought for them? Walangkar's petition to re-enter the army was met in 1942 by the establishment, at Ambedkar's urging, of a Mahar Regiment as a proud unit of the Indian army. Kamble's urging that the Mahar be accepted into the lower ranks of administration and police was met by the legal provision that a percentage of all governmental positions be reserved for the Scheduled Castes. Ambedkar's secular demands have been met, at least in theory, by the constitutional outlawing of any act of discrimination against Untouchables; his religious demands were obviated by the Buddhist conversion, and for those who did not convert there has been a general opening of Hindu temples, at least in urban areas. What still reigns is the general poverty level of most Scheduled Castes; sporadic but often intense enforcement of traditional subservience — at times violent — in the rural areas; subtle indications of inferiority in the cities — and something that can only be described as a lack of recognition of *manushki,* the full humanity of the Untouchable.

Looking at the Mahar story, it seems as if religious legitimation of their upward movement has been unimportant. The great changes wrought have come by secular government moves or economic opportunity. But Hinduism is more than a religion, and its hierarchy of social groupings has been correlated not only with status but also Junction. When one studies the Mahar movement as a group change in function, it becomes clear that the simple view of education and urbanization equaling modernization is not good enough. One must look at the nature of the function the Buddhist leadership now performs not only in terms of occupation but in terms of the traditional caste structure of Maharashtra. And one must consider this caste structure in order to understand why all Ambedkar's efforts, and those following him, failed to build a class movement, an organization of the Depressed Classes and the exploited in general, and has remained limited to the Mahars (and to smaller groups of other castes in areas outside Maharashtra).

Given this view, one asks: what new function could a Mahar Untouchable have whose traditional role was to serve the village as remover of pollution, low-status functionary in the bureaucratic system, entertainer in folk-music and folk-drama, and, of course, agricultural labour? When he becomes highly educated, urbanized, politicized, he does not yearn for the land (which he has never owned in viable quantities); he has no artisan skill; he has no instinct for trade (no Marathi-speaking caste of any size has entered this field); he can only fill the traditional social role of the Maharashtrian Brahman: the administrative echelons and the cultural establishment. Entering government service has been encouraged by special-privilege acts of the Government of India; filling a cultural role has been on the Mahar's own initiative.

What seems to be happening today is that the Mahar as "Brahman" is seeking and winning societal approval for a cultural function: the creation of literature, which had a meaningful high status value in Maharashtrian society. And the approval must come from the cultural establishment, which is still largely Brahman. As Dileep Padgaonkar, quoted earlier, has said, the Dalit writer has "effectively rebelled, in life as in letters, against the middle-class Hindus who have monopolised cultural expression". Though the village enemy may well be Maratha, whose caste dominates the land agriculturally and politically, the ideological enemy, the "mirror-image" in Arun Ramble's poems, and in many others, is still the Brahman. And yet paradoxically the very poets who translated the Dalit literature in the Special Issue of the *Times Weekly* are Brahman!

But all the years of effort have still left the bulk of the Mahars, now Buddhists, in the village. What is especially interesting in the Mahar movement is its leadership: for however elite they themselves may have become, the Mahar leaders have sought to extend the legitimacy won in the exercise of their new function to those still caught in the lower reaches of society. This cohesiveness is what has made the Mahar struggle in Maharashtra a movement of different quality than that Untouchables efforts toward higher social status. The tie of the Dalit poets with the Dalit Panthers is not a coincidence. The new Mahar, the Buddhist, the poet, with his new "tongue" proclaims the human worth of all his fellows.

References

Ambedkar, Bhimrao Ramji, *Mukti Kon Pathe?* (What Path Freedom) (Bombay: Bharat Bhushan Printing Press, 1936).

— *Annihilation of Caste with a Reply to Mahatama Gandhi* (Ambedkar: Ambedkar School of Thought, 1945, 3rd edition, First published in 1936).

— *The Untouchables. Who were they and why they became Untouchables* (New Delhi: Amrit Book Co.1948).

— "Report of Dr. Babasaheb Ambedkar's Speech in Nagpur" in *Prabuddh Bharat,* Translated by Rekha Damle and Eleanor Zelliot from the Marathi (27 October 1956).

— *The Buddha and His Dhamma* (Bombay: Siddharth College, 1957).

The Depressed Classes, "Bombay Depressed Classes Decision" in *The Depressed Classes: a Chronological Documentation*. Part I (Ranchi: Rev. Fr.J. Jans S.J., Catholic Press, 1935). Part II-Part VII (Kurseong: St. Mary's College, 1935-37, published in one volume).

Dhananjay Keer, *Dr. Ambedkar, Life and Mission* (Bombay: Popular Prakashan, 1962, 2nd edition).

Robert J. Miller, and Pramod Kale,' 'The Burden on the Head is Always There" in J. Michael Mahar ed., *The Untouchables in Contemporary India*. (Tucson: University of Arizona, 1972), pp. 317-590.

H.N. Navalkar, [petition] "To The Right Honourable The Earl of Crewe" in *The Life of Shivram Janba Kamble and Brief History of Poona Parvati Satyagraha* (Pune: S.J. Kamble, 1930), pp. 142-57.

M.N. Srinivas, "Sanskritization in *Social Change in Modern India* (Berkeley: University of California Press, 1966), pp. 1-45.

Times Weekly Supplement, "Special Issue on Dalit Literature" (Bombay, 25 November, 1973).

Gopalnak Viththalnak Walangkar,' To His Excellency the Commander-in-Chief of Bombay Presidency, at Poona, from the Anarya Doshpariharakham at Dapoli", 1894. *Manuscript* translated by D.R. Maheshkar with accompanying *pad* by Pandit Kondiram in the Khairmode Collection of the University of Bombay—Library.

Note: This English version of the 22 oaths has been taken, without correction, from a pamphlet published by the Buddhist Society of India, New Delhi, no date.

Eleanor Zelliot, "Buddhism and Politics in Maharashtra" in Donald E. Smith ed., *South Asian Politics and Religion* (Princeton: Princeton University Press, 1966), pp. 91-212.

—. "Dr. Ambedkar and the Mahar Movement", Unpublished Ph.D. dissertation submitted to University of Pennsylvania, 1969.

—. "Learning the Use of Political Means: The Mahars of Maharashtra", in Rajni Kothari ed., *Caste in Indian Politics* (New Delhi: Orient Longmans, 1970), pp. 29-69. Also in this volume.

—. "The 19th Century Background of the Mahar and Non-Brahman Movements in Maharashtra", in *The Indian Economic and Social History Review*, Vol. 8, No. 3, 1970.

— "Gandhi and Ambedkar: A Study in Leadership" in J. Michael Mahar ed., *The Untouchables in Contemporary India* (Tucson: University of Arizona Press, 1972), pp. 69-95.

13

Organization of Buddhists in India: Activities and Observances

The Buddhist Conversion Movement

The contemporary Buddhist conversion movement in India arose neither from a missionary enterprise which carried its own organizational structure and leadership, nor from the Buddhaization of a highly developed existent religious structure. Unlike any other mass conversion in history, this new religious movement was almost completely on its own. The massive conversion which began in 1956 largely affected low castes, particularly the Mahars of Maharashtra, who had been involved for decades in battle for political, social and religious rights. Buddhism was chosen as the religion of conversion because of its qualities of rationality, equality and intellectual creativity because—it offered a way out of the psychological imprisonment of the Hindu caste system. Buddhism as an organized religion, however, was almost non-existent in India at that time, and the ex-Untouchables who chose to convert had to create leadership, structure, religious observances and activities from very indirect models, and what they created had to be a religion that would fit their own needs.

The leader of this conversion movement, Dr. B.R. Ambedkar, had been interested in Buddhism most of his adult life. He had read books on Buddhism which had become a minor part of India's discovery of her own past in the twentieth century; he had met some of the men who had, as individuals, become interested in Buddhism; he had travelled to Ceylon and Burma to see living Buddhism in Buddhist countries; and he had written *The Buddha and His Dhamma,* a rationalized life of the Buddha and a selection of texts, chiefly from Pali sources.

Moreover, he had prepared his followers psychologically for a conversion from Hinduism from 1935 on, beginning with his own statement that he "would not die a Hindu". But the conversion was held suddenly, dramatically and without much organizational preparation on 14 October 1956, and within two months of it Ambedkar was dead. He had died a Buddhist, and he had set in motion a movement that soon involved over three million people. But although the inspiration of Ambedkar's own example and his invitation to others to follow him were powerful directives, the organization of the new religion was at a bare minimum.

The structural and leadership elements developed during the long struggle for social and political rights and for educational opportunities were pressed into service to provide the thrust and direction of the religious movement. Without the living example of a Buddhist society before them, the "new Buddhists"[1] had to create a meaningful religious life from the sources available to them: Dr. Ambedkar's precepts, traditional Buddhism as they understood it from the texts, and non-Indian Buddhists with whom they came in contact. Most importantly, they had to build that Buddhist society in the light of the needs of the Buddhist converts, most of them from formerly Untouchable castes, in the context of a dominant Hindu society.

Now, fifty years after the conversion, the movement has slowed in garnering numbers.[2] There were 180,823 Buddhists in India in 1951, before the conversion; 3,250,227 Buddhists in 1961, and 3,812,325 Buddhist in 1971, according to the Indian Census. The great bulk of the Buddhists are in Maharashtra, 3,264,000 Buddhists, but there are sizable numbers in urban centres outside that state: 10,000 in Andhra Pradesh, 81,800 in Madhya Pradesh, 14,100 in Karnataka, 78,000 in the city of Delhi, 8,400 in Orissa, 1,300 in the Punjab, 3,500 in Rajasthan, 1,100 in Tamil Nadu, 42,200 in Uttar Pradesh and 39,600 in West Bengal.[3] There is no single leader, there is no overall organization, but there is flourishing, creative, controversial Buddhist society which has evolved patterns of Buddhism both innovative and traditional.

This study looks at some of the visible elements of contemporary Buddhist society in India, i.e., the place of Dr.

Ambedkar in their activities and observances; the buildings that house Buddhist activities; the leadership which teaches, preaches and conducts ritual; the sorts of public holidays and festivals which are observed. The Buddhist tradition, the Mahar tradition and the surrounding Indian tradition all have marked the practices of the Buddhist converts. Much that seems innovative to the Buddhist tradition will be found to be a necessary carry-over from the convert's past or an almost unconscious response to the prevailing Indian (largely Hindu) present. The observations were made in three separate year-long visits to India, 1964-5,1971 and 1975-6. The perspective is limited to Maharashtra, although much of what is observed would also be found among Buddhist groups in a number of cities outside that state.

The Role of Ambedkar

The presence of a picture of Dr. Ambedkar in all Buddhist *viharas* and at all Buddhist functions seems to set the Indian Buddhists apart from the main Buddhist tradition. The inclusion of "Babasaheb" Ambedkar as an object of reverence is the most visible innovation in the practice of contemporary Buddhists in India. The Buddha and Babasaheb in plaster, stone, poster-art and painting, in song and drama and story, seemingly of near-equal importance, rarely one without the other, are continual evidence that contemporary Indian Buddhism proudly combines its own tradition with that of the main Buddhist tradition. Ambedkar is neither worshipped nor prayed to nor, of course, is the Buddha. No *puja* is performed, no *novas* (vows) are made to either figure, so their functions are not those of a Hindu god. But at every occasion, both figures are garlanded, the Buddha first; incense is lit; and Bhagwan Gautam Buddha and Parampujya Dr. Babasaheb Ambedkar are addressed before the speaker acknowledges the Chairman of the function and "Brothers and Sisters".

Honouring Ambedkar: Efforts have been made to place Dr. Ambedkar in the traditional Buddhist framework. Some Buddhists acknowledge Dr. Ambedkar as Bodhisattva in recognition of his role in bringing modern Indian converts into Buddhism, i.e., as a saviour. This use has been justified by, at least, one traditionally trained Theravada Buddhist bhikshu. Other Buddhists reject the Bodhisattva concept as Mahayana Buddhism, which they see as inferior to the rational, non-supernatural, humanity-centered religion they believe the Buddha taught. Another broadly accepted way of honoring Ambedkar is to add the diminutive of his first name, Bhimrao, to the list of refuges, i.e., *Bhimam saranam gachchami,* so that the "Three Jewels" become four :

I go for refuge to the Buddha;

I go for refuge to the Dhamma (doctrine)

I go for refuge to the Sangha (order of monks)

I go for refuge to Ambedkar.

These efforts to honour Dr. Ambedkar within the framework of the Buddhist tradition are an affront to some outside the conversion movement. Those who understand the importance of Dr. Ambedkar in the earlier struggle for political, social and religious rights are more charitable in accepting the continuing homage paid to him. That homage can best be understood by reference to the Indian tradition of the *guru* (teacher or master), a concept most explicit in Hinduism but also found in heterodox sects and in secular life in India. The use of the term "Bodhisattva", the inclusion of Ambedkar as a refuge, is an attempt to use Buddhist concepts for the basic Indian idea of the need for a teacher to show the way to religious insight and personal freedom. The old practice of *guru-shishya* (master-pupil) is often expanded in modern India to a generalized acceptance of the importance of one special person — parent, teacher, ideal, hero—as a chief inspiration in life. The key is that the guru figure is the one who brings his disciple into self-realization, into freedom, i.e., the man who "saves" him.

Ambedkar himself claimed that he had three gurus: The Buddha, the fifteenth century iconoclastic saint-poet Kabir, and the nineteenth century radical social reformer, Mahatma Jotiba Phule. In turn, his followers feel that he has been responsible for almost all the educational, social and political progress in their lives and in addition has shown them the way to a religion which is both honourable and honoured, a religion which negates the religious concepts that made them untouchable in the eyes of society. Many feel that Ambedkar has quite literally saved them, and often highly educated Buddhists feel more strongly about Ambedkar as guru than those who have not benefited so much from the movement.

Ambedkar is by no means a guru in the way that Maharshi Mahesh Yogi or Bhagwan Shree Rajneesh or any of the many contemporary cult figures are gurus. He is a guru in a less specific but totally Indian way. One's guru does not need to be saintly in character or religious in profession; he needs only to be the one who points toward enlightenment. The picture of Dr. Ambedkar, usually clad in a blue business suit, a book in his hand, a fountain pen is his pocket, placed beside the picture of the yellow-robed Buddha, makes clear the very human sort of guru he was.

One of the many contemporary songs sung to folk tunes or film music by Buddhist singing groups illustrates the combination of social and religious enlightenment Ambedkar represents :

He gave us the conversion at Nagpur

He threw his light in the darkness

He never was the slave of anyone

He showed us the way of Buddha

He gave us salvation.[4]

The importance of this concept is also expressed in a more sophisticated way by Namdeo Dhasal, a political radical and a poet of the new Dalit school of literature, which is chiefly composed of educated Buddhists. In this excerpt from one of Dhasal's poems, "they" refers to the forefathers of today's ex-Untouchables; "fakir" is used in Marathi for a Muslim saint, and Dhasal has used it here probably to avoid a reference to Hinduism :

Turning their backs to the sun, they journeyed through centuries;

Now, now, we must refuse to be pilgrims of darkness

After a thousand years we were blessed

with a sunflower-giving fakir;

Now, now, we must like sunflowers turn our face to the sun.[5]

- Whether he is called Boddhisattva, a refuge, a guru or a fakir, Ambedkar is honoured as the one who in his lifetime showed the way and who continues after his death to be seen as the wisest and most inspiring of men.

The Vihara : Meeting-place for the Buddhists

The new buildings dedicated to the Buddhist religion in Maharashtra as well as the old buildings converted to Buddhist use are called *viharas,* the technical term for the residence of the Buddhist monks. The words for temple in Marathi, *deul* and *mandir,* are studiously avoided, and the only term for a gathering place in the old Buddhist tradition seemed to be *vihara.* The need of today's Buddhists, however, is not so much living quarters for bhikshus as a meeting place for the laity, a place where the image of the Buddha can be kept, the community can gather for lectures on Buddhism or for *vandana,*[6] and children can be instructed. As in the case of other lay elements in Buddhist structure, there was no living model for the place of gathering of the Buddhist community available in India, and so the multipurpose *vihara* came into being.

The *vihara* is most often a plain rectangular structure, embellished, where possible, with architectural detail from the most accessible models of Buddhist structures: the caves of Ajanta and the stupa of Sanchi. These buildings are newly built whenever the Buddhists of some locality have the money and the cooperative spirit to create a symbol of their newly accepted faith. In many villages, the *caudi* (community hall) of the old *Maharwada* (the quarters of the Mahar, somewhat removed from the village proper), does double service as community meeting room and center for Buddhist activities. There have been few Hindu temples converted to Buddhist use, probably because few were completely in the hands of those Mahars who converted.

No one has undertaken the immense amount of travelling over Maharashtra and in the cities of the Buddhist conversion elsewhere to record the presence of *viharas,* nor is there any organizational record, since the building of a Buddhist center is an entirely local matter. The ones seen range from a small community shrine, large enough only to accommodate a statue of the Buddha in the slums of Delhi, to a large building with an elaborate stupa on top in Pulgaon, Maharashtra, where Buddhists constitute a large, economically secure, factory-worker community. Most *viharas* serve the Buddhist community in several ways. Daily or weekly *vandana,* memorial services and meetings for religious observances are held in the *viharas,* although few are large enough to accommodate all Buddhists in the locality and great occasions require that a pavillion be erected near the *vihara.* Many *viharas* are used for educational and social as well as religious purposes. In some, there are rooms for visiting or resident bhikshus. Others combine a room for the image of the Buddha with a room for a pre-school or a kindergarten. Such a *vihara* was dedicated in Wardha in May 1976. Residents of the area, many of them casual labor on the railway, collected money for some twenty years and then built a small building. The lower room is a *balwadi* (children's school) dedicated to Mahatma Phule; above, underneath a Sanchi-like dome, is a small room dominated by a Buddha image brought from Thailand and a photograph of Dr. Ambedkar, with quotations from both the Pali scriptures and Dr. Ambedkar painted on the walls.

The *vihara* of Buddhists today is not an imitation of a Hindu temple. There is no *pujari* or ritual priest, there is no stream of individual worshippers paying homage to the image. The *vihara* serves chiefly as a symbol of the community's faith and as a center for the community to gather as Buddhists. And since knowledge is seen as a Buddhist virtue, both Buddhist and secular education can easily be combined with its religious function.

The Leadership of the Buddhists

At the time of the conversion in 1956, there were few Buddhist bhikshus in India, and none who spoke Marathi as their native tongue. The oldest Buddhist Bhikshu then in India, Mahasthaveer Chandramani of Burma, came to Nagpur for the initial conversion ceremony and gave Dr. Ambedkar diksha. From then on, anyone who had converted to Buddhism during the mass meetings at Nagpur could convert others, and the stress was on the individual's commitment in a public ceremony. Another huge ceremony was held in Bombay ten days after the death of Ambedkar in December 1956, and here Bhikshu Anand Kausalyayan, a Hindi-speaking monk, initiated thousands into the new religion through the use of the Three Jewels (or three refuges) and the oaths of declaration of acceptance of Buddhism. There were few trained bhikshus available for diksha and teaching, however, and the burden of leadership in the early days of the movement fell upon the political leadership from Ambedkar's Republican Party. Religious conversion from the hands of political leaders may have seemed strange to outsiders, but for those in the movement, these were the men who knew them, who had worked with Ambedkar, who had long ago given up Hinduism as a religion of inequality and superstition.

Another group of leaders soon rose at the local level. These were the students — young men and a few women trained in the colleges that Ambedkar had founded. Some had studied Pali, all had sought out some knowledge of Buddhism in the intense and joyful early days of the conversion. They conducted marriages and memorial services in a simple ritual devised by Ambedkar, founded classes for children and study groups for adults, joined in Young Men's Buddhist Associations and women's service groups. They published pamphlets on Buddhism in Marathi, wrote songs to be sung in community meetings, and, whenever they could, found a travelling Buddhist bhikshu or an educated sympathetic Hindu to speak on Buddhist ideology at public meetings.

The overall organization of the Buddhists in India was less effective than that at the local level. The Buddhist Society of

India, centered in Bombay and led by Dr. Ambedkar's son, Yeshwant Ambedkar, was established by Dr. Ambedkar in 1955. Theoretically the center of Buddhist activities, the Buddhist Society of India has given little direction to the movement, and the ties between the center and its local branches are very loose. The center was dominated by political leaders, and as factions began to appear in Ambedkar's party, they affected the religious organization also.[7] The non-political leadership which arose on the local level could not effect a strong central leadership, but neither could the lack of a center affect the vitality of the new movement. The Buddhist Society of India has now completed the Dr. Ambedkar Memorial Shrine, a multipurpose *vihara* on the seashore at Shivaji Park in Bombay, the site where Dr. Ambedkar was cremated. The *viharas* in the towns and villages of Maharashtra, however, reflect local commitment and local leadership.

Now, after fifty years, it seems clear that Buddhism in India will continue its strong emphasis on the laity and lay leadership. It is still the lay leadership that performs most of the teaching and preaching, writes most of the religious material which continues to flow from the movement, collects the money and plans the *vihara*. But there are increasing numbers of Marathi-speaking bhikshus, appearing it seems not so much from the need of the community as out of their own individual commitment to Buddhism. Some go to Bodh Gaya or some other Buddhist center in North India for training, a few to Thailand, and a few others to Ceylon. One young man is now in Japan with the Nichiren sect. Most of the Marathi-speaking bhikshus are young and highly educated; many are working on doctoral degrees in Pali, archaeology or some other field related to the Buddhist past. The only Maharashtrian center for the training of bhikshus is that at Nagpur under the care of Bhandant Anand Kausalyayan, a former Punjabi Hindu who became a bhikshu in Ceylon in 1930. The Ven. Kausalyayan moved to Nagpur in 1970, has built a home and training center on the grounds where the 1956 conversion took place, and has educated dozens of young men, about fifteen of whom have been ordained as bhikshus.

The function of the bhikshu among the Buddhists in Maharashtra seems to be primarily teaching, although it seems also true that the very presence of a bhikshu is an important symbol of the identity of a Buddhist group. In the 1960s, the Ven. Sangarakshita of England and Kalimpong devoted half of each year to teaching in Maharashtra and Gujarat. He preached many sermons, his English being interpreted into Marathi by one of the young Buddhist students, and he also conducted *samnera,* a period of ten days or so in which Buddhist laity lived as monks. A Thai bhikshu, Vivekananda, also travelled widely in Maharashtra, giving simple lectures on Buddhist morality. A number of Thai bhikshus study at the University of Poona or Deccan College in Pune, and some of these establish working relationships with Maharashtrian Buddhists, particularly in Buddhist Sunday schools for children, but none are in India permanently. Some Tibetan monks have moved through Maharashtra, but those who met knew no English, Marathi or Hindi and so served the community by making clay images of the Buddha and reciting some texts in hastily learned Pali. In 1975 a Tamil-speaking Bhikshu was teaching meditation and performing some medical service both in Bombay and in the railroad porters colony in Pune. Singhalese, Burmese and Japanese bhikshus have been of service to the community at various times, their effectiveness dependent upon their ability to communicate and their attitude toward the still generally economically and socially depressed community.

The appearance of Marathi-speaking bhikshus with roots in the community may create a situation in which religious leaders become more essential to the community. However, to be effective, they will have to be highly educated, able to preach and teach, totally ethical, willing to be completely identified with the community, and free from any political ambition.

Such a sangha is now emerging, but there are not enough bhikshus to serve each Buddhist community. And along with the appearance of Marathi-speaking bhikshus, the creative lay leadership continues to function. Three examples will serve to indicate its direction: two dedicated professors teach Pali to over

2000 students at the complex of colleges in Aurangabad established by Ambedkar, and are deeply involved in plans for a Buddhist center, with a resident bhikshu, which will reach far beyond the student body. Another striking example is that of a young woman in Pune who combines works as a clerk in a government office with study for a law degree. She performed so well in a class taught by Thai Bhikshus in her community that she was sent to a Buddhist conference in Thailand. Since her return she has participated in numerous weddings, funerals and other ritual occasions, leading the Pali *vandana* and giving talks on Buddhism. A third example of lay leadership is the most ambitious of all. Waman Godbole, one of the planners of the Nagpur Conversion in 1956, called an All-India Buddhist Dharma Conference in Nagpur in December 1975. Eight bhikshus from many traditions and hundreds of lay leaders participated in the conference, with tens of thousands coming to the public sessions and taking part in processions. Godbole hopes for a structured organization that will unify all Buddhists in India. He recognizes that it took twenty years to plan such a conference, however, and is content to work slowly and patiently to build a functioning umbrella Buddhist organization. Godbole is a well-educated Buddhist layman who continued with his railway job to support himself and who did not marry in order to devote his life to the movement.

Leadership among Buddhists in Maharashtra has had to emerge out of a vacuum over the last fifty years. The Buddhist leaders are not related to the old Mahar religious leadership, which in any case lost its importance when Ambedkar's movement became committed to leaving Hinduism in the 1930s. The new Buddhist leader, whether a member of the sangha or a lay person, is effective only if he or she can share a knowledge of Buddhism and if he or she is committed to the service of the community.

The Holy Days Observed by the Maharashtrian Buddhists (Observances)

The four great observances of the contemporary Buddhists in India — Dhamma Diksha Day, Buddha Jayanti, Ambedkar's death memorial day, and Ambedkar Jayanti — reveal their determination to preserve hard-won glory of their past as well as to state their commitment to Buddhism.

The anniversary of the day of the conversion, 14 October, is celebrated as *Dhamma Diksha day*. Those who can, return to the field in Nagpur where the 1956 conversion was held for a great ceremony; others hold local observances of varying sorts. In Aurangabad, the Buddhist caves just outside the city are the focus of a procession, Pali *vandana* and later games for the children, while speeches and song services are held in the colleges.

Buddha Jayanti, the day of observance of the Buddha's birth, has been observed since 1950, when Ambedkar arranged for the celebration as a public occasion in Delhi. The Jayanti is a time for speeches, music, drama on Buddhist themes and occasionally a solemn procession.

Ambedkar's death anniversary, 6 December, is a time for quiet and sorrowful gatherings, and talks or music by one of the many singers or singing groups in the community predominate.

Ambedkar's birth anniversary, 14 April, on the other hand, is a noisy and joyful occasion. Here the borrowings from the processions found in Hinduism, Islam and Jainism are clear. As in the Muslim Moharram or the Hindu Ganapati festival, local groups form committees which plan their contribution to the citywide procession. In Pune, the central point is the statue of Dr. Ambedkar near the railway station, and groups of dancing, shouting youngsters and older men march from their scattered localities to Ambedkar Square. The Maharashtrian dance game *legim* is often played by the marchers, as in the Ganapati festival, although the Buddhists have at least one girls' group, which the Hindus do not. One group rented the city zoo's elephant in 1976 to carry Ambedkar's photograph in the procession, but generally the marchers try to out-do each other in spirit rather than constructing elaborate floats.

A Jayanti held at the Aundh Raod Buddhist locality near Pune illustrates the mood of this day. Dozens of boys and a few older men drummed and danced their way the twenty miles to Ambedkar Square and back. A meeting then began at about 9 o'clock that night, presided over by one of the exhausted participants. Speeches were made by a young Marathi-speaking bhikshu from another slum locality in Pune, a Maratha caste convert to Buddhism who had just attended a Buddhist conference in Thailand, and this American scholar who is considered an authority on Ambedkar's life. The speeches were followed by a local drama group. Every social group, male and female, and every political faction in the locality was invited to participate in an effort to unite the community, and no outside political leaders were asked to attend. The events of the day reached the children, the young people and the adults of the community in one phase or another. The procession was sheer fun, the speeches of the Bhikshus and the Buddhist converts contained heavy doses of ethics and morality, and the drama provided both entertainment and a glimpse of the Buddhist past.

While these observances bear some resemblance to Hindu or other Indian holy days or festivals, particularly in the idea of the public processions and the exhibiting of the photographs of the "gurus", the Buddha and Dr. Ambedkar, they are unlike Hindu occasions in their emphasis on teaching and their rationality. There is no one astrologically timed sacred moment, no one hallowed sacred space. There is no need for a religious figure to give an auspicious presence, blessing or rite. There is no spirit-possession, no religious ecstasy. These four observances are times for community spirit, for education, for remembrance.

The innovations of the contemporary Buddhist movement in India represent those elements in the past of the Buddhists which are important to their present progress: the work of Dr. Ambedkar, their social unity in the face of continued prejudice and occasional violence, their rejection of Hinduism as a religion of inequality, irrationality and superstition. Nevertheless, there is also some retention of Hindu or Indian elements among the modern Buddhists—the guru idea, the public processions, the days honouring the birth or death of great men. It must be remembered that the Buddhists of India are a minority in a dominant Hindu society, and as in the case of other minorities—Muslims, Christians, Sikhs and Jains— the ways of showing identity, loyalty and group spirit which are a part of Indian culture have coloured Buddhist celebrations.

The outward symbols of traditional Buddhism most stressed are those which carry inner meaning of the conversion: honour, equality, rationality, humanism. The image of the Buddha used is a simple one; he is the enlightened one, not a god. The study of Pali is important not only as the language of the Theravada texts but as a symbol of commitment to the Buddhist world. Pali ritual phrases are used in group performance of *vandana,* partly to produce a moment of group unity and partly to show that this is the holy language of Buddhism, as Sanskrit is the holy language of Hinduism. The Buddhist art and holy places of the past are honoured by contemporary Buddhists as proof of past greatness and part of their own heritage. The decorated caves of Ajanta, Elora, Aurangabad, Nasik and Junnar are visited with reverence and awe, and many make pilgrimages of Sanchi, Sarnath or Bodh Gaya.

Along with the amalgam of traditional Buddhism, the Mahar past and the socio-religious practices of Hindu society in general, the Buddhists of India seem to have created some new and interesting developments on their own. The multipurpose *vihara* and the initiative and responsibility of the lay leader are the most striking of these. Wherever it has gone, Buddhism has adapted itself to the needs of the surrounding culture. The contemporary Buddhists of India are not an exact copy of Singhalese, Burmese, Thai, Cambodian or Japanese Buddhists. As in those societies, Buddhism has retained some of its ancient lineaments while allowing those who claim commitment to it to change it in accordance with their own needs.[8]

Refereces

1. The Indian press and many Westerners use the term "Neo-Buddhist" for the concerts to Buddhism in the Ambedkar movement. The Buddhists themselves point out that the words "Neo-Muslim" or "Neo-Christian" are not used, and they find "Neo-Buddhist" a patronizing and unacceptable term.
2. Growth among Buddhists during 1960's showed a 17 per cent increase, in contrast to a 24 per cent increase for Hindus, 31 per cent for Muslims, 32 per cent for Sikhs 33 per cent for Christians. Buddhists claim that many outside Maharashtra would convert but for the fact that they lose their privileges as the Scheduled Castes (scholarishps, reserved government jobs and other benefits) upon conversion, except in the State of Maharashtra.
3. These figures, which have been rounded to the nearest hundred, are from the *Census of India* 1971. Series 1, Paper

2 of 1972; Religion. Those areas where numbers of Tibetans obviously account for Buddhists figures have been omitted, but some refugees and some carry-over Buddhist groups in Bengal and Orissa may account for several thousands in these figures.

4. From "Majha Bhimraya" (My Bhim, the king), a song collected by Russ Geyer for an undergraduate research paper on the songs of the Buddhists, Pune, 1969.
5. From "Atta" in *Golpitha* by Namdeo Dhasal (Pune: Nilkanth Prakashan, reprint 1975).
6. *Vandana* is defined in Molesworth's dictionary as "adoring, worshipping, rendering reverence or homage", and is used in place of the words describing Hindu prayer or ritual, *prarthana* or puja. *Vandana* generally consists of the *trisharana* and other Pali Buddhist textual material.
7. Some political leaders have done yeoman work in the promotion of Buddhism: Dadasaheb Gaikwad has built a complex of schools and a *vihara* in Nasik and D.T. Rupavate in Ahmadnagar; B.C. Kamble and his followers have been active in Buddhist teaching; R.S. Bhandare has kept his interest in Buddhism even after leaving the Republican Party for the Congress, and he is said to be responsible for the translation of the *Tripitika* into Hindi by the Government of Bihar. Nevertheless, the factions among the political leadership have resulted in factions among local Buddhists, and there is now an attempt to place Buddhist activities and organizations in a totally non-political context.
8. For further reading, see Adlle Fiske, "Scheduled Caste Buddhist Organizations" in J. Michael Mahar ed., *The Untouchables in Contemporary India,* Tucson: University of Arizona Press, 1972; the work of D.C. Ahir, the major writer of the movement in English, particularly *India's Debt to Buddhism* (New Delhi: Maha Bodhi Society of India, 1964); and *Buddhism in Modern India* (Nagpur; Bhikku Niwas Prakashan, 1972); and two of my articles, "Buddhism and Politics in Maharashtra, in Donald E. Smith ed., *South Asian Politics and Religion* (Princeton: Princeton University Press, 1966) and "The Psychological Dimension of the Buddhist Movement in India" in G.A. Oddie ed., *Religious Conversion and Revival Movements in South Asia in Medieval and Modern Times* (Delhi: Manohar, 1977).

14
Identity and Organization of Buddhists in India

The 1971 Census recorded the number of Buddhists in India as 3,812,325, i.e., less than one per cent of the population but this was a startling increase over the number of Buddhists noted in 1951. All but a few hundred thousand of these Buddhists have been converted since the 1956 Buddhist conversion of Dr. B.R. Ambedkar, an ex-Untouchable leader, and around eighty-five per cent of the contemporary Buddhists live in the State of Maharashtra, Ambedkar's home territory. The 1971 figure represents a 17.025 per cent increase over 1961, less than any other religious group in India, but the Buddhist movement is still very much alive. In this chapter we study the identity and organization of the converted Buddhists and observations of other Buddhist groups in India, i.e., the Tibetan refugees and the Buddhists of Bengal.

Tibetan Buddhism

An estimate of the number of Tibetans in India ranges around 500,000, chiefly in refugee settlements in Mysore, Assam, West Bengal, Madhya Pradesh and Himachal Pradesh. The Dalai Lama is the spiritual head of these Buddhists, and the monastic system is preserved through training centers for monks at Dharmshala in Himachal Pradesh[1] and at Mundgod in Karnataka. The Buddhism prevalent in old Tibet is preserved as much as possible by the refugees, and the resettlement of most Tibetans in groups in specific localities works toward the retainment of their culture.

There is little contact between Tibetan Buddhism and those converted since 1956, and little expectation of future interaction. Language is one basic problem, the form of Tibetan Buddhism another. One instance of interaction illustrates this:

I met two Tibetan monks living in the guest room of a very simple *vihara* in a very small poor Buddhist community outside Pune in Maharashtra. They had been there several weeks, had learned enough Pali to chant some formula familiar to the Maharashtrian Buddhists, and were making plaster Buddha images from moulds they had brought with them to repay the hospitality they were given. No other communication was possible, and I expect the connection did not last long. Robert and Beatrice Miller have told me that a young Buddhist boy from Maharashtra was taken to Dharmshala by Tibetans for training in the 1960s, but was returned home as he was too immature.

Tibetans are invited on the rare occasions when Buddhists in Maharashtra call for an All-India Buddhist conference. But it is unrealistic to expect the two groups to find much common ground. The Tibetan identity is all-important to the refugee Buddhists; they have little to gain from integration with a group of very low social and economic status. On the other hand, the recently converted Buddhists have no monastic or even priestly tradition; respect for leadership is based on the teaching ability of the bhikshu, and only secondarily on his institutional role.

Eastern India Buddhists

The second group of older Buddhists in the subcontinent is almost equally removed from the mass of Buddhists in Maharashtra in terms of distance, language and organizational structure. These are the Bengali Indian Buddhists (as distinct from Burmese Buddhists living in Bengal and Bangladesh) who have retained their identity as Buddhists from pre-Muslim times, and have undergone a revival in the mid-nineteenth century which reintroduced Theravada Buddhist ideas, practices, and training for bhikshus. These Buddhist remnants exist in Orissa, Bengal and possibly Assam, but the largest number live in the district of Chittagong, now in Bangladesh. The 1970 Chittagong Census count of Buddhists is near 80,000, most of them Barua Magh, a reference to the ancient center of Buddhism in Maghada, i.e., "the great Maghadas".

Something of a reformation began among these Bengal Buddhists who were almost submerged in Hinduism in 1856 when a Burmese bhikshu stopped by in Chittagong on his pilgrimage to Bodh Gaya and stayed there for two years to preach Theravada Buddhism to those he saw as corrupted Buddhists. Coincident with this, a young Barua Magh had discovered Theravada Buddhism through a Singhalese in Calcutta, and after his ordination as a bhikshu in Ceylon ordained in turn a new generation of Bengali bhikshus. The revival has produced schools and large-scale Buddhist festivals in Chittagong, and in Bengal a number of scholars. The most famous, B.M. Barua, dominated Pali and Buddhist scholarship in Calcutta for twenty-five years.

Although there is some contemporary study of the Eastern Indian Buddhists by Heinz Bechert and[2] others, the fullest report on the organization of the Buddhists of that area available now is that of the *Chittagong Gazetteer,* and since it repeats in large part the information given in 1908 Gazetteer, we will not venture to comment on the current organization beyond saying that it seems to depend upon the Sangha and upon popular festivals organized around holy places in the Chittagong region.

Identity and Organization of Buddhists

The identity and organization of the Buddhists in India whose conversion stems from the Ambedkar movement is a complex matter. The current life of the movement is based on local organizations and leadership, and its current creative edge is often the work of a single man. A great deal can be said, however, about what Buddhist identity means to the mass of these Buddhists, and scattered impressions of Buddhist organizations reveal a pattern which probably holds throughout Maharashtra and in the larger cities of India.

The Census figures on Buddhists in India probably indicate the minimum number. Only in the state of Maharashtra do Buddhists qualify for the government benefits of "contemporary discrimination" (the phrase is Mark Galanter's) which means scholarships, aid in housing and reservation of jobs in government organizations to ex-Untouchables. In other states, religious conversion means the cutting off of all these privileges, and in Maharashtra itself, the benefits at the Central Government level are not available to Buddhists. Consequently, only those who are financially secure or extraordinarily committed can afford to register themselves as Buddhists.

At its simplest, the identification with Buddhism of both official and non-official Buddhists is twofold: identity with one of India's greatest cultural periods, and, perhaps more important, identity with an anti-caste religion of rationality and egalitarianism. An interesting, if not numerically significant, group of Indians looked at Buddhism in this light before Dr. Ambedkar's conversion. Tagore and Nehru were among them, along with a number of high caste Hindu intellectuals. Dharmanand Kosambi, Rahul Sankrityayan and Jagdish Kashap (respectively, Pali scholar, writer, and founder of the revived Nalanda University, as well as the uncle of A.K. Narain) were also members of the Sangha, at least for a time. Several hundred lesser figures also became Buddhists or extolled that religion as the purest form of Hinduism.[3] Curiously enough, there were also at least two low-caste movements toward Buddhism, one in Madras and one in Rajasthan, which have not been recently investigated.[4]

The identification with Buddhism on the part of low-caste converts involves more than an intellectual attraction, however; it contains a large component of psychological freedom. A well-known Buddhist lawyer, writer and government official, Shankarrao Kharat, stated this simply and strongly :

> I have accepted the Buddhist Dhamma. I am a Buddhist now. I am not a Mahar, nor an Untouchable, nor even a Hindu. I have become a human being. I have now become equal with high-caste Hindus. I am equal with all. I am not low born or inferior now. With the acceptance of Buddhism my Untouchability has been erased. The chains of Untouchability which shackled my feet have now been shattered. Now I am a human being like all others. I am no longer the slave and menial servant of high caste Hindus. I will never again accept servile labour from the high caste Hindus. I have become independent. I am now free. I have become a free citizen of independent India.

One also senses the great sense of psychological freedom in the hundreds of songs written by amateur musicians and sold in cheap paper pamphlets at any gathering of Buddhists. One such song by a Buddhist from Akola in Maharashtra who uses the pen name "Dinbandhu", brother of the poor, "The Hindu faith, the hateful faith—we threw it out", and includes such lines as :

> The rope of slavery has been broken.
>
> We'll rise up to the heights of the sky;
>
> Our deeds will make the world seem small.

Another song by a professional folk musician, Waman Kardak, récounts the events of the conversion day, 14 October 1956, in Nagpur with this chorus :

> We have thrown away the rags
>
> which never did cover our shame.

and ends, "The humble were freed from the valley of Untouchability".

The sense of inner freedom, however, is only partially meaningful in outer matters. While it can give the ex-Untouchable greater ambition and great courage, it does not create much difference in the minds of non-Buddhists. *Bauddh* or *Nav-bauddh* (new Buddhist, a term the Buddhists themselves reject) in Maharashtra is a synonym for Mahar, since the vast majority of the converts were from that caste. The ex-Untouchable does not reach a position of equality automatically with conversion, but it does affect his attitude toward himself and his rights.[5]

In addition to the sense of release from being untouchable, there is a sense of belonging to a great past, an identity that supersedes current low status. There are many ways for the Buddhist convert to express this identity. Chief among them is to claim, as Ambedkar did in *The Untouchables* (New Delhi: Amrit Book Company, 1948), that Untouchables had been Buddhists in an earlier period, and indeed the very reason for their Untouchability was that they, as staunch and recalcitrant Buddhists, had refused to join the Hindu revival of the middle ages. Few Untouchables have ever used the *karma* theory of past bad deeds to explain their low status; almost all untouchable myths of origin all over India use some ancestral error, usually based on good intentions, to account for their despised place, or claim pre-Aryan status, or ex-Kshatriyahood. The theory of previous Buddhist identity fits well into the untouchables' need for an honorable past, a cultural heritage that can be claimed with pride, and even the unlettered find this mythic background comforting.

There are an astonishing number of visual and verbal references to the Buddhist past within the current movement. Pali is taught in all the colleges founded by Dr. Ambedkar and his followers, and studied by literally thousands of students. Local groups teach Pali chants to children in a sort of Buddhist Sunday School, and it is heartening to see the little ones reel off seemingly endless scripture.

Buddhist Structures

Whenever possible, architectural features from Buddhist structures, usually the caves at Ajanta or the stupa at Sanchi, are worked into school buildings or the *viharas* erected by local groups. Some Buddhists go on pilgrimage to Bodh Gaya, Sarnath or Sanchi; a great many visit the caves of Ajanta and Ellora. Actually, a good many of the guides and the guards at the caves are Buddhists, since the position is one for which there are reserved places in the government scheme, and these guides at times act as if they truly owned the caves, treating them as if they were contemporary places of special holiness. Buddhist caves at Aurangabad, Junnar and Nasik are used as sites for festival occasions such as the celebration of the Buddha's birth by local Buddhists. The Buddha Jayanti is observed in all local Buddhist groups, and while it is not quite the popular and exuberant festival of Ambedkar's birth, it can be a very impressive occasion in the cities.

Buddhist Literature

Much of the expression of a relationship with the Buddhist past is in literature. A Buddhist from Maharashtra oversaw the publication of the *Tripitika* in Hindi while he was Governor of Bihar. A Buddhist from Nagpur took upon himself to publish an archaeologist's findings on the location of Kapilavastu. Another Maharashtrian Buddhist published a well-received novel about the Buddha's wife, and a Pune based Buddhist playwright (a government servant) has written a play based on the conversion of a courtesan by the Buddha.

Perhaps even more interesting are the subtle ways in which Buddhist concepts are used by the writers in the contemporary Dalit Sahitya (literature of the oppressed) movement in Marathi, a recent phenomenon that has given birth to a whole new school of literature.[6] There is no such straightforward exultation in Buddhism as in the popular song literature; indeed, some of the best-known writers, such as Baburao Bagul, never mention Buddhism, although he has told me that it was the conversion to Buddhism which freed the ex-Untouchables to write! But where a reference to Buddhism does enter, it is obviously a profoundly meaningful part of the writer's mental resources. Daya Pawar's poem on the Bodhi Tree, the tree under which the Buddha was sitting when enlightenment came, appears in an autobiography which barely mentions Buddhism otherwise :

I have seen this tree choking with grief
Its roots are deep like a bodhi-tree's
But the bodhi tree, at least, flowered.
This tree is scorched in all seasons.

The sorrows that try to burst through every vein
The leaves fallen off like leper's fingers...
What is this disease? To bough after bough
        is tied a prop.
It bears death-like tortures, because it cannot die.
I have seen this tree choking with grief.

(Translated by Priya Adarkar in her presentation of excerpts from *Balut,* by Daya Pawar, translated as "For Them the Chaff: The Dalit Story" in *Imprint,* January 1980.)

Another poem by Daya Pawar uses the figure of Angulimal, a bandit of exceptional cruelty who was converted by the Buddha, as metaphor for the society of today :

O Siddhartha,
You made a tyrant like Angulimal tremble.

We are your humble followers.

How should we confront this ferocious Angulimal?

O Siddhartha,

If we fight tooth and claw,

Try to understand us.

Try to understand us.

(The full poem, translated by Vidya Dixit, Jayant Karve and Eleanor Zelliot, appears in the *Bulletin of Concerned Asian Scholars,* X:3 (1978, p. 3, and in section IV of this volume). The same figure of Angulimal is used in a totally different way by the prize-winning Buddhist poet, Tryambak Sapkale (who is also a train conductor on the Dhond-Manmad line in Maharashtra), who sees society as the cruel being who created Angulimal.

All these things help to build the kind of proud cultural past that few Untouchable groups can claim. They are part of what Richard Lambert once called "the vital dimension of self-respect" which is an essential element in any egalitarian social movement. Dr. Ambedkar dedicated his book, *The Untouchables,* to the Untouchable Bhakti saints, Nandnar, Ravidas and Chokhamela, the group that represented about the only claim to cultural contribution the Untouchables ever had. The Buddhist past which he opened up to his followers in the year of his death is an even deeper mine of riches, an endless source of meaningful imagery and a claim to a proud heritage.

It is clear that the identity of the Buddhists converted in Ambedkar's movement goes beyond caste identity, but it is still clearly bound up to that movement. A few Buddhists go to international conferences on Buddhism or on world religions, but for most identity is still in the context of the Hindu world, and when they stretch beyond this, it is through a very personal understanding of the meaning of Buddhism for them as individuals.

The full range of Buddhist organizations in India includes as much variety as the ways of identification with Buddhism, and is less easy to generalize about. No one knows the exact extent of organized groups among the Buddhists in India, not even in Maharashtra. Activity is almost entirely on the local level, there is no effective overall organization and there few people who travel widely enough to know the developments in more than one area. The notes on organization here are not comprehensive; rather an attempt has been made to use examples to point up the nature of institutions and leadership among the Buddhists.[7]

Buddhist Organization in Maharashtra

Two, perhaps, three, organizations in Maharashtra aspire to guide the Buddhist movement. Dr. Ambedkar himself founded the Buddhist Society of India before the conversion, but left no ongoing structure. Its leadership passed into the hands of Ambedkar's son, an ineffective and somewhat tragic figure, who was the token head until his death. The Society has achieved the building of the Dr. Ambedkar Memorial Shrine on the seashore in Shivaji Park, Mumbai, an expensive and gaudy affair that serves both as shrine and, it was hoped, a place for bhikshus to stay. Local societies often call themselves Buddhist Society of India groups, but there is no direct link with, certainly no guidance from, the central organization. The Bauddha Mahasabha, is another group which has translated into Marathi and published Ambedkar's *The Buddha and His Dhamma.*[8]

A more ambitious organization is that of Waman Godbole in Nagpur. One of the planners of the conversion in Nagpur in 1956 (an occasion which drew perhaps as many as a half-million people and was organized in five weeks), Godbole, called an All-India Buddhist Dharma Conference in 1975. Eighty-five bhikshus and hundreds of laymen from many Buddhist traditions, including the Tibetan and Bengali, attended, and the name of a Barua can be noted as a Vice-President of the conference. The Dalai Lama, however, was unable to come. Godbole planned to slowly build an organization that will unite all Buddhists in India, standardize *viharas* and increase conversions. A well-educated layman who continued his railway job to support himself and did not marry in order to devote his life to the movement. He said that it took twenty years to plan the Dharma conference and was willing to plan for another twenty to achieve some further results.

Buddhist Bhikshas and Monks

It is often said that Buddhism is a monastic religion. What then of the Sangha among the Buddhists of India? Needless to say, there is no centrally-trained, well-organized group in Maharashtra. There are perhaps eighty bhikshus functioning in one way or another in the State and in a few other areas of India, representing many traditions and many countries. The largest group, perhaps fifteen to twenty, has been trained by Anand Kausalyayan, a former Punjabi Hindu who became a bhikshu in Ceylon in 1930, and moved to Nagpur in 1970, supporting himself by heading a Hindi language promotion organization. The bhikshus trained by Kausalyayan were Marathi-speakers who also took degrees at Nagpur University, often even a Ph.D. in Pali or archaeology, fields which could be related to the Buddhist past. Kausalyayan also conducted classes in Buddhism for groups of young men.

Other Marathi-speaking bhikshus were trained in Thailand, Bodh Gaya, or a center in Yeotmal (about which little is known). Besides perhaps 25 or 30 bhikshus from Maharashtra itself (probably ex-Mahars, although no one who has become a bhikshu will talk about his former caste), there are a dozen other varieties of bhikshus in Maharashtra alone: a Japanese rather unwillingly serving Buddhists from the locality at the Worli Buddhist temple in Bombay built by the Birlas; an enthusiastic Nichiren Japanese bhikshu using his drum in lieu of English or Marathi to communicate in Nagpur; a Tamil-speaking bhikshu who has a dispensary in the slums of Pune and teaches meditation in several places; several Singhalese bhikshus, at least two of whom have stayed in Maharashtra for years; Thai bhikshus studying at Deccan College or the University of Poona who work with Buddhist groups in Pune, and bhikshus and *Shramanera* from England.

The Buddhist establishment from England offers the most unusual solution to the problem of the leadership of Buddhists in India. Work among the new converts began shortly after the conversion ceremony with bhikshu Sangarakshita, an English

Buddhist convert, who conducted training sessions and often went with a Thai bhikshu to both urban and rural groups. With a base in Kalimpong, Sangarakshita visited the Buddhists of Maharashtra and Gujarat several months of each year in the 1960s. He had returned from a new center in England to the area, establishing one of his English converts, a robed but not ordained Buddhist, in Pune to teach Buddhism. Lokamitra (friend of the people) lives in a Buddhist housing colony, holds classes in Buddhism in Pune and publishes a Marathi periodical. The goal of the group is to educate, and the establishment of a Sangha is not seen as necessary or desirable.

Can Buddhism function as a lay religion? Are a large group of bhikshus necessary for the continuance of the conversion movement and the education of the converts? There is some evidence that Dr. Ambedkar distrusted the Sangha. On a visit to Ceylon some five years before the conversion, he criticized the Sangha to its face for its lack of response to people's needs, and at a meeting in Sarnath, he again attacked the members of the Sangha from various countries for "parasitical behaviour". As he himself said, it was a "grave omission" in Buddhism to have an initiation into the Sangha and not into the Dhamma itself, and for his own conversion and that of his followers in 1956, he initiated such a ceremony.

If an example of a "leaderless" religious organization in Maharashtra can be stretched a bit, it can show how such a religious group can function and flourish. The Bhakti movement which had included the saints Ambedkar revered is still strong and vital in Maharashtra after 700 years. It has no clear leadership patterns, but it does have a series of "texts", including songs, which are sung in local groups, a yearly pilgrimage to Pandharpur, and standards of morality accepted by all. The single outward sign of a *warkari* is a necklace of tulsi beads. The temples at Pandharpur and at lesser sites such as Alandi and Dehu do have temple priests—these, however, are not *warkaris* or members of the sect, and it is not necessary to enter the temple, only to make the group pilgrimage. Local leadership, the tradition, and the songs are what hold the group together. (See G.A. Deleury, *The Cult of Vithoba*, (Pune: Deccan

College Postgraduate and Research Institute, 1960). Many contemporary Buddhists, and a few scholars, think the Bhakti movement has strong connections with Buddhism, and that the image of Vithoba at Pandharpur is brought from an earlier Buddhist holy center. But that argument is not the point here; rather it is that the foci of the contemporary Buddhist movement consist of somewhat the same things: local leadership, the Ambedkar tradition, the songs, festivals and rituals developed by the contemporary Buddhists.

The continuance, growth and creativity of the current Buddhist movement, unless it should develop a Sangha more quickly than now seems possible, is dependent upon lay leaders, usually based in a close-knit locality. In larger cities all over India Buddhist groups include members from a number of ex-Untouchable castes, drawn together as educated men and women in search for a new religious ethos, but in Maharashtra itself all but a handful of the Buddhists share the Mahar past. Two instances of local leadership which resulted in impressive achievements during the past five years illustrate the way in which Buddhism is organized in Maharashtra.

In Aurangabad, a college educated Buddhist with a clerk's job at one of Ambedkar's colleges has supervised the building of a small *vihara* which serves chiefly as a meeting place for the teaching of children and for speeches by passing dignitaries in a locality that is totally Buddhist. The *vihara* is simple; the gates which set it off from the crowded slum street use a wrought-iron design based on the Bodhi Tree which is both unique and quite beautiful. In Wardha, where railway labour gathered pennies for 20 years, another educated Buddhist with a senior level railway job has designed and constructed a *vihara* which houses a pre-school for children and, also has a small domed room, Sanchi style, for pictures of Ambedkar and the Buddha, a Buddha image, and scriptures inscribed on the wall. Neither of these *viharas* had a bhikshu in residence, although in both cases the local community would have welcomed one who was dedicated to teaching them.

Like the *warkari* or Bhakti tradition, the Buddhist movement also has its festival days which are celebrated by the entire community. Ambedkar's birth and death days, Buddha Jayanti, and the anniversary of the conversion on 14 October are the most important of these, and they are observed in such a way as to involve the whole community and to make a statement to the outside world. But unlike the *warkari* tradition, the Buddhist movement in Maharashtra has no place, no Pandharpur, no physical center. Nothing in the present or past Buddhist tradition in Maharashtra offers such a center, not even the Ajanta and Ellora caves, which are government-owned. The "physical" center continues to be Babasaheb Ambedkar, and the attempts at centers build on this fact. The Bombay center is built on the site where Ambedkar was cremated. Kausalyayan's center in Nagpur is on the ground where the mass conversion took place in 1956. A visionary Buddhist in Nagpur has grand, rather impractical plans to build a training center for bhikshus at Mahu in Madhya Pradesh, the birthplace of Babasaheb Ambedkar.

Dr. Ambedkar serves as a focal point both for the illiterate and, even more profoundly, for the educated. He fills three traditional ties of loyalty: the planner for progress: social, political and religious; the guru, i.e., the one who showed the way; and, in Buddhist terminology, a Boddhisattva. The idea of the business-suited, bespectacled, often impious Ambedkar as Boddhisattva sets some Buddhists' teeth on edge, but in terms of bringing the masses into Buddhism, in "saving" them from the world's evils, he fulfilled the role of Boddhisattva as modern Buddhists in Maharashtra understand it. The idea was actually conceived by Kausalyayan, an ordained bhikshu since 1930, and his teaching included a quadruple "refuge": I take refuge in the Buddha, I take refuge in the Sangha, I take refuge in the Dhamma, I take refuge in Bhim (Bhimrao Ramji Ambedkar.) *Bhimam saranam gachchami* can still be heard at the end of the Pali *trisaranam* chant in many places.

But in spite of the inspiration of Ambedkar's writings, the use of the other material on Buddhism, chiefly in Marathi, and the energy of local leadership, there is a great sense of need for teachers among Maharashtra's Buddhists, and a continual search to find ways to create a Sangha. Almost immediately after the conversion, six or eight boys were sent to Ceylon for training. They returned in a few months, troubled by teasing on what seems to have been a caste basis in the Buddhist schools. Tibetan monks took a village boy with them on one of their journeys through the state, and his parents gladly let him go, but he was returned within a year for being too young. Nichiren monks took a Nagpur boy to Japan, with his parents' full blessing, and there seems to be a real sense of service in this training effort. Pictures of the boy in his *shramanera* robes, and in his Japanese baseball suit, are sent periodically to the parents.

Basically, however, there is no traditional base for a priesthood or a Sangha among the ex-Untouchables of Maharashtra. The Hindu situation before the conversion was even more amorphous and confused than the current Buddhist structures. *Gosavis, potrajas,* an occasional *warkari* leader, children dedicated to the god Khandoba, *devrishis* there were, but no priestly class or access to the Brahman priests, and certainly no tradition of celibate scholarship and piety. It seems wasteful to many for an intelligent, highly educated young man to do work that will not aid in his family's growth nor his family's future. And bhikshus who are not intelligent, moral, well educated and totally dedicated are not acceptable to the community!

The pattern of organization that prevails now will probably hold for years: young men and women conducting *vandana* (Buddhist "prayer"), training schools, song festivals, etc., in their localities; older men who have raised their families turning to the building of *viharas,* the translation of books and texts, attendance at Buddhist conferences. An occasional bhikshu may visit; the wealthier and most committed localities may be able to arrange for a resident monk's presence. Literature at all levels; translation of Pali and English books into Marathi, the production of popular songs, the creation of new material from Buddhist imagery, will continue at an increased pace. Babasaheb Ambedkar will continue to be the centre and the inspiration. It may be enough. At the very least, the Buddhist movement has added new dynamism, new forms of organization and new movements of creativity to the social movement Dr. Ambedkar set in motion some sixty years ago. And it is very conscious of its newness and its needs. Just a year and a half ago, I was rocked out of my bed in a Buddhist locality in Nagpur at 5:30 in the morning by Pali chanting played over a loudspeaker at a decibel not even a Carleton student stereo could achieve. I protested: do the Muslims and Sikhs living on the fringes of the Buddhist area want to hear this public proclamation of your religion? My Buddhist host said: the community needs this at this stage. Perhaps later there will be better ways to inform ourselves about Buddhism.

Notes

1. Pradyumna P. Karen, *The Changing Face of Tibet* (Lexington: The University Press of Kentucky, 1976), pp. 58-9.
2. Heinz Bechert, "Contemporary Buddhism in Bengal and Tripura", *Educational Miscellany,* IV. 3 & 4 (Dec. 1967-March 1968), pp.1-25.
3. Eleanor Zelliot, "The Indian Rediscovery of Buddhism, 1855-1956" in A.K. Narain ed., *Studies in Pali and Buddhism* (New Delhi: D.K. Publishers. "Scheduled Caste Buddhist Organizations", in J. Michael Mahar ed., *The Untouchables in Contemporary India* (Tucson: University of Arizona Press, 1972).
5. S.K. Thorat, "Passage to Adulthood: Perceptions from Below", in Sudhir Kakar ed., *Identity and Adulthood* (Delhi: Oxford University Press, 1979).
6. Eleanor Zelliot, "Dalit—New Cultural Context of an Old Marathi Word", *Contributions to Asian Studies* XI, 1978 (1978a).
7. Owen M. Lynch, *The Politics of Untouchability* (New York: Columbia University Press, 1969).
8. B.R. Ambedkar, *The Buddha and His Dhamma* (Bombay: Siddharth College Publication I, 1957).

Other References

Tibetan Buddhists in India

Beatrice D. Miller, "Lamaist Laity and Sangha in West Bengal, India", *Religious Ferment in Asia,* Robert J. Miller ed. (Lawrence: University Press of Kansas, 1974).

Office of Tibet. Report. 1969.

Bengali Buddhists

Sukomal Chowdhury, "Renaissance of Buddhism in Bengal in the Modern Period", *Maha Bodhi,* 79, 1971, pp. 410-19.

Hara Prasad Sastri, *Discovery of Living Buddhism in Bengal* (Calcutta: Sanskrit Press Depository, 1897).

The Contemporary Buddhist Movement in India

D.C. Ahir, *Buddhism in Modern India* (Nagpur: Bhikku Niwas Prakashan, 1972).

— "80 Years of Buddhism in India", *Maha Bodhi,* 79 (1971), pp. 219-21.

Iravati Karve and Hemlata Acharya, "Neo-Buddhism in Maharashtra", *Journal of the University of Poona,* Humanities Section, 15 (1962), pp. 130-33.

Joanna Macy, and Eleanor Zelliot, "Tradition and Innovation in the Contemporary Buddhist Movement in India", *Studies in the History of Buddhism,* edited by A.K. Narain (Delhi: B.R. Publishing Corporation, 1980).

Beatrice Miller, "Revitalization Movements: Theory and Practice, as Evidenced Among the Buddhists of Maharashtra", in M.C. Pradhan et al. ed., *Anthropology and Archaeology: Essays in Commemoration of Varier Elwin* (London: Oxford University Press, 1969).

— "The Psychological Dimension of the Buddhist Movement in India", in G.A. Oddie ed., *Religion in South Asia* (New Delhi: Manohar, 1977).

— "Religion and Legitimation in the Mahar Movement", in Bardwell L. Smith ed., *Religion and Legitimation in South Asia* (Leiden: E.J. Brill, 1978).

15

The Buddhist Literature of Modern Maharashtra

The Buddhist literature of Maharashtra is only fifty years old, stemming from the conversion of Dr. B.R. Ambedkar on 14 October 1956, in Nagpur. Bhimrao Ramji Ambedkar,[1] born into the Untouchable Mahar caste, had announced that he would leave Hinduism way back in 1935, after a series of temple entry and political frustrations. But he continued his remarkable career as educator, writer, lawyer and statesman without actual conversion until near the time of his death in December 1956. Such was his prestige, however, and so well prepared were his followers, that more than four million converts to Buddhism have followed in his footsteps. The great majority of these are in Ambedkar's own area of Maharashtra, and among his own caste of Mahars, but a sizeable group comes from the urban areas of other states in India[2] and there are even a few high caste Hindu converts to Buddhism, drawn to that religion from the period of the rediscovery of Buddhism in India.[3]

An impressive range of material on Buddhism has been produced by Ambedkar's movement, although its content is very uneven. The following four groupings of Buddhist literature reveal the special nature of this Buddhist conversion and cast light on the way in which Buddhists think of themselves. The literature, most of it in Marathi, has been given here so as highlight to the most important thrusts of the conversion movement (1) guides to ritual and practice and histories of the conversion; (2) literature on the history and legends of Buddhism; (3) songs about Dr. Ambedkar and the conversion; (4) creative literature by Buddhists of the educated elite.

The Pali Scriptures—Study and Translation

The study of Pali, translations from Pali scriptures, and the reprinting of literature written by earlier Indian Buddhists, all reinforce the idea that today's Buddhists are part of the classical Buddhist tradition, dormant but not dead during the previous millennium. In 1948, long before the conversion, Dr. Ambedkar expressed the idea that Untouchables had been Buddhists in the past.[4] They had been pushed aside when neo-Brahmanism rose to engulf Buddhist tradition and reassert militant Hinduism. This premise is accepted without question by present Buddhist converts from low-caste communities. It has proved to be a very satisfactory explanation of untouchability and a very meaningful way to develop pride in one's past. Though it is not explicated in literature, the idea of a proud Buddhist past underlies the current attitude toward Pali, Buddhist literature, and Buddhist art. The importance of this theory can be seen in the choice of Nagpur, home of the Nagas, early followers of the Buddha, as the base of the conversion movement in 1956. The discovery of a major Buddhist site at Pauni, near Nagpur, several years ago, was hailed with delight by Buddhists. The Pali scriptures, rather than the Sanskrit scriptures of Mahayana Buddhism, are used in the current movement. Dr. Ambedkar felt that the Pali tradition was purer and more rational; it is also more logical that rebels against Brahmanism would want Pali rather than Sanskrit as their religious language.

Ambedkar Book

Dr. B.R. Ambedkar's *The Buddha and His Dhamma* (Bombay: Siddharth Publications, 1957), stories from the Pali scriptures as well as interpretations of Buddhism from a rational, humanistic viewpoint dominate. Even though Ambedkar's book is basic to the movement, a Marathi translation did not appear until 1970. Vasant Moon of Nagpur published a Marathi analysis in 1960, and Anand Kausalyayan published translation of the book in 1961, with notes on the Pali sources, which Ambedkar had not felt necessary to publish. The stories and the moral interpretations found in *The Buddha and His Dhamma,* however, circulated widely from the beginning of the conversion movement. The book is arranged in almost biblical fashion, with every verse numbered. The life and teachings of the Buddha are spelled out in very simple fashion, and Ambedkar's interpretation is humanistic and rational — no mythic material is included. The final chapter, "The Man who was Siddharth Gautama", lays emphasis on the Buddha's humanity, compassion, and sense of equality. In the sections on the Buddha's thought, the ideas of transmigration of soul, of rebirth according to past deeds, and of the individual soul *(atman)* are rejected as not being part of the Buddha's teaching, as also is, of course, the Hindu concept of *chaturvarna* (four fold caste structure).

Other Buddhist Works

Although Ambedkar's book is clearly most important, a number of other Buddhist interpretations are much used in the movement. Dharmanand Kosambi (1876-1948), a Brahman scholar who became a Buddhist early this century, published *Bhagwan Buddha,* a life of the Buddha, which stresses, rationality, and which Ambedkar undoubtedly read; it has been reprinted at least twice since its initial publication in 1940. Kosambi's *Buddha, dharma ani sangha,* which appeared in 1910, is in its fifth printing and is widely distributed in Buddhist book stores. The Maharashtra State Literature Committee, a body that feels considerable responsibility to represent all Marathi-speaking groups, has reprinted Kosambi's *Buddhalila-sarasamgraha,* which first appeared in 1914. A Buddhist in Pune told me that he felt Kosambi's *Hindi samskrti ani ahimsa* (Culture and Non-violence), which appeared in 1935, was one of the most important books for a Buddhist.

The work of other earlier Indian Buddhist converts is also important, although none were from the Untouchable community or from Maharashtra. Bhikshu Anand Kausalyayan, who established a Buddhist training centre in Nagpur after the conversion, has published nineteen books and pamphlets in Hindi, a language understood throughout eastern Maharashtra. Rahul Sankrityayan (1893-1963) is popular among younger left-wing Maharashtrian Buddhists who can read his Hindi works. *The Essence of Buddhism* by P. Lakshman Narasu, an early Tamil-speaking Buddhist, was republished by Ambedkar himself, and seems to be known to all English-educated Maharashtrian Buddhists, but has not been translated into Marathi.[5]

A very new group of Buddhist literature stems from an English bhikshu Sangarakshita, who lived in India for twenty years and worked closely with the early conversion movement. Within the last few years, Sangarakshita's young English Buddhist converts have established centers for teaching and publishing in Pune, Bombay, and Ahmedabad, and a retreat near the ancient Buddhist cave at Bhaja, and their many publications are readily available. A magazine appears monthly in Marathi, and a great many pamphlets in Marathi and English are published. A sizeable group of highly educated Marathi-speaking lay leaders do almost all the teaching within this movement.

Translations from Pali had appeared within the community even before much education in Pali language was available. D.P. Ranpise in Pune secured the help of a sympathetic Brahman Pali scholar, P.V. Bapat, to publish some work in Pali and Marathi shortly after the conversion. A number of translations of the *Dhammapada*[6] have appeared, and the Hindi translation of the *Milinda panha* by bhikshu Jagdish Kashyap, an early high caste convert to Buddhism, was translated into Marathi by Haribhau Pagare and published in Bombay in 1961. Some Buddhists own the *Tripitaka* in Hindi, a massive work undertaken by the Bihar Government, it is told, under the direction of R.D. Bhandare, a Buddhist from Maharashtra who was then Governor of Bihar.

Pali is very important in the conducting of life-passage rituals among today's Buddhists, and in the *vandana* (Buddhist prayers) that take place in the *viharas* across Maharashtra. It is also important as a subject taught in the vast complex of colleges established by Ambedkar and by his followers. Given the stress, it is strange, that more Pali scriptures do not appear in Marathi translation. It is also perhaps a bit unexpected that more of the basic English works on Buddhism have not been translated into Marathi. It is almost as if the movement finds its intellectual understanding only in the work of those who, like Ambedkar, Kosambi and Sangarakshita, know how to relate Buddhism to the hopes, dreams, and social conditions of the lowest of the castes in the Indian system.

Guides on Buddhist Ritual: Studies of the Meaning of Conversion

Since classical Buddhism in India left life-passage rituals in the hands of the Hindus, today's Buddhists have had to invent their own marriage and naming ceremonies, their own funeral rites, their own patterns for holy days. Ambedkar was aware of the need for Buddhist rituals, and prepared twenty-three oaths which were to be taken as part of the conversion to Buddhism. These promises are a mixture of declaration of faith in Buddhist principles and rejection of Hindu gods and social systems.[7] No more elaborate conversion ceremony has been devised. As on the first mass conversion day in Nagpur on 15 October 1956, would be Buddhists still recite the oaths and are given *diksha* by either a bhikshu, if one is available, or by a lay Buddhist.

Ambedkar also prepared a little guide to Buddhist ritual, but this has been preceded by a great many other manuals and guidebooks. Typical of title is the *Bauddhasamaskar-path* of V.R. Ranpise, which was first published in 1957, and was in its fourth edition by 1964, having reached a total of 10,000 copies. Its title might be translated "Readings in the Practice of Buddhism", since that is the thrust of the pamphlet. The Pali chants heard all over the Dalit areas of the Maharashtrian world, *"namo Buddhaya"*, *"saranattaya"* (The Three Refuges), and the *"panchshila"* (The Five Moral Vows) begin the pamphlet. *Vandana* or prayer-meditations on the Buddha, the *dhamma,* and the *sangha* follow, together with prayers for protection. The *Jayamangala-atthagatha* (The Eight Auspicious Sentences), *Maha-mangala-sutta* and the *Ratanasutta* follow, with a Marathi translation. A long section on ceremonies—for weddings, deaths, entering school and other occasions—comes next, with considerable attention to who may be called an *upasak*, a lay member, and what standards of conduct must be followed by one who leads. A list of Buddhist names for boys and girls is included. The pamphlet ends with ways to observe the various *purnimas* (full-moon days), and the various holidays such as Diwali and Holi associated with Hinduism.

Probably no religious conversion ever began with as much emphasis on the laity. Even now, thirty years after the conversion, there are not nearly enough trained bhikshus in many communities, and given the pressure on young men to help their families, the life of an indigent ascetic may be one that few are able to take. The creativity of the movement still lies with local lay leaders, and their degree of devotion and inventiveness determines the practice of their localities much more than any action by the Buddhist Society in Bombay, or the center established by Waman Godbole in Nagpur, important though these centers are. The number of inexpensive pamphlets that are produced locally to aid Buddhist practice is not so large as the number of song pamphlets intended for the spreading of the message or the celebration of various holy days, but it is impressive.

There are also histories of the conversion itself, and the events and circumstances that led up to it. Shankarrao Kharat, a highly respected author, produced the first of these with *Da. Babasaheb Ambedkarance dhammantar* (Dr. Babasaheb Ambedkar's Conversion), published in Pune in 1966, and three professors from Dr. Ambedkar College at Mahad published a *Nagpurchi dhamma kranti* (the religious revolution of Nagpur) in 1981, which indicates the perception of the conversion as a revolution. D.L. Ramteke, a Maharashtrian Buddhist, has attempted a history of Buddhism as well of the conversion in an English work, *Revival of Buddhism in Modern India* (New Delhi: Deep and Deep Publications, 1983), which is the most ambitious effort to date to present the entire movement to non-Marathi speakers. All of these stress the social significance of the conversion, and although Ramteke devotes the latter part of this book to the ideals of Buddhism, it is the social ethics of Buddhism that are stressed.

Although a close study of the Buddhist periodicals which appear in Marathi[8] such as *Dhammarajya,* published in Pune, have not been carried out, but it seems that masses issues being discussed among Buddhists do not appear in them. Many ponder what the Buddhist response can and should be to the violence that is increasingly used against them. Having denied the validity of caste, some see a conflict in accepting the benefits given on a caste basis, albeit to a caste that has suffered discrimination. Some wonder if Buddhist philosophy is too passive, not militant enough for an oppressed group. Others wonder how Buddhism can be made a uniting rather than a separating factor in India today. The training of bhikshus, and the necessity for bhikshus, is another issue which the community seems not to want to discuss in print. Perhaps, anything smacking of criticism is seen as better discussed verbally than in public.

The great flood of confessional literature in Christianity which delineates the meaning of that faith has some counterpart in Marathi, but is also not well developed. A sensitive essay entitled "Passage to Adulthood: Perceptions from Below" by a young Buddhist, S.K. Thorat, appeared in *Identity and Adulthood,* edited by Sudhir Kakar (Delhi: Oxford University Press, 1979). The autobiography of Daya Pawar, *Balute* (a gift in Kind for hereditary work: the Mahar was a *balutedar* in the village community), was published by the Bombay Granthali Prakashan in 1978 and won much attention, but Pawar's insight on the conversion is not as startingly meaningful as on his life as an Untouchable. The publishing of autobiography has now become a major trend among Dalit writers, but the preoccupation is still the struggle for *manuski* (human dignity) with Buddhism being accepted as a necessary but unexplained part of that struggle for those writers from a Mahar background. True, confessional religious literature is not part of the Hindu religious tradition, and perhaps one should not expect it; and perhaps it is significant that the closest thing to an accounting of the conversion process is in K.N. Kadam's *Buddhism as Rationalism and Humanism,* a set of essays written between 1950 and 1981 and published in mimeograph form for private Circulation - and Kadam was educated in Jesuit schools!

The History and Legends of Buddhism

Interest in the Buddhist past is very high among today's converts, and the re-telling of the legends of Buddhism takes many forms. Two books in Marathi tell of pilgrimages to Buddhist holy places all over India. V.R. Ranpise published *Baudhairnchi Bharatatila pavitra tithakshetre* (The Holy Places of the Buddha in India) in Pune in 1962, and the following year L.N. Ankush Guruji published *Majhe Bauddha tirthatana* (My Buddhist Pilgrimage) in Bombay: both are sizeable pamphlets intended to serve as guides as well as notes on the author's experiences. Two other publications deal with pilgrimage places in a rather unexpected manner. Chandrabhan Kisan Naranavare, known as "Chandranag" of Nagpur, has published a pamphlet intending to prove that the hill of Ramtek north of Nagpur was originally a Buddhist place. M.D. Panchbahi published *Kapilavastu,* a scholarly work by K.M. Srivastava of the Archaeological Survey of India, when he feared that interpretation of the site of the Buddha's birth would not be published officially.

At least two Ph.D. theses on the Buddhist past reflect the writer's own religious concerns. B.R. Kamble's *Caste and Philosophy in Pre-Buddhist India* (Aurangabad: Parimal Prakashan, 1979) is a contribution to the ongoing debate about the relationship of the sixth century Hinduism to Buddhism. Bhau Lokhande produced "The Influence of Buddhism on Marathi *Sant*-Literature" for his Nagpur University Ph.D. in 1975-76, and this discussion of the importance of Buddhist thought to the dominant bhakti cult in Maharashtra has been published in Marathi as *Marathi Santa Sahityavara Bauddha dharmacha prabhava* (Nagpur Ashok Prakashan, 1979).

Histories, that are not original scholarship are also important. D.C. Ahir, a Hindi-speaking Buddhist from Delhi, includes among his many books one called *India's Debt to Buddhism* (New Delhi: Maha Bodhi Society of India, 1964), a title which reflects the sentiment of the Maharashtrian Buddhists about the importance of the Buddhist past.[9] M.S. Moray, a Marathi-speaking Buddhist employed in government service in Gujarat, has published the *History of Buddhism in Gujarat* (Ahmedabad: Saraswati Pustak Bhandar, 1985) and has earlier published three books in Marathi which retold the stories of the Chinese travelers to India and the early history of Buddhism in Maharashtra as outlined by R.G. Bhandarkar and B.C. Gokhale. Moray writes about the past but is very conscious of the present: "Let us again, therefore, give India that glory which was its during the Buddhist period".

Buddhist legends and stories are presented in many ways. A very respectable novel on the life of the Buddha's wife,

Murlidhar Bhosekar's *Siddhathachi Yashodhara* (Pune: Ravind Prakashan, 1975) was well received, and he thereafter published another, *Kapilvastucha raj kumar* (the Prince of Kapilvastu) in 1977. Sugandha Shinde of Nagpur published a children's story of the life of the Buddha, and a play on Amrapali. B.S. Shinde's *Vasavadatta,* a play about the courtesan who became a Buddhist nun, has been presented in Pune with a cast from a Buddhist locality, and Shinde has more recently formed *a* Dalit Rangabhumi (Dalit Theater Company), which has great interest in performing plays on classical Buddhist themes as well as modern problem theater.

Buddhist stories and legends which contain social messages are most popular, stories in which untouchability is ignored, in which courtesans become respected nuns, in which princes give up their thrones for the good of the common man. Classic tales are adapted for amateur theater in many localities, just as classic Buddhist architecture is adapted for *viharas* and Buddhist school buildings. In Buddhism, ex-Untouchables may lay claim to a proud past, and the importance of justifiable pride to an oppressed people cannot be overstressed.

The Songs of the Buddhist Movement

Perhaps the best way to understand what the conversion means to the unsophisticated masses is to look at the song literature of the Maharashtrian Buddhists. Sold in cheap pamphlet form at all Buddhist occasions—the birth and death anniversaries of Dr. Ambedkar, the Buddha Jayanti (birthday), the anniversary of the conversion ceremony in Nagpur— these songs reflect a popular, unsophisticated celebration of Buddhism, with "Babasaheb" Ambedkar given prime attention as the saviour of his people. Some of the following translations were made by somewhat educated converts, and their sometime in accurate but touching English has been left untouched since the originals are not available.[10] It should be understood that "he" and "Bhim" refer to Bhimrao Ramji Ambedkar.

Rajananda Gadapyle in *Jagati Pramjota* (The Awakened Torch of Life), written shortly after the 1956 conversion, touches on a number of themes :

> The light of enthusiasm is spread everywhere
> and the teaching of Buddha is happy.

The evil days of slavery are gone.

and the sorrowful songs are gone.

Bhim gave us the great hymn *Buddham sarnam gachchami* (I Go for Refuge to the Buddha) and by attaining the perfection of this hymn we become the riders of our own chariot

The torch of revolution is burning in every heart.

A Buddhist life is smitten with humanity.

He turned the wheel of revolution.

He died the maker of an age.

All the ten directions give praise,

India gives praise.

Dinbandhu, the pseudonym of an Akola-based writer, dwells chiefly on the theme of release :

The Hindu faith, the hateful faith-

We threw it out!

Today we took the Buddha's way. (Chorus)

Today we cut the bonds of slavery,

Today is the joy of victory,

The old religion lies in pieces,

The new religion is ever new joy.

Every drop of blood is fired up today!

Come on, let's tell all the world,

Let's tell the sun, the moon, the stars,

the rivers, mountains, corners of the earth,

Say: listen, hear this voice,

New religion, new birth today is ours!

Who is Untouchable now?

Who is Chandal, the Atishudra?

Bhimrao gave the gift of life,

He turned cow dung into gold,

He showed the path of peace and equality!

An unknown poet in a song recorded by an American student puts the Buddhist message this way :

Neither todays nor yesterdays.
Neither war nor brutality.
This is a religion of socialism, this Buddhism.

Another anonymous poet transposes a Buddhist precept into simple language :

In Buddhism first comes the duty.
Mere speech is not religion,
Otherwise life would end in madness.
If you do not behave as you talk
What sense is there?

Ranu Bhima of Pune refers to the past, as do many of the songs, claiming the glory of earlier Buddhism as his own :

Bring to this country once again
The blessed name
Which made land of thy birth sacred
To all the distant lands!
Let the great awakening under the Bodhi tree
    be fulfilled.
Let the open doors that are barred
    and the resounding conch shell
Proclaim thy arrival at Bharat's gate.
Let, through innumerable voices,
    the gospel of an unmeasurable love
    announce thy call.

Another song from the same source refers to the train, a reflection of the importance of the railroad in bringing Mahars from the villages to service on the tracks in the 19th and early 20th centuries, the first step toward freedom from village servitude :

Bhim's train has come, has come ... ring the bell.
It is in India, and the Untouchables are sitting on it.
There are tracks of touchability . .. tell, o please tell.

The tracks should come together ... tie them, o please tie them. The main station is Delhi. We must go there.

Lord Buddha is the Ticket Master ...

The way in which Bhimrao Ambedkar and the Buddha are linked, and the way in which Buddhism must be related to the ongoing struggle of the ex-Untouchables for equality, is shown in a touching and rather unusually pacifistic song recorded in the Nagpur area.[11]

Bhimjayanti and Buddhajayanti are celebrated.
Buddha gave the message of peace to the world
And Bhim gave us the *Panchashila.*
Following the advice of the *Panchashila*
We gave up the language of revolution
And made our enemy our friend.

Waman Kardak, the best known and the most sophisticated of the folk poets, summarizes the social meaning of the conversion in his song, "14th October", the day on which Ambedkar himself converted :

We have thrown away the rags
which never did cover our shame ... (Chorus)
The drum of bravery was beaten;
The frame of *chaturvarna* was broken.
Bhim's promise to himself was fulfilled
The humble were freed
 from the valley of untouchability.[12]

Dalit Sahitya and Buddhist Literature

Stress on education, a passionate desire to make their suffering understood, and an intense need to contribute to culture has produced a school of literature in Marathi called Dalit Sahitya—the literature of the oppressed. Probably the single most important development in Marathi literature in the past ten years, Dalit Sahitya seems to be only marginally concerned with the Buddhist conversion. Baburao Bagul, a powerful short story writer, when asked about this, answered simply that something must be completely absorbed and understood before it can be written about. He also added that the Buddhist conversion set the Untouchable free to be creative! An example of this point can be found in a folder entitled "Buddhist Revolutionary Poems", published privately in Bombay in 1980, which begins with a quotation from P. Lakshmi Narasu's *The Essence of Buddhism,* about the relation of Buddhism and aesthetic aspirations and closes with a note that the poetry manifests "the Buddhist way of righteousness", although Buddhism is not specifically mentioned in the poems themselves. The pamphlet was published by Ashok Chakravarti and collected, translated and edited by Gautam Shinde, which seems to be a joint Bengali-Maharashtrian as well as a high-caste-Buddhist venture.

The poet Daya Pawar who won considerable honour and fame for his autobiography, *Balute,* has used Buddhist symbols and concepts in at least three poems. A rather bitter poem which appears in the English translation of excerpts from *Balute* by Priya Adarkar *(Imprint:* January 1980) begins with :

I have seen this tree choking with grief

Its roots are deep like a bodhi-tree's

But the bodhi tree, at least, flowered

And this tree is scorched in all seasons.

A particularly touching short story in this Buddhist literary tradition is one entitled *Ani Buddha marun padla* (And the Buddha Died), in Arjun Dangle's collection *Hi bambhavarachi manasa* (Pune: Mangova, 1979). A young Buddhist student attempts to get the Buddhists in his village to let the Untouchable Mangs (traditional enemies of the Untouchable Mahars, the caste which became Buddhist) use their well. He refuses to give money to help build a Buddhist temple when they will not. But then his father dies, and since he must have help with the funeral, he agrees to contribute. Then, as he looks down at his dead father's face, he sees the Buddha has died.

Perhaps it is fitting that we end with a story written by a highly educated Buddhist about village Buddhists, and that the sophisticated work of the poets here balances the exuberant but unsophisticated folk songs given earlier. Today's Buddhists are both illiterate and highly educated, they are village labourers and professors in universities, their social class varies enormously, but they are bound together by a common belief that the Buddhist conversion has freed them, and that the way taught them by Bhimrao Ambedkar is the only way for them to possess full human rights, human dignity, and pride in what they are.

References

1. The fullest biography of Dr. Ambedkar is still Dhananjay Keer's *Dr. Ambedkar: Life and Mission* (Bombay: Popular Prakashan, 1971, 3rd edition). All of Dr. Ambedkar's shorter writing will eventually appear in the *Dr. Babasaheb Ambedkar Writings and Speeches* series edited by Vasant Moon under the sponsorship of the Education Department, Government of Maharashtra. [Thus far, ten volumes have appeared—the first in 1979.]
2. See Owen Lynch, "Dr. Ambedkar—Myth and Charisma" and Adele Fiske, "Scheduled Caste Buddhist Organisations" in *The Untouchables in Contemporary India,* J. Michael Mahar ed. (Tucson: University of Arizona Press, 1972) for notes on Buddhists outside Maharashtra. D.C. Ahir of New Delhi is probably the most prolific writer from India's Buddhist community today in English. Jullundar in Punjab has a major Buddhist publishing center under the leadership of L.R. Balley and Bhagwan Das.
3. I have described the pre-Ambedkar interest in Buddhism in "The Indian Rediscovery of Buddhism, 1855-1956" in A.K.Narain ed., *Studies in Pali and Buddhism* (Jagdish Kashap Memorial Volume) (New Delhi: D.K. Publishers' Distributors, 1978).
4. Dr. B.R. Ambedkar, *The Untouchables* (New Delhi: Amrit Book Company, 1948).
5. P. Lakshmi Narasu (1860-1935), was evidently of a low caste, but not an Untouchable. A professor at Madras Christian College, he advocated conversion to Buddhism as an antidote to the caste system. *The Essence of Buddhism,* first published in 1907, was again published by Thacker and Company with an introduction by Ambedkar in 1948, and republished in Delhi by the Bhartiya Publishing House in 1976.

6. The *Dhammapada* seems to be by far the most meaningful of the Buddhist scriptures to the new Buddhists. I know of at least six translations, one of them in the traditional *ovi* meter of Marathi folk poetry, and another in the *abhang* genre used in the all important saint-poet literature of the bhakti movement in Maharashtra [One of the founders of the Dalit Panthers, Raja Dhale, is now translating the *Dhammapad.*]
7. I have reproduced the Buddhist's oaths in my article "Religion and Legitimation in the Mahar Movement", in Bradwell L. Smith ed., *Religion and Legitimation of Power in South Asia* (Leiden: E.J. Brill, 1978) and in this volume.
8. The number of publications is impressive, and at times it seems there is a journal in each town, if only for a short while. Among the more unusual journals, which deal with Buddhism as well as other issues are *Asmitadarsh,* an excellent Dalit literary journal published by Gangadhar Pantawahe in Aurangabad, and *Outcry,* a periodical published in English by the Dr. Ambedkar Mission, a group of staunch Buddhist migrants in Toronto, Canada.
9. Another interpretation of the contemporary Buddhist view of history by a non-Maharashtrian convert is by W.R. Vijayakumar, "A Historical Survey of Buddhism in India" in T.S. Wilkinson and M.M. Thomas eds., *Ambedkar and the Neo-Buddhist Movement* (Bangalore: Christian Institute for the Study of Religion and Society; Madras: Christian Literature Society, 1972).
10. Three young undergraduate students in the Associated Colleges of the Midwest's India Studies Program during the last fifteen years have collected Buddhist songs, many of them gleaned directly from singers during Buddhist occasions. I regret that I cannot credit James H. Fisher, Russell Geyer, and John A. Luke more specifically for the songs they have provided.
11. Indira V. Junghare, "Songs of the Mahars: An Untouchable Caste of Maharashtra India", *Ethnomusicology,* XXVII, 2, 1983, p. 290.
12. Published in *Watchal* (Movement) (Prabhodan Prakashan, Aurangabad, 1972). The full poem is translated by Jayant Karve and Eleanor Zelliot in Peter Gaeffke and David A. Utz eds., *Identity and Division in Cults and Sects in South Asia* (Proceedings of the South Asia Seminar, University of Pennsylvania, 1980-81) (Philadelphia, 1984), p. 108.

16
Conclusion

The Dalit identity is the illustration of the consciousness of the Untouchables of India. It displays the political, social and economic awakening of all downtrodden people of the *Brahmanic* order. The Untouchables of India managed to develop the unity consciousness and became organized after the colonization of India. Before the colonization period, since those people have never met a different attitude other than the approach of their environment, they did not unite for the elevation of their situation. However, the existence of the British made sense for them. The British paid attention on their backwardness and developed awareness in aid of the Untouchables. Now they were receiving education and recruitment within the lines of governmental jobs and those steps were lessening the others touch-me-not-ism perception towards the Untouchables.

The democracy understanding of the Europeans was somehow transmitted to the natives of the sub-continent. This appreciation of democracy brought the Untouchables to aspire political representation and freedom of faith for them. Thus, it was the colonial power triggering the solidarity consciousness of the Untouchables and encouraging them for a rise up. Nevertheless the fixed rulers of India were willing to overthrow the foreign rule and to consolidate their ancient order once again. The Untouchables knew that, the meaning of consolidation of the ancient order meant to fortify the *varna* and to leave the Untouchables out of the social, economic, spiritual and political spheres. So as to prevent the foreseen problems sprang, the Untouchables had to take some measures like manipulating the constitution before the new India was formed. Hence all the mentioned ideas of overthrowing the inequalities among Indians, deleting the backwardness of the

Untouchables, making all equal before law were formed due to the inspirations from the colonial dominion.

While on one hand his colonial legacy was feeding the free will objects of the Untouchables, at the same time the British were taking the advantage of this developing consciousness. The British divide and rule policy corrupted the Indian caste system. India, being culturally, religiously, linguistically, socially and racially a diversified country, was a very fruitful colony for the British policy of divide and rule. With the intention of facilitating the control of such a broad land, the British did not hesitate to encourage separate groups to act unaccompanied by the others within India. In the name of bringing democracy, modernity and reforms the British Government presented the separate electorate idea for the main branches of India. This political structure stimulated initially the Muslims and Sikhs. The newly introduced political system culminated with communal hatred and partition of India into Muslim Pakistan. The British administration eased its job in India by acting as a political liberator. For distinct groups, the British were operating as if it was safeguarding their interests against the aged Hindu system. By doing like that, the British were weakening India, because an India in a pure solidarity could encounter against the British imperialism. Now, distinct groups were in their own peculiar struggle not against the British colonialism, but against the Indian governance.

This policy of the colonial dominion in India affected the Untouchables as well. It is unavoidably true that, the presence of a colonial body had a restraining effect on forming a modern Indian state. Due to its 'divide and rule' policy, the British prevented India being a unified nation in harmony. It rather led to self-realization of ethnic, social, local, religious and linguistic communities. It is the same for the case of the Dalits. By making some favours to the low classes, the British initially got the reliance of them. In the eyes of the Dalits, the British were the enemy of the enemy. The support they needed was provided by the colonial dominion. So they could wage their own independence struggle against the caste system. This rivalry amongst two branches of the Hindu society was for the advantage of the British rule, like any other cut away from this society. The Dalits consisted a huge percentage of the Indian society, for this reason any tension and hostility between the Untouchables and the rest of the society nourished the British policy. Like the enmity amid Muslims and Hindus, this inter-caste turmoil also provided the British a perfect field to function without restraints. So the eagerness of the Dalits relieved 'divide and rule' strategy. Dr. Ambedkar wore an enmity role neither against imperialism nor against the British. According to some sources, it was not because he was favouring imperialism or the British, but because he found it impossible to fight its mighty foes all together. In his several speeches he highlighted that British imperialism and Indian feudalism are equally destroying to the Indian nation and to the Dalits.[1]

Even though there had been several previous challenges against the *varna* order by different segments of the downtrodden people of India, it was the first time that all downtrodden people of India, including the Untouchables, *Sudras* and other agitated people of the caste system, could be organized to the extent rejecting the *varna* order and making political and social manoeuvres on behalf of bettering their position within the Indian society. These manoeuvres were realized under the leadership of Dr. Babasaheb Ambedkar. Even though the centre of the mentioned movement was the Maharashtra state, people of other states were inspired by their association and initiated protests against the caste system. It was Dr. Ambedkar arousing the belief and enthusiasm of people to raise their problem and to seek solutions besides organizing people around their case. Dr. Ambedkar died just after the conversion took place. By his death the movement lost its fervor and excitement and hitherto Dalits could not carry their case as it happened in the epoch of Ambedkar. So the glorious times of the Dalit movement covers only the time when Dr. Ambedkar guided and the movement was over by his loss. After his death, his trusted lieutenant Dadasaheb Gaikwad who appeared as a natural choice held the leadership. However, he never managed to achieve the same attraction of the Dalits. Even some of the Dalits blamed him of being a communist and trying to bring a communist nuance to the movement. He was labelled as a communist due to his economic programs. Moreover, some found him intellectually incapable to carry a social movement, because he was not a university graduate.[2]

Today, the implementation of *varna* order and discrimination among Indian citizens is restricted by the Indian Constitution since it was first enforced in 1950. Even though these ancient traditions do not still persist in cities, the rural areas are field of conflict even today. Sometimes the ex-Untouchables are attacked by the Hindu nationalists; they face pogrommes and mass killings and the Dalits, who are now Muslims, Christians or Buddhists, are still fighting against the oppressive character of the caste system. Some international organizations are taking some measures on behalf of saving the neo-Buddhists, Muslims and Christians. A sub-branch of United Nations (UN) the Committee on the Elimination of Racial Discrimination (CERD) openly condemned discrimination based on caste and similar forms of inherited status as human rights violations in 2002. In the resolution, India's Dalits recognized as a community discriminated against on the basis of descent. United Nations High Commissioner for Refugees (UNHCR) passed a resolution in 2004, appointing special rapporteurs, where the Dalits are still oppressed. So the violence committed against the Dalits could be find and as a result those terrorized people could easily refuge to other lands, where they can live in peace. The UN Commission on Human Rights also decided to appoint special rapporteurs to detect and to tackle the entrenched problem of caste-based discrimination. Except Kocheril Raman Narayanan, the tenth President of the Indian republic, the presidency of India has been kept by leaders affiliates of Brahman families. As for the prime ministers, from Jawaharlal Nehru, Lal Bahadur Shastri, Indira Gandhi, Morarji Desai, Choudhary Charan Singh, Rajiv Gandhi, to Atal Behari Vajpayee, none of them applied a special policy concerning Dalits, but did not forget to include in the state policy of keeping all citizens equal.

References

1. Teltumbde, *op. cit.*, p. 20.
2. *Ibid.*, p. 5.

Index